Math Fundamentals

GRADE 2

The following illustrations were created by the artists listed (provided through Shutterstock.com) and are protected by copyright: SmallAtomWorks, ririro (front cover); wavebreakmedia (page 7); Jollanda (page 103); Seamartini Graphics (page 106); BeatWalk (page 108); Viktorija Reuta (page 108)

Writing: Marti Beeck
Content Editing: Lisa Vitarisi Mathews, Kathleen Jorgensen
Copy Editing: Cathy Harber
Art Direction: Yuki Meyer
Cover Design: Yuki Meyer
Illustration: Ann Iosa, Mary Rojas
Design/Production: Yuki Meyer, Jessica Onken

Visit
teaching-standards.com
to view a correlation
of this book.
This is a free service.

Correlated to Current Standards

Congratulations on your purchase of some of the finest teaching materials in the world.

Photocopying the pages in this book is permitted for single-classroom use only. Making photocopies for additional classes or schools is prohibited.

For information about other Evan-Moor products, call 1-800-777-4362, fax 1-800-777-4332, or visit our website, www.evan-moor.com.

18 Lower Ragsdale Drive, Monterey, CA 93940-5746. Printed in USA.

004

CPSIA: McNaughton & Gunn, Saline, MI USA [11/2020]

Contents

What's in This Book

Math Fundamentals is your comprehensive resource for grade-level problem-solving and analysis practice. The broad scope of math skills ranges in difficulty on skill practice pages, allowing you to precisely target specific skills for each student.

- Each unit in this book corresponds to a Common Core cluster (the bold statements within a domain). The units are in the same order as the Common Core State Standards for easy reference; however, **the order does not suggest a teaching path**. (See page 8 for a suggested teaching path.)
- Each unit is divided into concept sections that include a student reference page showing multiple strategies and models, skill practice pages that progress from foundational to challenging, and a culminating problem-solving activity. These activities offer opportunities to investigate and analyze the concept, improve computational fluency, and apply the skill in student-friendly real-world contexts.
- The student pages may be assigned as individual practice or homework. They can also be used for small-group work or a whole-class lesson.

Teacher Page

Unit Overview

This page shows at a glance the concepts, skills, and mathematical practices in the unit.

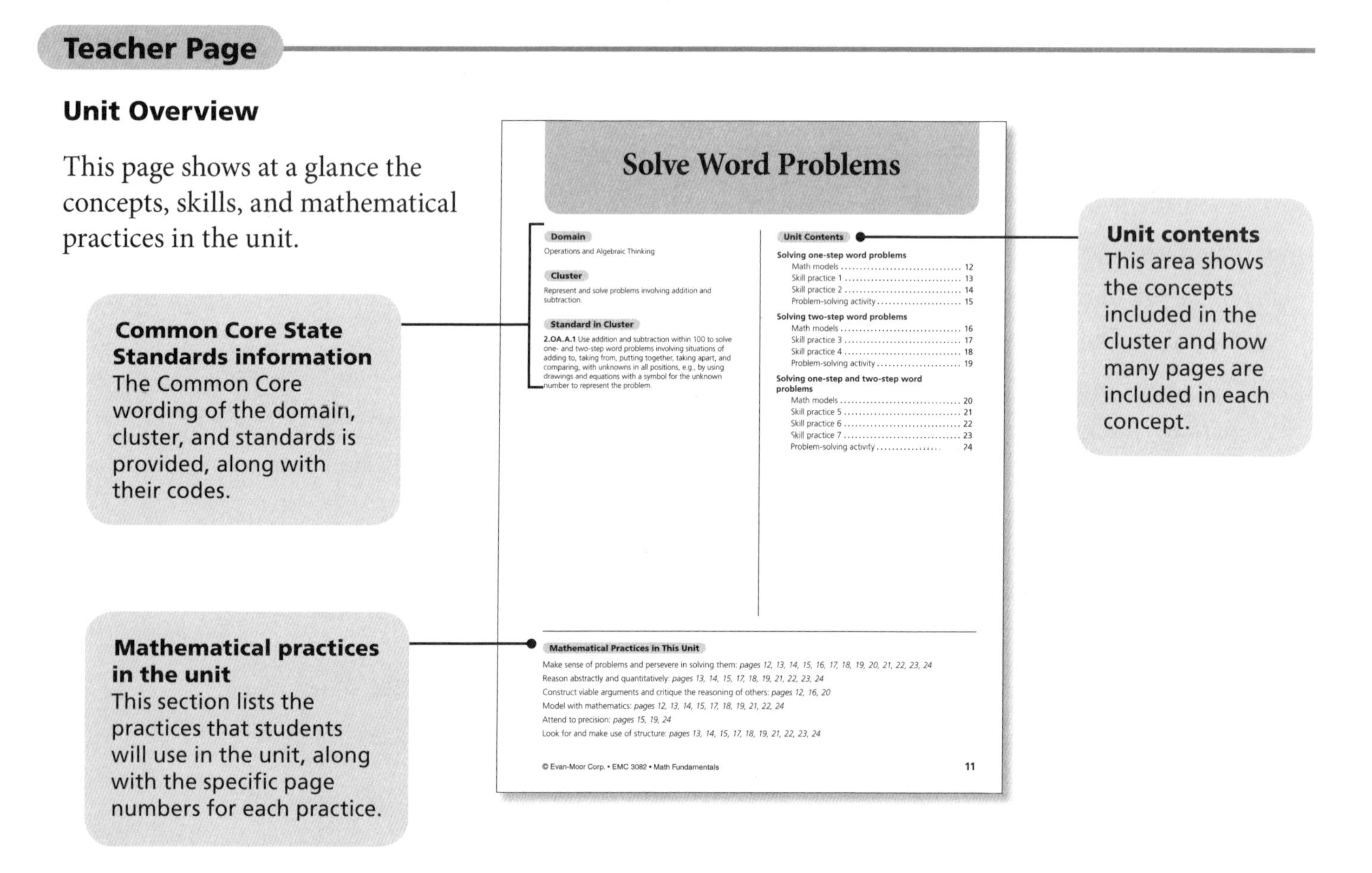
Common Core State Standards information
The Common Core wording of the domain, cluster, and standards is provided, along with their codes.
Mathematical practices in the unit
This section lists the practices that students will use in the unit, along with the specific page numbers for each practice.
Unit contents
This area shows the concepts included in the cluster and how many pages are included in each concept.

Solve Word Problems

Domain
Operations and Algebraic Thinking

Cluster
Represent and solve problems involving addition and subtraction.

Standard in Cluster
2.OA.A.1 Use addition and subtraction within 100 to solve one- and two-step word problems involving situations of adding to, taking from, putting together, taking apart, and comparing, with unknowns in all positions, e.g., by using drawings and equations with a symbol for the unknown number to represent the problem.

Unit Contents

Mathematical Practices in This Unit
Make sense of problems and persevere in solving them: *pages 12, 13, 14, 15, 16, 17, 18, 19, 20, 21, 22, 23, 24*
Reason abstractly and quantitatively: *pages 13, 14, 15, 17, 18, 19, 21, 22, 23, 24*
Construct viable arguments and critique the reasoning of others: *pages 12, 16, 20*
Model with mathematics: *pages 12, 13, 14, 15, 17, 18, 19, 21, 22, 24*
Attend to precision: *pages 15, 19, 24*
Look for and make use of structure: *pages 13, 14, 15, 17, 18, 19, 21, 22, 23, 24*

© Evan-Moor Corp. • EMC 3082 • Math Fundamentals 11

Student Pages

Math Models

These reference pages help students with each concept.

Multiple solving strategies with examples
Several example problems are shown, along with all work and answers so students can follow the steps. Multiple strategies or models are used so students can choose what best fits their thinking or the type of problem.

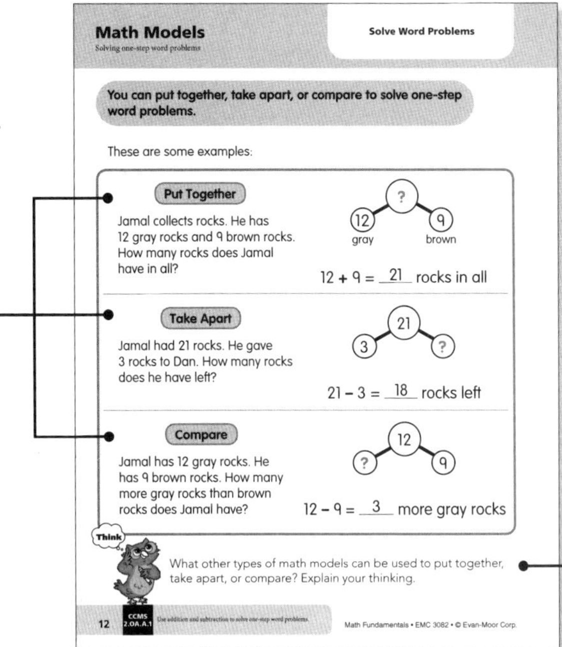

Math Models Solve Word Problems

You can put together, take apart, or compare to solve one-step word problems.

These are some examples:

Put Together

Jamal collects rocks. He has 12 gray rocks and 9 brown rocks. How many rocks does Jamal have in all?

12 + 9 = 21 rocks in all

Take Apart

Jamal had 21 rocks. He gave 3 rocks to Dan. How many rocks does he have left?

21 − 3 = 18 rocks left

Compare

Jamal has 12 gray rocks. He has 9 brown rocks. How many more gray rocks than brown rocks does Jamal have?

12 − 9 = 3 more gray rocks

Think

What other types of math models can be used to put together, take apart, or compare? Explain your thinking.

12 CCMS 2.OA.A.1 Math Fundamentals • EMC 3082 • © Evan-Moor Corp.

Reference page with many uses
- Introduce students to the types of problems they'll encounter.
- Print, project, or post it for reference as you teach the unit.
- Send it home as a resource for homework so parents can connect what they know with current methodology.

"Think" questions
"Think" questions help students apply what they have learned to a similar problem. The questions provide students an opportunity to talk about math strategies and to explain their thinking.

Skill Practice

These pages help students analyze concepts, gain fluency, and apply skills.

Example problem
The first skill practice page in each section includes an example to show students how to mark the answer and show their work.

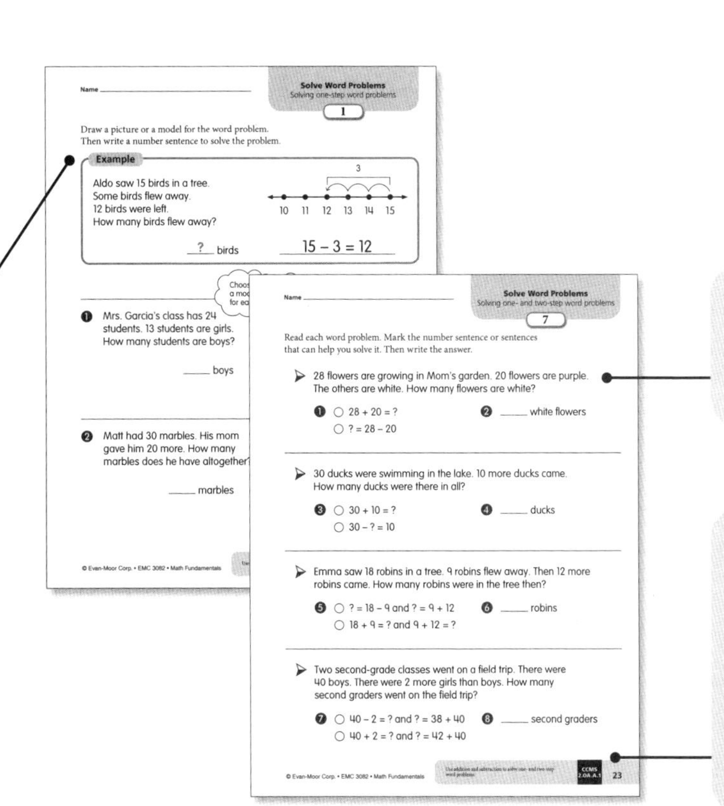

Name ______

Solve Word Problems
Solving one-step word problems
1

Draw a picture or a model for the word problem.
Then write a number sentence to solve the problem.

Example

Aldo saw 15 birds in a tree.
Some birds flew away.
12 birds were left.
How many birds flew away?

? birds 15 − 3 = 12

1. Mrs. Garcia's class has 24 students. 13 students are girls. How many students are boys?
   ______ boys

2. Matt had 30 marbles. His mom gave him 20 more. How many marbles does he have altogether?
   ______ marbles

© Evan-Moor Corp. • EMC 3082 • Math Fundamentals

Name ______

Solve Word Problems
Solving one- and two-step word problems
7

Read each word problem. Mark the number sentence or sentences that can help you solve it. Then write the answer.

28 flowers are growing in Mom's garden. 20 flowers are purple. The others are white. How many flowers are white?

1. ○ 28 + 20 = ?
   ○ ? = 28 − 20
2. ______ white flowers

30 ducks were swimming in the lake. 10 more ducks came. How many ducks were there in all?

3. ○ 30 + 10 = ?
   ○ 30 − ? = 10
4. ______ ducks

Emma saw 18 robins in a tree. 9 robins flew away. Then 12 more robins came. How many robins were in the tree then?

5. ○ ? = 18 − 9 and ? = 9 + 12
   ○ 18 + 9 = ? and 9 + 12 = ?
6. ______ robins

Two second-grade classes went on a field trip. There were 40 boys. There were 2 more girls than boys. How many second graders went on the field trip?

7. ○ 40 − 2 = ? and ? = 38 + 40
   ○ 40 + 2 = ? and ? = 42 + 40
8. ______ second graders

© Evan-Moor Corp. • EMC 3082 • Math Fundamentals CCMS 2.OA.A.1 23

Practice problems
Students practice math skills and work toward fluency.

Standard identifier
This indicates the specific skill within the cluster, along with its Common Core Math Standard code (includes a letter designating the cluster).

What's in This Book, *continued*

Student Pages, *continued*

Problem-Solving Activity

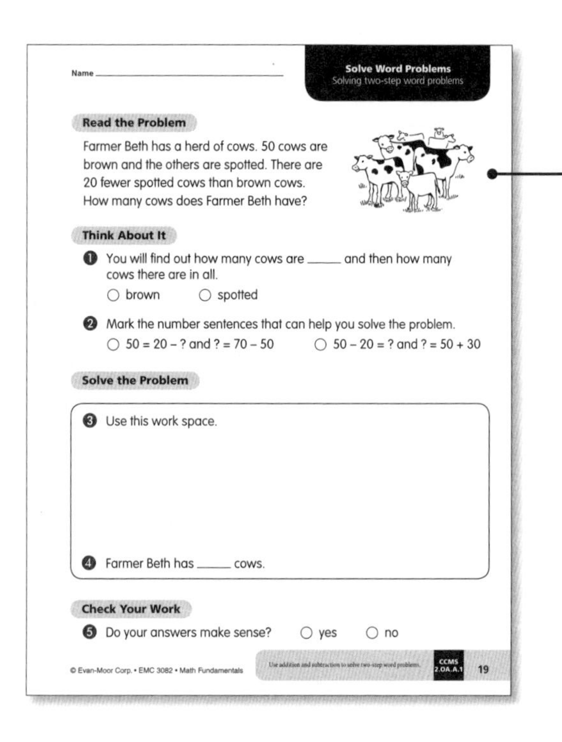
Name ______

Solve Word Problems
Solving two-step word problems

Read the Problem

Farmer Beth has a herd of cows. 50 cows are brown and the others are spotted. There are 20 fewer spotted cows than brown cows. How many cows does Farmer Beth have?

Think About It

1. You will find out how many cows are ____ and then how many cows there are in all.
   ○ brown ○ spotted
2. Mark the number sentences that can help you solve the problem.
   ○ 50 = 20 – ? and ? = 70 – 50 ○ 50 – 20 = ? and ? = 50 + 30

Solve the Problem

3. Use this work space.
4. Farmer Beth has ____ cows.

Check Your Work

5. Do your answers make sense? ○ yes ○ no

© Evan-Moor Corp. • EMC 3082 • Math Fundamentals CCMS 2.OA.A.1 19

Real-world problem
Students tackle a real-world problem. The activity leads students through unpacking the problem: analyzing what the problem asks for, figuring out what information is needed to calculate the answer, showing their work or model, arriving at a solution, and checking their work.

Answer Key

Correct Answers or Examples

The correct response or an exemplar response is shown on a reduced version of the actual page.

Teachers may establish their own criteria for evaluating and scoring work shown leading to an answer.

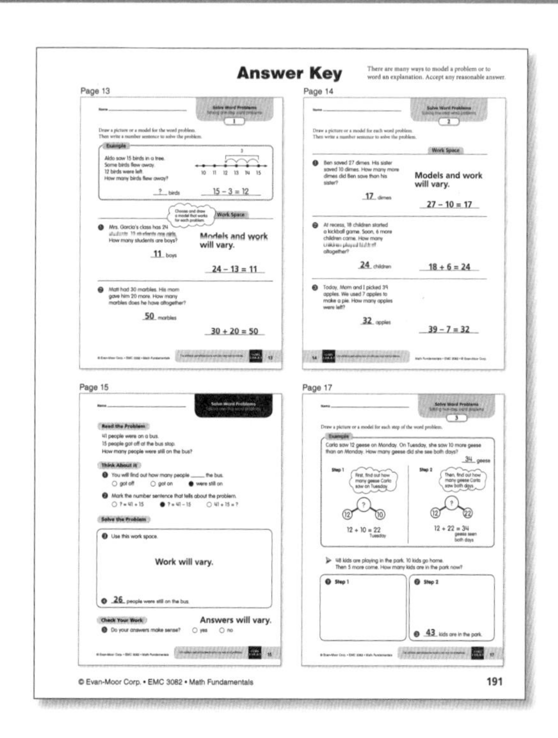
Answer Key

Page 13

Models and work will vary.

15 – 3 = 12

24 – 13 = 11

30 + 20 = 50

Page 14

Models and work will vary.

27 – 10 = 17

18 + 6 = 24

39 – 7 = 32

Page 15

Work will vary.

26 people were still on the bus.

Answers will vary.

Page 17

12 + 10 = 22

12 + 22 = 34

43 kids are in the park.

© Evan-Moor Corp. • EMC 3082 • Math Fundamentals 191

Math Models

Small-Group Instruction

The Math Models pages are intended to be used in a small-group instruction setting. Consider the following approach:

1. Read aloud the concept statement to students.
2. Guide students through each example. Lead them in a discussion about the strategies.
3. Read aloud and discuss the "Think" question at the bottom of the page. Encourage students to participate in the discussion and explain their thinking. This is an opportunity for you to check students' understanding of the math concept.

The models included are suggestions. A variety of widely used models are represented in the book, but feel free to add additional models or integrate those used in class. Where counters are pictured, you may have students use actual manipulative counters or work with representations of them, as you see fit.

Parent Education

Send home Math Models pages for parent education.

Many parents may have questions about the new math strategies their children are learning. The math models will help them better understand the concepts so they can support their children's math education.

Suggested Teaching Path

If you wish to use this book as a core resource, we suggest using the units in the following order:

1. **Add and Subtract Within 20 (page 25)**
   Adding within 20
   Subtracting within 20
2. **Understand Place Value (page 49)**
   Understanding three-digit numbers
   Understanding skip counting
   Reading and writing numbers
   Comparing numbers
3. **Make Equal Groups (page 35)**
   Determining odd and even numbers
   Using equations for even numbers
   Using arrays and repeated addition
4. **Use Math Strategies (page 67)**
   Adding within 100
   Subtracting within 100
   Adding up to four two-digit numbers
   Adding within 1,000
   Subtracting within 1,000
   Adding and subtracting 10 or 100: Mental math
   Explaining why addition strategies work
   Explaining why subtraction strategies work
5. **Solve Word Problems (page 11)**
   Solving one-step word problems
   Solving two-step word problems
   Solving one-step and two-step word problems
6. **Measure and Estimate Length (page 101)**
   Measuring length in customary units
   Measuring length in metric units
   Estimating length
   Measuring, comparing, and writing the difference
7. **Relate Addition and Subtraction to Length (page 119)**
   Solving word problems by using drawings and equations
   Representing lengths on a number line diagram
8. **Work with Time and Money (page 129)**
   Telling and writing time
   Using *a.m.* and *p.m.*
   Determining the value of money
   Solving word problems about money
9. **Represent and Interpret Data (page 147)**
   Interpreting a line plot
   Recording measurement data on a line plot
   Making picture graphs
   Making bar graphs
10. **Analyze Shapes (page 165)**
    Identifying and drawing triangles
    Identifying and drawing quadrilaterals
    Identifying and drawing pentagons and hexagons
    Identifying and drawing cubes
    Partitioning a rectangle
    Describing equal shares

Reproduce and distribute to students.

Strategies for Solving Word Problems and Activities

1. **Read the problem** carefully. Think about what it says.
2. **Draw a model** of the problem. It can be a picture, a diagram, or a chart of data.
3. **Think about what you need** to do to solve it.

   Do you need to
   - add or subtract?
   - skip count?
   - measure something?
   - write an equation?
   - figure out a piece of information before you solve the problem?

4. **Solve the problem.** Hint: Sometimes it will take two steps.
5. **Check your work.** Do your answers make sense?

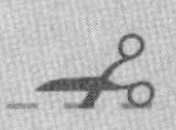

Strategies for Solving Word Problems and Activities

1. **Read the problem** carefully. Think about what it says.
2. **Draw a model** of the problem. It can be a picture, a diagram, or a chart of data.
3. **Think about what you need** to do to solve it.

   Do you need to
   - add or subtract?
   - skip count?
   - measure something?
   - write an equation?
   - figure out a piece of information before you solve the problem?

4. **Solve the problem.** Hint: Sometimes it will take two steps.
5. **Check your work.** Do your answers make sense?

The perfect companion to Evan-Moor's *Daily Math Practice*

Thousands of grade 1 through 6 classrooms use *Daily Math Practice* for focused practice and review. Multiple studies show that this type of distributed, or spaced, practice is a powerful strategy for achieving proficiency and retention of skills.

Student responses on the *Daily Math Practice* items will indicate which skills need additional practice or remediation. Use *Math Fundamentals* to provide the reteaching and additional practice. For example:

A student makes errors in week 31 of *Daily Math Practice*. Your assessment is that the student needs more practice with these skills.

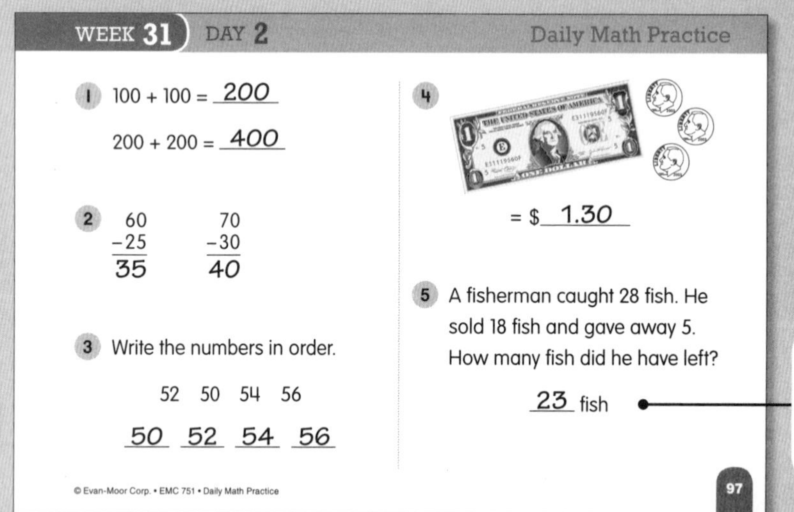

WEEK 31 DAY 2 Daily Math Practice

1. 100 + 100 = 200
   200 + 200 = 400
2. 60 − 25 = 35   70 − 30 = 40
3. Write the numbers in order.
   52 50 54 56
   50 52 54 56
4. = $ 1.30
5. A fisherman caught 28 fish. He sold 18 fish and gave away 5. How many fish did he have left?
   23 fish

© Evan-Moor Corp. • EMC 751 • Daily Math Practice 97

The student does not know how to solve two-step problems.

Use these pages from *Math Fundamentals* to reteach and practice the skills the student has not mastered.

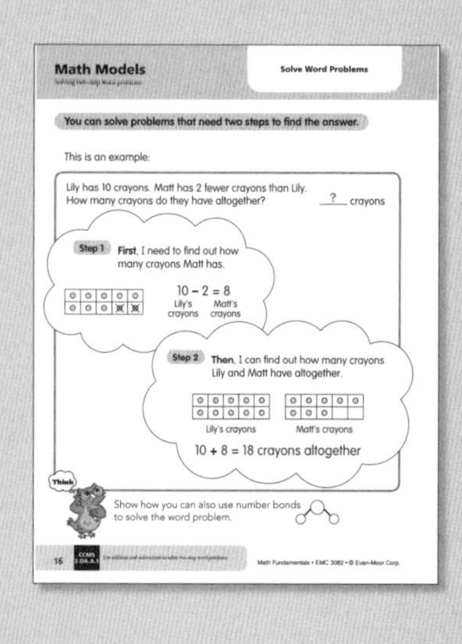

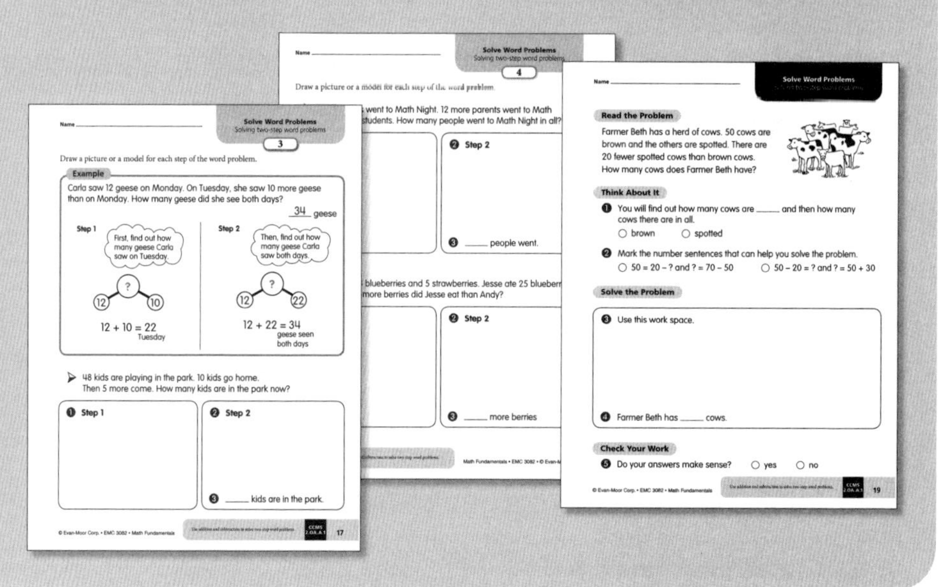

Solve Word Problems

Domain

Operations and Algebraic Thinking

Cluster

Represent and solve problems involving addition and subtraction.

Standard in Cluster

2.OA.A.1 Use addition and subtraction within 100 to solve one- and two-step word problems involving situations of adding to, taking from, putting together, taking apart, and comparing, with unknowns in all positions, e.g., by using drawings and equations with a symbol for the unknown number to represent the problem.

Unit Contents

Mathematical Practices in This Unit

Make sense of problems and persevere in solving them: *pages 12, 13, 14, 15, 16, 17, 18, 19, 20, 21, 22, 23, 24*

Reason abstractly and quantitatively: *pages 13, 14, 15, 17, 18, 19, 21, 22, 23, 24*

Construct viable arguments and critique the reasoning of others: *pages 12, 16, 20*

Model with mathematics: *pages 12, 13, 14, 15, 17, 18, 19, 21, 22, 24*

Attend to precision: *pages 15, 19, 24*

Look for and make use of structure: *pages 13, 14, 15, 17, 18, 19, 21, 22, 23, 24*

You can put together, take apart, or compare to solve one-step word problems.

These are some examples:

Put Together

Jamal collects rocks. He has 12 gray rocks and 9 brown rocks. How many rocks does Jamal have in all?

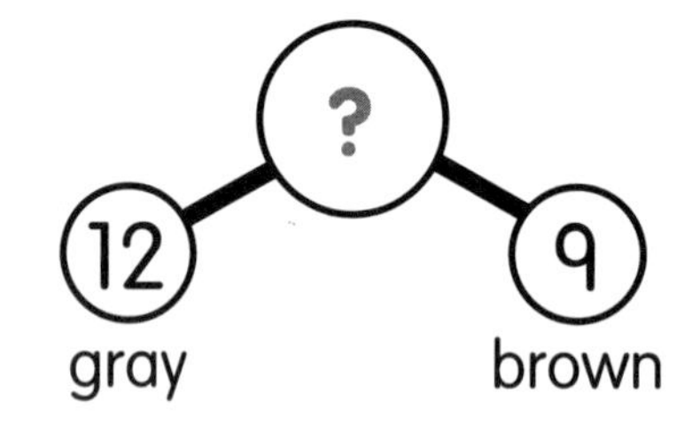

12 + 9 = 21 rocks in all

Take Apart

Jamal had 21 rocks. He gave 3 rocks to Dan. How many rocks does he have left?

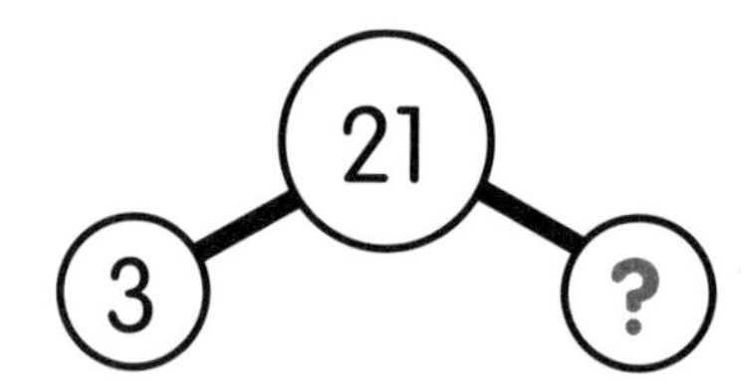

21 − 3 = 18 rocks left

Compare

Jamal has 12 gray rocks. He has 9 brown rocks. How many more gray rocks than brown rocks does Jamal have?

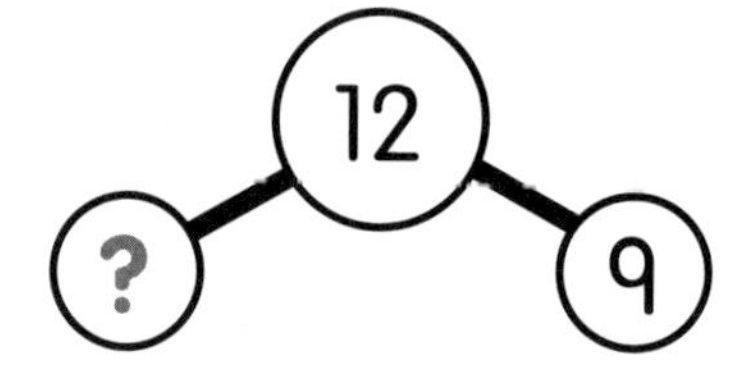

12 − 9 = 3 more gray rocks

What other types of math models can be used to put together, take apart, or compare? Explain your thinking.

Name ________________________________

Draw a picture or a model for the word problem.
Then write a number sentence to solve the problem.

Example

Aldo saw 15 birds in a tree.
Some birds flew away.
12 birds were left.
How many birds flew away?

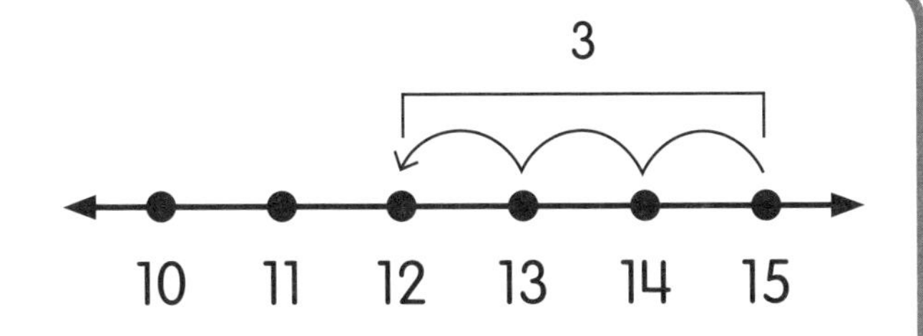

__?__ birds

15 – 3 = 12

Choose and draw a model that works for each problem.

Work Space

1. Mrs. Garcia's class has 24 students. 13 students are girls. How many students are boys?

_____ boys

____

2. Matt had 30 marbles. His mom gave him 20 more. How many marbles does he have altogether?

_____ marbles

____

Name ______________________________

Solve Word Problems
Solving one-step word problems

2

Draw a picture or a model for each word problem.
Then write a number sentence to solve the problem.

Work Space

1. Ben saved 27 dimes. His sister saved 10 dimes. How many more dimes did Ben save than his sister?

   _____ dimes

   ____

2. At recess, 18 children started a kickball game. Soon, 6 more children came. How many children played kickball altogether?

   _____ children

   ____

3. Today, Mom and I picked 39 apples. We used 7 apples to make a pie. How many apples were left?

   _____ apples

   ____

CCMS 2.OA.A.1 Use addition and subtraction to solve one-step word problems.

Name ______________________________

Read the Problem

41 people were on a bus.
15 people got off at the bus stop.
How many people were still on the bus?

Think About It

1. You will find out how many people _____ the bus.
   - ○ got off ○ got on ○ were still on

2. Mark the number sentence that tells about the problem.
   - ○ ? = 41 + 15 ○ ? = 41 – 15 ○ 41 + 15 = ?

Solve the Problem

3. Use this work space.

4. _____ people were still on the bus.

Check Your Work

5. Do your answers make sense? ○ yes ○ no

You can solve problems that need two steps to find the answer.

This is an example:

Lily has 10 crayons. Matt has 2 fewer crayons than Lily.
How many crayons do they have altogether? ___?___ crayons

Step 1 **First**, I need to find out how many crayons Matt has.

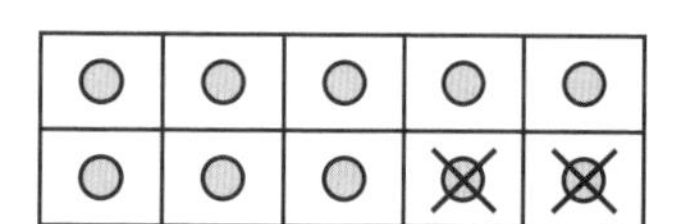

$10 - 2 = 8$
Lily's crayons Matt's crayons

Step 2 **Then**, I can find out how many crayons Lily and Matt have altogether.

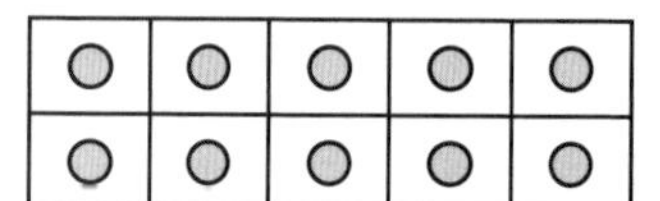

Lily's crayons

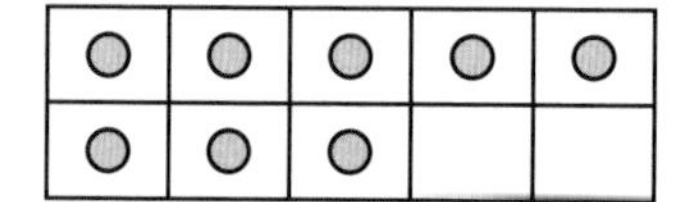

Matt's crayons

$10 + 8 = 18$ crayons altogether

Think

Show how you can also use number bonds to solve the word problem.

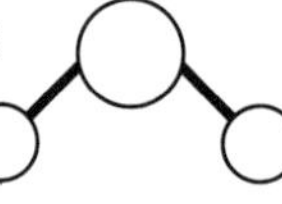

Name ______________________________

Draw a picture or a model for each step of the word problem.

Example

Carla saw 12 geese on Monday. On Tuesday, she saw 10 more geese than on Monday. How many geese did she see both days?

34 geese

Step 1

First, find out how many geese Carla saw on Tuesday.

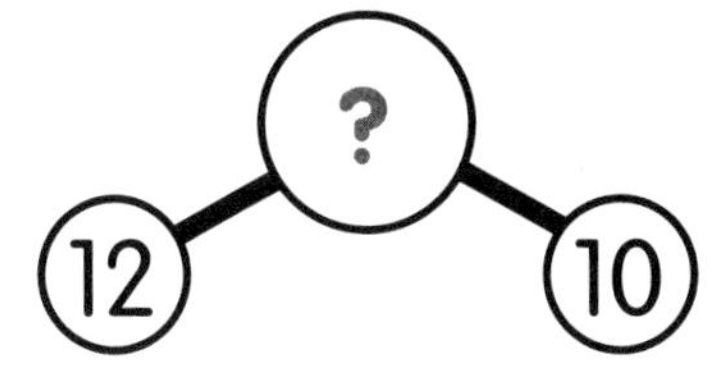

12 + 10 = 22
Tuesday

Step 2

Then, find out how many geese Carla saw both days.

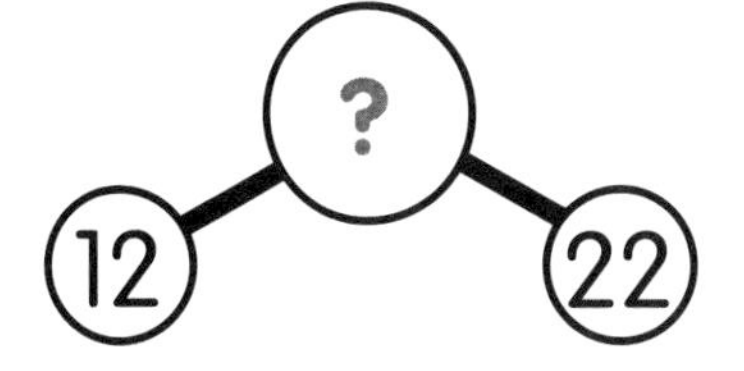

12 + 22 = 34
geese seen both days

48 kids are playing in the park. 10 kids go home. Then 5 more come. How many kids are in the park now?

❶ **Step 1**

❷ **Step 2**

❸ _____ kids are in the park.

Use addition and subtraction to solve two-step word problems.

CCMS 2.OA.A.1

Name ______________________________

Draw a picture or a model for each step of the word problem.

34 students went to Math Night. 12 more parents went to Math Night than students. How many people went to Math Night in all?

1 Step 1

2 Step 2

3 ______ people went.

Andy ate 18 blueberries and 5 strawberries. Jesse ate 25 blueberries. How many more berries did Jesse eat than Andy?

1 Step 1

2 Step 2

3 ______ more berries

CCMS 2.OA.A.1 Use addition and subtraction to solve two-step word problems.

Name ____________________

Read the Problem

Farmer Beth has a herd of cows. 50 cows are brown and the others are spotted. There are 20 fewer spotted cows than brown cows. How many cows does Farmer Beth have?

Think About It

1. You will find out how many cows are _____ and then how many cows there are in all.
   ○ brown ○ spotted

2. Mark the number sentences that can help you solve the problem.
   ○ 50 = 20 – ? and ? = 70 – 50 ○ 50 – 20 = ? and ? = 50 + 30

Solve the Problem

3. Use this work space.

4. Farmer Beth has _____ cows.

Check Your Work

5. Do your answers make sense? ○ yes ○ no

Math Models

Solving one- and two-step word problems

You can decide if a word problem needs one or two steps to solve.

These are **two** examples:

Mom made 24 cupcakes and 72 cookies for the bake sale. How many treats did she make in all?

__?__ treats

Step 1 I can add to solve.

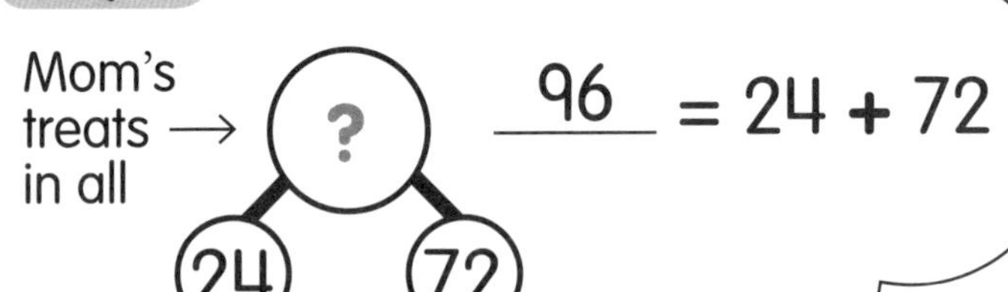

cupcakes cookies

Dad made 36 cookies for the bake sale. Aunt Sue made 12 more than Dad made. How many cookies did they make in all?

__?__ cookies

Step 1 **First**, I need to find out how many cookies Aunt Sue made.

Aunt Sue's cookies → ? ; 36 (Dad's), 12

36 + 12 = 48 (Aunt Sue's)

Step 2 **Then**, I can add the cookies to solve the problem.

cookies in all → ? ; Dad's 36, 48 Aunt Sue's

36 + 48 = 84

How can you tell if you need to use one or two steps in these word problems? Explain your thinking.

CCMS 2.OA.A.1 Use addition and subtraction to solve one- and two-step word problems.

Name ______________________

Solve each word problem with one or two steps. Show your work.

Example

Amy's team has 26 points. Sara's team has 32 points.
How many more points does Sara's team have? <u>6</u> more points

I can find out with one step.

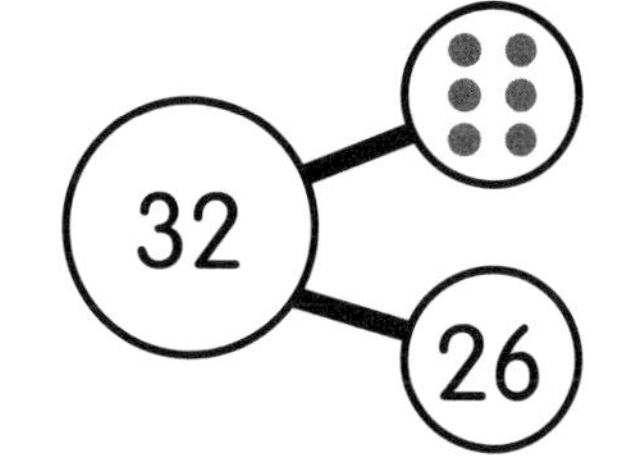

32 – <u>6</u> = 26

➤ Cam has 46 marbles. Tessa has 3 fewer than Cam.
How many marbles do they have altogether?

❶ Use this work space.

❷ _____ marbles

➤ Jan played jump rope for 30 minutes. Then she played hopscotch for 15 minutes. How many minutes did Jan play in all?

❸ Use this work space.

❹ _____ minutes

Use addition and subtraction to solve one- and two-step word problems.

CCMS 2.OA.A.1

Name ______________________________

Solve each word problem with one or two steps. Show your work.

51 children were swimming in a pool. 8 more children joined them. Then 12 children went home. How many children were still swimming?

1. Use this work space.
2. ______ children

Zoey had 37 books. Her grandma gave her 4 more. How many books does Zoey have now?

3. Use this work space.
4. ______ books

Chris rode his bike for 30 minutes on Monday and 45 minutes on Tuesday. Rita rode her bike for 60 minutes on Tuesday. How much longer did Chris ride his bike than Rita?

5. Use this work space.
6. ______ minutes

CCMS 2.OA.A.1 Use addition and subtraction to solve one- and two-step word problems.

Name ________________________________

Solve Word Problems
Solving one- and two-step word problems

7

Read each word problem. Mark the number sentence or sentences that can help you solve it. Then write the answer.

28 flowers are growing in Mom's garden. 20 flowers are purple. The others are white. How many flowers are white?

1. ○ 28 + 20 = ?
   ○ ? = 28 – 20
2. _____ white flowers

---

30 ducks were swimming in the lake. 10 more ducks came. How many ducks were there in all?

3. ○ 30 + 10 = ?
   ○ 30 – ? = 10
4. _____ ducks

Emma saw 18 robins in a tree. 9 robins flew away. Then 12 more robins came. How many robins were in the tree then?

5. ○ ? = 18 – 9 and ? = 9 + 12
   ○ 18 + 9 = ? and 9 + 12 = ?
6. _____ robins

Two second-grade classes went on a field trip. There were 40 boys. There were 2 more girls than boys. How many second graders went on the field trip?

7. ○ 40 – 2 = ? and ? = 38 + 40
   ○ 40 + 2 = ? and ? = 42 + 40
8. _____ second graders

Name ______________________

Solve Word Problems
Solving one- and two-step word problems

Read the Problem

Alex read a book for 20 minutes. His little sister, Lara, read for 5 minutes less than him. How many minutes did Alex and his sister read altogether?

Think About It

1. This word problem will take _____ steps to solve.
   ○ one ○ two

2. Mark the number sentence that tells how many minutes Lara read.
   ○ 20 + 15 = ? ○ ? = 20 – 5 ○ ? = 20 + 5

3. Mark the number sentence that tells how many minutes Alex and Lara read altogether.
   ○ 20 + 15 = ? ○ 15 + ? = 20 ○ 20 – ? = 5

Solve the Problem

4. Use this work space.

5. Alex and Lara read _____ minutes altogether.

Check Your Work

6. Do your answers make sense? ○ yes ○ no

CCMS 2.OA.A.1 Use addition and subtraction to solve one- and two-step word problems.

Add and Subtract Within 20

Domain

Operations and Algebraic Thinking

Cluster

Add and subtract using mental strategies.

Standards in Cluster

2.OA.B.2 Add and subtract within 20.

2.OA.B.2 Fluently add and subtract within 20 using mental strategies. By the end of Grade 2, know from memory all sums of two one-digit numbers.

Unit Contents

Mathematical Practices in This Unit

Make sense of problems and persevere in solving them: *pages 26, 27, 28, 29, 30, 31, 32, 33, 34*

Reason abstractly and quantitatively: *pages 27, 28, 29, 31, 32, 33, 34*

Construct viable arguments and critique the reasoning of others: *pages 26, 30*

Model with mathematics: *pages 27, 28, 29, 31, 32, 34*

Attend to precision: *pages 29, 34*

Look for and make use of structure: *pages 26, 30*

Math Models

Adding within 20

You can use thinking models to add.

These are some examples:

Count on

12 + 3 = 15

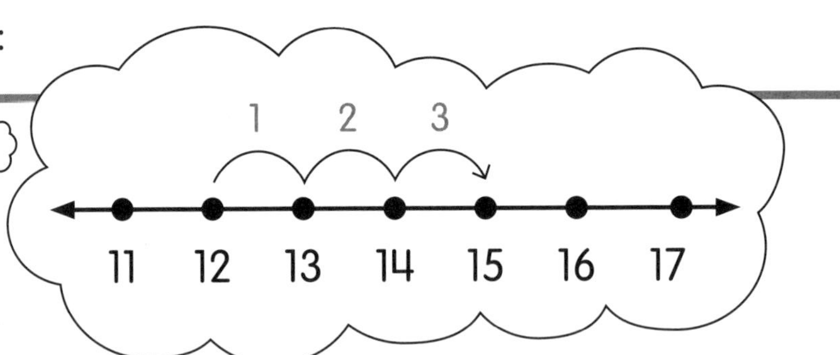

Make a ten

7 + 5 = 12

7 + 5 = ?
7 + ③ ② = ?
10 + 2 = 12

Use a number sentence that you already know.

Doubles fact

8 + 9 = 17

I know 8 + 8 = 16.
So 8 + 9 = 17.

Easier fact

9 + 7 = 16

I know 10 + 7 = 17.
So 9 + 7 = 16.

Add **8 + 4 = ?** in your mind. Explain your thinking.

Name ______________________

Find each sum. Show a way to think about it.

Example

6 + 8 = __?__

6 + 8 = ?
④②+ 8 = ?
4 + 10 = __14__

❶ 9 + 5 = ____

❷ 7 + 8 = ____

❸ 15 + 2 = ____

Name ____________________

Find each sum. Show a way to think about it.

1. 5 + 7 = ____

2. 12 + 2 = ____

3. 11 + 5 = ____

4. 6 + 9 = ____

CCMS 2.OA.B.2 Fluently add using mental strategies.

Name ______________________________

Read the Problem

Jack's team made 8 goals last week.
They made 9 goals this week.
How many goals did Jack's team make in all?

Think About It

1. You will find out how many goals they _____.
   - ○ missed
   - ○ made
   - ○ want

2. Mark the number sentence that can help you solve the problem.
   - ○ $8 + 1 = 9$
   - ○ $9 - 8 = 1$
   - ○ $8 + 8 = 16$

Solve the Problem

3. Use this work space.

4. Jack's team made _____ goals in all.

Check Your Work

5. Do your answers make sense? ○ yes ○ no

Math Models

Subtracting within 20

You can use thinking models to subtract.

These are some examples:

Count back

$17 - 2 = \underline{15}$

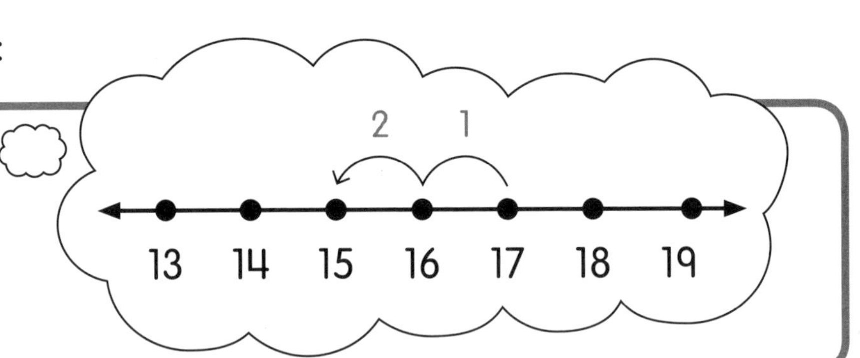

Lead to a ten

$14 - 5 = \underline{9}$

$14 - 5 = ?$

$14 - (4)(1) = ?$

$10 - 1 = 9$

Use a number sentence that you already know.

Doubles fact

$13 - 7 = \underline{6}$

I know $14 - 7 = 7$.
So $13 - 7 = 6$.

Related addition fact

$15 - 9 = \underline{6}$

I know $6 + 9 = 15$.
So $15 - 9 = 6$.

Subtract **17 − 8 = ?** in your mind. Explain your thinking.

Name ______________________

Find the difference. Show a way to think about it.

Example

12 – 7 = __?__

I know 12 – 6 = 6.
So 12 – 7 = __5__.

1 15 – 8 = ______

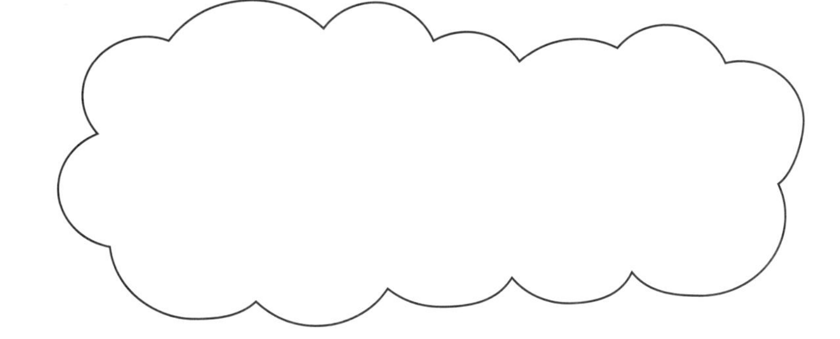

2 ______ = 18 – 4

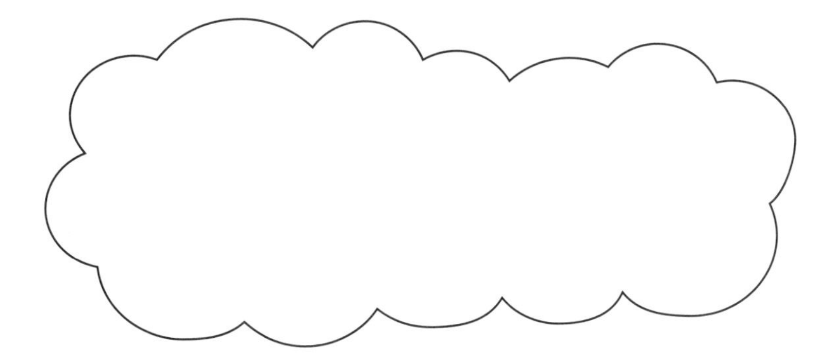

3 11 – ______ = 6

Name ______________________________

Find the difference. Show a way to think about it.

1. $13 - 4 =$ ____

2. $17 -$ ____ $= 8$

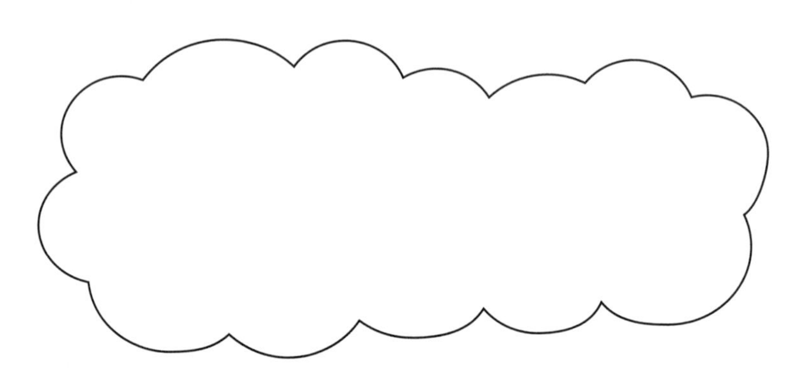

3. ____ $= 17 - 2$

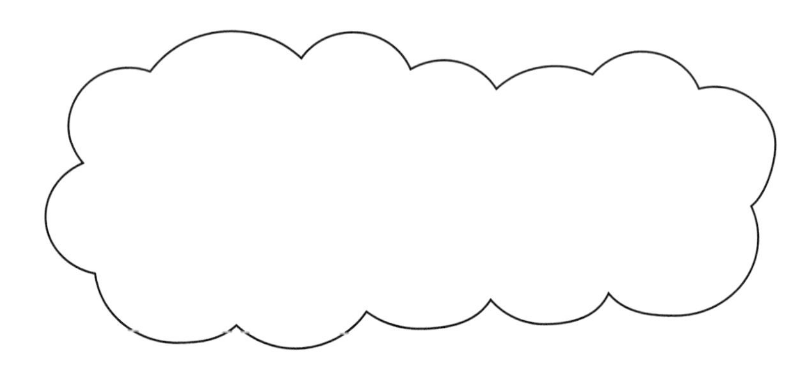

4. $20 -$ ____ $= 9$

CCMS 2.OA.B.2 Fluently subtract using mental strategies.

Name ______________________________

Mark the number sentence that can help you solve each subtraction problem. Then write the missing number.

Example

11 − 6 = __5__

○ 11 + 6 = 17
● 10 − 5 = 5

❶ _____ − 16 = 3

○ 16 + 3 = 19
○ 19 − 3 = 16

❷ 17 − _____ = 9

○ 16 + 8 = 24
○ 16 − 8 = 8

❸ 13 − 5 = _____

○ 10 − 2 = 8
○ 15 − 3 = 12

❹ 13 − _____ = 7

○ 13 + 6 = 19
○ 6 + 7 = 13

Fluently subtract using mental strategies.

CCMS 2.OA.B.2

Name ______________________

Read the Problem

At the game, Joy's team had 17 players. 2 players went home sick. How many players were left?

Think About It

1. You will find out how many players were _____.

   ○ on the team ○ left ○ sick

2. Mark the thinking model that can help you solve the problem.

○ 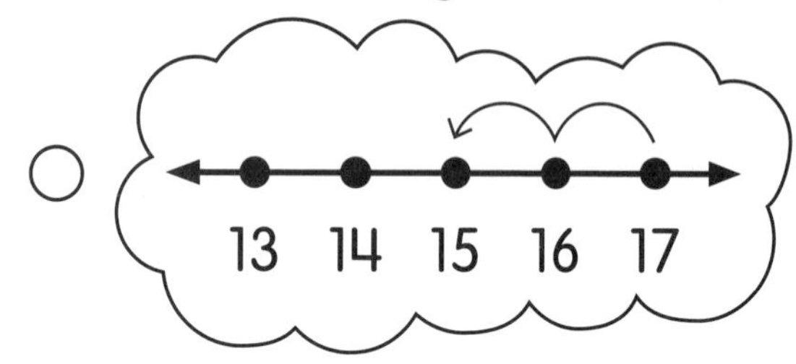

○ 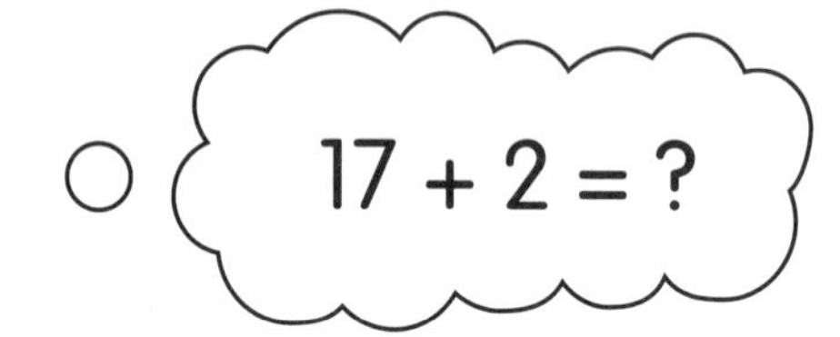

Solve the Problem

3. Use this work space.

4. _____ players were left.

Check Your Work

5. Do your answers make sense? ○ yes ○ no

CCMS 2.OA.B.2 Fluently subtract using mental strategies.

Make Equal Groups

Domain

Operations and Algebraic Thinking

Cluster

Work with equal groups of objects to gain foundations for multiplication.

Standards in Cluster

2.OA.C.3 Determine whether a group of objects (up to 20) has an odd or even number of members, e.g., by pairing objects or counting them by 2s; write an equation to express an even number as a sum of two equal addends.

2.OA.C.4 Use addition to find the total number of objects arranged in rectangular arrays with up to 5 rows and up to 5 columns; write an equation to express the total as a sum of equal addends.

Unit Contents

Mathematical Practices in This Unit

Make sense of problems and persevere in solving them: *pages 36, 39, 40, 43, 44, 48*

Reason abstractly and quantitatively: *pages 39, 43, 48*

Construct viable arguments and critique the reasoning of others: *pages 36, 40, 44*

Model with mathematics: *pages 39, 41, 42, 43, 46, 48*

Attend to precision: *pages 37, 38, 41, 42, 45, 46, 47*

Look for and make use of structure: *pages 36, 37, 38, 40, 41, 42, 44, 45, 46*

Math Models

Determining odd and even numbers

You can tell if a group of objects is an odd or even number of things.

A pair means **two**. You can make pairs to show **odd** or **even**.

Odd	Even
5	6
9	10
17	18

Odd numbers shown as pairs will have one number left over.

Even numbers can be shown as pairs.

Think

How can counting by twos help you decide if the number **11** is an even or odd number? Explain your thinking.

CCMS 2.OA.C.3 Determine whether a group of objects has an odd or even number.

Name ________________________________

Write the number of objects in each group. Then mark **even** or **odd**.

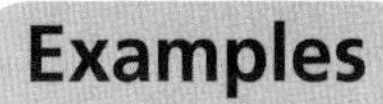

Examples

4

● even ○ odd

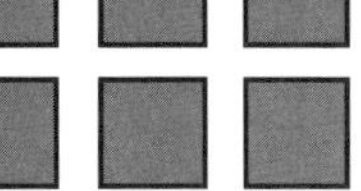

7

○ even ● odd

1

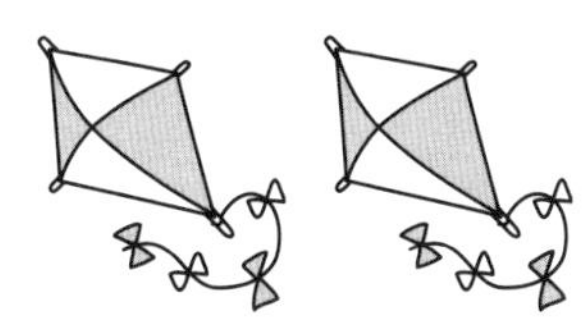
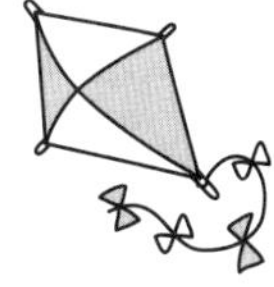

____

○ even ○ odd

2

____

○ even ○ odd

3

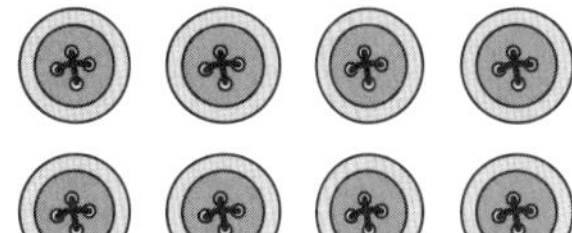

____

○ even ○ odd

4

____

○ even ○ odd

Name ______________________

Make Equal Groups
Determining odd and even numbers

2

Write the number of objects in each group. Then mark **even** or **odd**.

1. 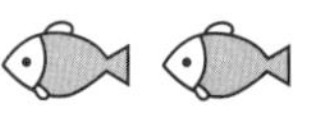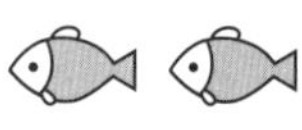 ______

   ○ even ○ odd

2. 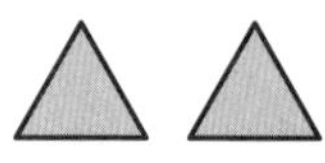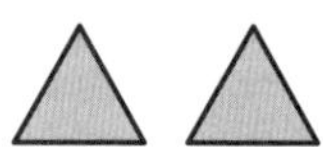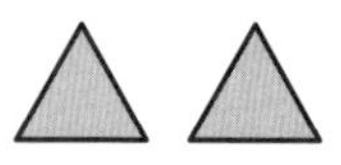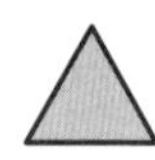 ______

   ○ even ○ odd

3.  ______

   ○ even ○ odd

4. 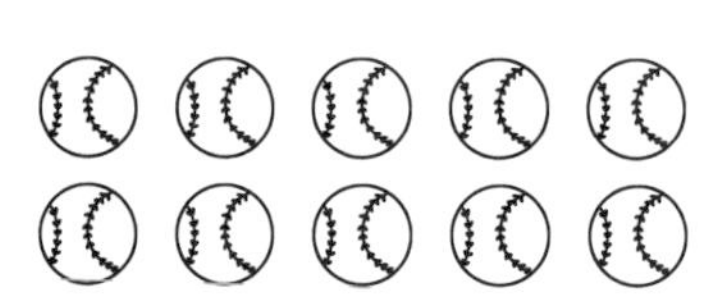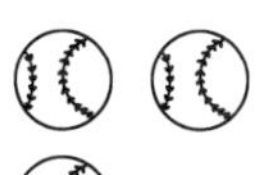 ______

   ○ even ○ odd

5.  ______

   ○ even ○ odd

6. 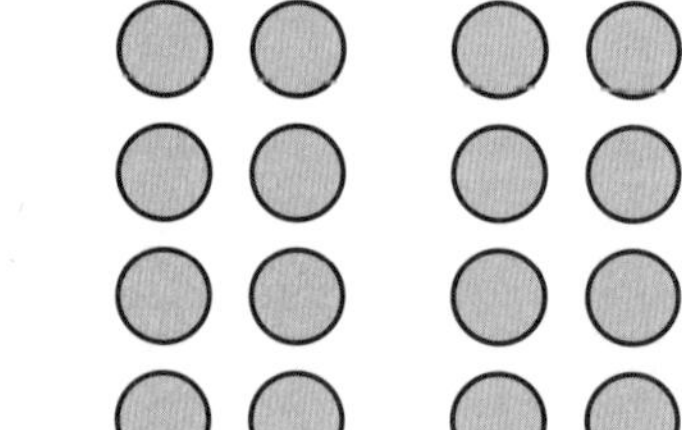 ______

   ○ even ○ odd

CCMS 2.OA.C.3 Determine whether a group of objects has an odd or even number.

Name ______________________________

Read the Problem

9 girls and 9 boys rode on the bus. How many children rode on the bus altogether? Was there an odd number of children?

Think About It

❶ First, you will find out how many _____ rode on the bus.

○ girls ○ boys ○ girls and boys

❷ Mark the number sentence that tells about the problem.

○ $9 = ? - 9$ ○ $? = 9 + 9$ ○ $? - 9 = 9$

Solve the Problem

❸ Use this work space.

❹ _____ children rode on the bus altogether.

❺ There was an odd number of children. ○ yes ○ no

Check Your Work

❻ Do your answers make sense? ○ yes ○ no

Determine whether a group of objects has an odd or even number.

CCMS 2.OA.C.3

Math Models

Using equations for even numbers

You can write a doubles number sentence that tells about an even number.

These are some examples:

Even Number	Model	Number Sentence
2	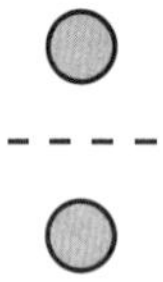	1 + 1 = 2
8	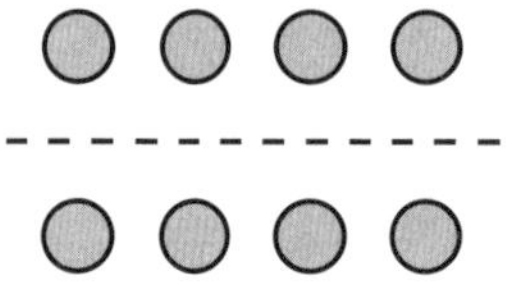	4 + 4 = 8
14	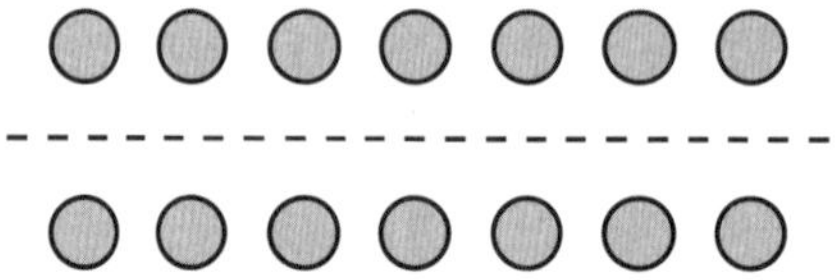	7 + 7 = 14
20	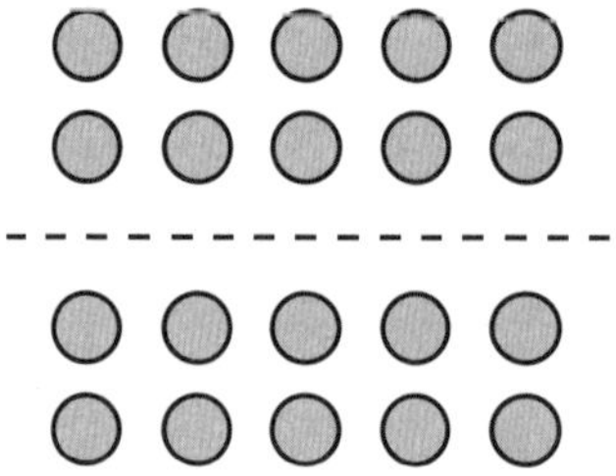	10 + 10 = 20

Think

Jared says he can't write a doubles number sentence for the sum of **9**. Do you agree? Explain your thinking.

CCMS 2.OA.C.3 Write an equation to express an even number as the sum of two equal addends.

Name ______________________________

Make Equal Groups
Using equations for even numbers

3

Write a doubles number sentence that tells about each even number.

Example

Model	Number	Doubles number sentence
	10	5 + 5 = 10

1.  6 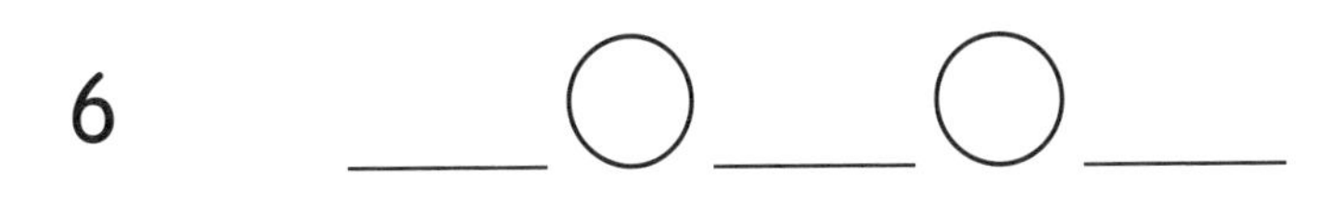

2. 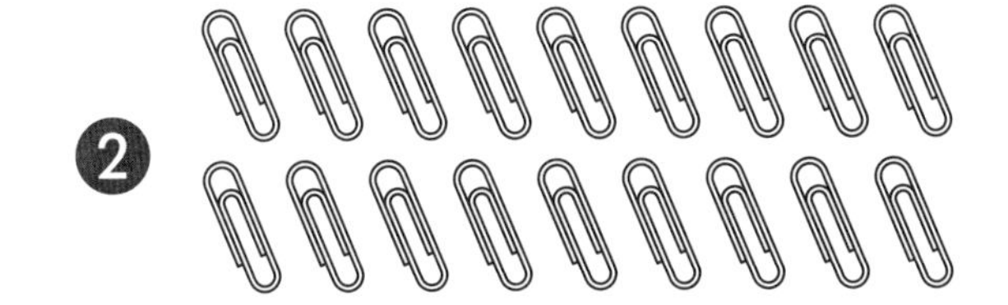 18 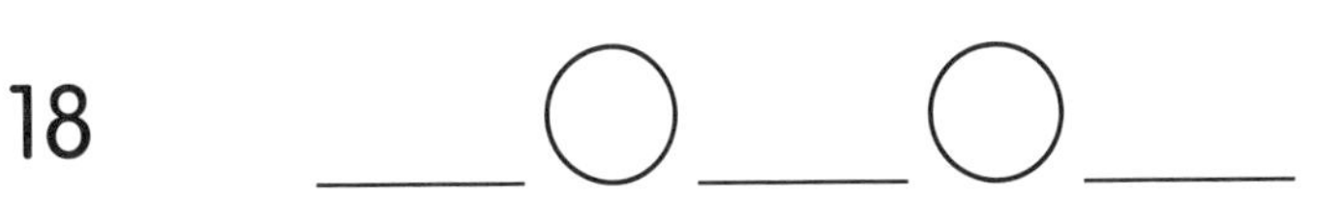

3. 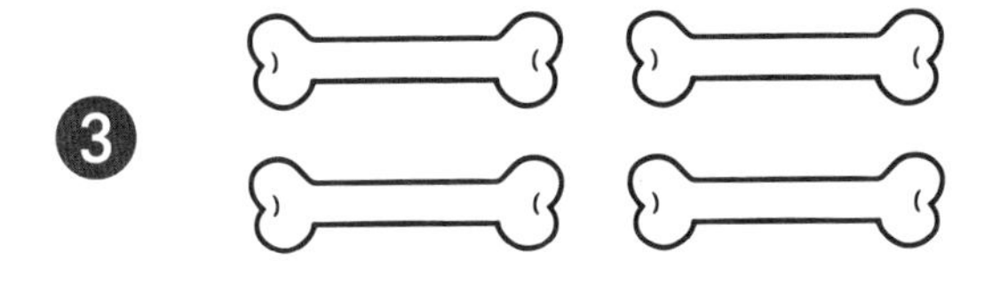 4 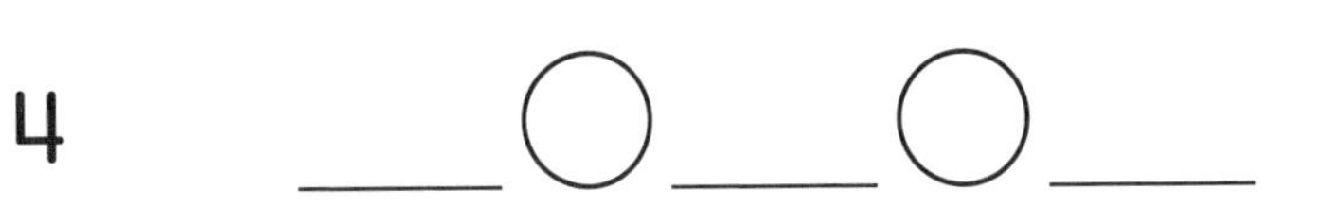

4.  12 ___ ◯ ___ ◯ ___

Write an equation to express an even number as the sum of two equal addends.

CCMS 2.OA.C.3

Name ____________________

Make Equal Groups
Using equations for even numbers

4

For each number sentence, draw pairs of objects to show how many. Then write the sum.

Example

$4 + 4 = \underline{8}$

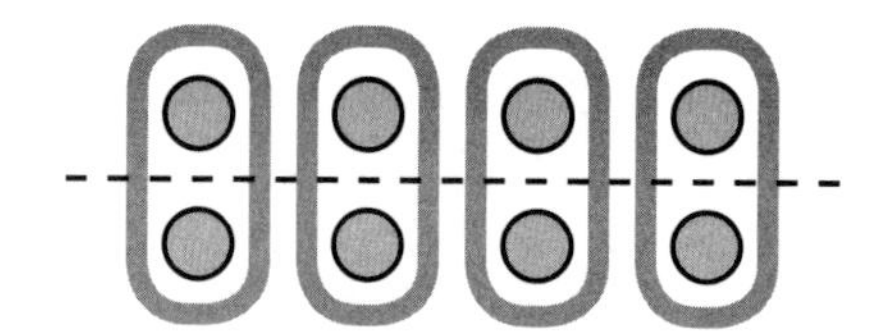

Work Space

1. $3 + 3 =$ _____

2. $5 + 5 =$ _____

3. $8 + 8 =$ _____

4. $10 + 10 =$ _____

CCMS 2.OA.C.3 Write an equation to express an even number as the sum of two equal addends.

Name ______________________________

Read the Problem

The players on two teams lined up to shake hands.

It looked like this: **Team 1** ○ ○ ○ ○ ○ ○ ○ ○ ○

Team 2 ○ ○ ○ ○ ○ ○ ○ ○ ○

You will write a doubles number sentence below that tells how many players there were altogether.

Think About It

1. You will find out how many players there were ______.
   - ○ on each team
   - ○ altogether
   - ○ on one team

2. The number of players on each team is ______.
   - ○ equal
   - ○ different
   - ○ greater than 10

Solve the Problem

3. Use this work space to write the doubles number sentence that tells about the problem.

   ____ ○ ____ ○ ____

4. There were ______ players altogether.

Check Your Work

5. Do your answers make sense? ○ yes ○ no

You can use repeated addition to find the number of objects in an array.

An **array** is a set of objects that shows equal groups in rows and columns.

rows

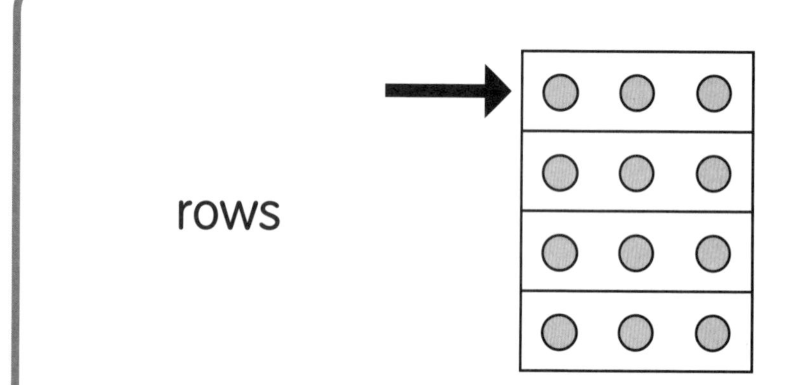

$3 + 3 + 3 + 3 = 12$

columns

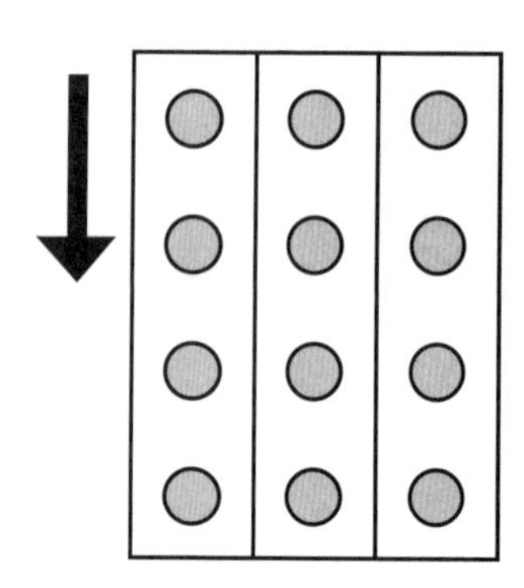

$4 + 4 + 4 = 12$

If you write two repeated addition number sentences for this array, will they be the same? Explain your thinking.

Name ______________________________

Make Equal Groups
Using arrays and repeated addition

5

Look at the **rows** in each array. Write the number of objects in each row.
Then complete the number sentence.

Example

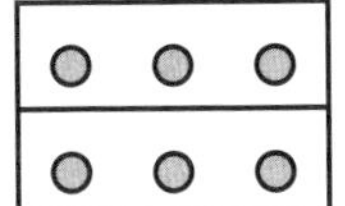

There are 2 rows of <u>3</u>.

<u>3</u> + <u>3</u> = <u>6</u>

1

There are 3 rows of ____.

____ + ____ + ____ = ____

2

There are 5 rows of ____.

____ + ____ + ____ + ____ + ____ = ____

3

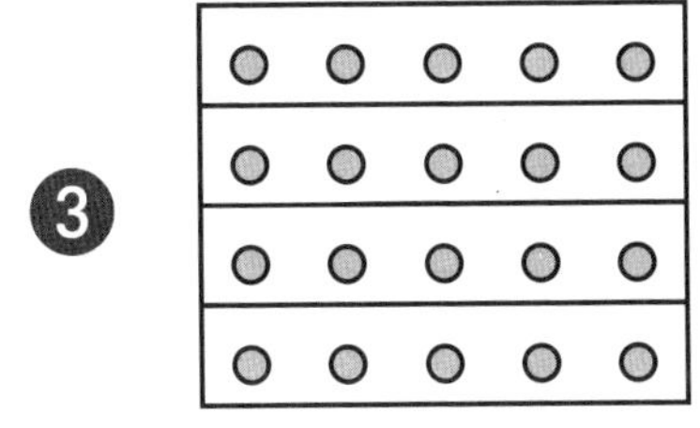

There are 4 rows of ____.

____ + ____ + ____ + ____ = ____

Name ______________________

Make Equal Groups

Using arrays and repeated addition

6

Look at the **columns** in each array. Write the number of objects in each column. Then complete the number sentence.

Example

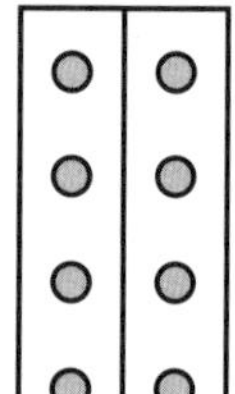

There are 2 columns of __4__.

__4__ + __4__ = __8__

1. 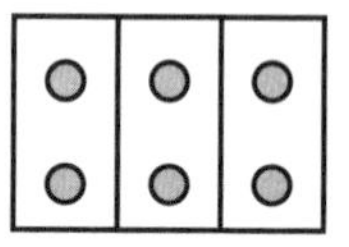

There are 3 columns of ____.

____ + ____ + ____ = ____

2. 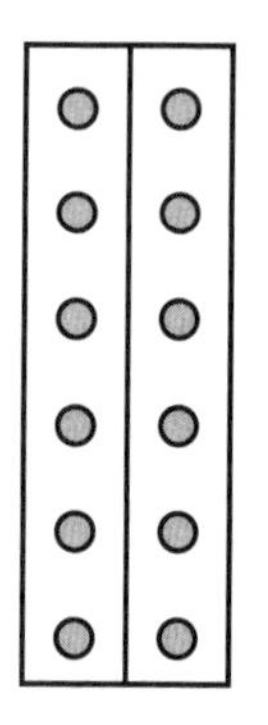

There are 2 columns of ____.

____ + ____ = ____

3. 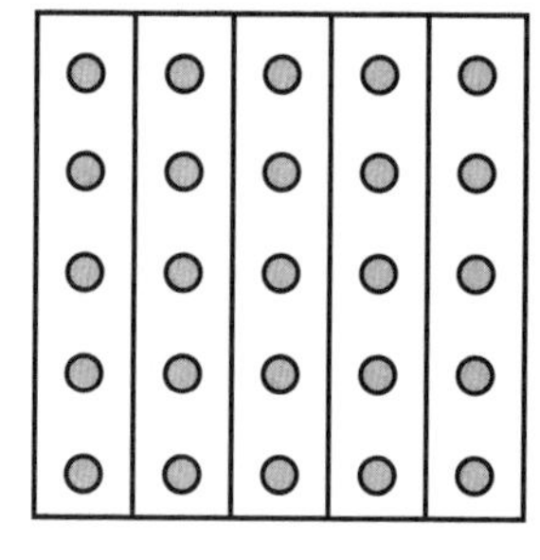

There are 5 columns of ____.

____ + ____ + ____ + ____ + ____ = ____

CCMS 2.OA.C.4 Use addition to find the total number of objects arranged in arrays.

Name ______________________________

Mark the number sentence that tells about each array.

1. 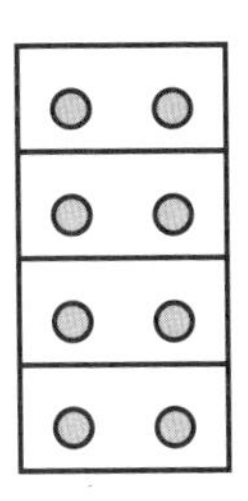

- ○ 2 + 2 + 2 + 2 = ?
- ○ 2 + 2 + 2 = ?
- ○ 4 + 4 + 4 = ?

---

2. 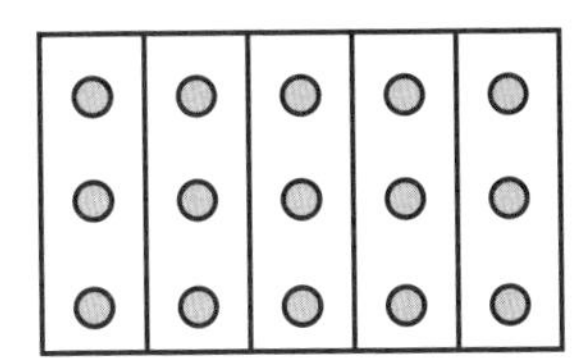

- ○ 5 + 5 + 5 + 5 = ?
- ○ 3 + 3 + 3 = ?
- ○ 3 + 3 + 3 + 3 + 3 = ?

3.

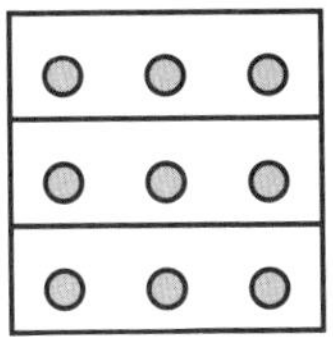

- ○ 3 + 3 + 3 = ?
- ○ 3 + 3 = ?
- ○ 3 + 3 + 3 + 3 = ?

---

4. 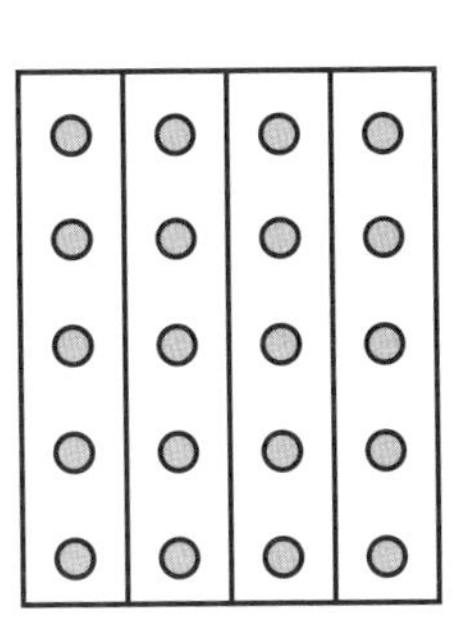

- ○ 4 + 4 + 4 + 4 = ?
- ○ 5 + 5 + 5 + 5 = ?
- ○ 5 + 5 + 5 = ?

Name ___________________________

Make Equal Groups
Using arrays and repeated addition

Read the Problem

Nadia went to the city. She saw a building with a lot of windows. It looked like this:

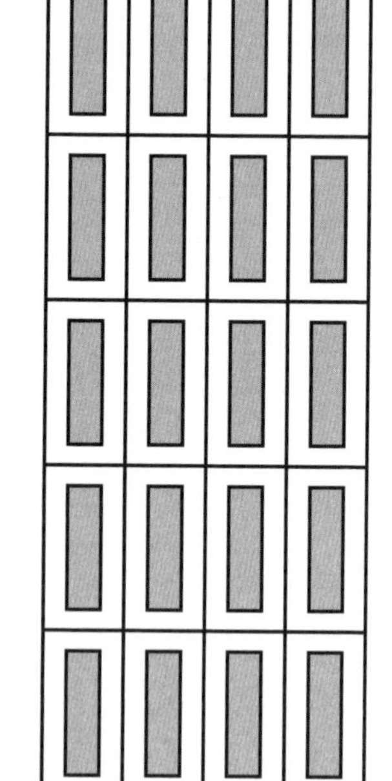

You will write a repeated addition number sentence below to find out how many windows Nadia saw.

Think About It

1. You will find out how many _____ Nadia saw.
   - ○ buildings ○ cities ○ windows

2. Each row has _____ windows.
   - ○ 5 ○ 4 ○ 16

Solve the Problem

3. Use this work space to write the repeated number sentence.

4. Nadia saw _____ windows on the building.

Check Your Work

5. Do your answers make sense? ○ yes ○ no

CCMS 2.OA.C.4 Use addition to find the total number of objects arranged in arrays.

Understand Place Value

Domain

Number and Operations in Base Ten

Cluster

Understand place value.

Standards in Cluster

2.NBT.A.1 Understand that the three digits of a three-digit number represent amounts of hundreds, tens, and ones; e.g., 706 equals 7 hundreds, 0 tens, and 6 ones. Understand the following as special cases:

2.NBT.A.1.a 100 can be thought of as a bundle of tens—called a "hundred."

2.NBT.A.1.b The numbers 100, 200, 300, 400, 500, 600, 700, 800, 900 refer to one, two, three, four, five, six, seven, eight, or nine hundreds (and 0 tens and 0 ones).

2.NBT.A.2 Count within 1,000; skip-count by 5s, 10s, and 100s.

2.NBT.A.3 Read and write numbers to 1,000 using base-ten numerals, number names, and expanded form.

2.NBT.A.4 Compare two three-digit numbers based on meanings of the hundreds, tens, and ones digits, using >, =, and < symbols to record the results of comparisons.

Unit Contents

Mathematical Practices in This Unit

Make sense of problems and persevere in solving them: *pages 50, 53, 54, 57, 58, 61, 62, 66*

Reason abstractly and quantitatively: *pages 52, 53, 56, 57, 59, 60, 61, 63, 64, 65, 66*

Construct viable arguments and critique the reasoning of others: *pages 50, 54, 58, 61, 62*

Model with mathematics: *pages 53, 57, 61, 66*

Attend to precision: *pages 53, 57, 61, 66*

Look for and make use of structure: *pages 51, 52, 55, 56, 59, 60, 63, 54, 65*

Look for and express regularity in repeated reasoning: *pages 54, 55, 56, 57*

Math Models

Understanding three-digit numbers

You can understand the meaning of hundreds, tens, and ones.

Let's look at a three-digit number:

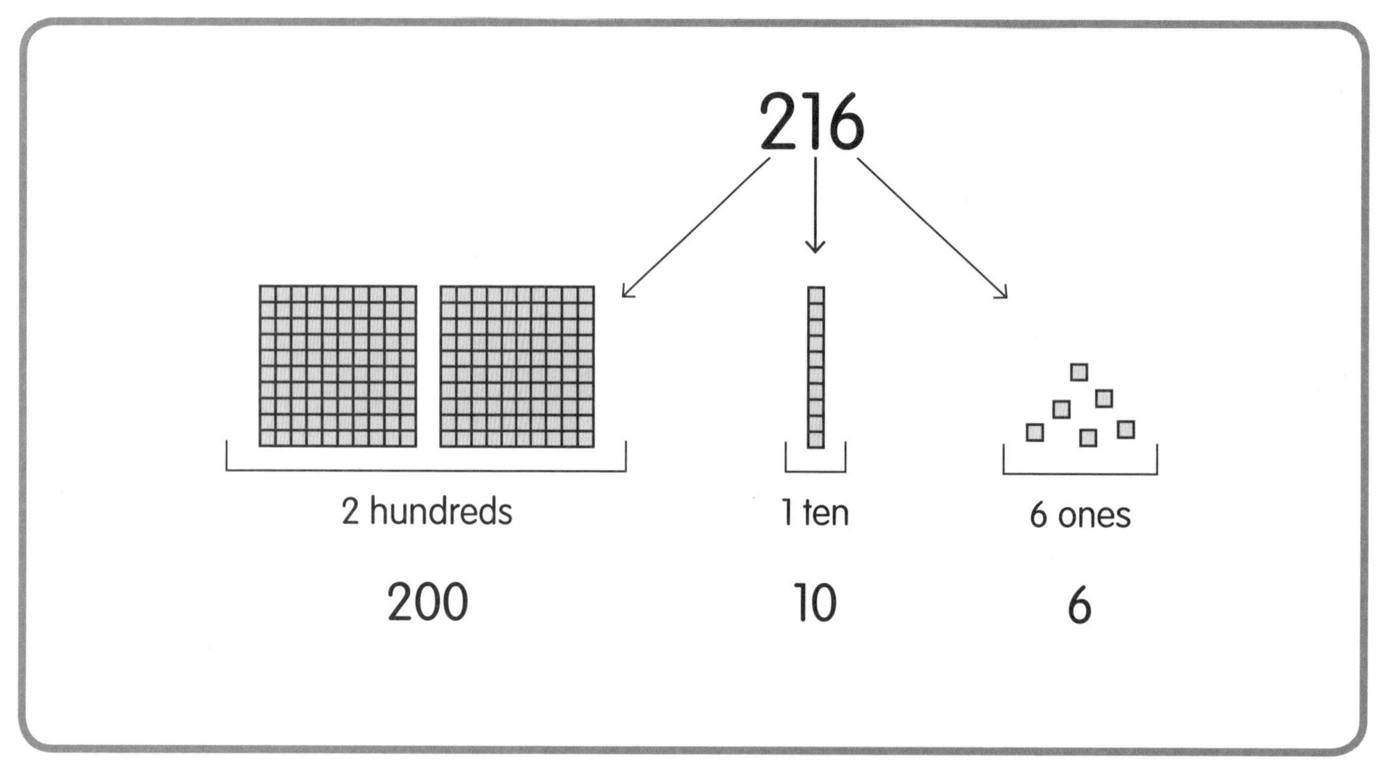

How many tens are in **100**? How many tens are in **1,000**? Explain your thinking.

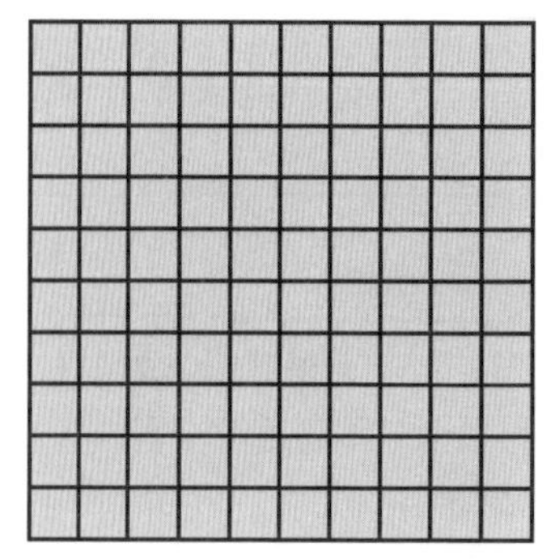

CCMS 2.NBT.A.1 Understand hundreds, tens, and ones in a three-digit number.

Name ______________________________

Mark the number that names each picture.

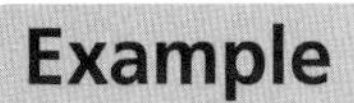

Example

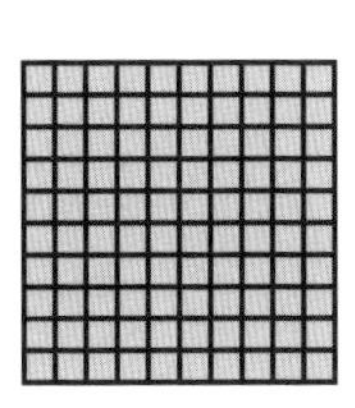 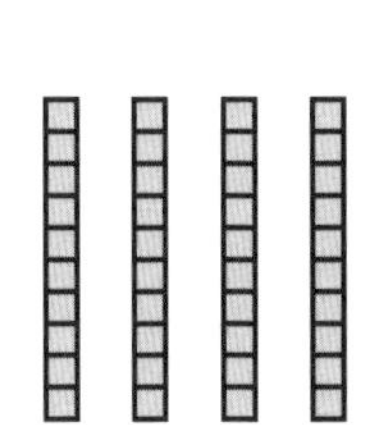 

- ○ 242
- ○ 424
- ● 142

❶ 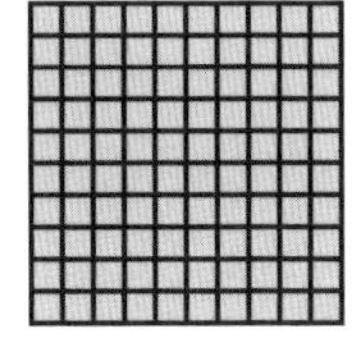 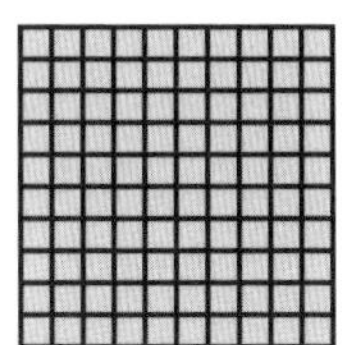 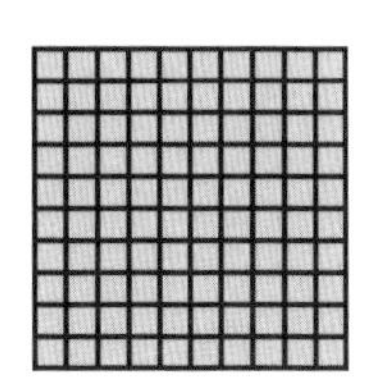 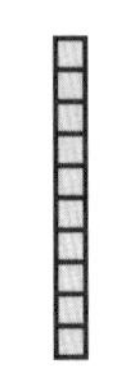

- ○ 310
- ○ 301
- ○ 131

❷ 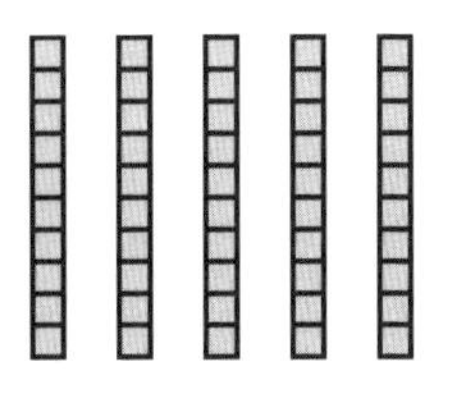

- ○ 65
- ○ 155
- ○ 55

❸ 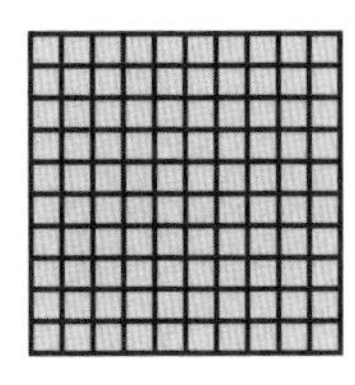

- ○ 24
- ○ 204
- ○ 114

❹ 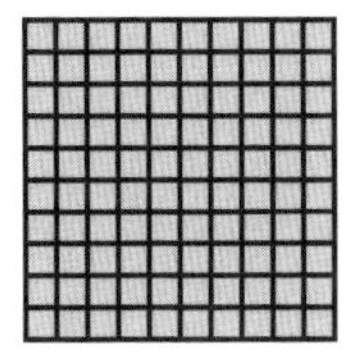 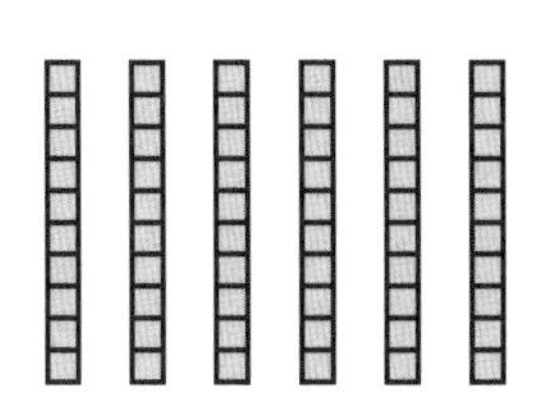

- ○ 601
- ○ 116
- ○ 161

Name ________________________________

Understand Place Value
Understanding three-digit numbers

2

For each number, mark the value of the underlined digit.

1. 483
   - ○ 4
   - ○ 40
   - ○ 400

2. 929
   - ○ 9
   - ○ 90
   - ○ 900

3. 523
   - ○ 50
   - ○ 500
   - ○ 5

4. 627
   - ○ 200
   - ○ 20
   - ○ 2

5. 701
   - ○ 70
   - ○ 1
   - ○ 0 tens

6. 390
   - ○ 900
   - ○ 90
   - ○ 9

CCMS 2.NBT.A.1 Understand hundreds, tens, and ones in a three-digit number.

Name ____________________

Read the Problem

Malik said, "I am thinking of a number.
It has 4 hundreds, 6 tens, and 9 ones.
What is the number that I am thinking of?"

Think About It

1. You will find the _____ number that Malik is thinking of.
   ○ 1-digit ○ 2-digit ○ 3-digit

2. To find the number, you will need to think about _____.
   ○ subtraction ○ place value ○ skip counting

Solve the Problem

3. Use this work space.

4. Malik is thinking of the number _______.

Check Your Work

5. Do your answers make sense? ○ yes ○ no

Understand hundreds, tens, and ones in a three-digit number.

CCMS 2.NBT.A.1

Math Models

Understanding skip counting

You can skip count by 5s, 10s, and 100s.

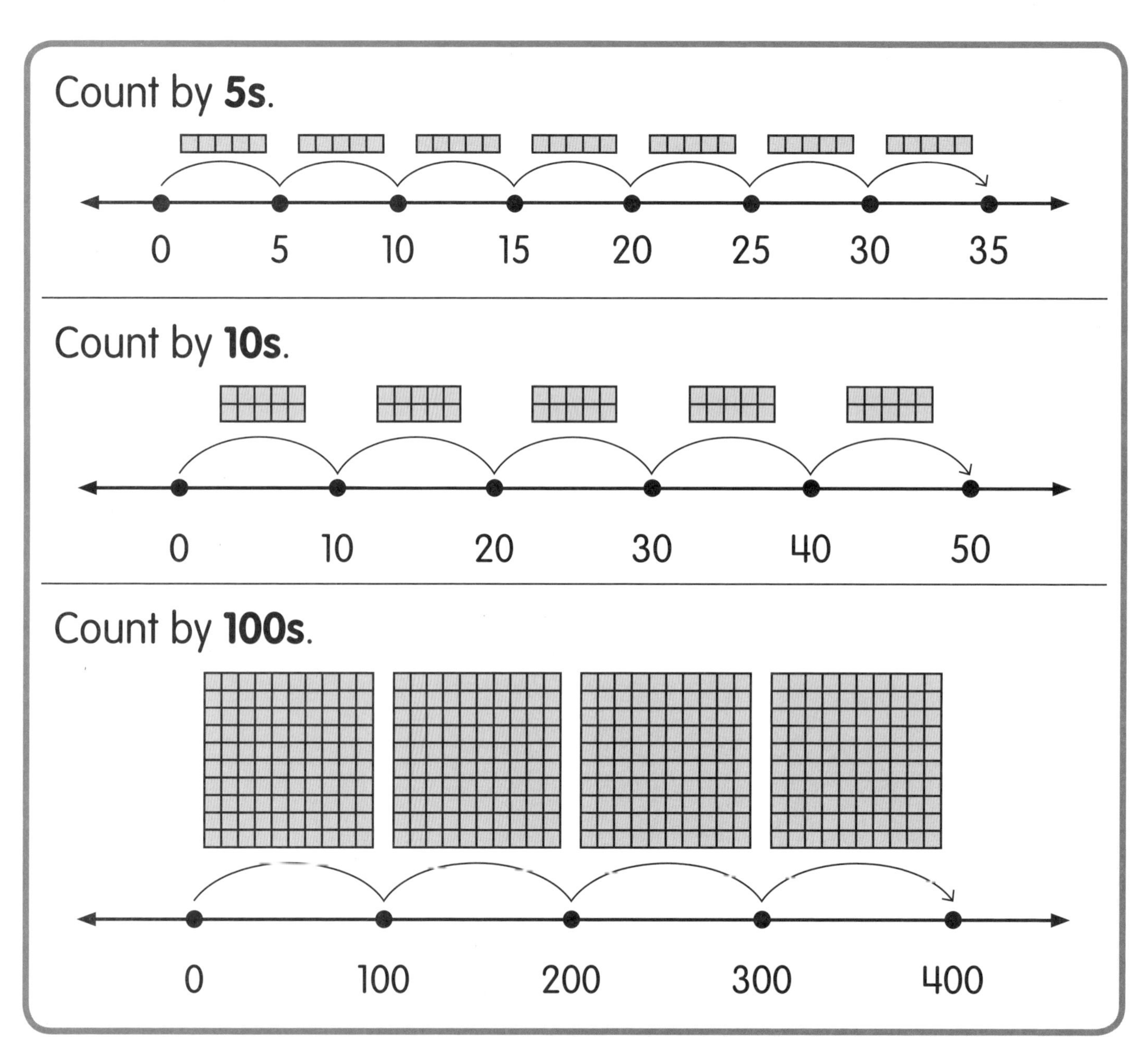

Count aloud by ones from **950** to **1,000**.
Then count back by ones from **1,000** to **950**.

CCMS 2.NBT.A.2 Count within 1,000. Skip count by 5s, 10s, and 100s.

Name ______________________________

Skip count to tell how many cubes there are in all.

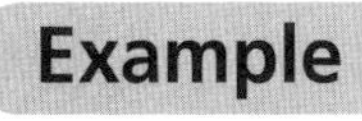

Example

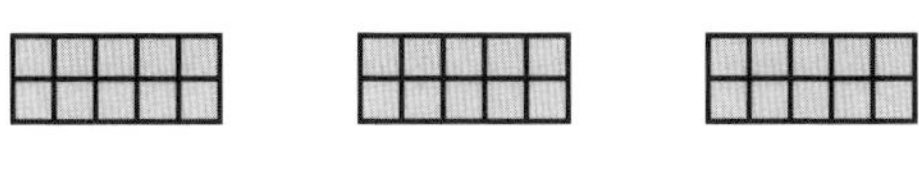

10 20 30

30 cubes

❶ ______ cubes

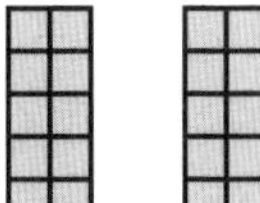

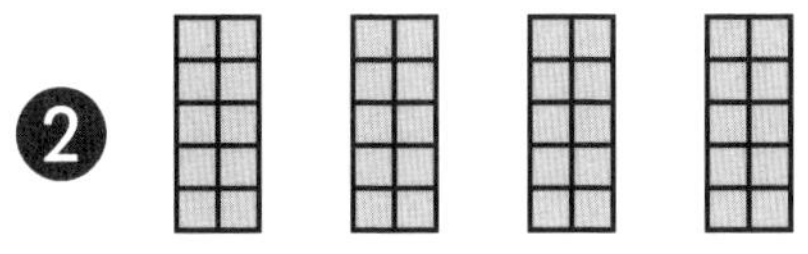

❷ ______ cubes

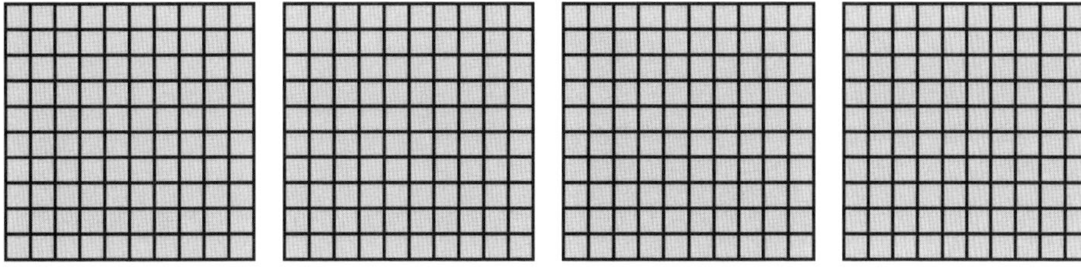

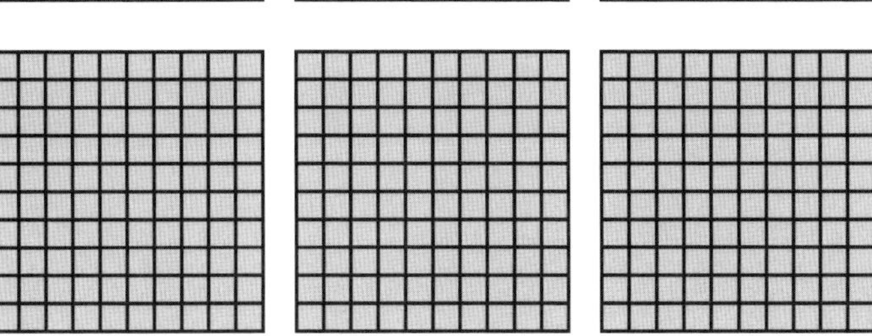

❸ ______ cubes

Count within 1,000. Skip count by 5s, 10s, and 100s.

CCMS 2.NBT.A.2

Name ______________________________

Continue each skip counting pattern. Write the missing numbers.

Example

500, 600, 700, 800, 900, 1,000

1. 45, 50, ____, ____, ____, ____

2. 100, 200, ____, ____, ____, ____

3. 110, 120, ____, ____, ____, ____

4. 325, 330, ____, ____, ____, ____

5. 700, 710, ____, ____, ____, ____

6. 300, 400, ____, ____, ____, ____

 CCMS 2.NBT.A.2 Count within 1,000. Skip count by 5s, 10s, and 100s.

Name ______________________________

Read the Problem

Mrs. Phan needs to count pencils. There are 10 boxes, and each box holds 100 pencils. Write the numbers below that Mrs. Phan will say as she counts each box. Then write the total number of pencils.

Think About It

1. You will count by _____.
   ○ fives ○ tens ○ hundreds

2. The first number that Mrs. Phan will say is _____.
   ○ 10 ○ 100 ○ 110

Solve the Problem

3. Write the numbers Mrs. Phan will say.

4. There are ________ pencils.

Check Your Work

5. Do your answers make sense? ○ yes ○ no

You can read, write, and expand numbers.

These are some ways to show a number:

Base Ten Numeral	Written Form	Expanded Form
96	ninety-six	90 + 6
163	one hundred sixty-three	100 + 60 + 3
527	five hundred twenty-seven	500 + 20 + 7
904	nine hundred four	900 + 4

How can you show **1,000** in expanded form? Explain your thinking.

CCMS 2.NBT.A.3 Read and write numbers to 1,000. Use base ten numerals, number names, and expanded form.

Name ____________________

Read each number. Then write the number **two** ways.

Example

five hundred fifty-two

500 + 50 + 2

552

1. seven hundred twenty-eight

   ____ + ____ + ____

   ____

2. three hundred sixty-seven

   ____ + ____ + ____

   ____

3. nine hundred ninety-nine

   ____ + ____ + ____

   ____

4. one hundred forty-one

   ____ + ____ + ____

   ____

5. twenty-four

   ____ + ____

   ____

6. five hundred eighty-two

   ____ + ____ + ____

   ____

Read and write numbers to 1,000. Use base ten numerals, number names, and expanded form.

CCMS 2.NBT.A.3

Name ______________________________

Mark a different form for each number.

❶ 268

- ○ 200 + 60 + 8
- ○ 800 + 20 + 6
- ○ 26 + 8

❷ 605

- ○ six hundred fifty
- ○ six hundred five
- ○ sixty-five

❸ 347

- ○ 300 + 70 + 4
- ○ 300 + 40 + 7
- ○ 700 + 30 + 4

❹ 480

- ○ forty-eight
- ○ four hundred eight
- ○ four hundred eighty

❺ 893

- ○ 800 + 30 + 9
- ○ 300 + 80 + 9
- ○ 800 + 90 + 3

❻ 1,000

- ○ one thousand
- ○ one hundred
- ○ ten thousand

Name ______________________________

Read the Problem

Mr. Ramos asked his students to write the number **625** a different way. Elena wrote **600 + 20 + 5**. Do you agree? Explain why or why not.

Think About It

1. You will find out if _____ is another way to write **625**.
   ○ 600 + 20 + 5 ○ 200 + 60 + 5

2. The number **6** in **6̲25** has a value of _____.
   ○ 6 ones ○ 6 tens ○ 6 hundreds

Solve the Problem

3. I agree that 600 + 20 + 5 is another way to write 625.
   ○ yes ○ no

4. I ____________ agree because ______________________________
   do do not

   ____

   ____.

Check Your Work

5. Do your answers make sense? ○ yes ○ no

Math Models

Comparing numbers

You can compare three-digit numbers.

Use (>), (=), and (<).

To compare numbers, start with the largest place value digit.

<u>4</u>89  <u>5</u>21

Four hundreds are **less** than five hundreds.

So 489 (<) 521.

If the hundreds digits are the same, then compare the tens digits.

4<u>8</u>9  4<u>6</u>2

Eight tens are **more** than six tens.

So 489 (>) 462.

Kelly says that **999 < 1,000**. Darius says that **1,000 > 99**. Who is correct? Explain your answer.

CCMS 2.NBT.A.4 Compare two three-digit numbers based on meanings of the hundreds, tens, and ones digits.

Name ____________________

Compare the numbers. Write **>**, **=**, or **<** in the circle to make a true number sentence.

Examples

384
495

384 (<) 495

900
899

900 (>) 899

❶
627
627

627 ◯ 627

❷
197
313

313 ◯ 197

❸
501
298

298 ◯ 501

❹
720
711

720 ◯ 711

Compare two three-digit numbers based on meanings of the hundreds, tens, and ones digits.

CCMS 2.NBT.A.4

Name ____________________

Compare the numbers. Write **>**, **=**, or **<** in the circle to make a true number sentence.

❶ 798
987

987 ◯ 798

❷ 601
700

700 ◯ 601

❸ 599
995

599 ◯ 995

❹ 360
245

245 ◯ 360

❺ 731
731

731 ◯ 731

❻ 1,000
100

1,000 ◯ 100

CCMS 2.NBT.A.4 Compare two three-digit numbers based on meanings of the hundreds, tens, and ones digits.

Name ____________________

Write a number sentence using **>**, **=**, or **<** that compares each number pair.

❶ 608 529 ____ ◯ ____

❷ 212 198 ____ ◯ ____

❸ 398 426 ____ ◯ ____

❹ 321 123 ____ ◯ ____

❺ 593 593 ____ ◯ ____

❻ 923 932 ____ ◯ ____

Compare two three-digit numbers based on meanings of the hundreds, tens, and ones digits.

CCMS 2.NBT.A.4

Name ______________________________

Read the Problem

Anton has 139 marbles. Marcel has 151 marbles.
Who has the most marbles?
Use **>**, **=**, or **<** to write a number sentence below.

Think About It

1. You will find out who has _____ marbles.
   ○ the fewest ○ the most ○ an equal number of

2. To compare **139** and **151**, I need to look at the _____ digits.
   ○ ones ○ tens ○ hundreds

Solve the Problem

3. Use this work space.

4. ______________ has the most marbles.

5. _____ ◯ _____

Check Your Work

6. Do your answers make sense? ○ yes ○ no

CCMS 2.NBT.A.4 Compare two three-digit numbers based on meanings of the hundreds, tens, and ones digits.

Use Math Strategies

Domain

Number and Operations in Base Ten

Cluster

Use place value understanding and properties of operations to add and subtract.

Standards in Cluster

2.NBT.B.5 Fluently add and subtract within 100 using strategies based on place value and properties of operations.

2.NBT.B.6 Add up to four two-digit numbers using strategies based on place value and properties of operations.

2.NBT.B.7 Add and subtract within 1,000, using concrete models or drawings and strategies based on place value, properties of operations, and/or the relationship between addition and subtraction; relate the strategy to a written method. Understand that in adding or subtracting three-digit numbers, one adds or subtracts hundreds and hundreds, tens and tens, ones and ones; and sometimes it is necessary to compose or decompose tens or hundreds.

2.NBT.B.8 Mentally add 10 or 100 to a given number 100–900, and mentally subtract 10 or 100 from a given number 100–900.

2.NBT.B.9 Explain why addition and subtraction strategies work, using place value and the properties of operations.

Unit Contents

Unit Contents, *continued*

Mathematical Practices in This Unit

Make sense of problems and persevere in solving them: *pages 68, 71, 72, 75, 76, 79, 80, 83, 84, 88, 89, 92, 93, 96, 97, 100*
Reason abstractly and quantitatively: *pages 71, 75, 79, 83, 88, 92*
Construct viable arguments and critique the reasoning of others: *pages 68, 72, 77, 80, 84, 90, 93, 97*
Model with mathematics: *pages 71, 75, 79, 83, 88, 92, 96, 100*
Attend to precision: *pages 68, 72, 77, 80, 84, 90, 93, 94, 95, 96, 97, 98, 99*
Look for and make use of structure: *pages 68, 72, 77, 80, 84, 90, 93, 97*

Math Models

Adding within 100

You can choose different ways to add two-digit numbers.

These are some ways to think about adding:

Decompose and compose.

$55 + 37 = ?$

$(50)(5) + (30)(7) = ?$

$50 + 30 + 5 + 7 = ?$

$80 + 12 = ?$

$80 + (10)(2) = ?$

$90 + 2 = 92$

Count on.

$27 + 2 = ?$

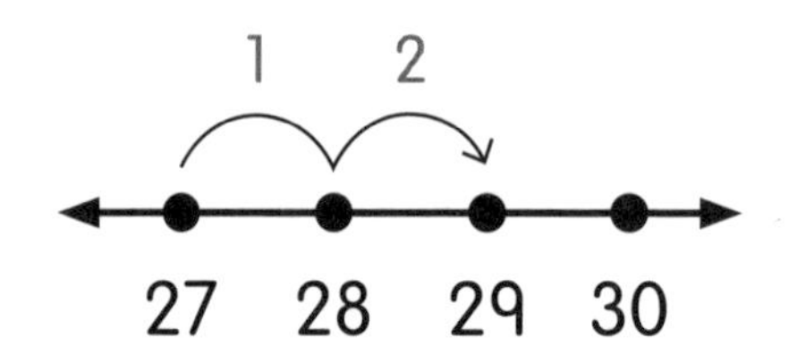

Use friendly numbers.

$16 + 9 = ?$

$16 + 10 - 1 = ?$

$26 - 1 = 25$

Solve **63 + 50 + 17 = ?** Explain your thinking and tell about a way you can solve it.

CCMS 2.NBT.B.5 Fluently add within 100 using strategies based on place value and operations.

Name ____________________

Solve each problem. Draw or write to show your thinking.

Example

52 + 16 = 68

50 + 2 + 10 + 6 = ?

50 + 10 + 2 + 6 = ?

60 + 8 = 68

Work Space

1. 43 + 31 = ____

2. 27 + 54 = ____

3. 62 + 9 = ____

Name ____________________

Solve each problem. Draw or write to show your thinking.

Work Space

1. $38 + 7 =$ ____

2. $73 + 19 =$ ____

3. $22 + 55 =$ ____

4. $47 + 23 =$ ____

CCMS 2.NBT.B.5 Fluently add within 100 using strategies based on place value and operations.

Name ______________________________

Read the Problem

Lian has 43 pennies in her piggy bank. She has 27 pennies in a jar. How many pennies does she have in all?

Think About It

❶ You will find out how many pennies Lian has _____.

○ in a jar ○ left over ○ in all

❷ You will need to compose a ten to solve the problem.

○ yes ○ no

Solve the Problem

❸ Use this work space.

❹ Lian has _____ pennies in all.

Check Your Work

❺ Do your answers make sense? ○ yes ○ no

You can choose different ways to subtract from two-digit numbers.

These are some ways to think about subtracting:

Subtract tens and tens.
Subtract ones and ones.

$84 - 62 = ?$

$80 - 60 + 4 - 2 = ?$

$20 + 2 = 22$

Use base-ten blocks.

$42 - 23 = ?$

42	
− 23	
19	

Count back.

$62 - 3 = ?$

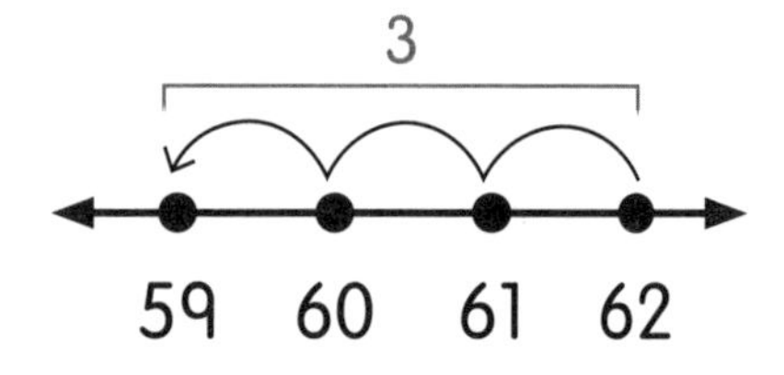

Count up.

$51 - 48 = ?$

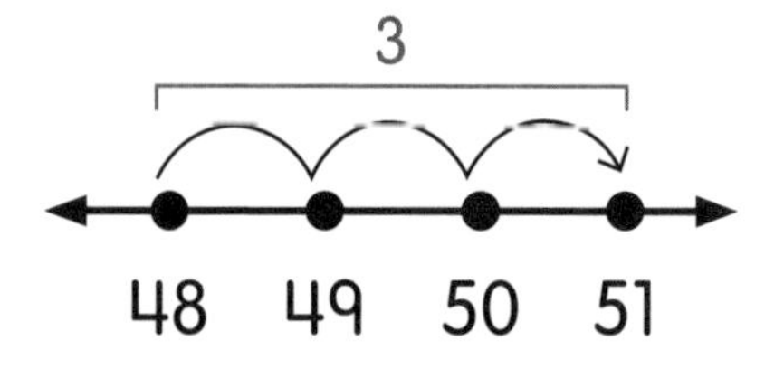

Solve **30 – 15 = ?** Explain your thinking and tell about a way you can solve it.

Name ______________________________

Solve each problem. Draw or write to show your thinking.

I need to decompose a ten.

Example

73 − 47 = 26

```
  73
− 47
----
  26
```

Work Space

1. 51 − 3 = ____

2. 97 − 21 = ____

3. 74 − 14 = ____

Name ______________________

Solve each problem. Draw or write to show your thinking.

Work Space

1. 81 – 2 = ____

2. 29 – 14 = ____

3. 73 – 59 = ____

4. 96 – 68 = ____

CCMS 2.NBT.B.5 Subtract within 100 using strategies based on place value, operations, and the relationship between addition and subtraction.

Name ___________________________________

Read the Problem

Enzo has 75 marbles. Gina has 69 marbles.
How many fewer marbles does Gina have?

Think About It

1. You will find out how many _____ marbles Gina has.
   ○ more ○ fewer ○ extra

2. You will need to decompose a ten.
   ○ yes ○ no

Solve the Problem

3. Use this work space.

4. Gina has _____ fewer marbles.

Check Your Work

5. Do your answers make sense? ○ yes ○ no

Subtract within 100 using strategies based on place value, operations, and the relationship between addition and subtraction. CCMS 2.NBT.B.5

Math Models

Adding up to four two-digit numbers

Use Math Strategies

You can add tens and ones in any order to find the sum of two-digit numbers.

These are examples:

Make tens partners.

$$28 + 16 + 14 + 12 = ?$$

$$40 + 30 = 70$$

I noticed that 8 and 2 make 10, so I can add 28 + 12 easily. Also, 6 and 4 make 10, so I can add 16 + 14 easily.

Make hundreds partners.

$$81 + 50 + 19 + 22 = ?$$

$$100 + 50 + 20 + 2 = ?$$

$$100 + 70 + 2 = 172$$

I noticed that 1 and 9 make 10, so I can add 81 + 19 easily.

I broke apart 22. Then I composed the tens.

Now I can add the hundreds, tens, and ones.

The examples above are only two of many ways to solve the problem. Explain how you would group the numbers to solve them with your own thinking.

Name ____________________

Write the sum for each number sentence. Show the way that you grouped the tens and ones to solve the problem.

Example

$23 + 10 + 7 + 34 = \underline{74}$

$30 + 10 + 30 + 4 = ?$

$70 + 4 = 74$

❷ $32 + 8 + 17 + 3 =$ ____

❶ $46 + 18 + 14 =$ ____

❸ $25 + 9 + 15 + 4 =$ ____

Name ____________________

Use Math Strategies

Adding up to four two-digit numbers

6

Write the sum for each number sentence. Show the way that you grouped the tens and ones to solve the problem.

1. $69 + 11 + 3 =$ _____

3. $46 + 10 + 16 + 20 =$ _____

2. $23 + 35 + 25 + 17 =$ _____

4. $13 + 67 + 11 + 19 =$ _____

CCMS 2.NBT.B.6 Add up to four two-digit numbers.

Name ______________________________

Use Math Strategies
Adding up to four two-digit numbers

Read the Problem

Tanya kept track of how many minutes she read so far this week. She made this chart. How many minutes has Tanya read so far?

My Reading List

Day	Minutes
Monday	25
Tuesday	15
Wednesday	20
Thursday	27

Think About It

1. You will find out how many minutes Tanya read _____.
   ○ in three days ○ in four days ○ all week

2. Mark the way to break apart **25**.
   ○ 20 + 5 ○ 10 + 10 ○ 10 + 5

Solve the Problem

3. Use this work space.

4. Tanya has read _____ minutes so far.

Check Your Work

5. Do your answers make sense? ○ yes ○ no

Math Models

Adding within 1,000

You can write the hundreds, tens, and ones in expanded form to add numbers within 1,000.

Add the hundreds.
Add the tens.
Add the ones.

Here is an example of using expanded form:

$236 + 495 = ?$

First, I write each number in expanded form. I write one number below the other.

$200 + 30 + 6 = ?$
$+ 400 + 90 + 5 = ?$

Next, I add the hundreds, tens, and ones separately.

$600 + 120 + 11 = ?$

I need to break apart 120 and 11.

$600 + 100\ 20 + (10)(1)$

Now I can add the hundreds, tens, and ones.

$700 + 30 + 1 = 731$

The example above is only one of many ways to solve the problem. Explain how you would solve **162 + 368 = ?**

CCMS 2.NBT.B.7 Add numbers within 1,000, composing or decomposing when necessary.

Name ______________________________

Use what you know about ones, tens, and hundreds to find the sum.
Draw or write to show your thinking.

Example

$$\begin{array}{r} 200 + 70 + 3 \\ +\ 100 + 40 + 2 \\ \hline 300 + 110 + 5 \end{array}$$

First, I will write each number in expanded form.

110 → 100, 10

I need to break apart 110.

$400 + 10 + 5 = 415$

❷ $509 + 365 =$ ______

❶ $96 + 416 =$ ______

❸ $141 + 679 =$ ______

Name ____________________

Use what you know about ones, tens, and hundreds to find the sum.
Draw or write to show your thinking.

1. 29 + 342 = ______

2. 259 + 190 = ______

3. 640 + 187 = ______

4. 548 + 176 = ______

CCMS 2.NBT.B.7 Add numbers within 1,000, composing or decomposing when necessary.

Name ______________________________

Read the Problem

The sports store sold 312 soccer balls and 199 baseballs last year. How many soccer balls and baseballs did the store sell altogether?

Think About It

❶ You will find out how many soccer balls and baseballs were _____.

○ left ○ lost ○ sold

❷ Mark the way to break apart **312**.

○ 300 + 100 + 20 ○ 300 + 10 + 2 ○ 300 + 20 + 1

Solve the Problem

❸ Use this work space.

❹ The store sold _______ soccer balls and baseballs altogether.

Check Your Work

❺ Do your answers make sense? ○ yes ○ no

Add numbers within 1,000, composing or decomposing when necessary.

CCMS 2.NBT.B.7

Math Models

Subtracting within 1,000

You can use a place value chart to subtract numbers within 1,000.

Subtract hundreds from hundreds.
Subtract tens from tens.
Subtract ones from ones.

Example:

465 – 253 = ?

Hundreds	Tens	Ones
100 100 100 100	10 10 10 10 10 10	1 1 1 1 1

I show the first number, 465, using disks on a place value chart.

Next, I remove disks that make up the second number, 253.

The disks that are left show the answer: 212.

What can you do if you need to decompose and compose to make more tens and ones? Explain how you can solve **700 – 235 = ?**

CCMS 2.NBT.B.7 Add and subtract numbers within 1,000.

Name ____________________

Use what you know about ones, tens, and hundreds to find the difference. Draw or write to show your thinking.

Example

314 – 102 = 212

I show the first number on a place value chart.

Hundreds	Tens	Ones
100 100 100	10	1 1 1 1

Next, I remove disks that make up the second number.

❷ 173 – 45 = ______

❶ 508 – 329 = ______

❸ 701 – 256 = ______

Name ______________________________

Use what you know about ones, tens, and hundreds to find the difference. Draw or write to show your thinking.

1. 499 – 75 = ______

3. 381 – 167 = ______

2. 626 – 542 = ______

4. 700 – 155 = ______

Name ______________________

Mark the number sentence that can help you solve the subtraction problem. Then write the answer.

Example

$197 - 81 =$ 116

○ $197 + 81 = 278$
● $197 - 80 = 117$

❶ $638 - 202 =$ ______

○ $640 - 200 = 440$
○ $638 - 200 = 438$

❷ $710 - 100 =$ ______

○ $700 + 10 - 100 = 610$
○ $100 + 70 - 10 = 160$

❸ $175 - 10 =$ ______

○ $175 + 10 = 185$
○ $180 - 10 - 5 = 165$

❹ $520 - 70 =$ ______

○ $400 + 20 - 7 = 413$
○ $400 + 120 - 70 = 450$

Name ____________________

Read the Problem

There are 548 students at Oakdale School.
266 students are girls. How many students are boys?

Think About It

1. You will find out how many _____ go to Oakdale School.
   ○ girls ○ boys ○ boys and girls

2. Mark the number sentence that tells about the problem.
   ○ ? – 266 = 548 ○ ? = 548 + 266 ○ ? = 548 – 266

Solve the Problem

3. Use this work space.

4. _______ boys go to Oakdale School.

Check Your Work

5. Do your answers make sense? ○ yes ○ no

CCMS 2.NBT.B.7 Add and subtract numbers within 1,000.

Math Models

Adding and subtracting 10 or 100: Mental math

You can use mental math to add 10 or 100 to a number or subtract 10 or 100 from a number.

To add 10:

8̲4

Add one ten to the tens place.

84 + 10 = 9̲4

To subtract 10:

8̲4

Subtract one ten from the tens place.

84 – 10 = 7̲4

To add 100:

3̲52

Add one hundred to the hundreds place.

352 + 100 = 4̲52

To subtract 100:

3̲52

Subtract one hundred from the hundreds place.

352 – 100 = 2̲52

Use mental math to add these problems:

90 + 10 = ?

900 + 100 = ?

Explain your thinking.

Name ____________________

Read each sentence. Mark the correct number.

Example

10 more than 330 is ____.

- ○ 430
- ● 340

❶ 10 less than 423 is ____.

- ○ 413
- ○ 513

---

❷ 100 more than 603 is ____.

- ○ 613
- ○ 703

---

❸ 100 less than 279 is ____.

- ○ 179
- ○ 379

---

❹ 10 more than 890 is ____.

- ○ 900
- ○ 880

---

❺ 100 less than 105 is ____.

- ○ 50
- ○ 5

CCMS 2.NBT.B.8 Mentally add or subtract 10 or 100 to/from a given number.

Name ______________________________

Read each number sentence. Write the missing number.

Examples

253 + <u>100</u> = 353

553 – 10 = <u>543</u>

1. ______ + 10 = 160
2. 495 – ______ = 485
3. 715 + 100 = ______
4. ______ – 10 = 895
5. 1,000 – 100 = ______
6. 306 + ______ = 406
7. 575 – 10 = ______
8. ______ + 10 = 620
9. 210 – 100 = ______
10. ______ = 899 + 10

Name ____________________

Read the Problem

528 people went to the zoo on Sunday.
100 fewer people went to the zoo on Monday.
How many people went to the zoo on Monday?

Think About It

1. You will find out how many ______ people went to the zoo on Monday.
   ○ more ○ fewer ○ extra

2. Mark the value in **528** that will change when you find **100** fewer.
   ○ 8 ○ 20 ○ 500

Solve the Problem

3. Use this work space.

4. ______ people went to the zoo on Monday.

Check Your Work

5. Do your answers make sense? ○ yes ○ no

CCMS 2.NBT.B.8 Mentally add or subtract 10 or 100 to/from a given number.

Math Models

Explaining why addition strategies work

Use Math Strategies

You can explain why addition strategies work.

Sometimes you need to explain your addition math thinking. These are some sentence starter ideas:

- I decided...
- I decided to add because...
- I noticed...
- I thought...
- First, I..., Next, I..., Then, I...
- I agree/disagree with the results because...

Example:

$22 + 48 = ?$

I noticed that 2 ones + 8 ones equals 10.
First, I added 20 + 40 = 60.
Then, I added 60 + 10 = 70.

Shadia says that **525 + 100 = 425**. Do you agree? Use a sentence starter to explain your thinking.

Name ______________________________

Use Math Strategies
Explaining why addition strategies work

14

Solve each problem. Write to explain your thinking.

Example

485 + 100 = 585

I decided to look at the digits in the hundreds place. If 400 + 100 = 500, then I know 485 + 100 = 585.

Writing Space

328 + 102 = ______

19 + 48 = ______

150 + 50 + 7 = ______

CCMS 2.NBT.B.9 Explain why addition strategies work.

Name ______________________

Solve each problem. Write to explain your thinking.

Writing Space

$8 + 14 + 16 =$ ______

$42 + 28 + 12 =$ ______

$60 + 600 + 100 =$ ______

$40 + 100 + 3 =$ ______

Name ___________________________

Read the Problem

186 children and 42 adults went to the science fair.
How many people went to the science fair in all?

Think About It

1. You will find out how many _____ went to the science fair.
   ○ children ○ adults ○ people

2. Mark the way that you will solve the problem.
   ○ add ○ compare ○ subtract

Solve the Problem

3. Use this work space to write about your thinking.

   ____

   ____

   ____

   ____

   ____

4. _______ people went to the science fair.

Check Your Work

5. Do your answers make sense? ○ yes ○ no

Math Models

Explaining why subtraction strategies work

You can explain why subtraction strategies work.

Sometimes you need to explain your subtraction math thinking. These are some sentence starter ideas:

- I decided...
- I decided to subtract because...
- I noticed...
- I compared...
- First, I..., Next, I..., Then, I...
- I agree/disagree with the results because...

Example:

Petro says that $102 - 50 = 51$.

Do you agree?

I disagree with the results because
if I subtract $100 - 50 = 50$,
then $102 - 50 = 52$.

If you know that **235 + 20 = 255**, do you know the answer to **255 – 235 = ?** Explain your thinking.

Name ____________________

Solve each problem. Write to explain your thinking.

Example

628 – 30 = 598

I noticed that 28 is close to 30.
First, I broke 30 into 28 + 2.
Next, I did 628 – 28 = 600,
and then 600 – 2 = 598.

Writing Space

373 – 100 = ______

If 287 + 13 = 300,
then 300 – 13 = ______.

901 – 10 = ______

Name ______________________

Solve each problem. Write to explain your thinking.

Writing Space

482 – 79 = ______

316 – 100 = ______

If 950 + 50 = 1,000,
then 1,000 – 50 = ______.

601 – 10 = ______

Name ______________________________

Use Math Strategies
Explaining why subtraction strategies work

Read the Problem

Kanika has 172 baseball cards. Cedro has 10 fewer baseball cards than Kanika. Cedro says he has 182 cards.
Do you agree? ○ yes ○ no

Think About It

1. You will find out if Cedro has _____ cards.
   ○ 172 ○ 182 ○ 72

2. Mark the value in **172** that will change when you find **10** fewer.
   ○ 100 ○ 70 ○ 2

Solve the Problem

3. Use this work space to write about your thinking.

____

____

____

____

____

4. Cedro has _______ baseball cards.

Check Your Work

5. Do your answers make sense? ○ yes ○ no

Measure and Estimate Length

Domain

Measurement and Data

Cluster

Measure and estimate lengths in standard units.

Standards in Cluster

2.MD.A.1 Measure the length of an object by selecting and using appropriate tools such as rulers, yardsticks, meter sticks, and measuring tapes.

2.MD.A.2 Measure the length of an object twice, using length units of different lengths for the two measurements; describe how the two measurements relate to the size of the unit chosen.

2.MD.A.3 Estimate lengths using units of inches, feet, yards, centimeters, and meters.

2.MD.A.4 Measure to determine how much longer one object is than another, expressing the length difference in terms of a standard length unit.

Unit Contents

Mathematical Practices in This Unit

Make sense of problems and persevere in solving them: *pages 102, 105, 106, 109, 110, 113, 114, 117, 118*

Reason abstractly and quantitatively: *pages 103, 104, 107, 108, 111, 112, 115, 116*

Construct viable arguments and critique the reasoning of others: *pages 102, 105, 106, 109, 110, 114*

Model with mathematics: *pages 105, 109, 113, 117, 118*

Use appropriate tools strategically: *pages 102, 103, 104, 105, 107, 108, 111, 112, 115, 116, 117*

Attend to precision: *pages 105, 109, 113, 118*

Math Models

Measuring length in customary units

You can choose a tool to measure the length of an object in inches, feet, and yards.

Pictures of these objects and their measurements are smaller than their real size.

Inches	Feet	Yards
	There are 12 inches in 1 foot.	There are 3 feet in 1 yard.
 6 inches	 10 feet	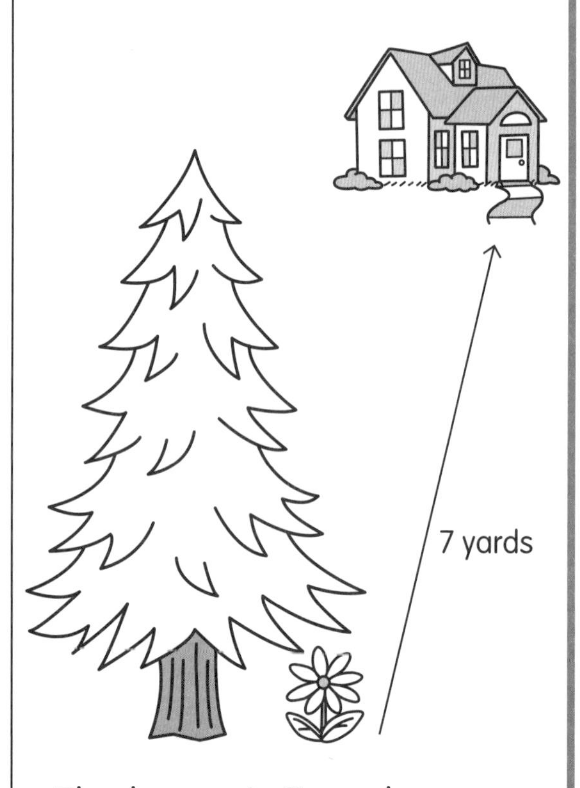
The plant is 6 inches tall.	The tree is 10 feet tall.	The house is 7 yards away.

What things can you measure best with a measuring tape? Explain your thinking.

Name ______________________________

Measure and Estimate Length
Measuring length in customary units

1

Mark the length that makes sense for each object.

Example

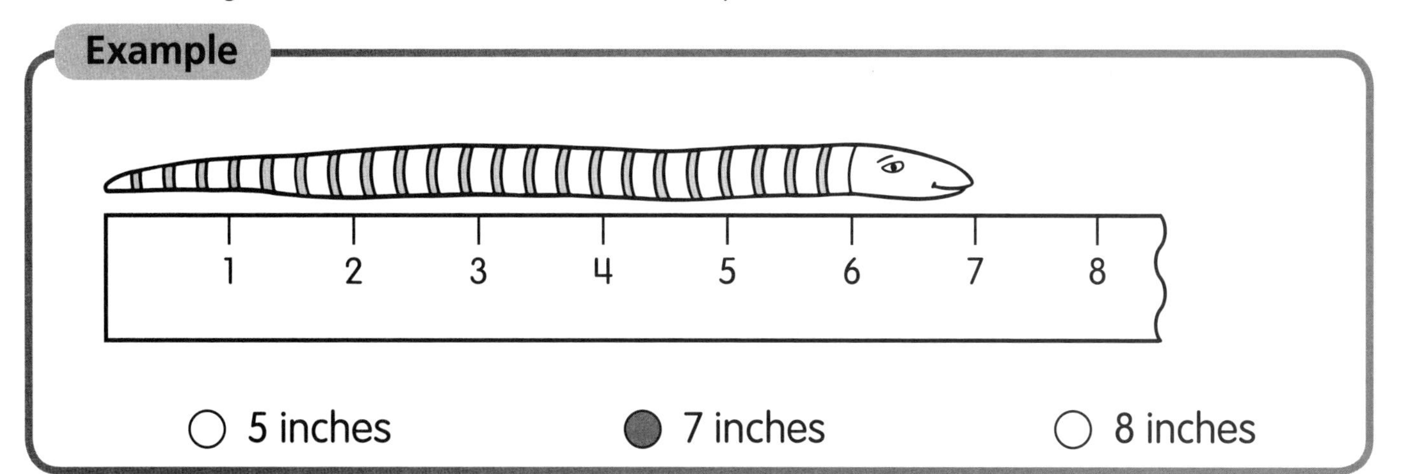

○ 5 inches ● 7 inches ○ 8 inches

1

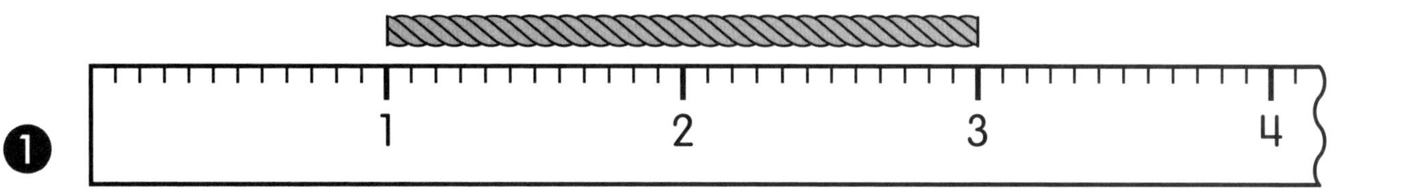

○ 2 feet ○ 3 feet ○ 4 feet

2

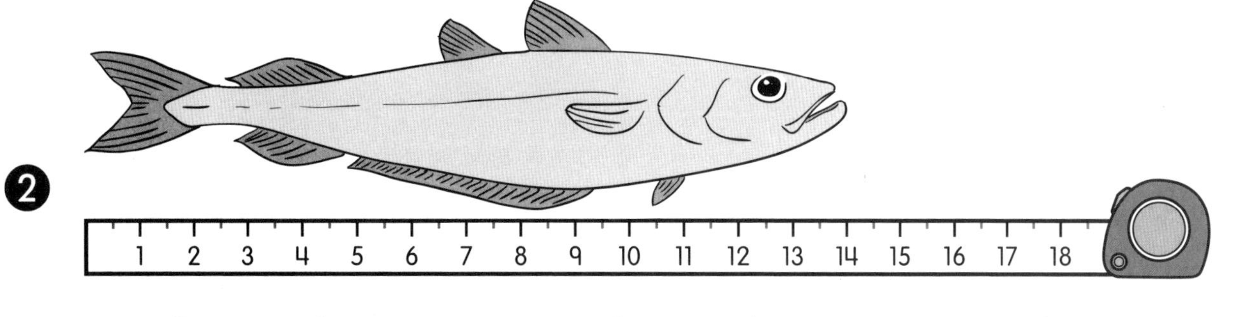

○ 16 inches ○ 11 inches ○ 14 inches

3

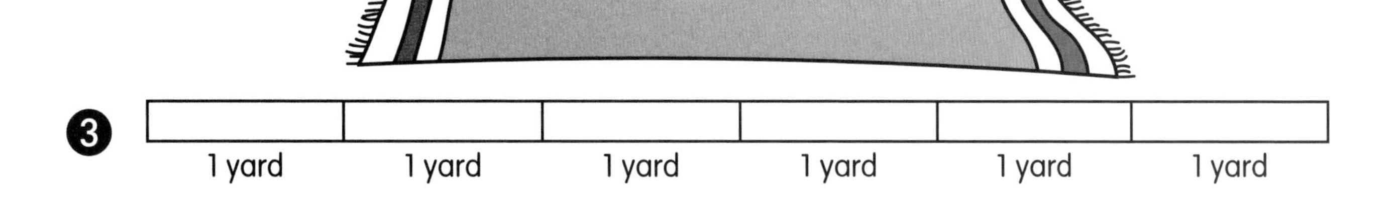

○ 5 yards ○ 4 yards ○ 3 yards

Name ____________________

Measure and Estimate Length
Measuring length in customary units

2

Mark the length that makes sense for each object.

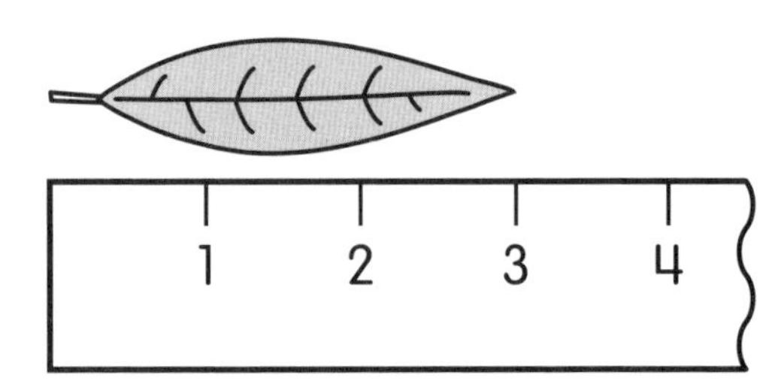

- ○ 3 inches
- ○ 3 feet
- ○ 3 yards

2

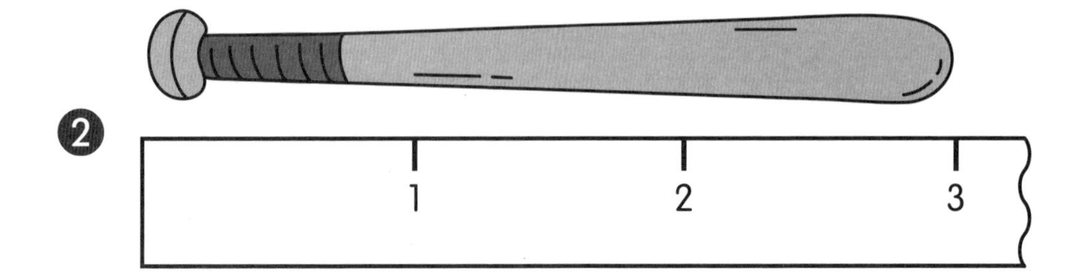

- ○ 3 inches
- ○ 3 yards
- ○ 3 feet

3

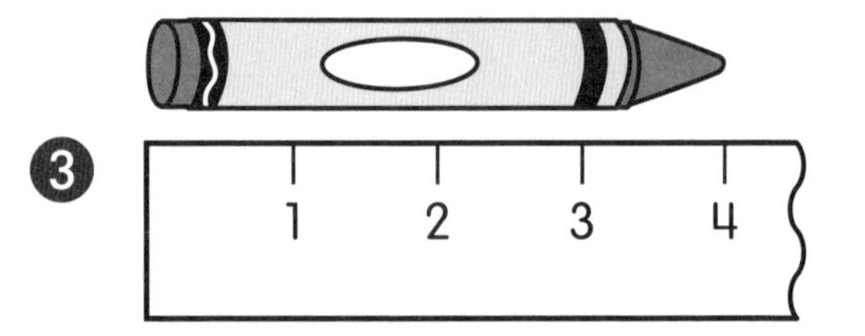

- ○ 4 inches
- ○ 4 feet
- ○ 4 yards

4

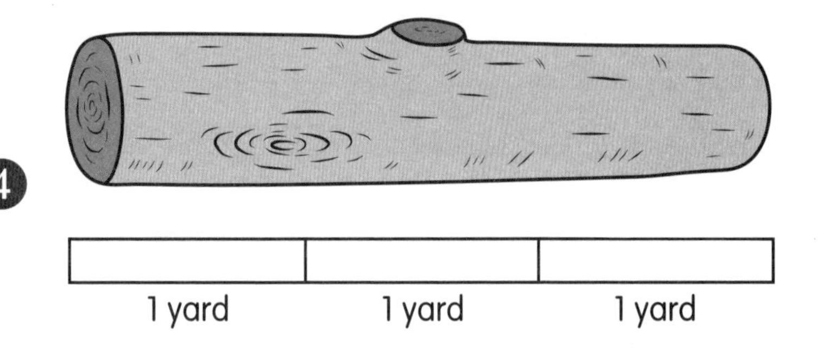

- ○ 3 inches
- ○ 3 feet
- ○ 3 yards

CCMS 2.MD.A.1 Select and use appropriate tool to measure the length of an object.

Name ____________________

Read the Problem

Jon measured these two plants. He measured one with an inch ruler and one with a centimeter ruler. He thinks the second plant is taller because the number is bigger. Do you agree? Measure the first plant in inches and the second plant in centimeters. Then explain your thinking below.

Think About It

1. You will find out if the second plant's measurement is _____ the first plant's.
   - ○ smaller than ○ larger than ○ the same as

2. You will need to know that centimeters are _____ inches.
   - ○ smaller than ○ larger than ○ the same as

Solve the Problem

3. Measure the plants. Explain your thinking.

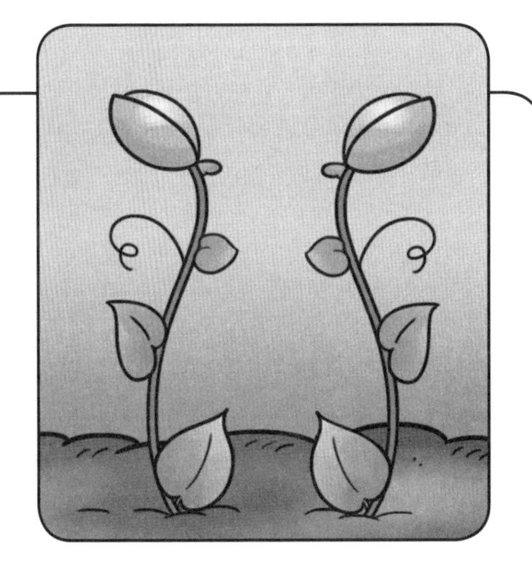

4. I agree that the second plant is taller. ○ yes ○ no

Check Your Work

5. Do your answers make sense? ○ yes ○ no

Describe how two measurements relate to the size of the unit chosen.

CCMS 2.MD.A.2

You can choose a tool to measure the length of an object in centimeters and meters.

These are two examples:

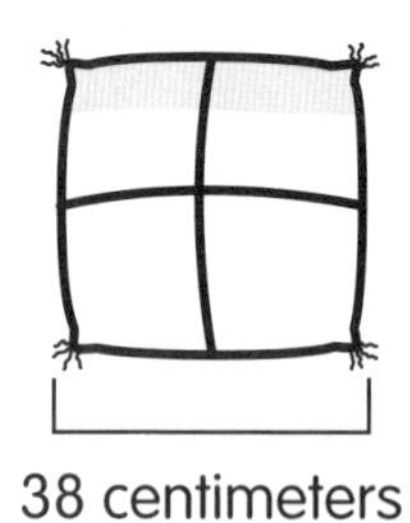

The pillow is 38 centimeters wide.

There are 100 centimeters in 1 meter.

The sofa is 2 meters long.

Name an object that you would measure with a centimeter ruler.
Name an object that you would measure with a meter stick.

Name ________________________________

Mark the length that makes sense for each object. Pictures of these objects and measuring tools are smaller than their real size.

Example

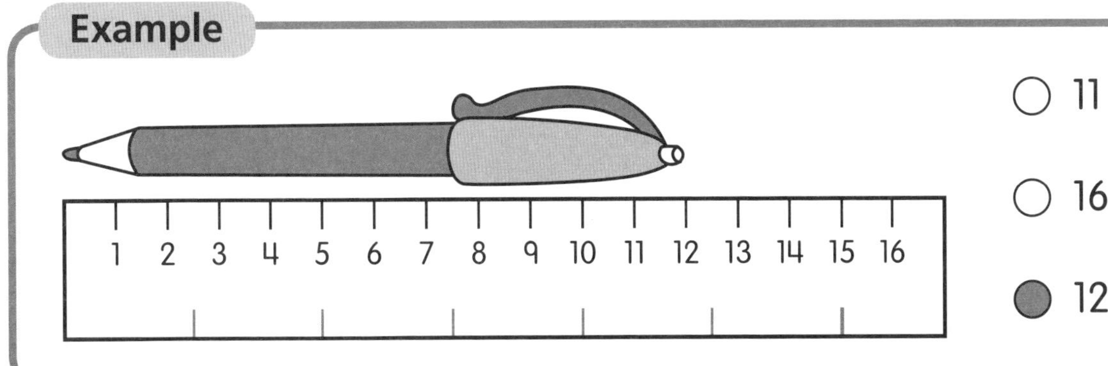

- ○ 11 meters
- ○ 16 centimeters
- ● 12 centimeters

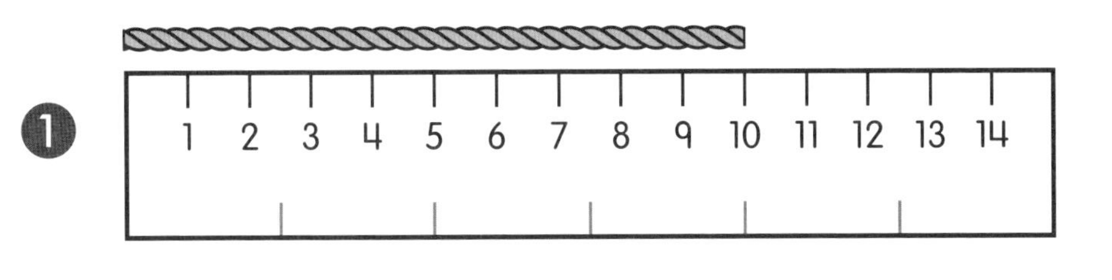

1.
- ○ 14 centimeters
- ○ 10 centimeters
- ○ 8 meters

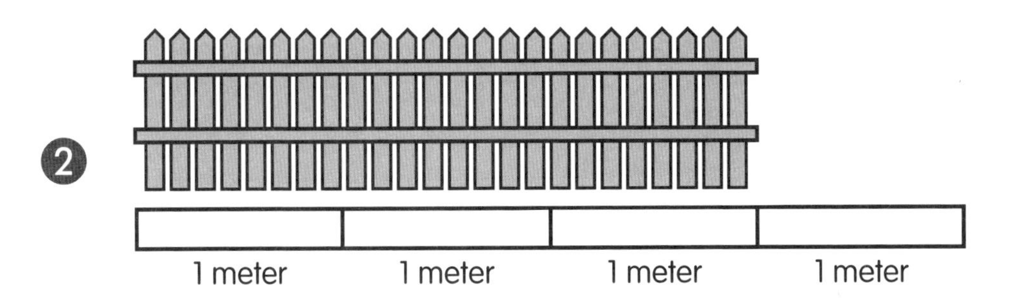

2.
- ○ 3 meters
- ○ 4 meters
- ○ 4 centimeters

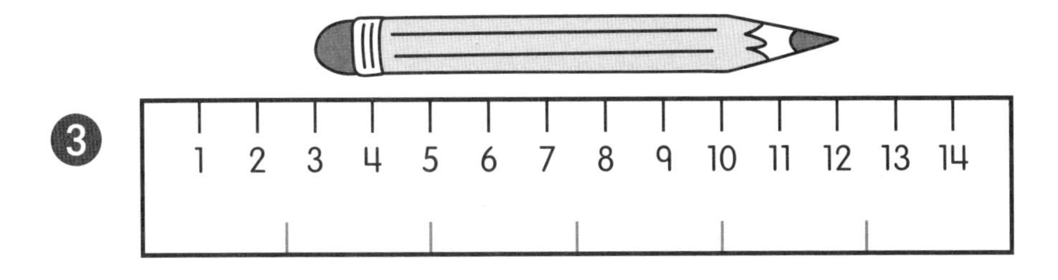

3.
- ○ 9 centimeters
- ○ 12 centimeters
- ○ 12 meters

Name ______________________________

Mark the length that makes sense for each object. Pictures of these objects and measuring tools are smaller than their real size.

1.

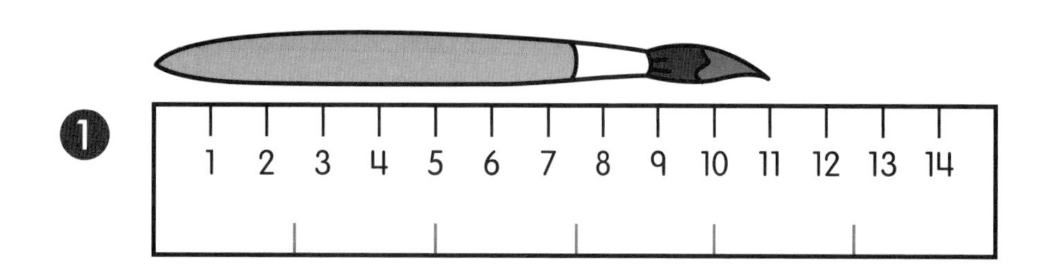

- ○ 12 centimeters
- ○ 9 centimeters
- ○ 11 centimeters

2.

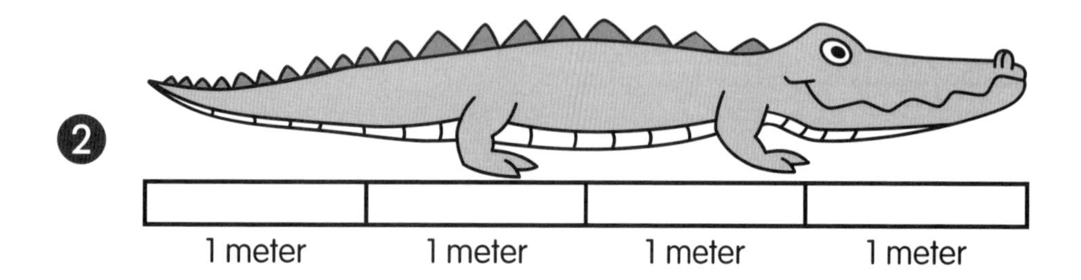

- ○ 13 centimeters
- ○ 4 meters
- ○ 5 meters

3.

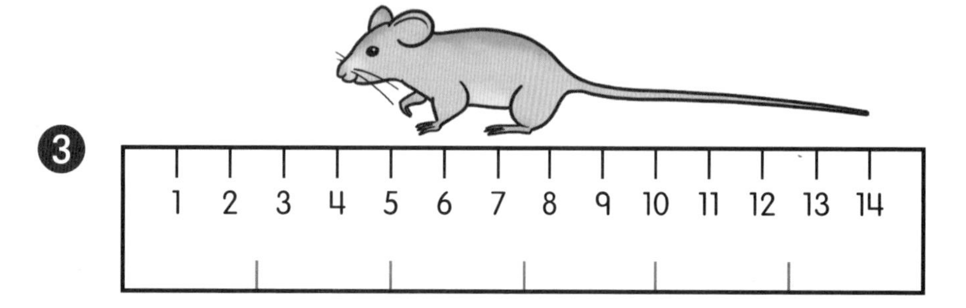

- ○ 14 centimeters
- ○ 10 centimeters
- ○ 4 centimeters

4.

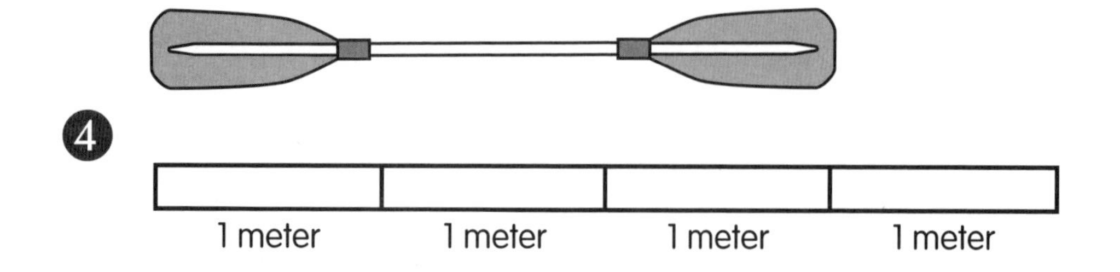

- ○ 3 meters
- ○ 4 meters
- ○ 4 centimeters

Name ______________________________

Read the Problem

Yasmin wants to measure her garden. Should she use a centimeter ruler or a meter stick? Draw or write below to explain your thinking.

Think About It

1. You will find out the best tool to ______ a garden.
   ○ plant ○ measure ○ draw

2. You will need to know that there are ______ centimeters in a meter.
   ○ 3 ○ 12 ○ 100

3. Centimeters are often used to measure ______ things.
   ○ small ○ big

Solve the Problem

4. Use this work space to explain your thinking.

5. Yasmin should use a ____________________ to measure her garden.

Check Your Work

6. Do your answers make sense? ○ yes ○ no

Math Models

Estimating length

You can estimate the length of objects.

Units of Length	Size of Objects	Examples
centimeters or inches	small	Fairy Tales
feet	medium	
yards or meters	large	

Think

What will happen if you measure a large object twice—first in centimeters and then in meters? Explain your thinking.

CCMS 2.MD.A.2 2.MD.A.3 Describe how two measurements relate to the size of the unit chosen. Estimate lengths using units of inches, feet, yards, centimeters, and meters.

Name ______________________________

Mark the best estimate for the length of each object.

Example

The paper clip is 1 inch long.
About how long is the string?

- ○ 2 inches
- ● 4 inches
- ○ 6 inches

1 The bead is 1 centimeter long.
About how long is the chain?

- ○ 5 centimeters
- ○ 20 centimeters
- ○ 11 centimeters

---

2 The bat pictured is actually 1 yard long.
About how long is the rug?

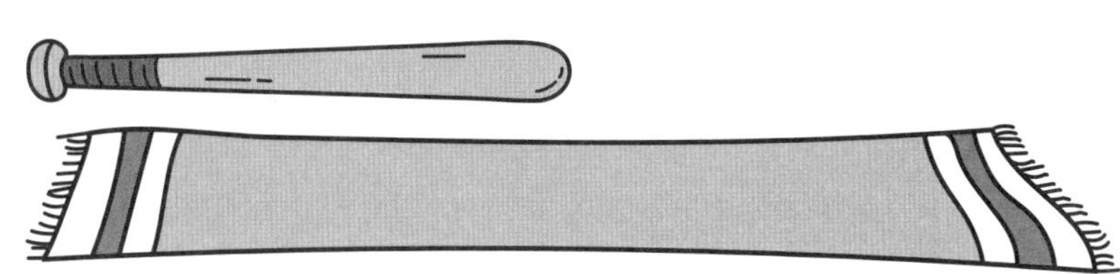

- ○ 3 feet
- ○ 3 yards
- ○ 2 yards

---

3 The stick pictured is actually 3 feet long.
About how long is the ladder?

- ○ 6 feet
- ○ 9 feet
- ○ 12 feet

Estimate lengths using units of inches, feet, yards, centimeters, and meters.

CCMS 2.MD.A.3

Name ________________________________

Mark the best estimate for the length of each object.

1. The ruler pictured is actually 1 foot long.
About how long is the board?

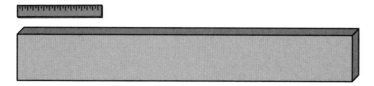

- ○ 2 feet
- ○ 1 yard
- ○ 4 feet

---

2. The eraser pictured is actually 2 inches long.
About how long is the spoon?

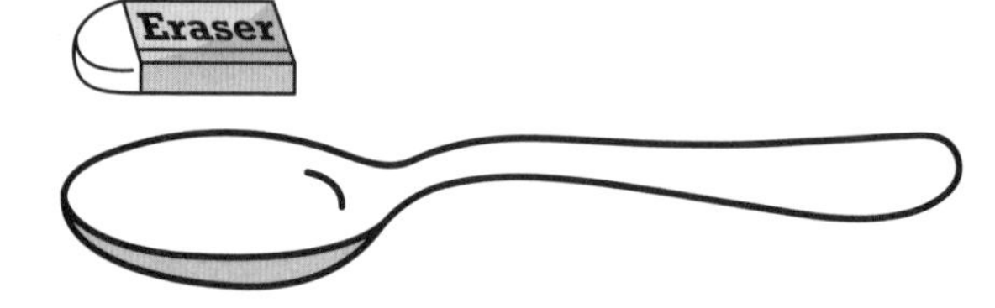

- ○ 8 inches
- ○ 4 inches
- ○ 6 inches

---

3. The window pictured is actually 1 meter tall.
About how tall is the door?

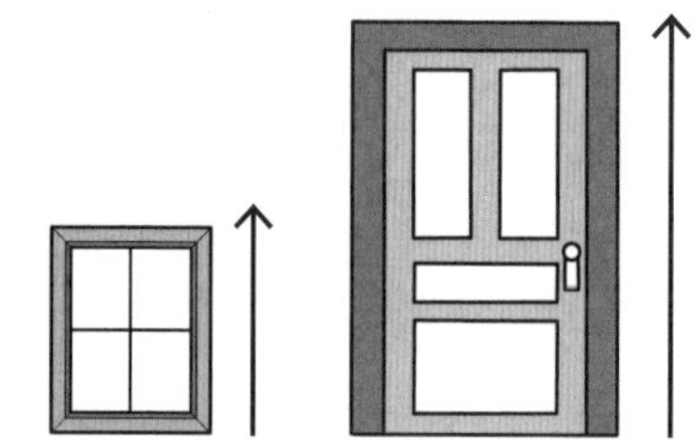

- ○ 3 meters
- ○ 2 meters
- ○ 100 centimeters

---

4. The leaf is 6 centimeters long.
About how long is the bug?

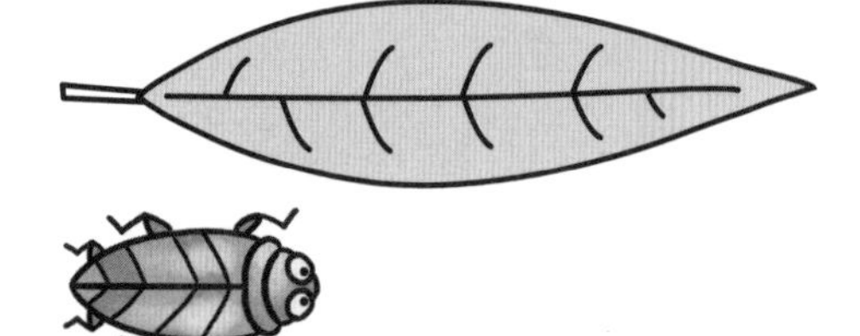

- ○ 5 centimeters
- ○ 3 centimeters
- ○ 2 centimeters

 CCMS 2.MD.A.3 Estimate lengths using units of inches, feet, yards, centimeters, and meters.

Name ______________________

Read the Problem

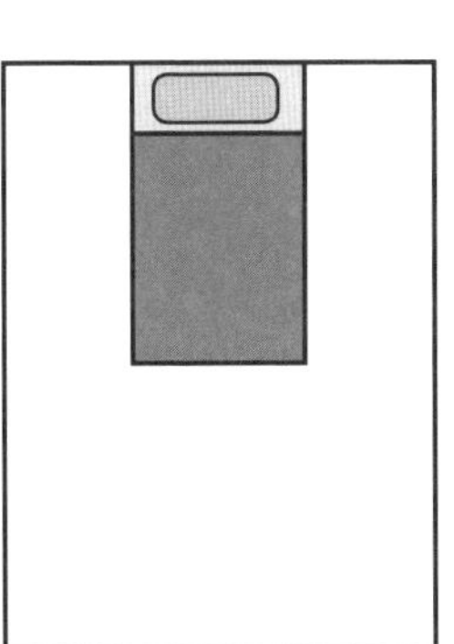

Look at the picture of Petro's bedroom. His bed is 7 feet long and 4 feet wide. About how long is the bedroom? About how wide is it? Draw or write below to explain your thinking.

Think About It

❶ You will estimate the size of _____.

○ Petro ○ Petro's room ○ Petro's bed

❷ The size will be in _____.

○ inches ○ yards ○ feet

Solve the Problem

❸ Use this work space to explain your thinking.

❹ Petro's bedroom is about __________ long and __________ wide.

Check Your Work

❺ Do your answers make sense? ○ yes ○ no

Estimate lengths using units of inches, feet, yards, centimeters, and meters.

CCMS 2.MD.A.3

Math Models

Measuring, comparing, and writing the difference

You can measure and compare the length of two objects and write the difference.

This is an example of comparing lengths:
How much shorter is the white pencil?

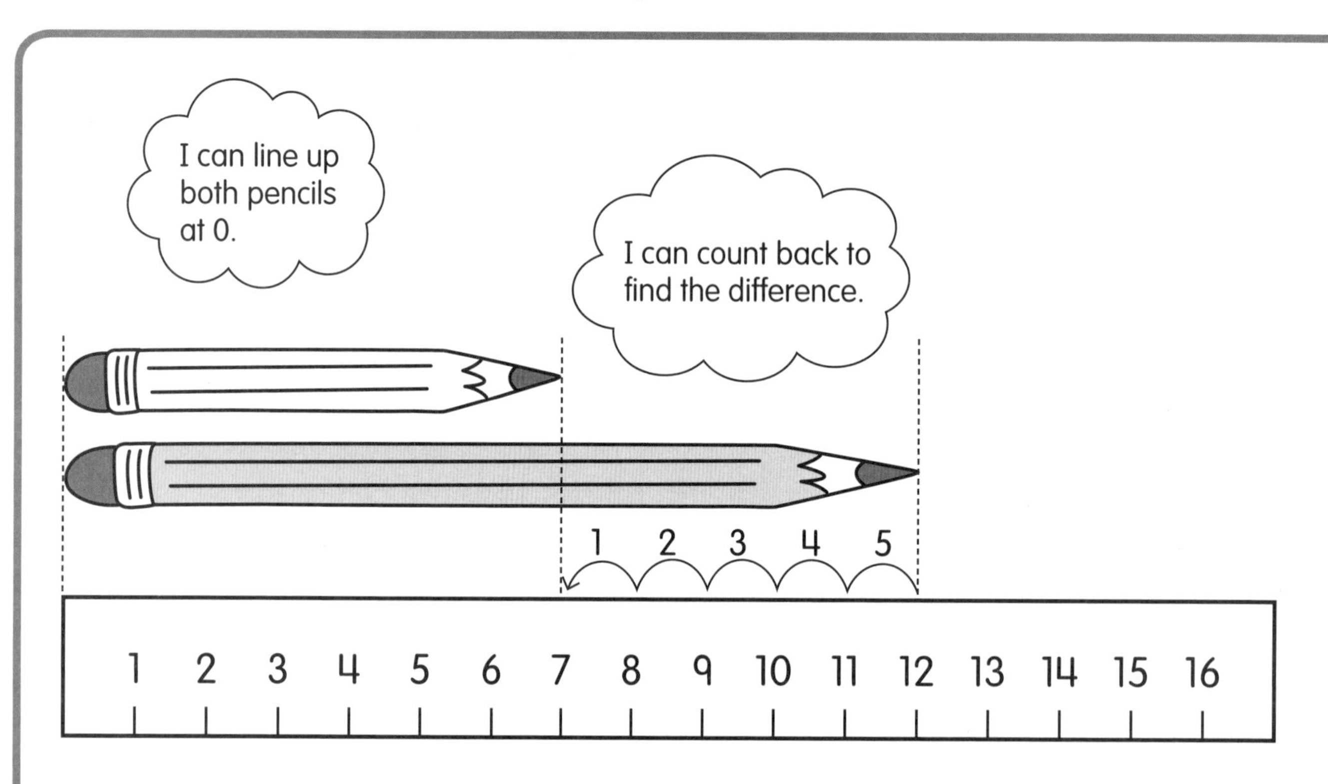

I can line up both pencils at 0.
I can count back to find the difference.
1 2 3 4 5
1 2 3 4 5 6 7 8 9 10 11 12 13 14 15 16
I can measure, and then write a number sentence.

12 cm – 7 cm = <u>5</u> centimeters

The white pencil is <u>5</u> centimeters shorter.

Think

One skateboard is 24 inches long. Another skateboard is 1 yard long. Which skateboard is longer? Explain your thinking.

Name ______________________________

Compare each pair of objects. Then complete the number sentence to answer the question.

Example

How much longer is the gray worm?

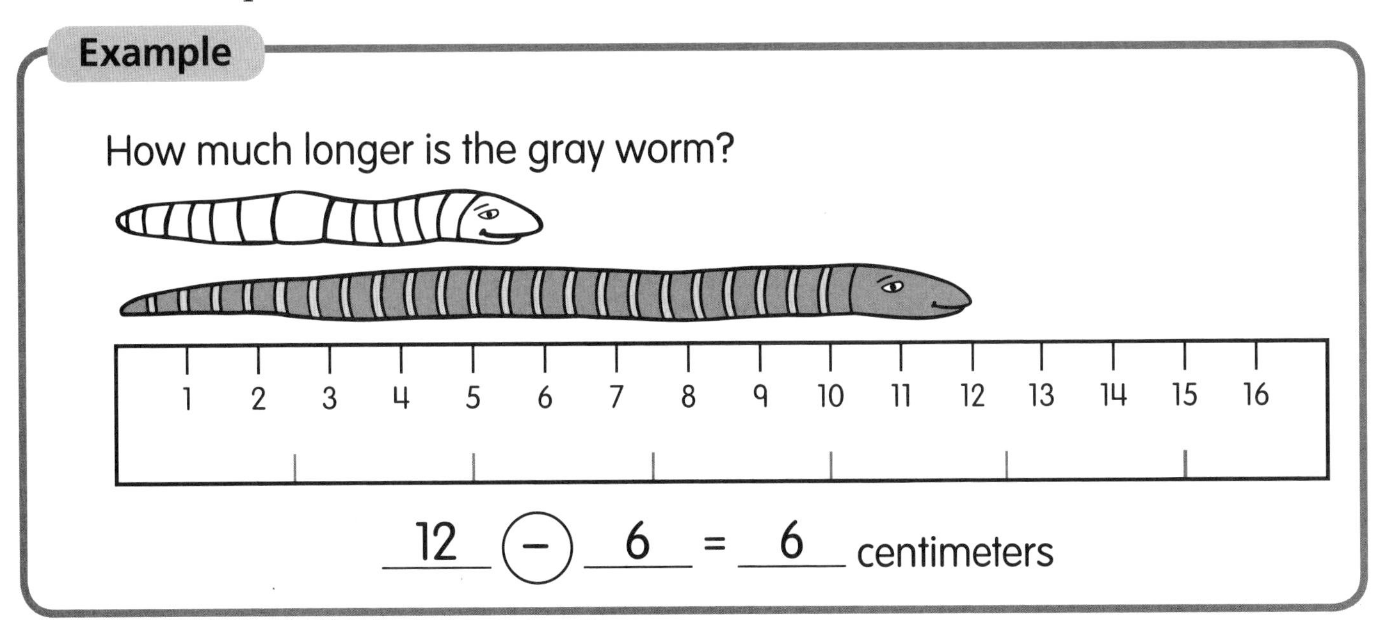

1. How much longer is the white ribbon?

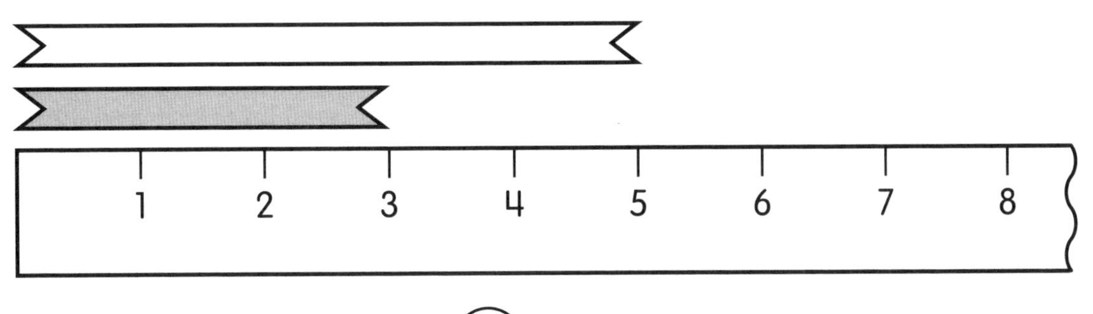

_____ ◯ _____ = _____ inches

2. How much shorter is the dark string?

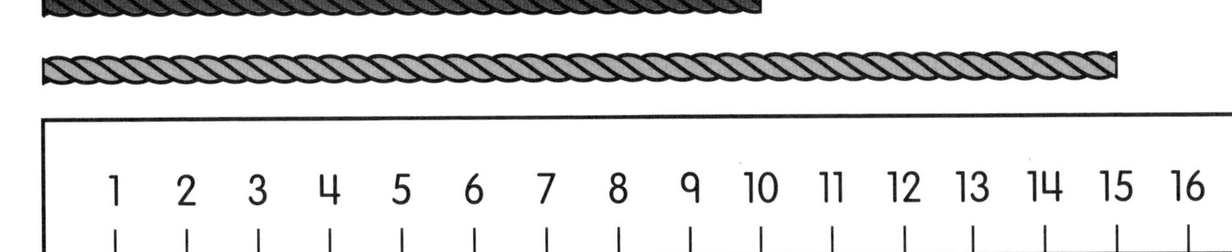

_____ ◯ _____ = _____ centimeters

Name ______________________________

Compare each pair of objects. Then complete the number sentence to answer the question.

1 How much farther did the spotted frog jump?

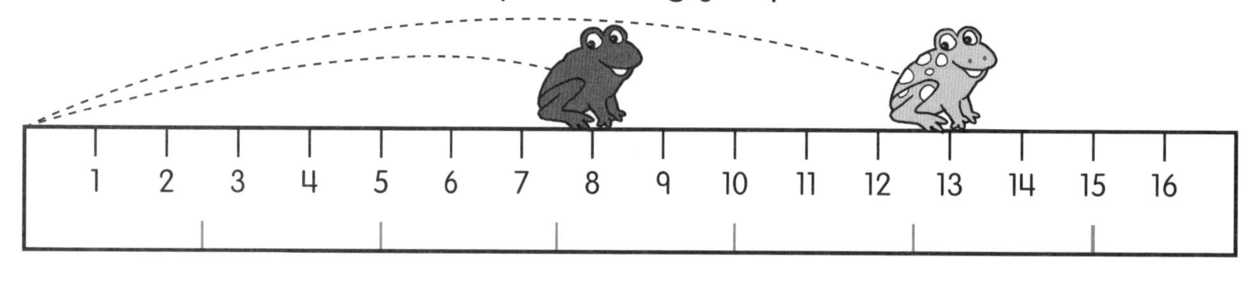

_____ ◯ _____ = _____ centimeters

---

2 How much longer is the striped straw?

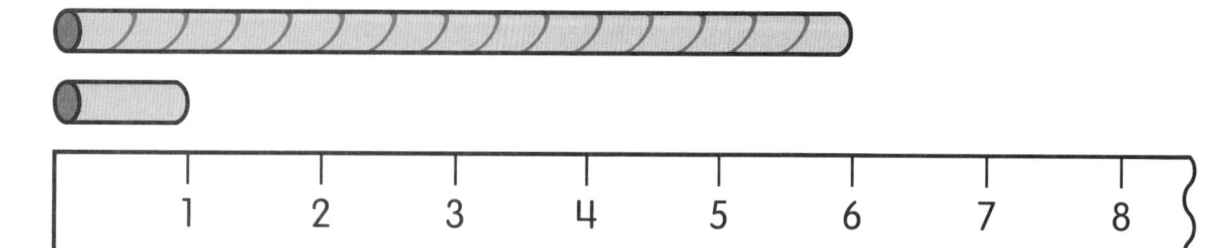

_____ ◯ _____ = _____ inches

---

3 How much shorter is the gray fish?

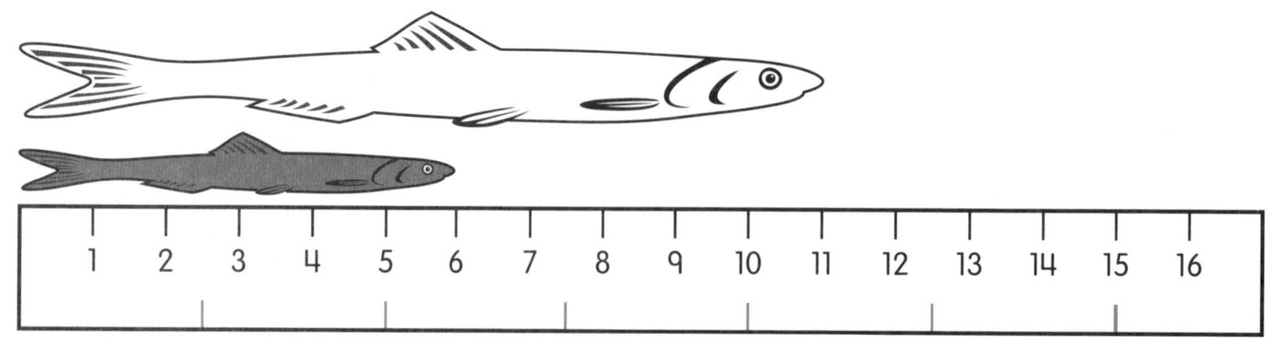

_____ ◯ _____ = _____ centimeters

Name ______________________________

Read each problem. Draw or write to show your thinking. Then write the answer.

Dad's car is 5 feet wide. Mom's car is 6 feet wide. The garage door is 12 feet wide. Will both cars fit in the garage?

1. Use this work space.

2. Both cars will fit in the garage. ○ yes ○ no

Erin is 47 inches tall. Brian is 51 inches tall. How many inches taller is Brian than Erin?

3. Use this work space.

4. Brian is ______ inches taller than Erin.

Name ______________________________

Read the Problem

Thalia swam across a pool that is 25 meters long. She wants to try swimming across a pool that is 50 meters long. How much farther will Thalia have to swim to get across a 50-meter swimming pool?

Think About It

1. You will find out how much _____ Thalia needs to swim.
   ○ slower ○ faster ○ farther

2. Mark the number sentence that can help you solve the problem.
   ○ 50 + 25 = ? ○ 50 – 25 = ?

Solve the Problem

3. Use this work space.

4. Thalia will have to swim _____ meters farther.

Check Your Work

5. Do your answers make sense? ○ yes ○ no

Relate Addition and Subtraction to Length

Domain

Measurement and Data

Cluster

Relate addition and subtraction to length.

Standards in Cluster

2.MD.B.5 Use addition and subtraction within 100 to solve word problems involving lengths that are given in the same units, e.g., by using drawings (such as drawings of rulers) and equations with a symbol for the unknown number to represent the problem.

2.MD.B.6 Represent whole numbers as lengths from 0 on a number line diagram with equally spaced points corresponding to the numbers 0, 1, 2, ..., and represent whole-number sums and differences within 100 on a number line diagram.

Unit Contents

Mathematical Practices in This Unit

Make sense of problems and persevere in solving them: *pages 120, 121, 122, 123, 124, 125, 126, 127, 128*

Reason abstractly and quantitatively: *pages 120, 121, 122, 123*

Model with mathematics: *pages 121, 122, 123, 124, 125, 126, 127, 128*

Attend to precision: *pages 120, 123, 124, 128*

Look for and make use of structure: *pages 120, 121, 124, 125, 126*

You can use addition and subtraction to solve word problems about length.

Word Problem:

Carli has two dogs named Spot and Lucky. Spot's tail is 16 inches long. Lucky's tail is 5 inches shorter than Spot's tail. How long is Lucky's tail?

These are **two** ways to solve the word problem:

Draw a picture.

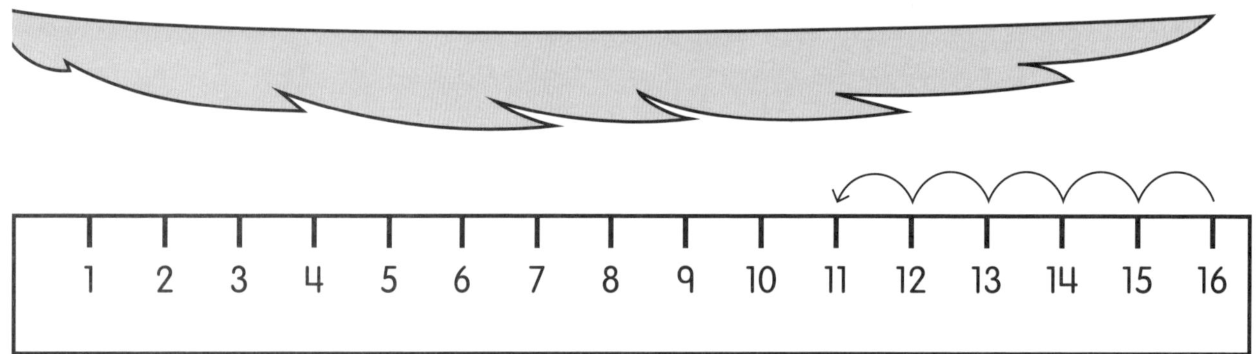

Write a number sentence.

difference
16 – 5 = ___?___ inches
Spot's tail — Lucky's tail

16 – 5 = __11__ inches

Lucky's tail is __11__ inches long.

Addie had a blue hair ribbon that was 36 inches long. She cut 10 inches off the end and gave it to her sister. How many inches long was Addie's ribbon then? Explain your thinking and tell about a way you can solve the problem.

Name ______________________________

Solve each word problem. Show your work.

Example

Sal's shoe is 22 centimeters long. Dad's shoe is 30 centimeters long. How many centimeters longer is Dad's shoe than Sal's?

Dad's shoe is __8__ centimeters longer than Sal's.

30 cm – 22 cm = 8 cm
(Dad's shoe) (Sal's shoe)

Work Space

1. On Monday, Simon Snail traveled 43 inches. On Tuesday, he traveled 15 inches. How many inches did Simon travel altogether?

   Simon Snail traveled ______ inches altogether.

2. Rosa's skateboard is 80 centimeters long. Corey's skateboard is 7 centimeters shorter than Rosa's. How long is Corey's skateboard?

   Corey's skateboard is ______ centimeters long.

Use addition and subtraction within 100 to solve word problems involving lengths that are the same units.

CCMS 2.MD.B.5

Name ______________________________

Relate Addition and Subtraction to Length
Solving word problems by using drawings and equations

2

Solve each word problem. Show your work.

Work Space

1. The running race was 50 meters long. Kari tripped and fell when she still had 21 meters to go. How many meters did Kari run before she fell?

   Kari ran _____ meters.

2. Grandpa has a rope that is 23 yards long. He wants to cut it so that he has two 12-yard ropes. Will Grandpa's plan work?

   ○ yes ○ no

3. Rafe is painting a fence. He already finished painting 54 feet of it. He has 20 more feet to go. How many feet of fence will Rafe have painted in all?

   Rafe will have painted _____ feet of fence.

CCMS 2.MD.B.5 Use addition and subtraction within 100 to solve word problems involving lengths that are the same units.

Name ______________________________

Relate Addition and Subtraction to Length
Solving word problems by using drawings and equations

Read the Problem

A sign at the fair says that children must be at least 42 inches tall to ride the roller coaster. Last year, Arlo was only 39 inches tall. Since then, he has grown more than 3 inches. Is Arlo tall enough to ride on the roller coaster now?

Think About It

1. You will find out how many inches tall Arlo _____.
   - ○ was last year
   - ○ is this year
   - ○ will be next year

2. Mark the number sentence that can help you solve the problem.
   - ○ $42 + 3 = ?$
   - ○ $39 + 3 = ?$
   - ○ $39 - 3 = ?$

Solve the Problem

3. Use this work space.

4. Arlo is tall enough to ride on the roller coaster now.
   - ○ yes
   - ○ no

Check Your Work

5. Do your answers make sense? ○ yes ○ no

Use addition and subtraction within 100 to solve word problems involving lengths that are the same units.

CCMS 2.MD.B.5

You can represent lengths on a number line diagram.

These are **two** examples:

Add

The garden path was 13 feet long. Mom used bricks to make the path 9 feet longer. How long was the path after Mom placed the bricks?

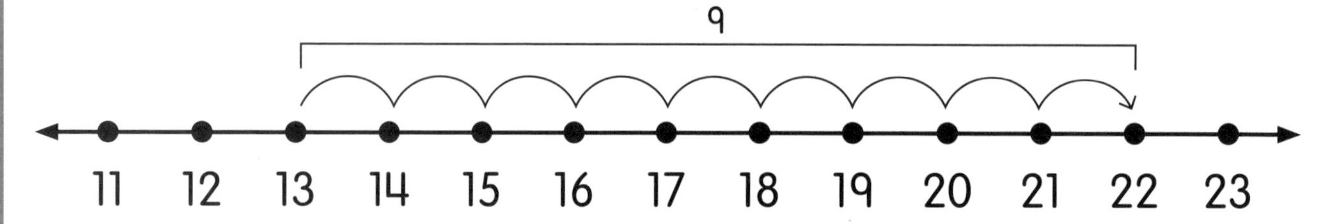

The path was 22 feet long.

Subtract

Kaya swam 50 meters without stopping. Her little brother, Awan, swam 46 meters. How many fewer meters did Awan swim than Kaya?

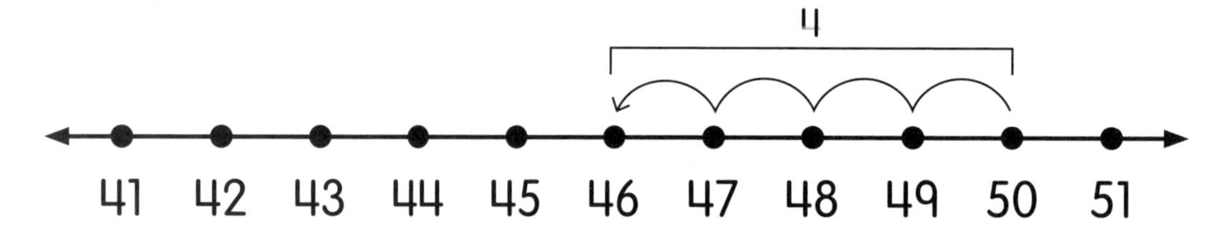

Awan swam 4 fewer meters.

Think

Would you use a number line to solve **96 inches – 42 inches = ?** Explain your thinking and tell about a way you can solve it.

Name ______________________

Use the number line to solve each word problem.

Example

The garden border is 15 meters long. If Dad wants a 22-meter-long border, how many more meters of border will he place?

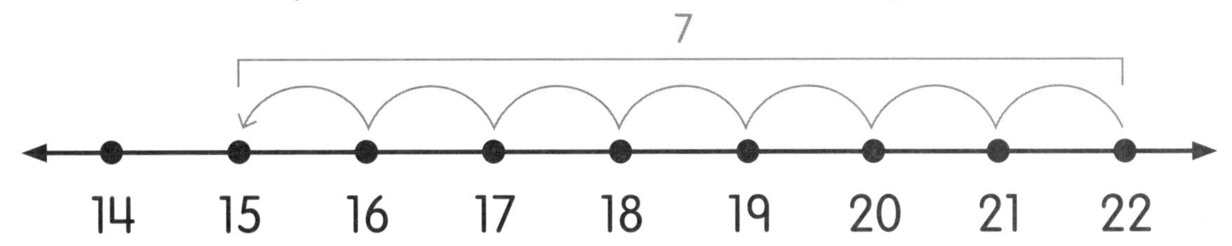

Dad will place __7__ more meters of border.

The library book is 27 cm long. It is 21 cm wide.
How many fewer centimeters wide than long is the book?

1.
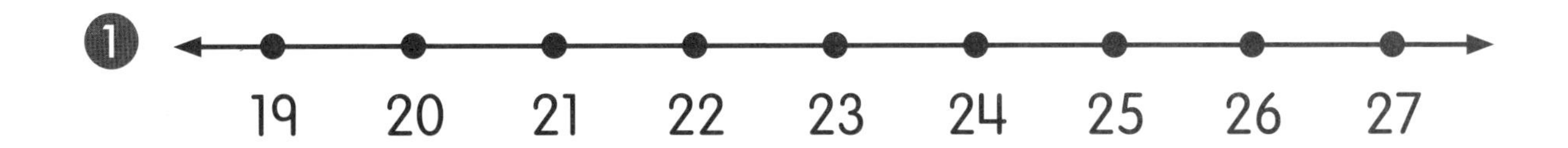

2. The book is _____ fewer centimeters wide than long.

A bee flew 22 yards to a blue flower. Then it flew 5 yards to a red flower. Finally, the bee flew 3 yards to a pink flower. How far did the bee fly?

3.
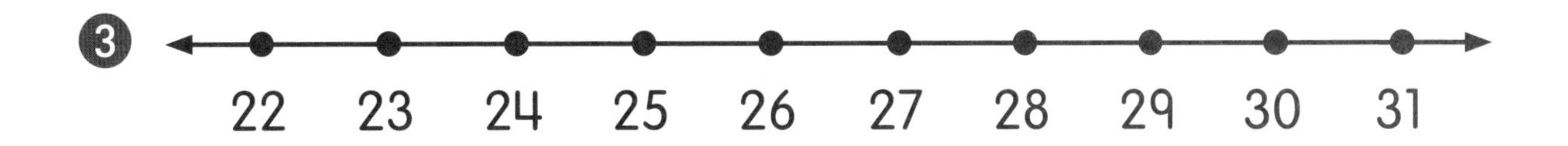

4. The bee flew _____ yards.

Name ____________________

Complete the number line to solve each word problem.

Example

A roll of paper is 50 feet long. Mrs. Davis needs to use 9 feet. How many feet of paper will she have left?

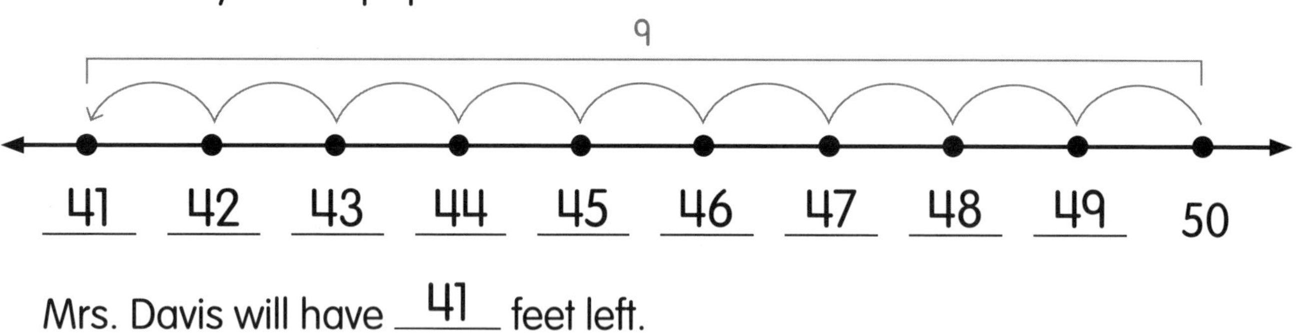

Mrs. Davis will have 41 feet left.

A plant was 6 inches tall. After two weeks, it was 13 inches tall. How many inches did the plant grow?

1 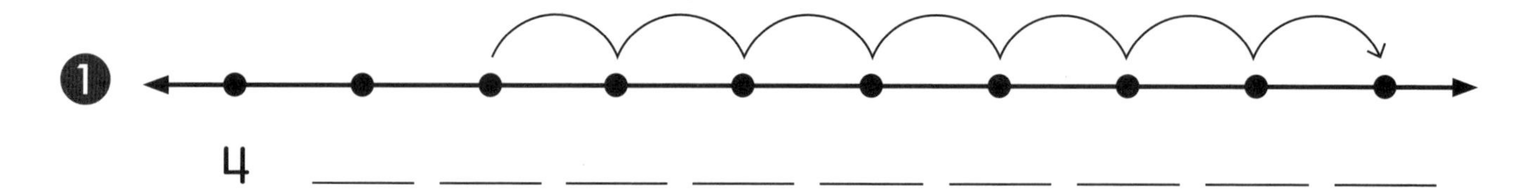

4 ____ ____ ____ ____ ____ ____ ____ ____ ____

2 The plant grew ____ inches.

At a party, a 10-foot table and an 8-foot table were placed end to end. What was the total length of both tables?

3 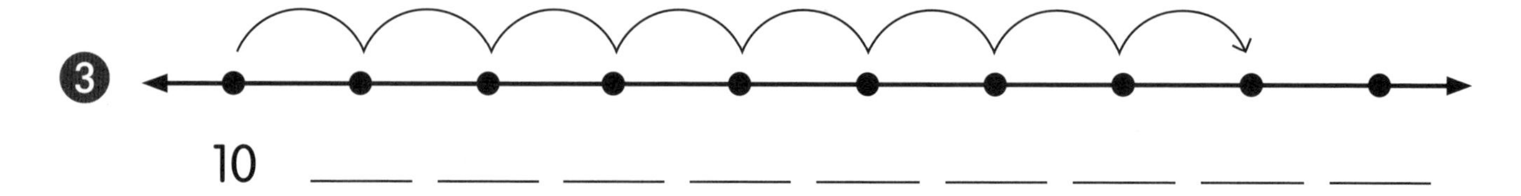

10 ____ ____ ____ ____ ____ ____ ____ ____ ____

4 The total length of both tables was ____ feet.

 CCMS 2.MD.B.6 Represent whole numbers as lengths for sums and differences.

Name ______________________________

Relate Addition and Subtraction to Length
Using a number line diagram

5

Complete the number line to solve each word problem.

A second-grade class made a paper chain that is 22 yards long. They want it to be 30 yards long. How many more yards of chain do the students need to add?

1 

2 The students need to add _____ more yards of chain.

A tree's trunk was 38 centimeters around. Now the tree's trunk is 45 centimeters around. How many centimeters did the tree's trunk grow?

3 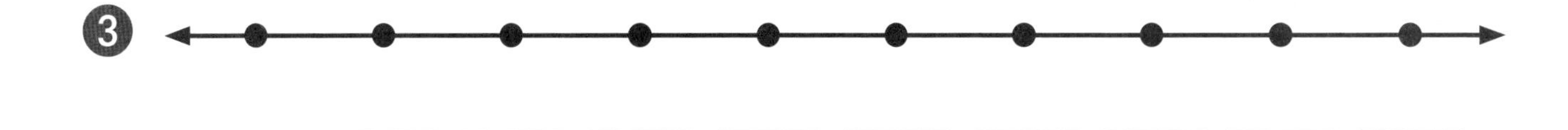

4 The tree's trunk grew _____ centimeters.

It takes 45 meters of string lights to reach across the front of our school. If we have 40 meters of string lights, how many more meters do we need?

5 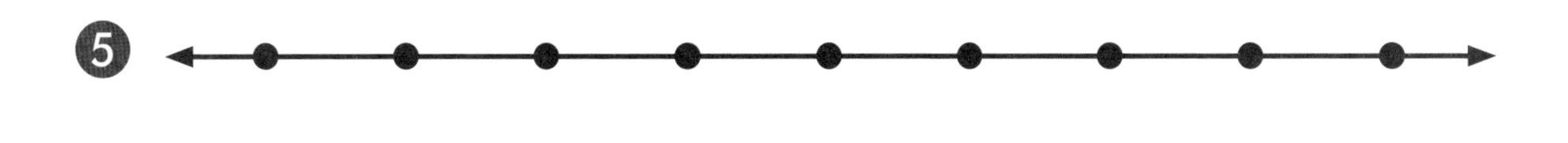

6 We need _____ more meters of string lights.

Name ______________________________

Relate Addition and Subtraction to Length
Using a number line diagram

Read the Problem

My dog, Toby, was 45 centimeters tall last month. Now he is 55 centimeters tall. How many centimeters did Toby grow since last month?

Think About It

1. You will find out ______.
   ○ how tall Toby is ○ how many centimeters Toby grew

2. Mark the number that is **not** needed on your number line.
   ○ 55 ○ 45 ○ 65

Solve the Problem

3. Use this work space to complete the number line.

4. Toby grew ______ centimeters since last month.

Check Your Work

5. Do your answers make sense? ○ yes ○ no

Work with Time and Money

Domain

Measurement and Data

Cluster

Work with time and money.

Standards in Cluster

2.MD.C.7 Tell and write time from analog and digital clocks to the nearest five minutes, using *a.m.* and *p.m.*

2.MD.C.8 Solve word problems involving dollar bills, quarters, dimes, nickels, and pennies, using $ and ¢ symbols appropriately.

Unit Contents

Mathematical Practices in This Unit

Make sense of problems and persevere in solving them: *pages 130, 133, 134, 137, 138, 139, 140, 141, 142, 143, 146*

Reason abstractly and quantitatively: *pages 133, 135, 136, 137, 140, 141, 142, 144, 145, 146*

Construct viable arguments and critique the reasoning of others: *pages 130, 134, 137, 138, 143*

Model with mathematics: *pages 133, 139, 140, 141, 142, 146*

Use appropriate tools strategically: *pages 130, 131, 132, 133, 138, 139, 140, 141, 142, 145, 146*

Attend to precision: *pages 133, 137, 142, 146*

Look for and make use of structure: *pages 130, 131, 132, 133, 138, 139, 140, 141, 142, 145, 146*

Math Models

Telling and writing time

You can tell the time on an analog or a digital clock.

Analog Clock

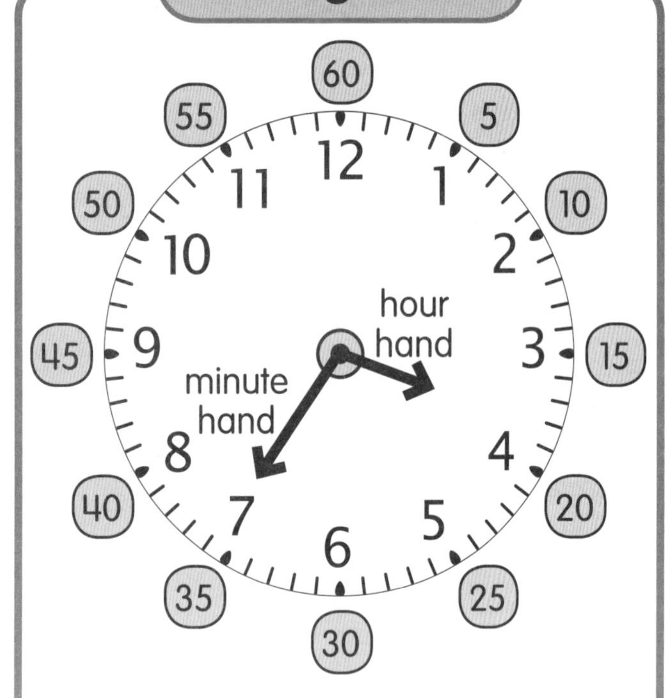

The short hand shows the **hour**.

The long hand points to the **minutes**.

This clock shows 3:35.

Digital Clock

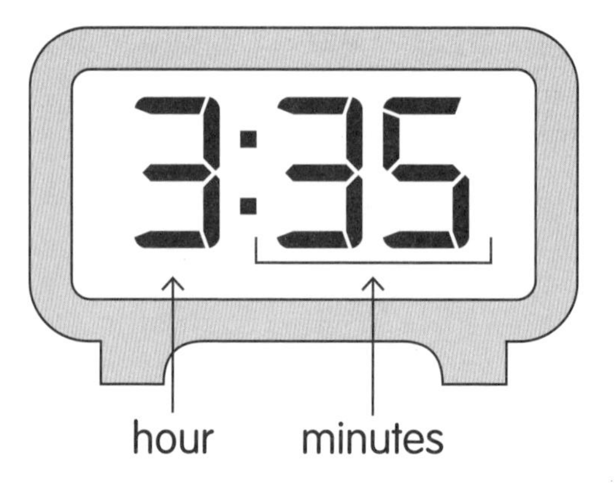

Read the **hour**: **3**:35.

Read the **minutes**: 3:**35**.

How would you write the time **five minutes past nine**? Explain your thinking and tell about your answer.

Name ______________________________

Draw a line from each analog clock to its matching digital clock.

Example

3:30

❶ 

❷ 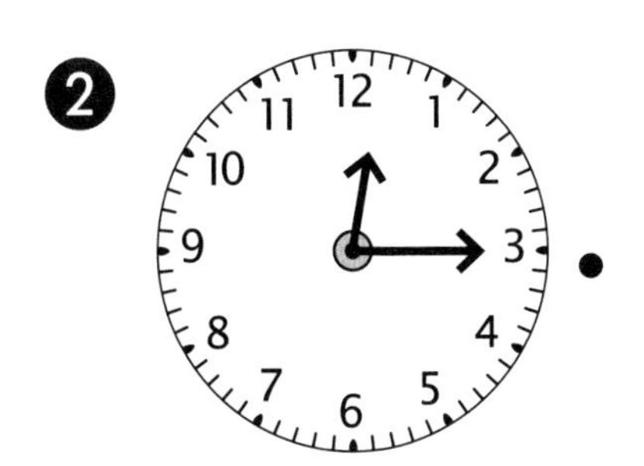

❸ 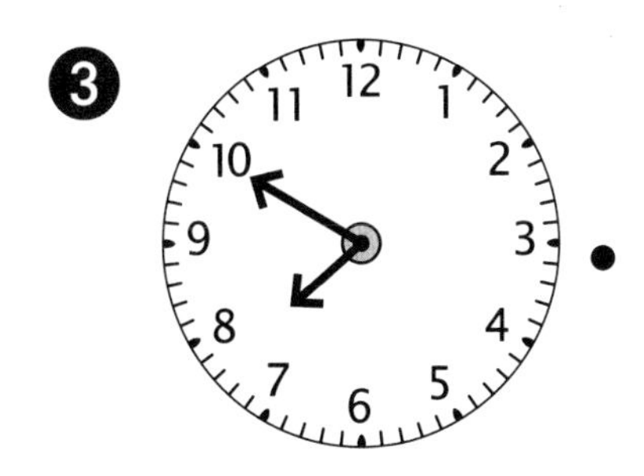

❹ 

Name ______________________________

Look at each analog clock. Write the matching time on the digital clock.

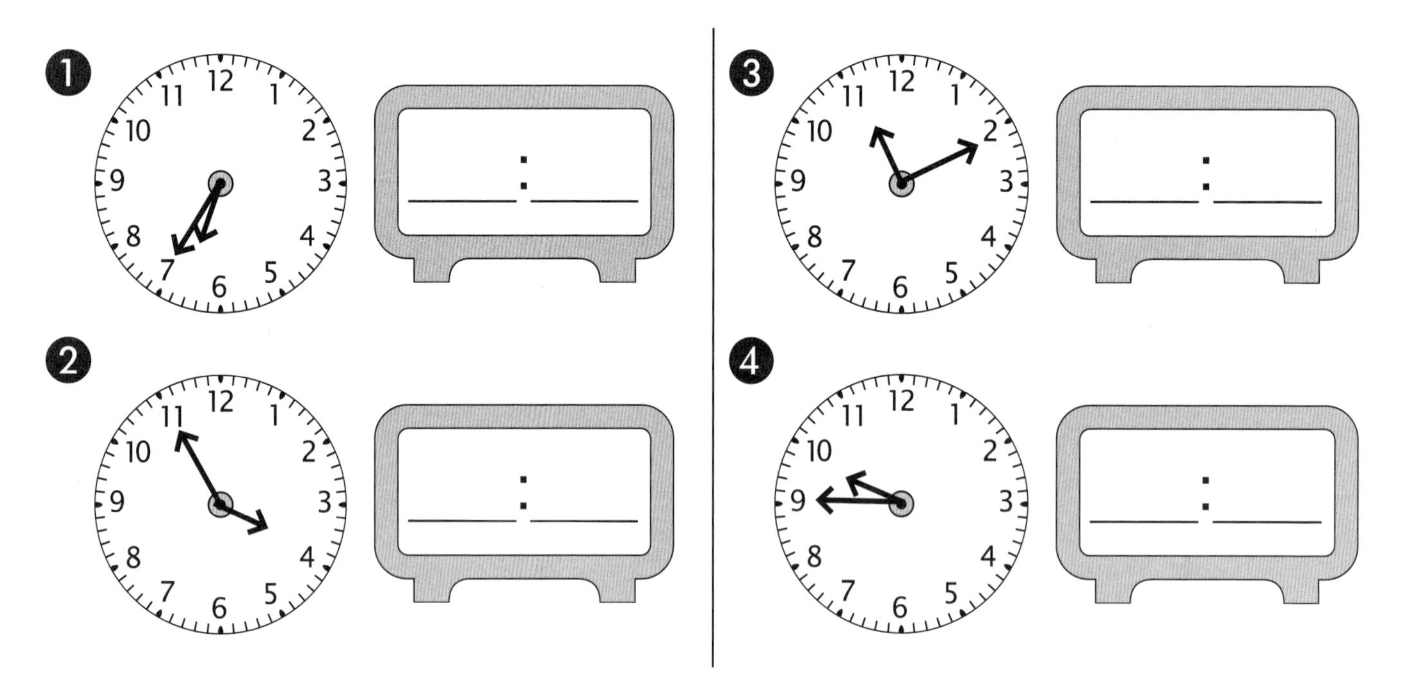

Look at both clocks. Write how much time has passed.

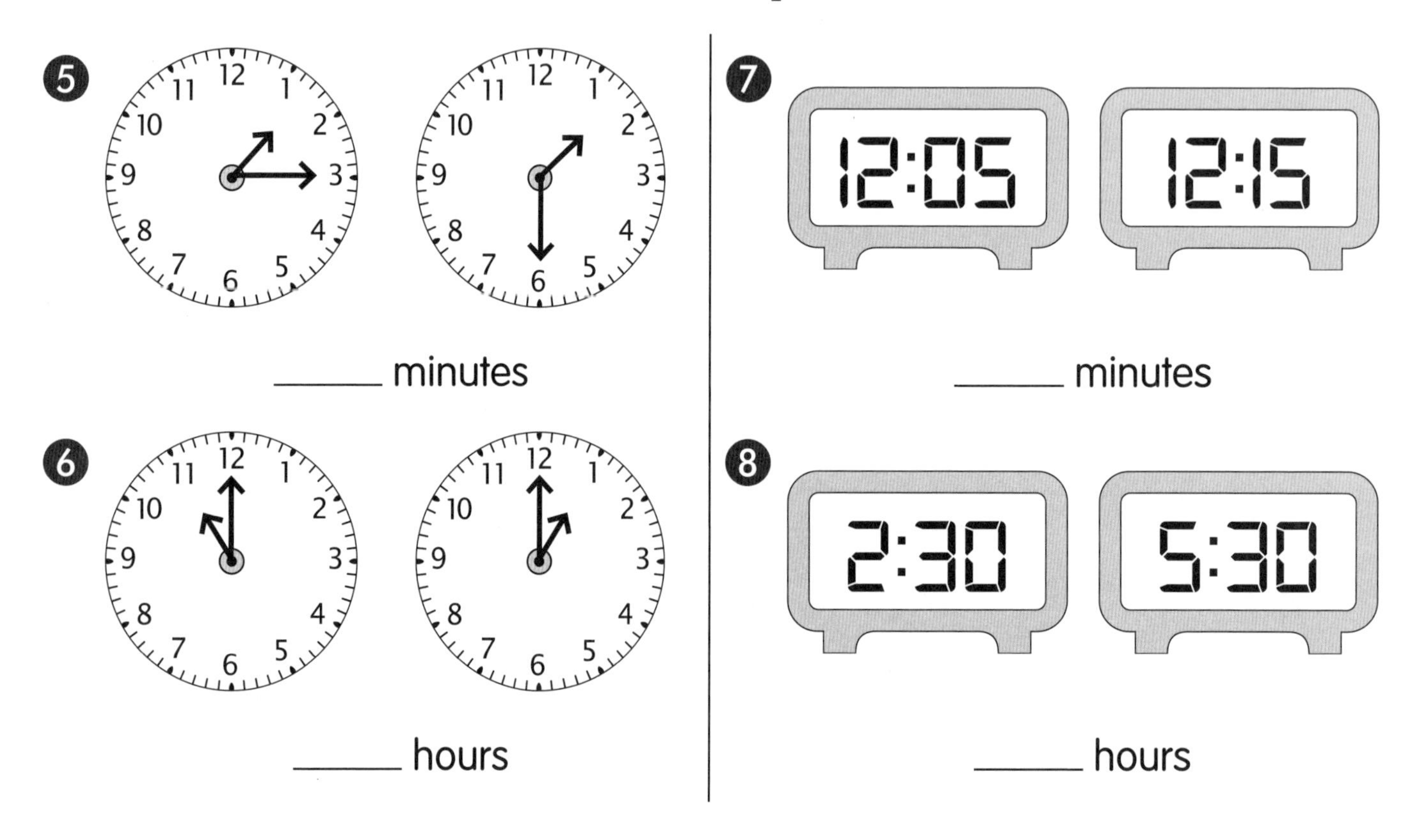

 CCMS 2.MD.C.7 Tell and write time to the nearest five minutes.

Name ______________________________

Read the Problem

It takes Jordy 15 minutes to walk to school. At what time should he leave home if school starts at 8:20?

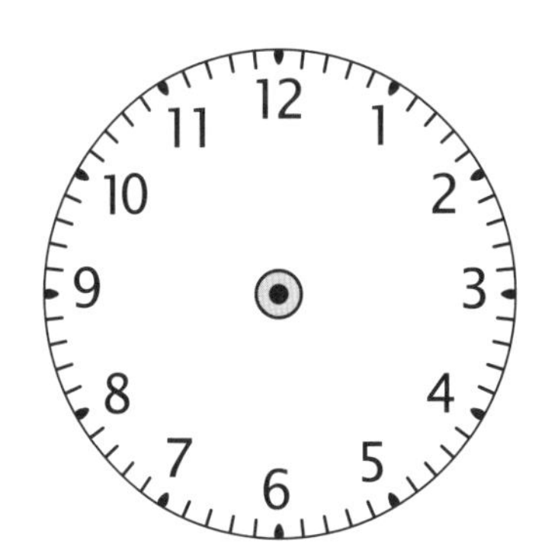

Think About It

1. You will find out at what time Jordy ______.
   ○ leaves home ○ leaves school ○ gets home from school

2. Jordy needs to leave home ______.
   ○ at 8:00 ○ before 8:00 ○ after 8:00

Solve the Problem

3. Use this work space.

4. Jordy should leave home at _____:_____.

Check Your Work

5. Do your answers make sense? ○ yes ○ no

You can tell time using a.m. and p.m.

a.m.

It is **a.m.** from

12:00 midnight to 11:59 before noon

p.m.

It is **p.m.** from

12:00 noon to 11:59 before midnight

Let's compare:

At 3:00 **a.m.**, it is nighttime.

At 3:00 **p.m.**, it is daytime.

Think

Why is it important to use **a.m.** or **p.m.**? Explain your thinking.

Name ______________________________

Mark **a.m.** or **p.m.** to show when each action is likely to happen.

Example

I eat breakfast. ● a.m. ○ p.m.

1. We see the sunset. ○ a.m. ○ p.m.

2. We get up in the morning. ○ a.m. ○ p.m.

3. I go to bed at night. ○ a.m. ○ p.m.

4. The school day begins. ○ a.m. ○ p.m.

5. We sit down for dinner. ○ a.m. ○ p.m.

Name ______________________________

Write or draw a picture of something you might do at each time.

❶ 2:00 a.m.	❹ 2:00 p.m.
❷ 8:30 a.m.	❺ 8:30 p.m.
❸ 12:00 midnight	❻ 12:00 noon

Name ______________________

Read the Problem

Our family went to the park at 11:20 a.m. We stayed there for 3 hours. My brother, Nate, says that we stayed at the park until 2:20 p.m. I say that we stayed until 2:20 a.m. Who is correct? Explain your thinking below.

Think About It

1. You will find out if we stayed at the park ______.
   - ○ for 3 hours
   - ○ until 2:20 a.m. or 2:20 p.m.
   - ○ until 11:20 a.m.

2. Mark something you would usually do at 2:20 a.m.
   - ○ eat
   - ○ play
   - ○ sleep

Solve the Problem

3. Use this work space to explain your thinking.

4. ______________ is correct.

5. We stayed at the park until 2:20 ________.

Check Your Work

6. Do your answers make sense? ○ yes ○ no

Math Models

Determining the value of money

You can count dollar bills, quarters, dimes, nickels, and pennies to find the value of money.

penny

one cent
1¢

count by **1s**

¢

nickel

one nickel
5¢

count by **5s**

¢

dime

one dime
10¢

count by **10s**

¢

quarter

one quarter
25¢

count by **25s**

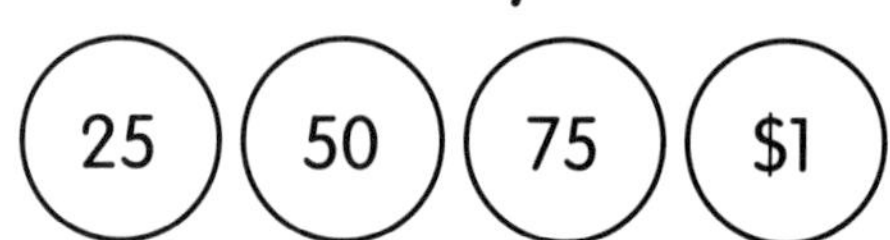

dollar

one dollar
$1 = 100¢

count by **1s**

1 2 3 4 5 $

Think

If you have 2 quarters, 3 dimes, 1 nickel, and 4 pennies, how much money do you have? Explain how to count to find the answer.

Name ______________________________

Mark the amount that is written correctly for each money group.

Example

○ $78

● 78¢

○ ¢78

❶

○ $225

○ $2.25¢

○ $2.25

---

❷

○ 58¢

○ $58

○ ¢58

---

❸

○ 1.15$

○ $1.15

○ ¢1.15

Name ________________________________

Work with Time and Money
Determining the value of money

6

Choose the set of coins that answers the question.

Example

Which set is worth 10¢?

1 Which set is worth 7¢?

2 Which set is worth 47¢?

3 Which set is worth $1?

Name ______________________________

Use what you know about money to solve each word problem.

Example

Tamara has one quarter and one dime in her pocket. She has two dimes and a nickel in her backpack. How much money does Tamara have altogether?

25 35 45 55 60

5

Tamara has 60 cents altogether.

Work Space

1. Matt found two quarters, one dime, and two pennies under his bed. How much money did he find?

   Matt found _____ cents.

2. Gino has two quarters. Jared has five dimes and one nickel. How much money does each boy have?

   Gino has _____ cents.

   Jared has _____ cents.

Solve word problems involving money.

CCMS 2.MD.C.8

Name ______________________________

Read the Problem

Nick has saved some money. He has pennies, nickels, dimes, quarters, and dollar bills. He wants to buy a kite for $2. Below, draw 3 different ways he can make $2.

Think About It

1. You will find out how to make _____.
   - ○ a kite ○ $2 ○ some money

2. **$2** is the same amount as _____.
   - ○ 2¢ ○ 20¢ ○ 200¢

Solve the Problem

3. Use this work space.

first way	second way	third way

Check Your Work

4. Do your answers make sense? ○ yes ○ no

 CCMS 2.MD.C.8 Solve word problems involving money.

You can add and subtract to solve word problems about money.

Use **$** and **.** to write dollars and cents together.

Malik had 55¢. Then he got a dollar bill for his birthday.
How much money does he have now?

55¢ + $1 = **$**1.55 (dollars . cents)

Linda had $6. She bought a dozen eggs for $4.
How much money does she have left?

$6 − $4 = $2

Think

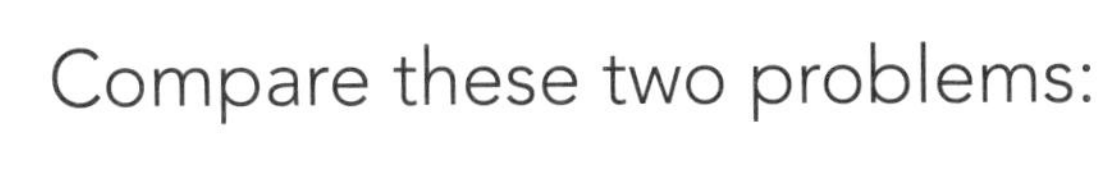

Compare these two problems:

2 + 3 = 5 **$2 + $3 = $5**

What is the same in both problems? What is different?

Name ________________________________

Use what you know about money to solve each word problem.

Example

At the big sale, a red bike was marked $10 off from $85. What was the sale price of the red bike?

The sale price was $_75_.

$$\begin{array}{r} \$85 \\ -\ \$10 \\ \hline \$75 \end{array}$$

Work Space

1. We bought an apple for 30¢ and a banana for 25¢. How much did we spend?

   We spent ______¢.

2. Keely wants to buy an art set that costs $25. She earned $14 doing chores. How much more money does Keely need?

   Keely needs $______ more.

 CCMS 2.MD.C.8 Solve word problems involving money.

Name ______________________________

Use what you know about money to solve each word problem.

Work Space

1. Rudy wants to buy a pencil box that costs $1. He has 2 quarters, 4 dimes, and 3 nickels. Does Rudy have enough money to buy the pencil box?

   ○ yes ○ no

2. Pencils cost 25¢ each. How many pencils can Marisa buy if she has 1 quarter, 2 dimes, and 3 nickels?

   Marisa can buy _____ pencils.

3. At the store, Carlos buys an eraser that costs 69¢. He gives the clerk 3 quarters. How much money will Carlos get back?

   Carlos will get back _____¢.

Name ______________________________

Read the Problem

Lauren wants to buy a balloon that costs 59¢.
If she gives the clerk a one-dollar bill, how much money will she get back?

Think About It

1. You will find out how much money Lauren will ______.
   - ○ pay ○ get back ○ save

2. Lauren will get back ______.
   - ○ less than 50¢ ○ more than 50¢ ○ more than 60¢

Solve the Problem

3. Use this work space to draw the coins Lauren will get back.
   Use the fewest coins possible.

4. Lauren will get back ______ cents.

Check Your Work

5. Do your answers make sense? ○ yes ○ no

Represent and Interpret Data

Domain

Measurement and Data

Cluster

Represent and interpret data.

Standards in Cluster

2.MD.D.9 Generate measurement data by measuring lengths of several objects to the nearest whole unit, or by making repeated measurements of the same object. Show the measurements by making a line plot, where the horizontal scale is marked off in whole-number units.

2.MD.D.10 Draw a picture graph and a bar graph (with single-unit scale) to represent a data set with up to four categories. Solve simple put-together, take-apart, and compare problems using information presented in a bar graph.

Unit Contents

Mathematical Practices in This Unit

Make sense of problems and persevere in solving them: *pages 148, 151, 152, 155, 156, 160, 165*

Reason abstractly and quantitatively: *pages 156, 157, 158, 159, 160 ,161, 162, 164*

Construct viable arguments and critique the reasoning of others: *pages 148, 152, 161, 165*

Model with mathematics: *pages 156, 157, 158, 159, 160, 161, 162, 164*

Attend to precision: *pages 149, 150 ,151 ,153 ,154, 155, 157, 158, 159, 161, 162, 163, 164*

Look for and make use of structure: *pages 148, 152, 156, 160*

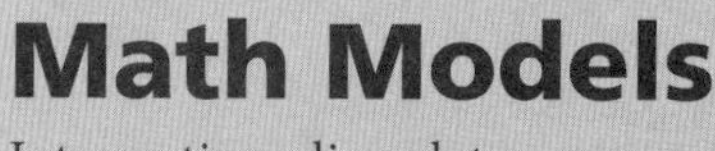

Interpreting a line plot

You can look at a line plot to see how often a number happens.

Mrs. Yoshi's class wants to find out how many pets each student has at home. Each student shared the number of pets he or she has. An **X** was placed on the line plot for each student.

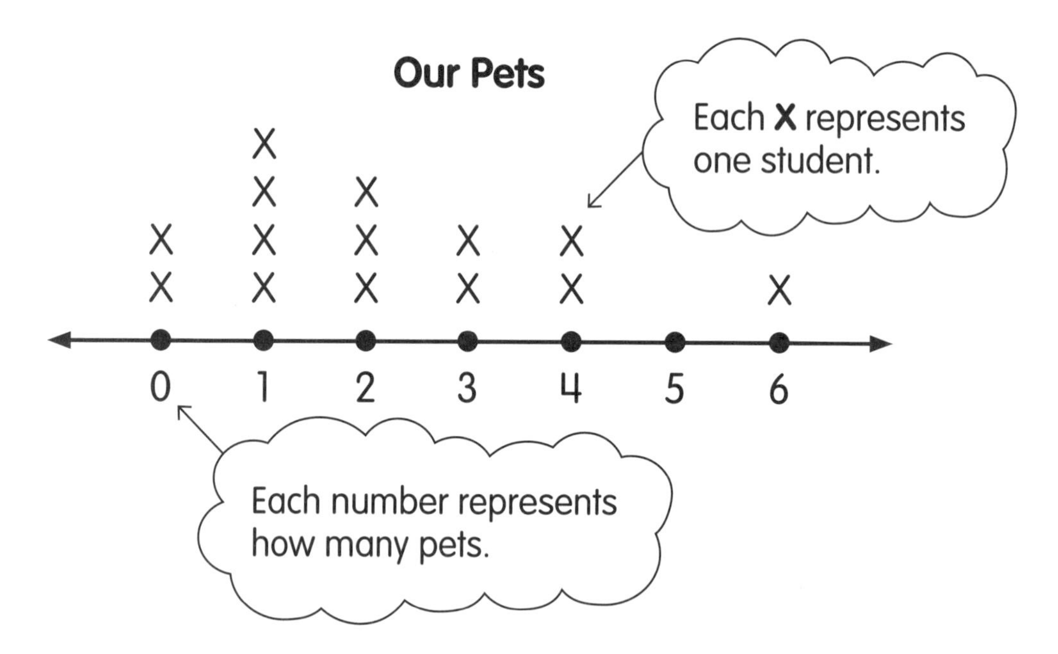

We can look at a line plot to find out facts. Here are some examples:

1. 4 students have one pet.
2. 2 students don't have a pet.
3. Students in Mrs. Yoshi's class have 30 pets in all.

Does a line plot remind you of a number line? Explain your thinking.

Name ______________________

Read the sentence. Then use the line plot to help you answer each question.

Example

This line plot shows how many books students read last week.

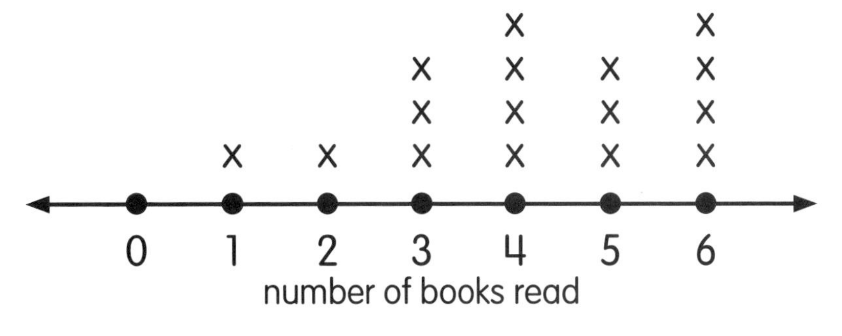

How many students read last week?

● 16 ○ 14 ○ 17

Baseball players counted how many hits they made last week.

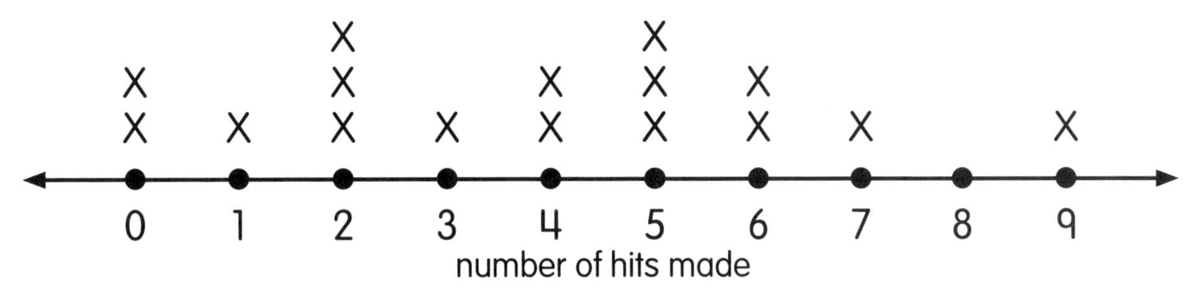

1. Each **X** represents a _____.

   ○ baseball player ○ hit ○ day of the week

2. Each number represents how many _____.

   ○ days of the week ○ baseball players ○ hits

3. _____ baseball players made fewer than 5 hits.

   ○ 4 ○ 7 ○ 9

Name ________________________________

Read the sentences. Then use the line plot to help you answer each question.

Swimmers on a team counted the number of laps they swam today. Each swimmer drew an **X** on the line plot to show the number of laps he or she swam.

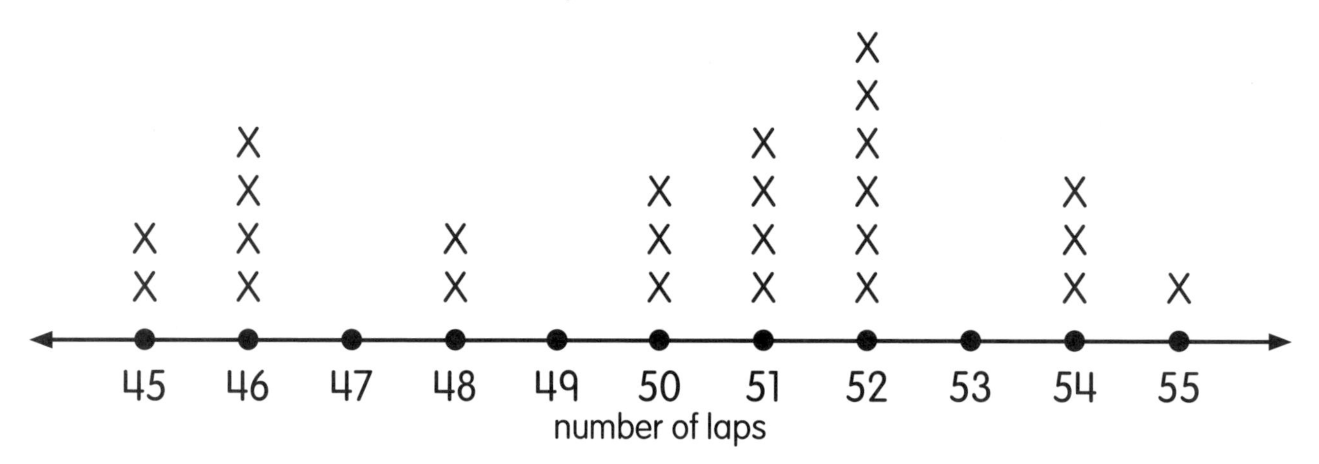

1. Each **X** represents a ______.
   - ○ lap
   - ○ swimmer
   - ○ pool

2. Each number represents the number of ______.
   - ○ swimmers
   - ○ pools
   - ○ laps

3. ______ swimmers swam more than 50 laps.
   - ○ 17
   - ○ 14
   - ○ 10

4. More swimmers swam ______ laps than any other number.
   - ○ 52
   - ○ 46
   - ○ 55

Name ______________________________

Read the Problem

Nathan's family picked apples at a farm. This list shows how many pounds of apples each person picked. Use the list to complete the line plot below.

Mom: 9 pounds	**Clara:** 5 pounds
Dad: 8 pounds	**Bennie:** 5 pounds
Nathan: 9 pounds	**Finn:** 4 pounds

Think About It

❶ You will make a ______.

○ number sentence ○ list ○ line plot

❷ Mark the numbers that belong in the line plot number line.

○ 4 to 9 ○ 5 to 9 ○ 4 to 11

Solve the Problem

Use this work space to complete the line plot.

Weight of Apples We Picked

❸ 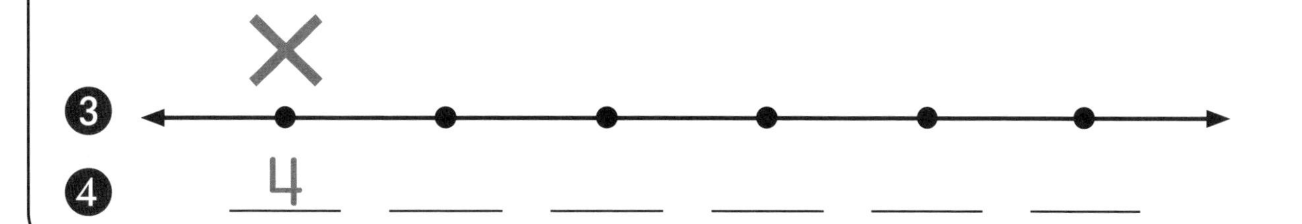

❹ 4 ____ ____ ____ ____ ____

Check Your Work

❺ Do your answers make sense? ○ yes ○ no

Math Models

Recording measurement data on a line plot

You can make a line plot to show measurement data.

Students in Room 11 measured the lengths of their pencils in centimeters. Then they made a data chart.

Pencil Lengths	Tally Marks
15 cm	II
16 cm	IIII
17 cm	III
18 cm	𝍸
20 cm	I

Each tally mark represents one pencil.

Then they used the data to make a line plot.

Pencil Lengths

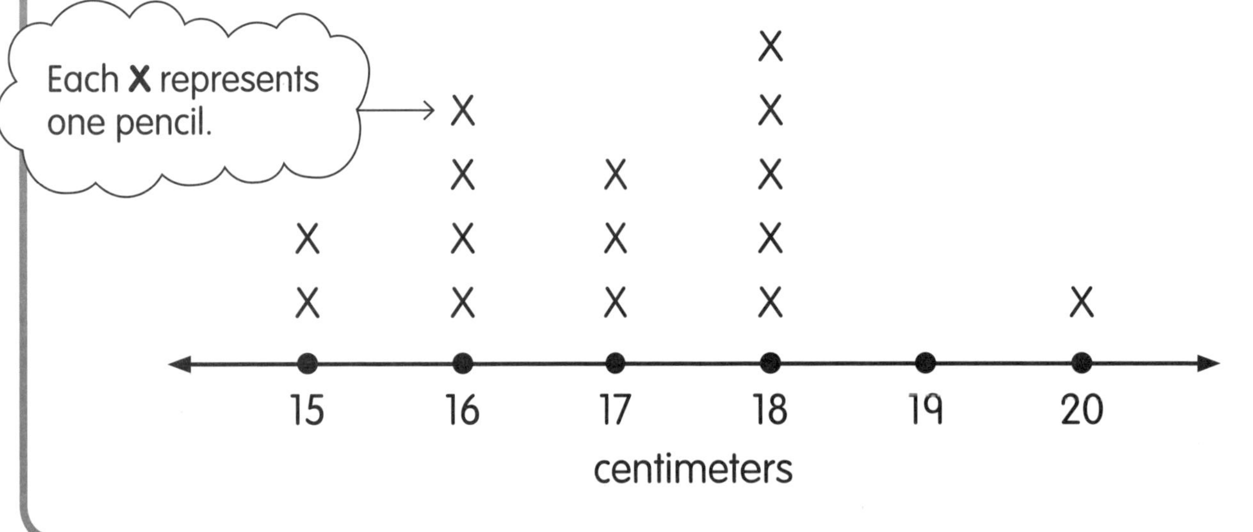

Look at the line plot. Is it important to include the number **19**, even though no pencils were 19 centimeters long? Explain your thinking.

Name ______________________

Read the word problem. Use the data chart to help you complete the line plot. Then answer the questions.

Example

Raj wanted to do an art project using ribbon scraps. He measured his ribbon pieces. The chart shows Raj's data.

Ribbon Lengths	
4 inches	II
5 inches	II
6 inches	I
7 inches	II
8 inches	III

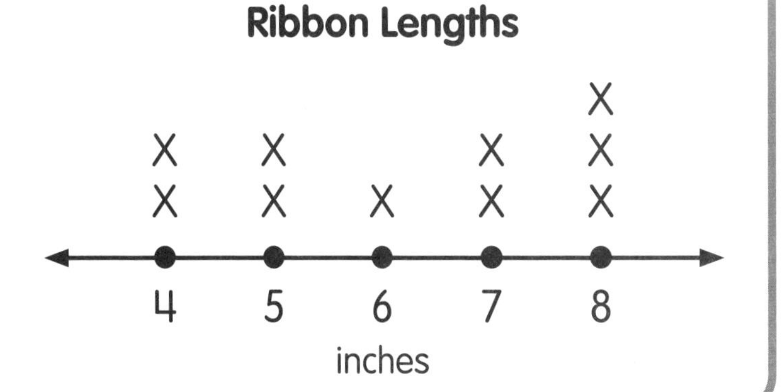

Cali measured her crayons to the nearest centimeter (cm). She made a chart to show the lengths. Use the chart to help you complete the line plot.

Crayon Lengths	
5 cm	II
6 cm	I
7 cm	II
8 cm	III
9 cm	IIII

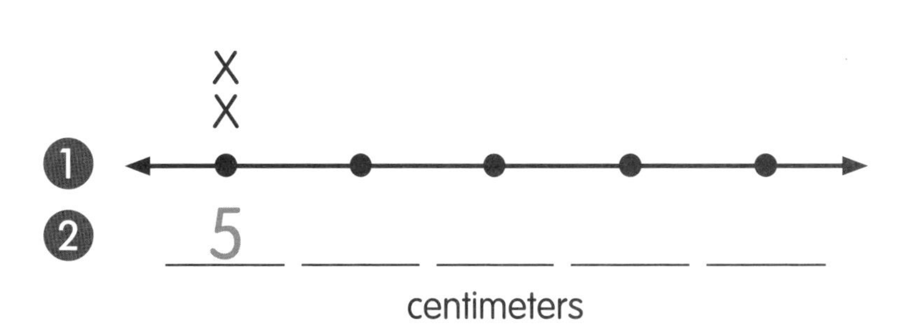

3. Each **X** represents a ______.
   - ○ centimeter ○ chart ○ crayon

4. Each number represents ______.
   - ○ a crayon ○ an inch ○ how many centimeters

Read the word problem and the data chart. Then complete the line plot. Answer the questions.

➤ Kyle and his friends each measured one of their feet to the nearest inch. Kyle made a chart to show the data. Use the chart to help you complete the line plot.

Our Foot Lengths	
6 inches	II
7 inches	III
8 inches	~~IIII~~
9 inches	IIII

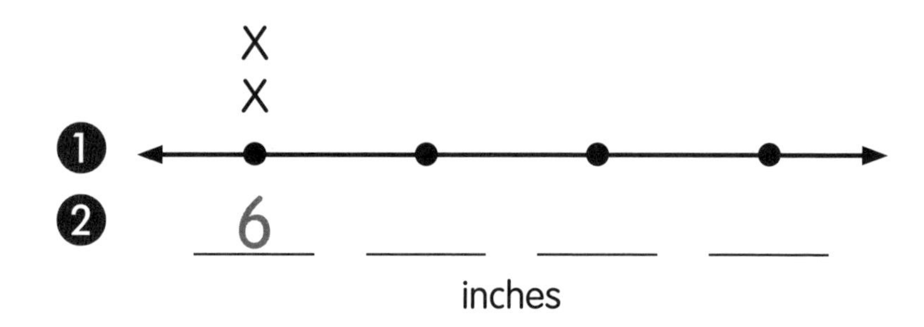

❸ Each **X** represents a ______.

○ person's foot ○ number of inches ○ number of feet

❹ Each number represents a ______.

○ foot ○ person ○ number of inches

❺ How many more people had 8- to 9-inch feet than 6- to 7-inch feet?

______ more people

Name ____________________

Read the Problem

Each kite needs 100 feet of kite-flying string to fly.
Use the data chart to help you make a line plot below.
Then find out how many kites can be flown.

String Lengths	
97 feet	III
98 feet	~~IIII~~ I
99 feet	~~IIII~~
100 feet	~~IIII~~ II

Think About It

1. You will find out how many _____.
   - ○ strings there are
   - ○ kites can be flown

2. Each **X** on your line plot will represent a _____.
   - ○ person
   - ○ kite-flying string
   - ○ number of feet

Solve the Problem

Use this work space to make a line plot.

3. ←――――――――――――――――――→

4. _____ kites can be flown.

Check Your Work

5. Do your answers make sense? ○ yes ○ no

Math Models

Making picture graphs

You can draw a picture graph to represent data.

A picture graph is used to compare data by using pictures or symbols.

Kendra counted the insects she saw in her backyard.

This chart shows the insects that Kendra saw in her yard.

Insects in My Yard	
ladybugs	I
bees	~~IIII~~
ants	~~IIII~~ II
butterflies	II

One tally mark represents 1 insect.

Then she used the data to make a **picture graph**.

Insects in My Yard	
ladybugs	🐞
bees	🐝 🐝 🐝 🐝 🐝
ants	🐜 🐜 🐜 🐜 🐜 🐜 🐜
butterflies	🦋 🦋

One picture represents 1 insect.

We can look at a picture graph to find out facts.
Here are some examples:

1. Kendra saw 15 insects in all.
2. She saw 8 flying insects.
3. Kendra saw 2 more ants than bees.

Can Kendra's picture graph be drawn to show the data going vertical ↑? Explain your thinking and what the graph would look like.

Name ______________________________

Read the sentences. Use the data chart to help you complete the picture graph. Then answer the questions.

Example

We saw different types of animals on our hike today.

Animals We Saw	
birds	𝍸 II
bugs	𝍸
rabbits	II
deer	III

Animals We Saw	
birds	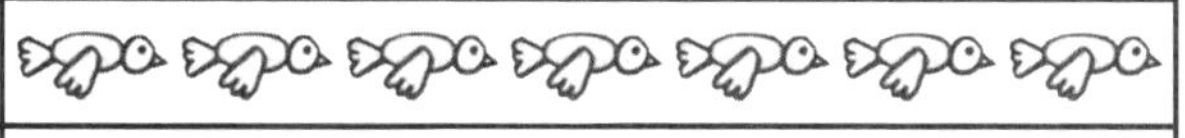
bugs	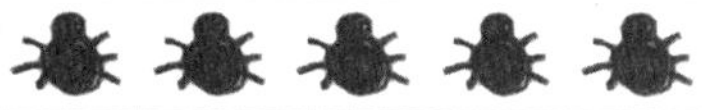
rabbits	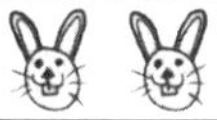
deer	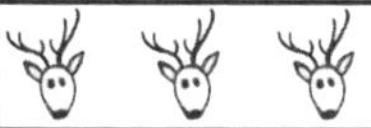

We saw _____ fewer deer than birds.

● 4 ○ 5 ○ 6

➤ Krista cleaned her room and found lots of things under her bed. Look at the data chart she made to help you complete the picture graph.

Things Krista Found	
socks	III
books	𝍸 I
crayons	𝍸 II
cups	II

	Things Krista Found	
	socks	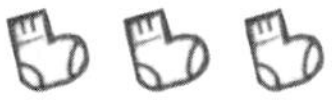
1	books	
2	crayons	
3	cups	

4 Krista found _____ more crayons than socks.

○ 5 ○ 4 ○ 3

5 Krista found _____ things in all.

○ 15 ○ 18 ○ 17

Name ______________________________

Read the sentence. Use the data chart to help you complete the picture graph. Then answer the questions.

Grandma has a plate of fancy cookies in different shapes.

❶

❷ There are _____ cookies in all.

○ 24 ○ 23 ○ 21

❸ There are _____ fewer triangle cookies than rectangle cookies.

○ 4 ○ 3 ○ 5

❹ There are more _____ cookies than any other shape.

○ circle ○ square ○ rectangle

Name ______________________________

Read the Problem

A second-grade class wants to make a picture graph to show what types of weather happened last week. Look at their data chart. Then draw a picture graph below that the class can make.

Our Weather	
sunny	𝍸 I
cloudy	𝍸 I
windy	III
rainy	I

Think About It

1. You will draw a _____ that the class can make.
   ○ picture graph ○ tally chart ○ line plot

2. A day can have _____ type(s) of weather.
   ○ only one ○ at least two ○ one or more

Solve the Problem

3. Use this work space to draw a picture graph.

Check Your Work

4. Do your answers make sense? ○ yes ○ no

Math Models

Making bar graphs

You can make a bar graph to compare and contrast data.

Mr. Safi asked students in his class in which season their birthdays take place.

The class made a chart that shows the number of birthdays that take place in each season.

Then the class used the data to make a bar graph.

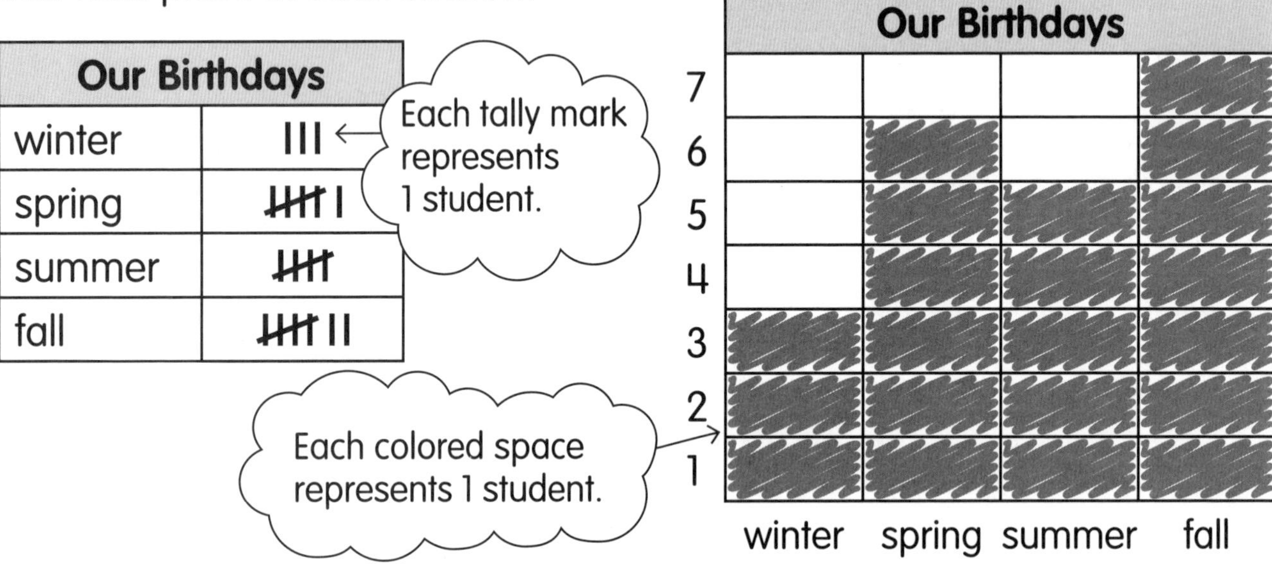

Our Birthdays	
winter	III
spring	卌 I
summer	卌
fall	卌 II

We can look at a bar graph to find out facts. This is an example:

In Mr. Safi's class, more students have a birthday in **fall** than in any other season.

Can a bar graph be drawn to show the bars going horizontal? Explain what it would look like.

Name ______________________________

Read the story. Use the data chart to help you complete the bar graph. Then answer the questions.

Dad spent all day baking treats. He made a chart to count how many cups of flour, sugar, berries, and apples he used.

Dad's Baking	
flour	𝍸
sugar	III
berries	IIII
apples	𝍸 I

1

Dad's Baking				
6				
5	▒			
4	▒			
3	▒			
2	▒			
1	▒			
	flour	sugar	berries	apples

2 Dad used more ______ than flour.

○ sugar ○ berries ○ apples

3 He used ______ cups of flour, sugar, berries, and apples in all.

○ 18 ○ 19 ○ 20

4 Dad used ______ cups of fruit altogether.

○ 8 ○ 9 ○ 10

Name ____________________

Read the story. Use the data chart to help you complete the bar graph. Then answer the questions.

Reenie and her friends each signed up to play a sport. The chart shows what she and her friends chose.

Sports	
track	IIII
swimming	III
baseball	~~IIII~~
soccer	~~IIII~~

1.

Sports					
track	▓	▓	▓	▓	
swimming					
baseball					
soccer					
	1	2	3	4	5

2. The fewest people signed up to do ______.
   ○ track ○ swimming ○ baseball

3. Five people signed up to do ______ and baseball.
   ○ track ○ swimming ○ soccer

4. ______ people signed up to play a sport that uses a ball.
   ○ 5 ○ 10 ○ 14

Name ______________________

Read the story. Then complete the tally chart.

➤ Erin, Skylar, Marcus, and Toby like to collect rocks.
They wrote the number of rocks they have collected so far.

	Name	Tally	Number of Rocks
	Erin	𝍸 |||	8
1	Skylar		11
2	Marcus		7
3	Toby		10

Now color one space on the bar graph for each rock that has been collected by each child.

4

Rocks											
Erin											
Skylar											
Marcus											
Toby											
	1	2	3	4	5	6	7	8	9	10	11

Name ______________________________

Read the Problem

Kenji made a data chart that shows how many of each animal he saw at the farm. Then his teacher asked him to make a bar graph. You will draw one below for Kenji.

Kenji's Chart

Animals I Saw	
cows	II
pigs	III
chickens	~~IIII~~ II
goats	~~IIII~~

Think About It

1. You will use the data to make a ______.
   - ○ list
   - ○ bar graph
   - ○ data chart

2. Each tally mark on the data chart represents one ______.
   - ○ animal
   - ○ farm
   - ○ student

Solve the Problem

3. Use this work space to make a bar graph.

Check Your Work

4. Do your answers make sense? ○ yes ○ no

Analyze Shapes

Domain

Geometry

Cluster

Reason with shapes and their attributes.

Standards in Cluster

2.G.A.1 Recognize and draw shapes having specified attributes, such as a given number of angles or a given number of equal faces. Identify triangles, quadrilaterals, pentagons, hexagons, and cubes.

2.G.A.2 Partition a rectangle into rows and columns of same-size squares and count to find the total number of them.

2.G.A.3 Partition circles and rectangles into two, three, or four equal shares, describe the shares using the words *halves, thirds, half of, a third of,* etc., and describe the whole as two halves, three thirds, four fourths. Recognize that equal shares of identical wholes need not have the same shape.

Unit Contents

Mathematical Practices in This Unit

Make sense of problems and persevere in solving them: *pages 166, 169, 170, 173, 174, 177, 178, 181, 182, 185, 186, 190*

Reason abstractly and quantitatively: *pages 178, 179*

Construct viable arguments and critique the reasoning of others: *page 178*

Model with mathematics: *pages 168, 172, 175, 176*

Attend to precision: *pages 167, 169, 171, 173, 177, 180, 181, 185*

Look for and make use of structure: *pages 182, 183, 184, 185*

Math Models

Identifying and drawing triangles

You can name and draw triangles.

A triangle has 3 straight sides and 3 angles. These are some examples:

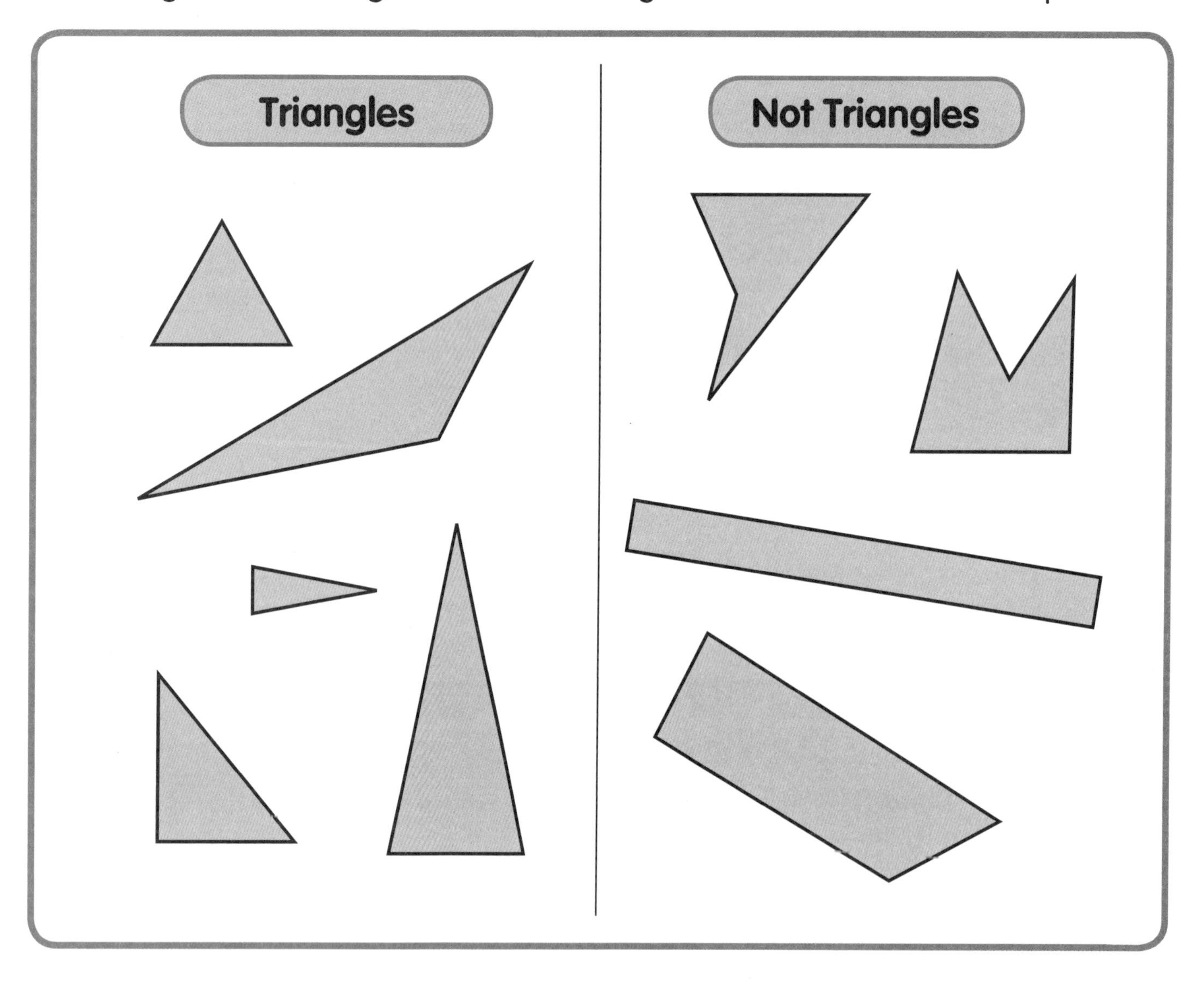

Find a triangle that has an angle that looks like each of these examples:

Hint: You can turn the chart to change the way you see the shapes. Explain your thinking.

Name ____________________

For each row, circle the triangle. Then draw the same triangle in the work space.

Example

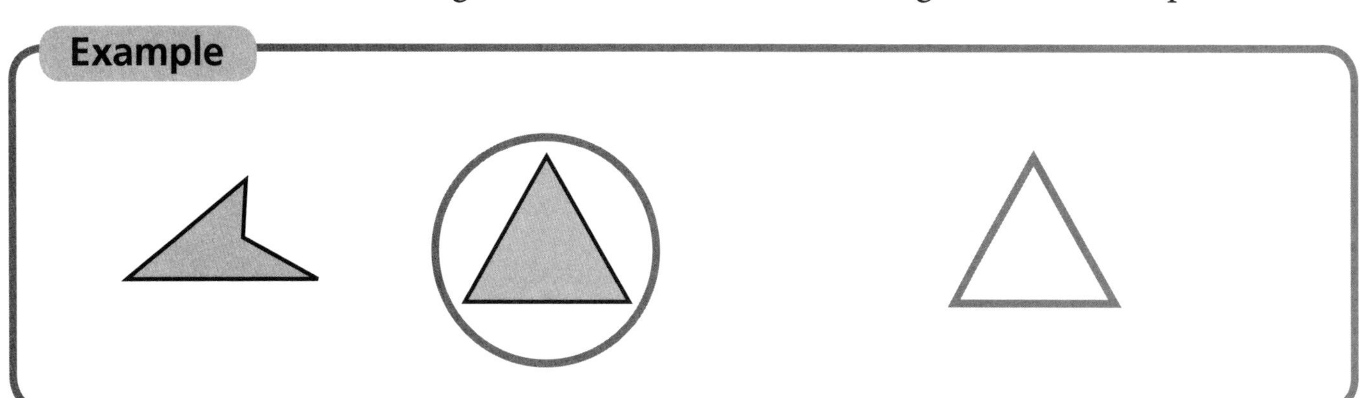

Work Space

 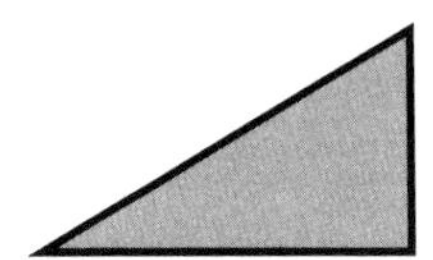 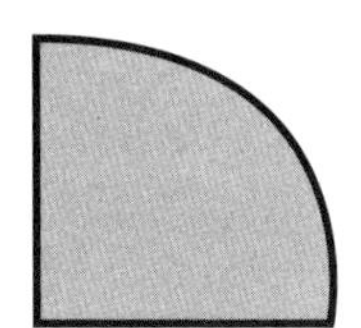

❷ 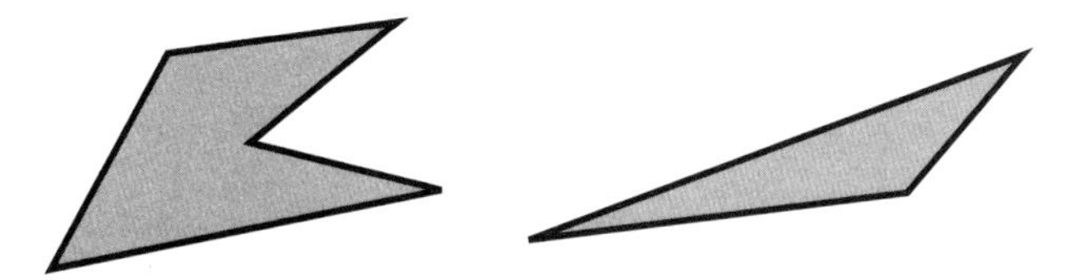

❸ 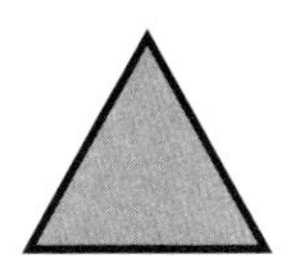 

 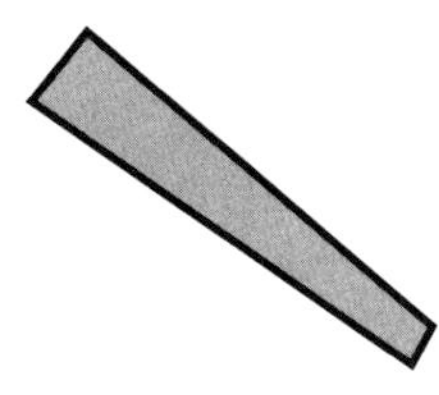 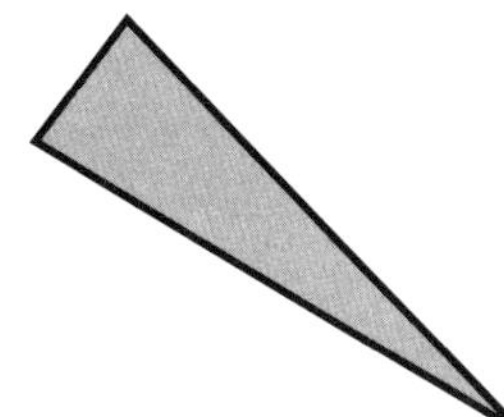

Name ______________________

Mark **yes** or **no** to show if each shape is or is not a triangle.
Then write to explain your thinking.

	Shape	Is it a triangle?	Explain why or why not.
	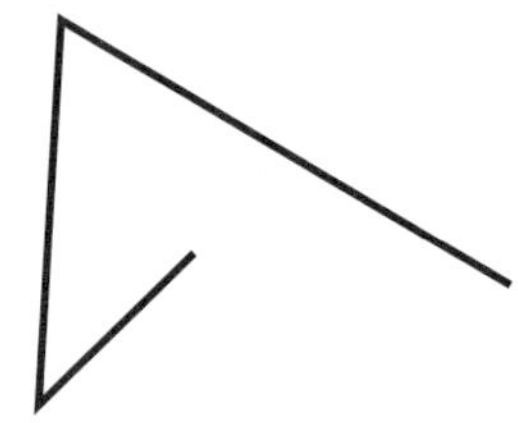	○ yes ● no	It is not closed.
1	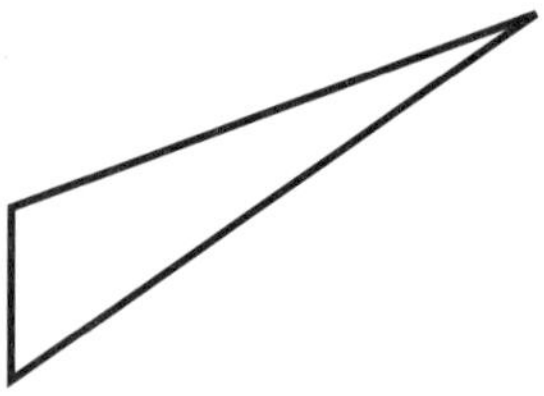	○ yes ○ no	
2	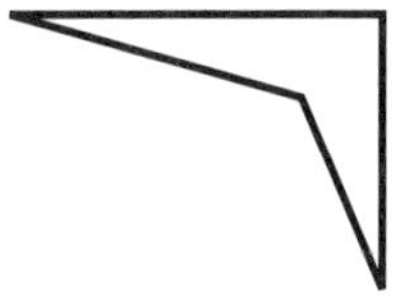	○ yes ○ no	
3	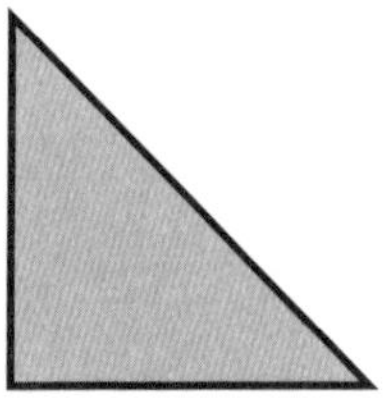	○ yes ○ no	

 CCMS 2.G.A.1 Recognize and draw triangles.

Name ______________________________

Read the Problem

Sven says that he can draw a triangle that has 2 sides that are the same length. Do you agree? Draw a triangle below that Sven can make.

Think About It

1. You will find out if a triangle can have 2 sides ______.
   ○ the same length ○ with curves ○ not touching

2. A triangle has 3 straight sides and ______.
   ○ 4 angles ○ 3 angles ○ 2 angles

Solve the Problem

3. Use this work space to draw Sven's triangle.

4. Sven can draw a triangle with 2 of its 3 sides the same length.
   ○ yes ○ no

Check Your Work

5. Do your answers make sense? ○ yes ○ no

Math Models

Identifying and drawing quadrilaterals

You can name and draw quadrilaterals.

A quadrilateral has 4 straight sides and 4 angles. These are some examples:

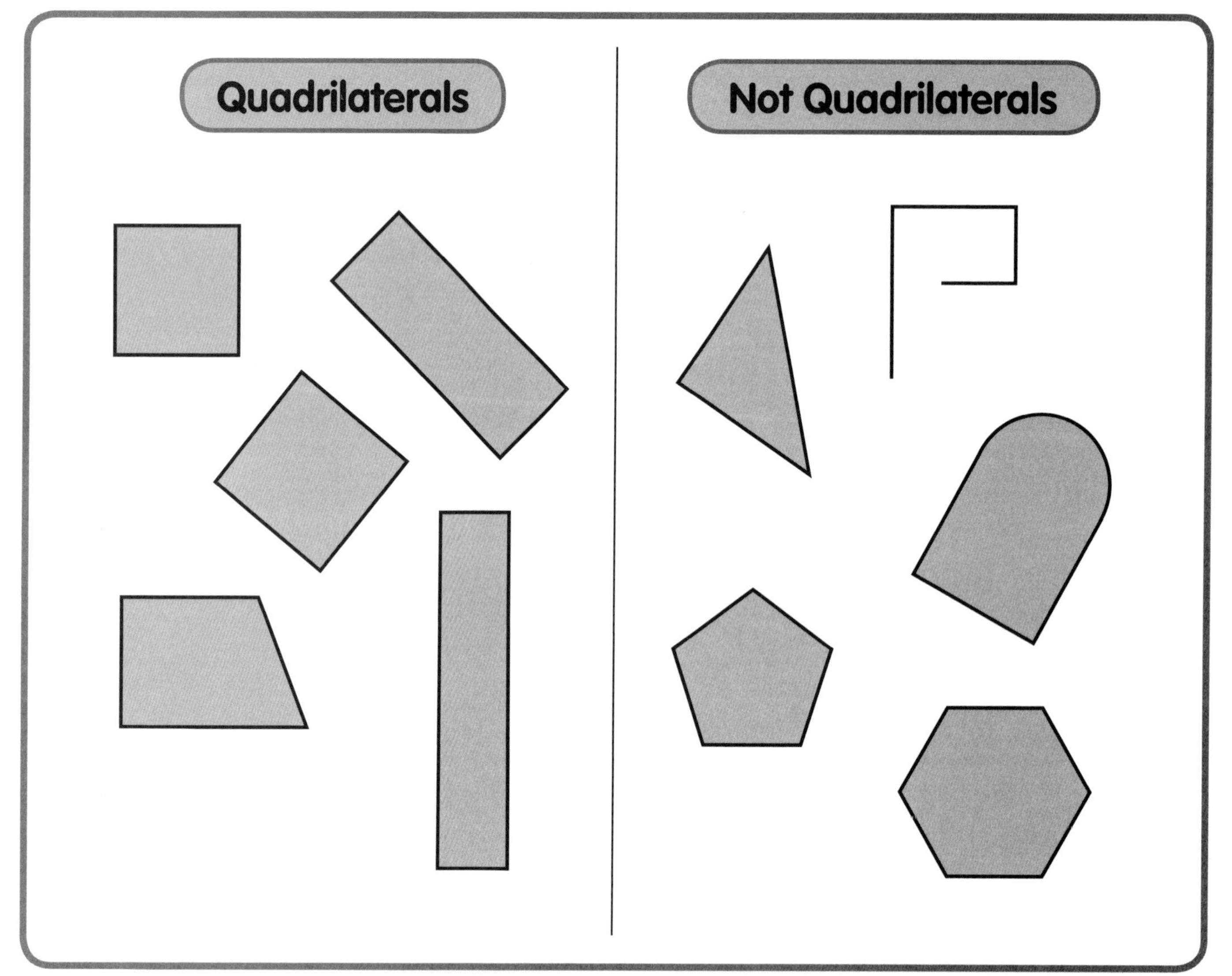

Look at the shapes that are **not** quadrilaterals. Explain how you know that each one is not a quadrilateral.

Name ______________________________

For each row, circle the quadrilateral. Then draw the same quadrilateral in the work space.

Example

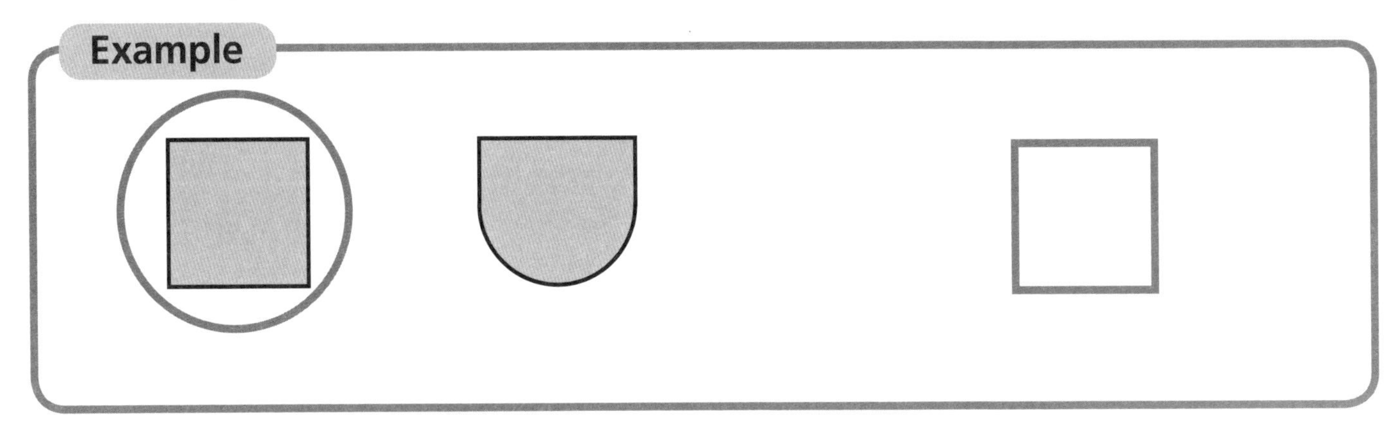

Work Space

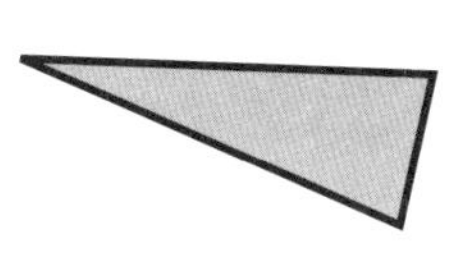

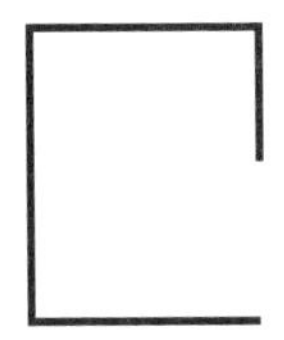
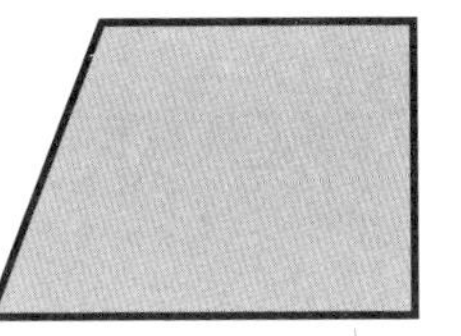

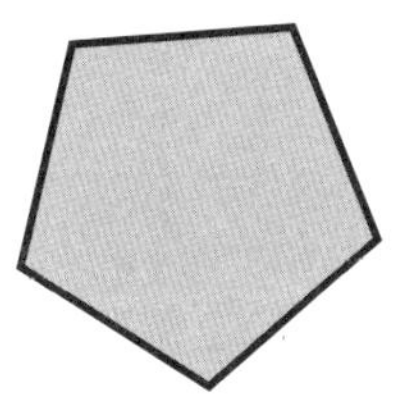
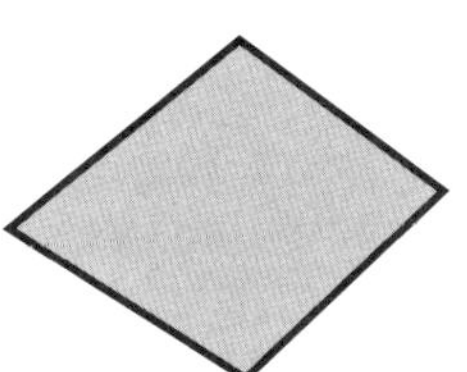

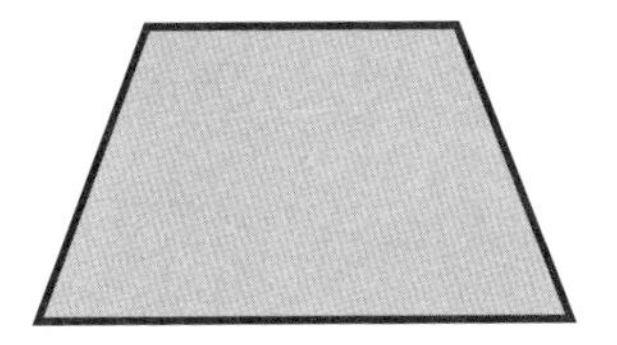

Recognize and draw quadrilaterals.

CCMS 2.G.A.1

Name ______________________________

Analyze Shapes
Identifying and drawing quadrilaterals

4

Mark **yes** or **no** to show if each shape is or is not a quadrilateral.
Then write to explain your thinking.

	Shape	Is it a quadrilateral?	Explain why or why not.
	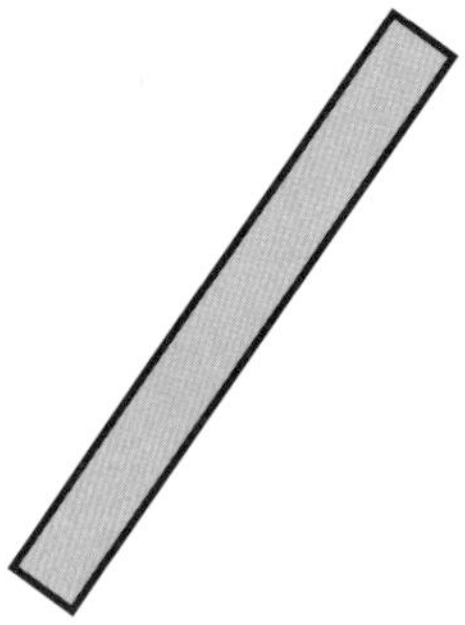	● yes ○ no	It has 4 straight sides and 4 angles.
1	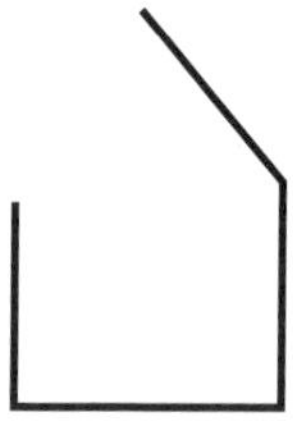	○ yes ○ no	
2	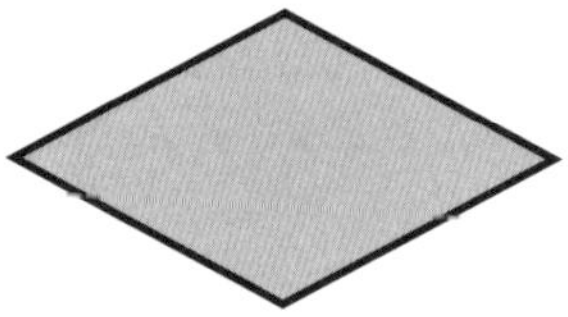	○ yes ○ no	
3		○ yes ○ no	

Name ______________________________

Read the Problem

Olivia is planning to make a new garden in her yard. She wants the shape to be a quadrilateral. Draw 3 different quadrilaterals below that she can use.

Think About It

1. You will draw 3 different ______.
   - ○ triangles ○ circles ○ quadrilaterals

2. A quadrilateral has ______ straight sides and 4 angles.
   - ○ 3 ○ 4 ○ 5

Solve the Problem

Use this work space to draw 3 different quadrilaterals.

3	4	5

Check Your Work

6. Do your answers make sense? ○ yes ○ no

Recognize and draw quadrilaterals.

CCMS 2.G.A.1

Math Models

Identifying and drawing pentagons and hexagons

Analyze Shapes

You can name and draw pentagons and hexagons.

Pentagons have 5 straight sides and 5 angles. Hexagons have 6 straight sides and 6 angles. These are some examples:

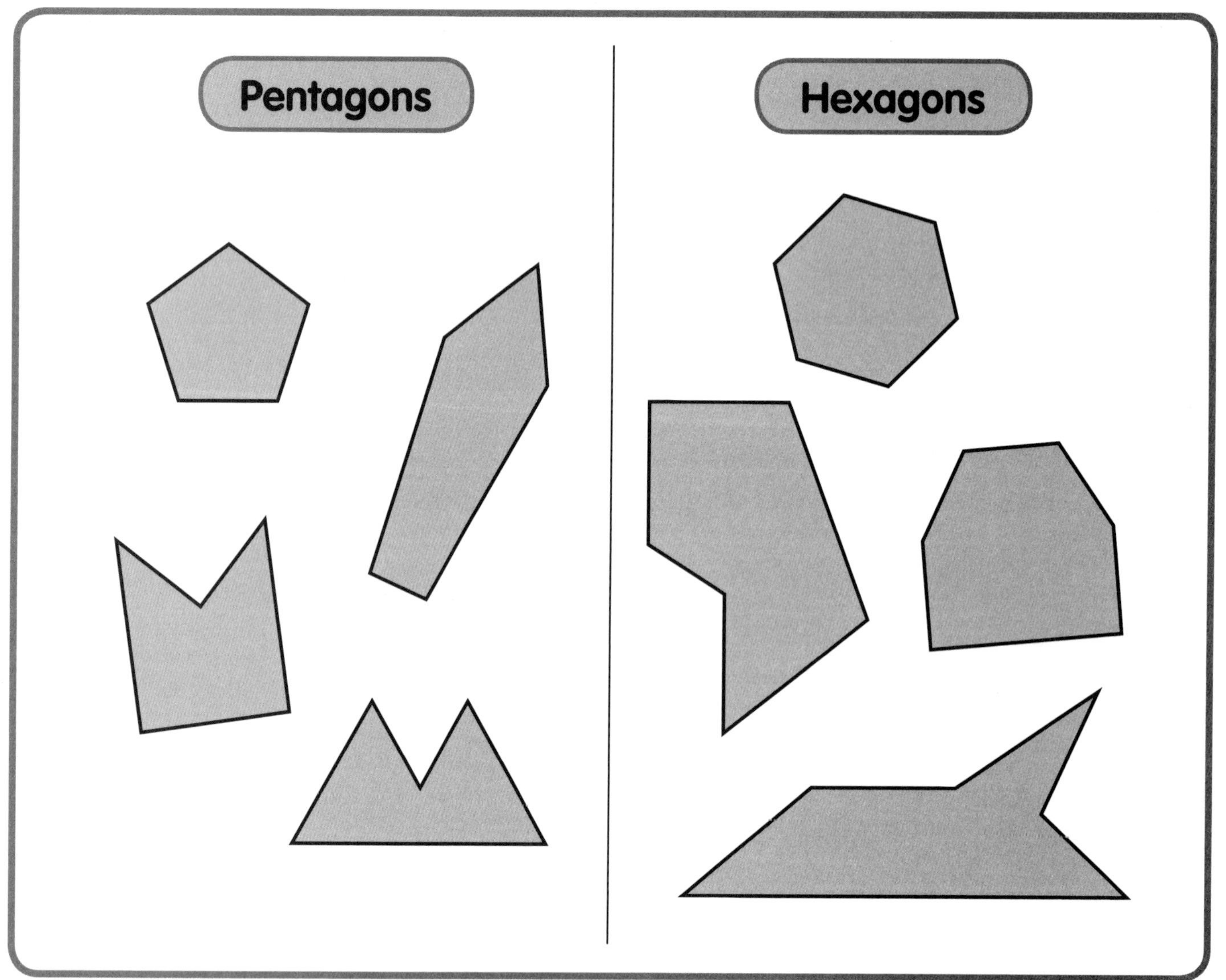

Does a hexagon have more angles than a pentagon? Explain your thinking.

Name ______________________________

For each row, mark the answer that describes each shape.
Then write to explain your thinking.

Example

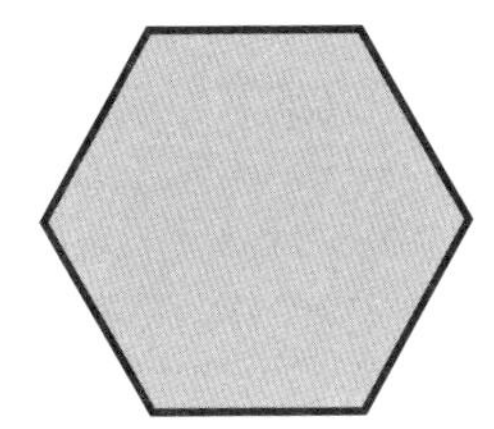

- ○ pentagon
- ● hexagon
- ○ other

It has 6 straight sides and 6 angles.

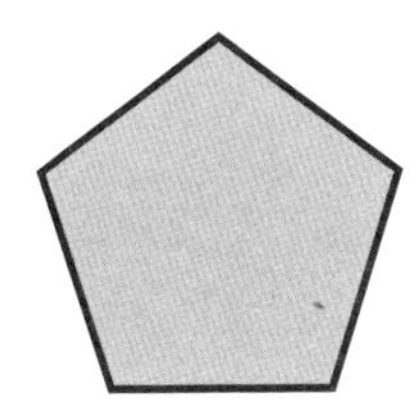

- ○ pentagon
- ○ hexagon
- ○ other

____
____
____

2

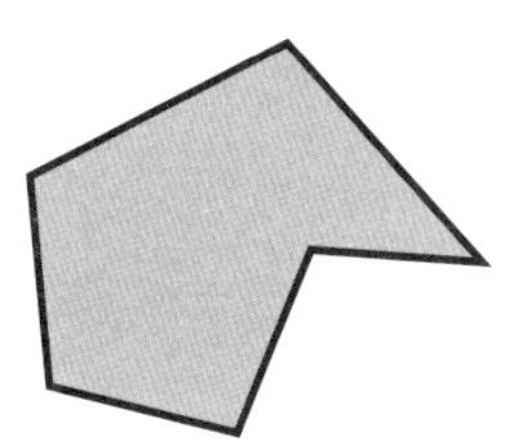

- ○ pentagon
- ○ hexagon
- ○ other

____
____
____

3

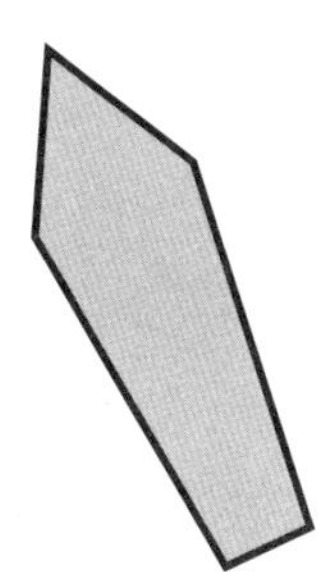

- ○ pentagon
- ○ hexagon
- ○ other

____
____
____

Name ______________________________

Analyze Shapes
Identifying and drawing pentagons and hexagons

6

For each row, mark the answer that describes each shape. Then write to explain your thinking.

1

○ pentagon
○ hexagon
○ other

2

○ pentagon
○ hexagon
○ other

3

○ pentagon
○ hexagon
○ other

4

○ pentagon
○ hexagon
○ other

CCMS 2.G.A.1 Recognize and draw pentagons and hexagons.

Name ______________________________

Read the Problem

The cells of a beehive look like this. Below, draw and name the shapes that make up a beehive.

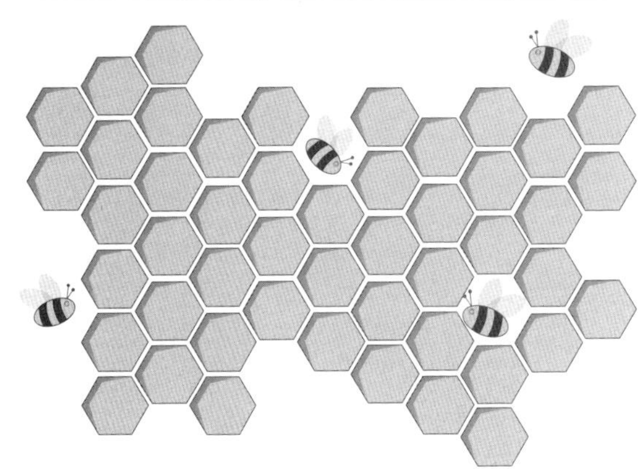

Think About It

❶ You will name the shapes that make up a _____.

○ beehive ○ bee ○ flower

❷ One beehive cell has _____ angles.

○ 5 ○ 6 ○ 7

Solve the Problem

❸ Use this work space to draw the shape.

❹ The beehive is made up of ________________.

pentagons hexagons

Check Your Work

❺ Do your answers make sense? ○ yes ○ no

You can name and draw cubes.

A cube is a 3-dimensional shape. It can be solid or hollow.

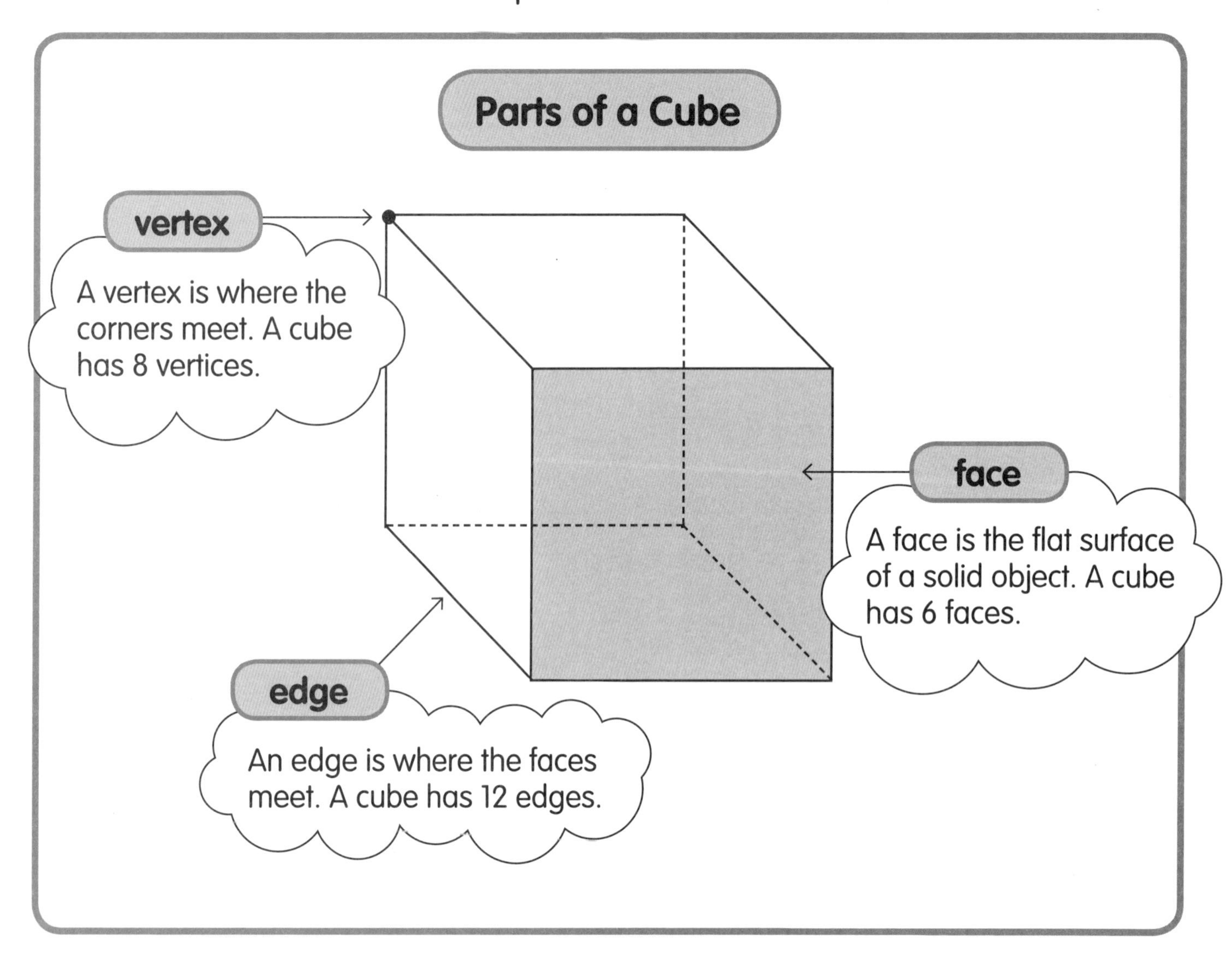

Parts of a Cube
vertex
A vertex is where the corners meet. A cube has 8 vertices.
face
A face is the flat surface of a solid object. A cube has 6 faces.
edge
An edge is where the faces meet. A cube has 12 edges.

Think

When you look at a wooden cube, can you see all the faces, edges, and vertices at the same time? Explain your thinking.

Name ____________________

Mark the correct answer for each question.

Example

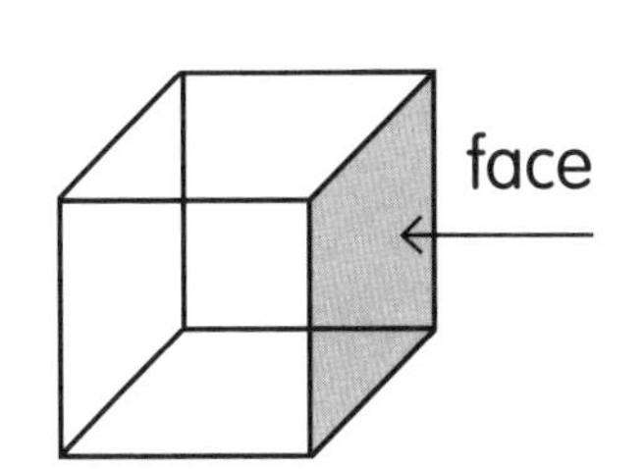

The shape of each face on a cube is a _____.

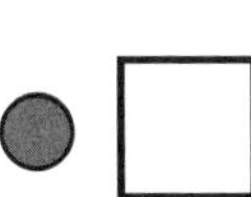 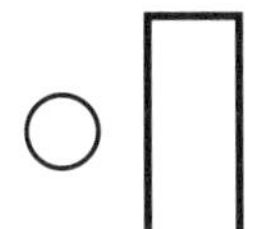 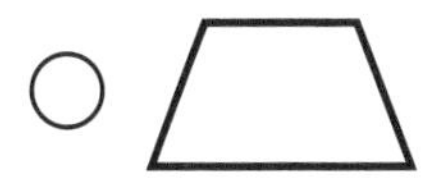

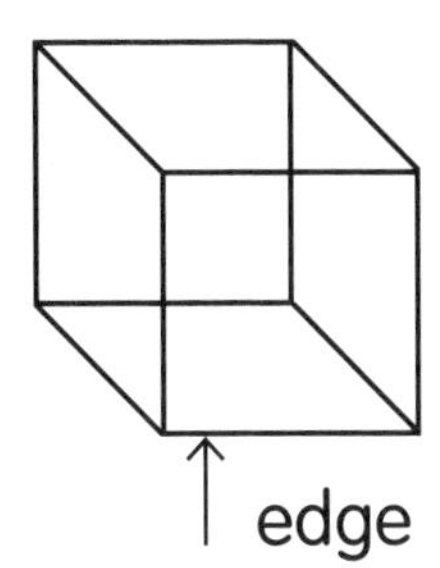

A cube has _____ edges.

○ 6 ○ 8 ○ 12

2

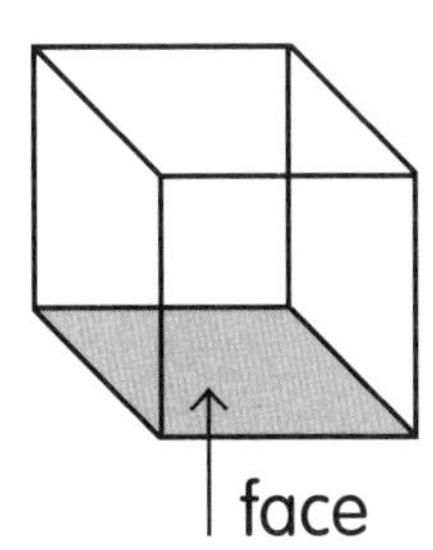

The shape of each face on a cube is a _____.

○ triangle ○ square ○ hexagon

3

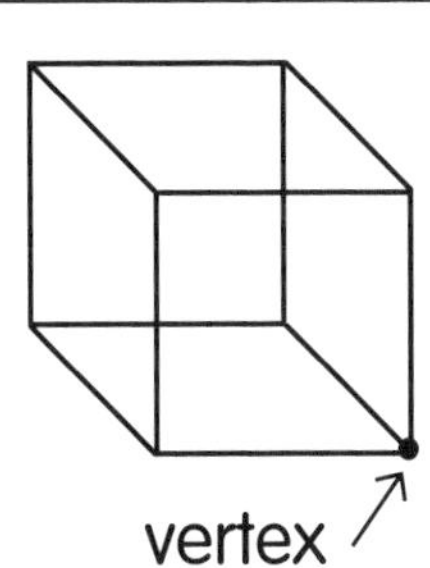

A cube has _____ vertices.

○ 4 ○ 8 ○ 12

4

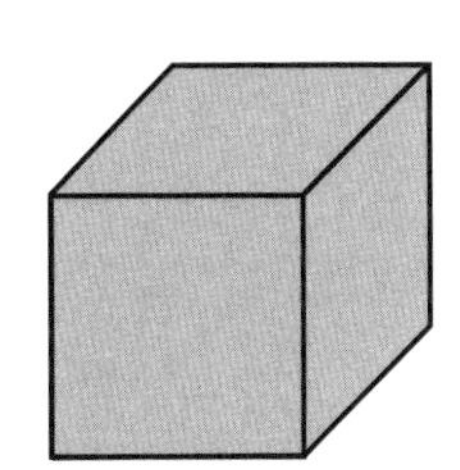

I see only 3 faces, but I know there are _____ faces.

○ 6 ○ 8 ○ 12

Recognize and draw cubes.

Name ______________________________

Follow the steps to draw a cube. Then write.

Example

First	Next	Last
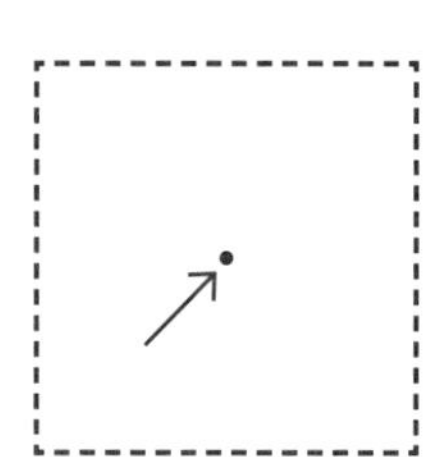	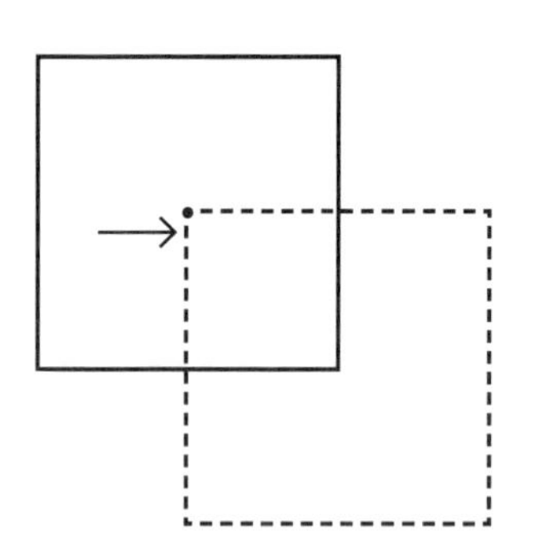	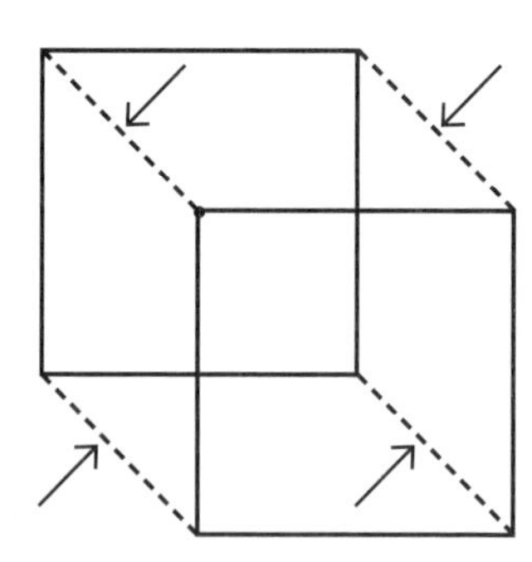
Draw a square. Draw a dot in the center.	Start at the dot. Draw another square the same size.	Draw straight lines to connect the corners.

1. Use this work space.

2. Explain how a cube is different from a square.

____

____

 CCMS 2.G.A.1 Recognize and draw cubes.

Name ______________________________

Read the Problem

Ian wants to trace around the face of a cube-shaped wooden block. If he puts the block on a sheet of paper and traces around the face, what shape will he make? Draw it below.

Think About It

❶ You will find out what shape the _____ of a block is.

○ angle ○ vertex ○ face

❷ The shape Ian traces will **not** have _____.

○ angles ○ curves ○ equal sides

Solve the Problem

❸ Use this work space to draw the shape.

❹ The shape is a ______________.

Check Your Work

❺ Do your answers make sense? ○ yes ○ no

Math Models

Partitioning a rectangle

You can find out how many squares make up a rectangle.

Here is an example:

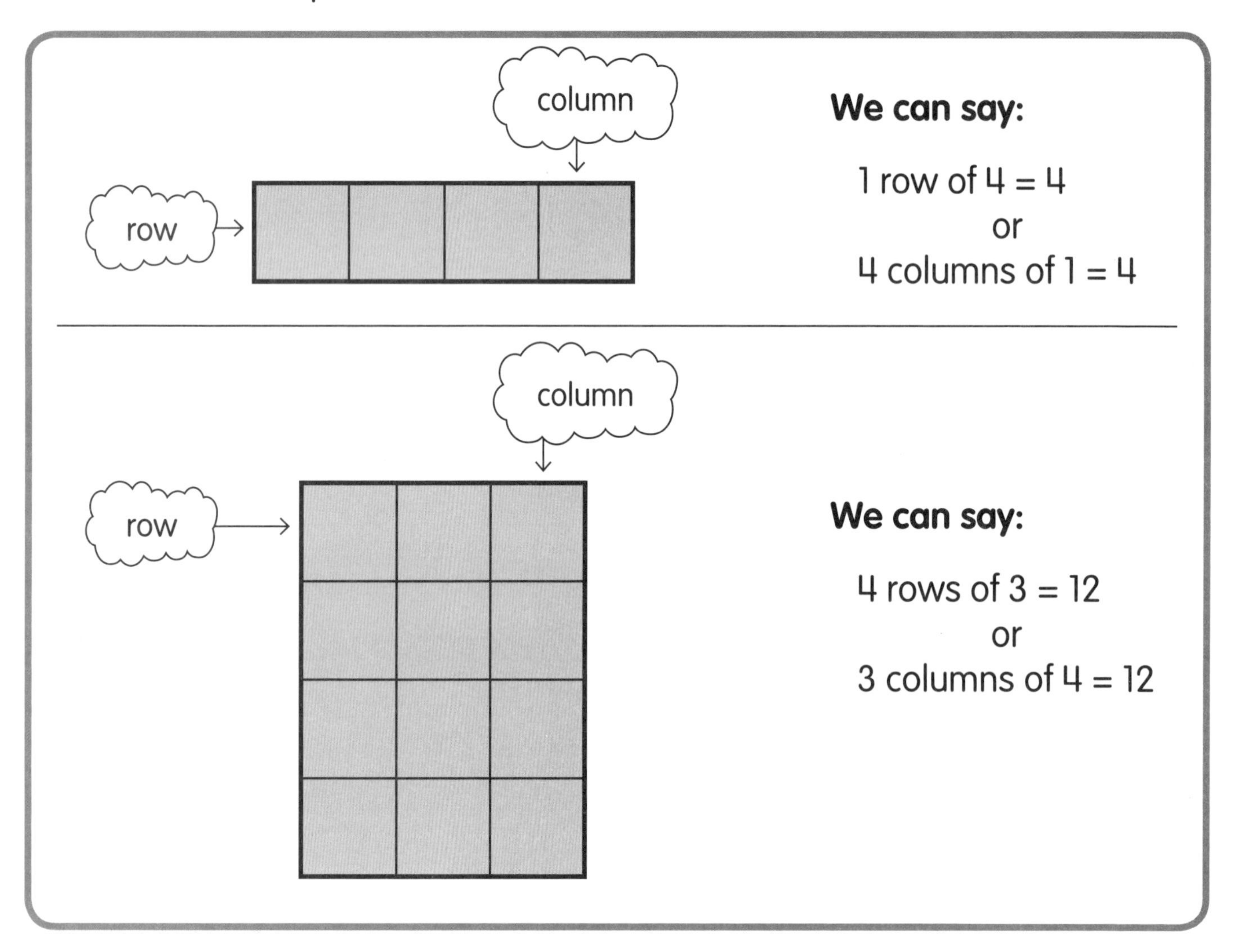

column
row
We can say:
1 row of 4 = 4
or
4 columns of 1 = 4
column
row
We can say:
4 rows of 3 = 12
or
3 columns of 4 = 12

Use 5 squares to make a rectangle. Draw and explain your thinking.

Name ______________________________

Complete the number sentence to show the number of squares that make up each rectangle.

Example

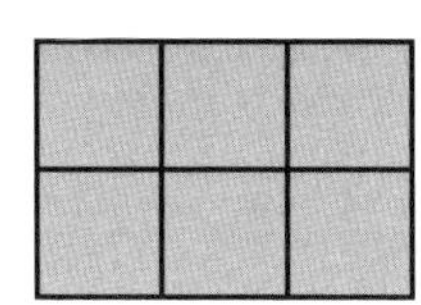

2 rows of 3 = 6

❶

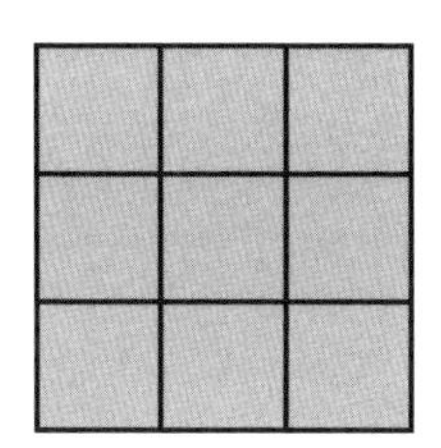

3 columns of 3 = ______

❷

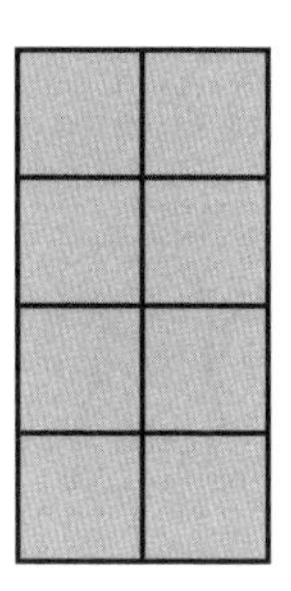

4 rows of 2 = ______

❸

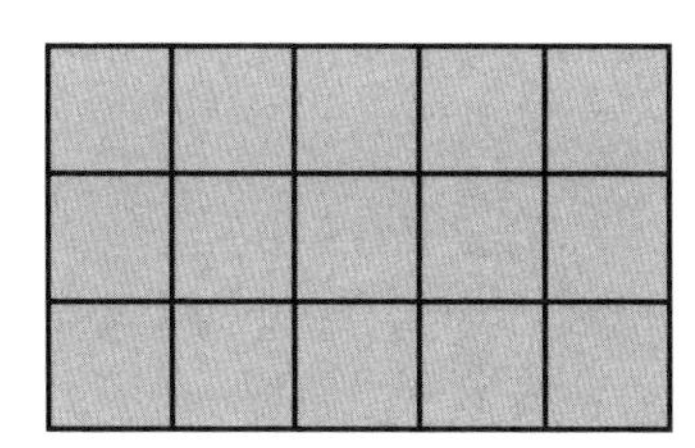

5 columns of 3 = ______

Name ______________________________

Complete the number sentence to show the number of squares that make up each rectangle.

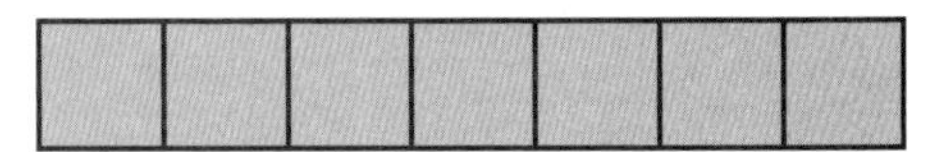

1 row of _____ = _____

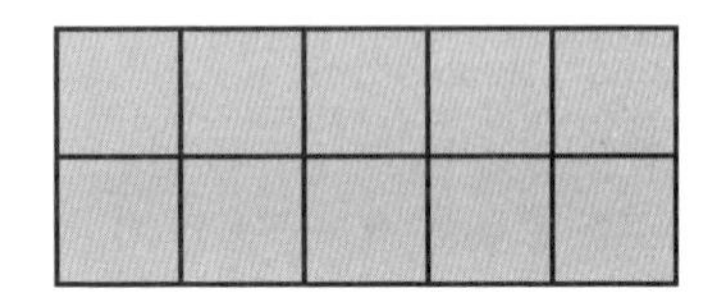

5 columns of _____ = _____

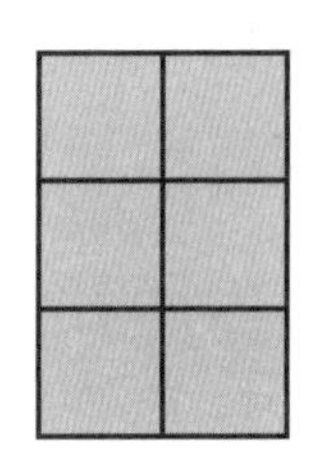

3 rows of _____ = _____

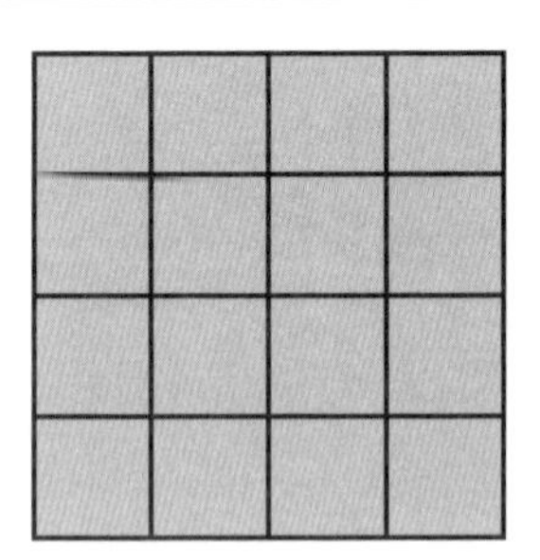

4 rows of _____ = _____

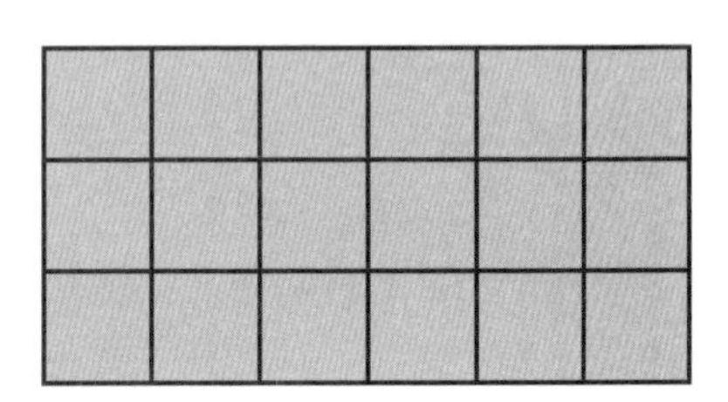

6 columns of _____ = _____

Name ______________________________

Read the Problem

Brandon baked a pan of brownies. It looked like this. Then he and his sister ate two brownies. How many brownies were left?

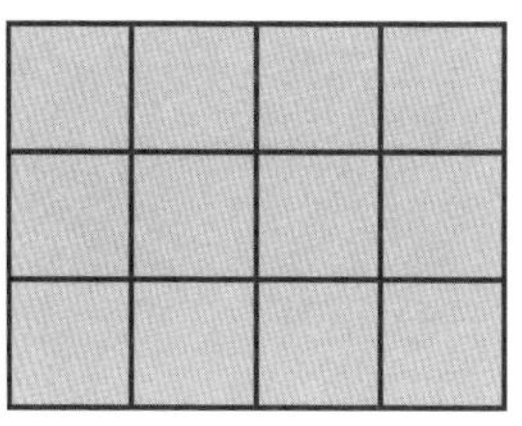

Think About It

1. You will find out how many brownies were ______.
   ○ eaten ○ made ○ left

2. The pan of brownies is ______.
   ○ 3 rows of 4 ○ 4 rows of 4 ○ 3 columns of 4

Solve the Problem

3. Use this work space.

4. ______ brownies were left.

Check Your Work

5. Do your answers make sense? ○ yes ○ no

Count rows and columns of squares in a rectangle.

CCMS 2.G.A.2

Math Models

Describing equal shares

You can describe equal shares of a whole.

Here are some examples:

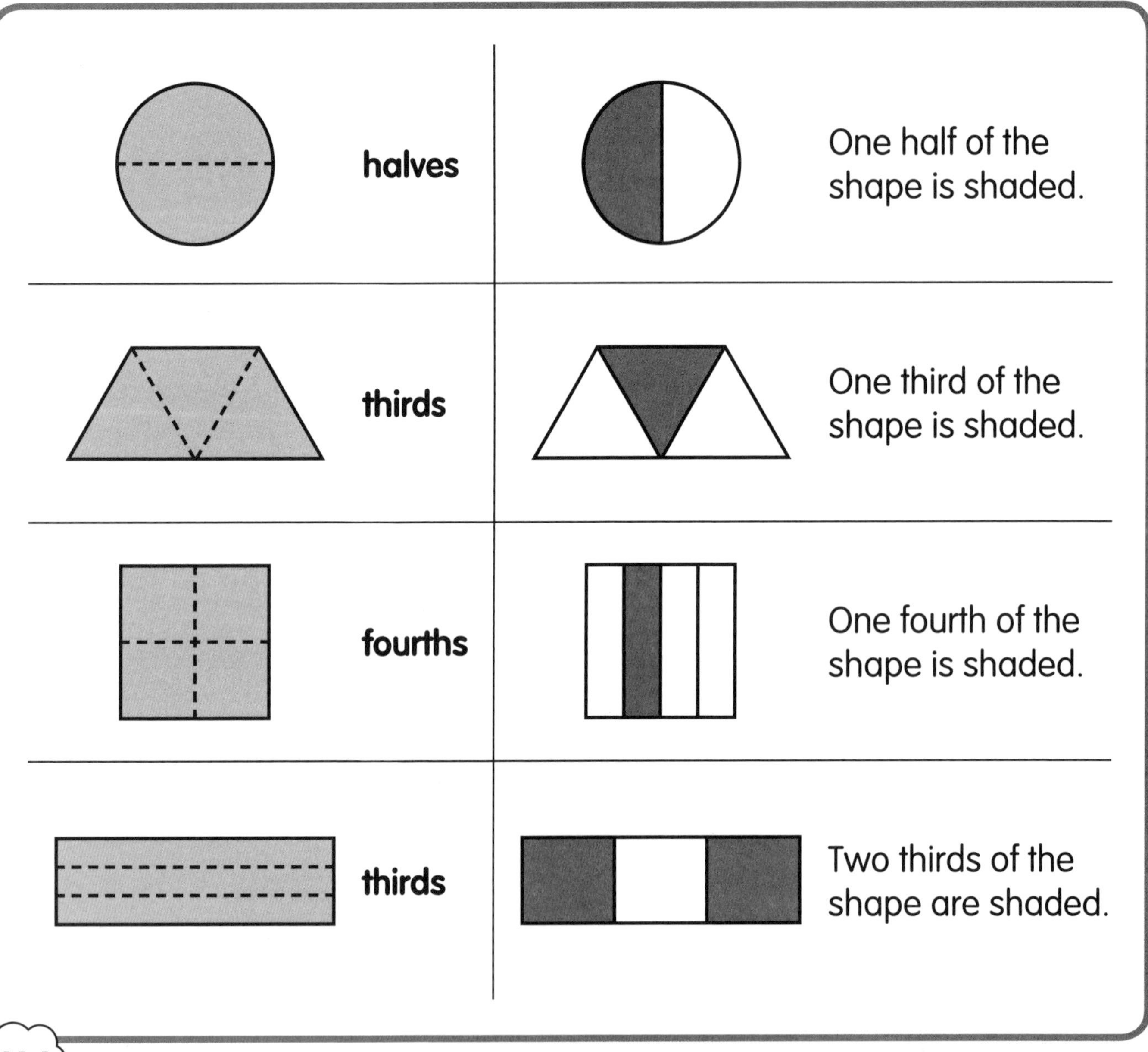
halves
One half of the shape is shaded.
thirds
One third of the shape is shaded.
fourths
One fourth of the shape is shaded.
thirds
Two thirds of the shape are shaded.

Think

A whole has how many halves? How many thirds? How many fourths? Explain your thinking.

CCMS 2.G.A.3

Describe equal shares of a whole.
Partition circles and rectangles into two, three, or four equal shares and describe using *halves, thirds,* or *fourths.*

Name ____________________

For each shape, mark the answer that names the shaded part or parts.

Examples

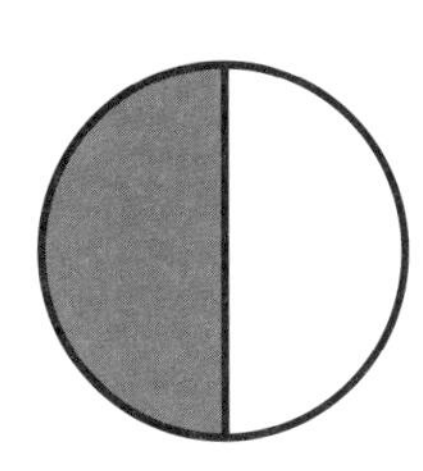

- ● one half
- ○ two halves
- ○ one whole

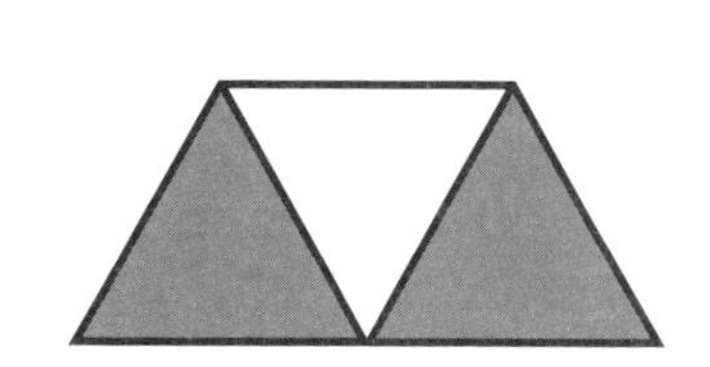

- ○ one third
- ● two thirds
- ○ one whole

1

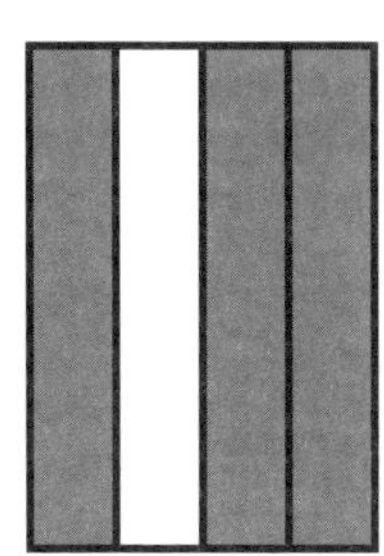

- ○ two thirds
- ○ one fourth
- ○ three fourths

2

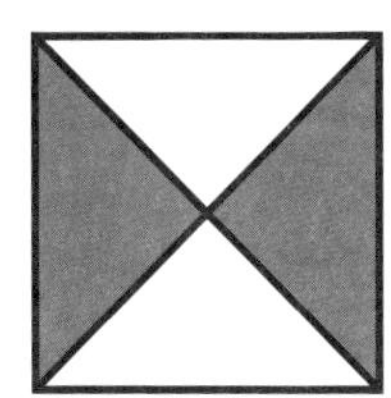

- ○ two thirds
- ○ two fourths
- ○ three fourths

3

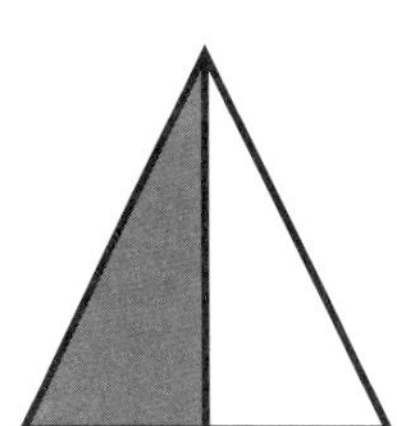

- ○ one half
- ○ one third
- ○ two halves

4

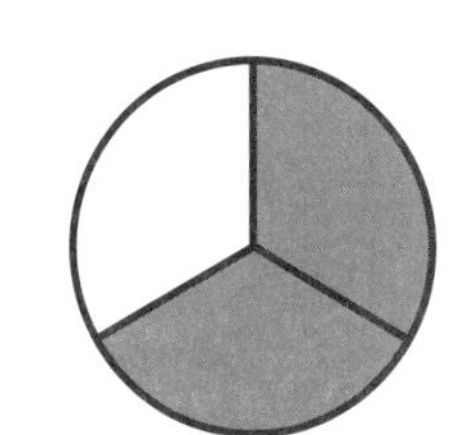

- ○ one third
- ○ one fourth
- ○ two thirds

5

- ○ one third
- ○ two thirds
- ○ one fourth

6

- ○ one fourth
- ○ two fourths
- ○ three fourths

Name ____________________

For each shape, color the part or parts as labeled.

Examples

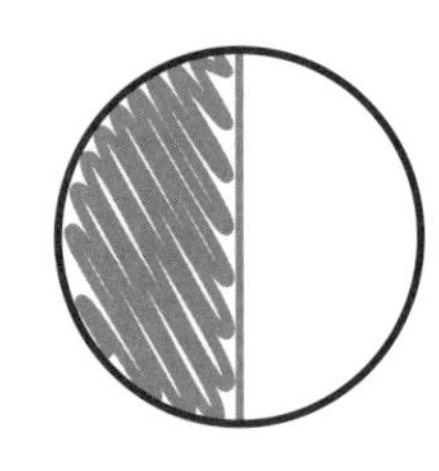

one half

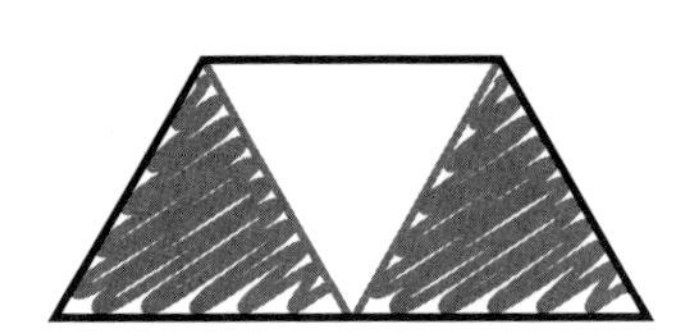

two thirds

1

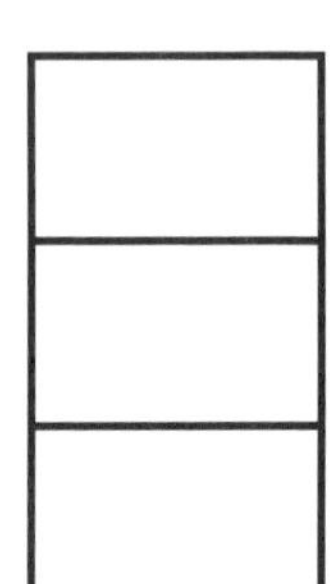

one third

2

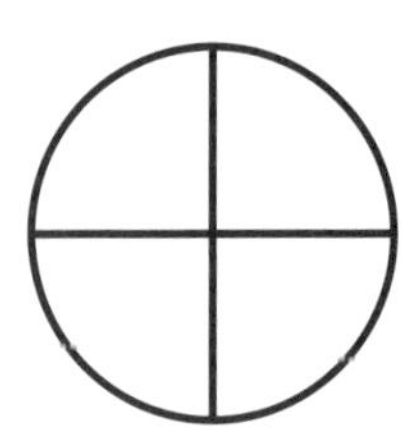

one whole

3

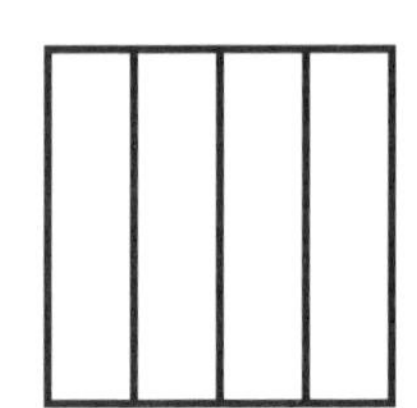

three fourths

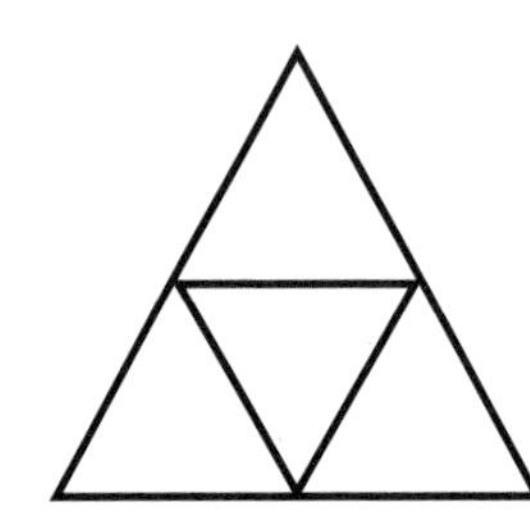

two fourths

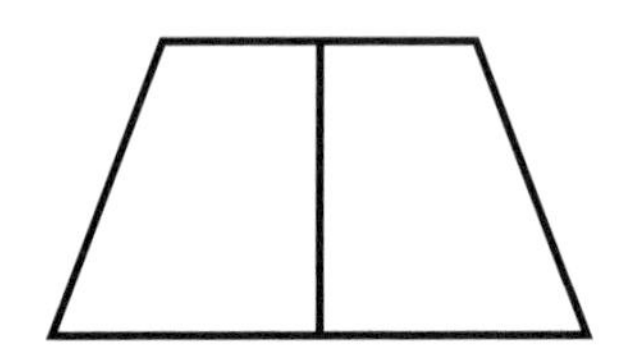

one half

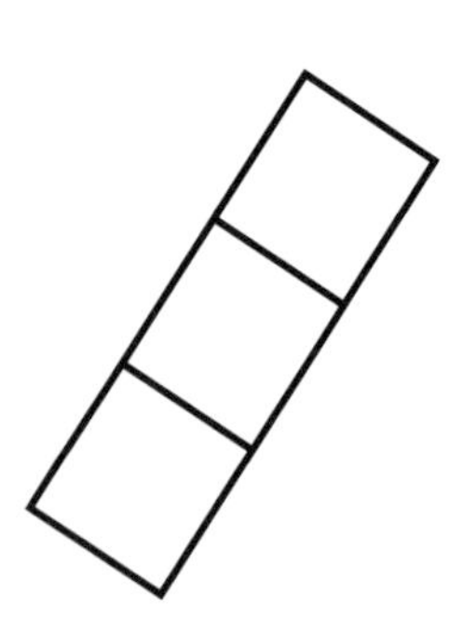

two thirds

CCMS 2.G.A.3 Describe equal shares of a whole.
Partition circles and rectangles into two, three, or four equal shares and describe using *halves, thirds,* or *fourths.*

Name ______________________________

Draw the partitions and color the parts to show each shape as labeled.

Examples

one fourth

one half

1. two fourths

2. one half

3. three fourths

4. one third

5. two thirds

6. two halves

Describe equal shares of a whole.
Partition circles and rectangles into two, three, or four equal shares and describe using *halves*, *thirds*, or *fourths*.

CCMS 2.G.A.3

Name ____________________

Read the Problem

Teri made a sandwich. She ate three fourths of it.
How much was **not** eaten? Draw the sandwich below.
Color the part Teri did **not** eat.

Think About It

1. You will find out how much was ______.
   - ○ made ○ eaten ○ not eaten

2. The sandwich is cut into ______.
   - ○ fourths ○ halves ○ thirds

Solve the Problem

3. Use this work space to draw the sandwich.

4. ____________ of the sandwich was **not** eaten.

Check Your Work

5. Do your answers make sense? ○ yes ○ no

CCMS 2.G.A.3

Describe equal shares of a whole.
Partition circles and rectangles into two, three, or four equal shares and describe using *halves, thirds,* or *fourths.*

Answer Key

There are many ways to model a problem or to word an explanation. Accept any reasonable answer.

Page 13

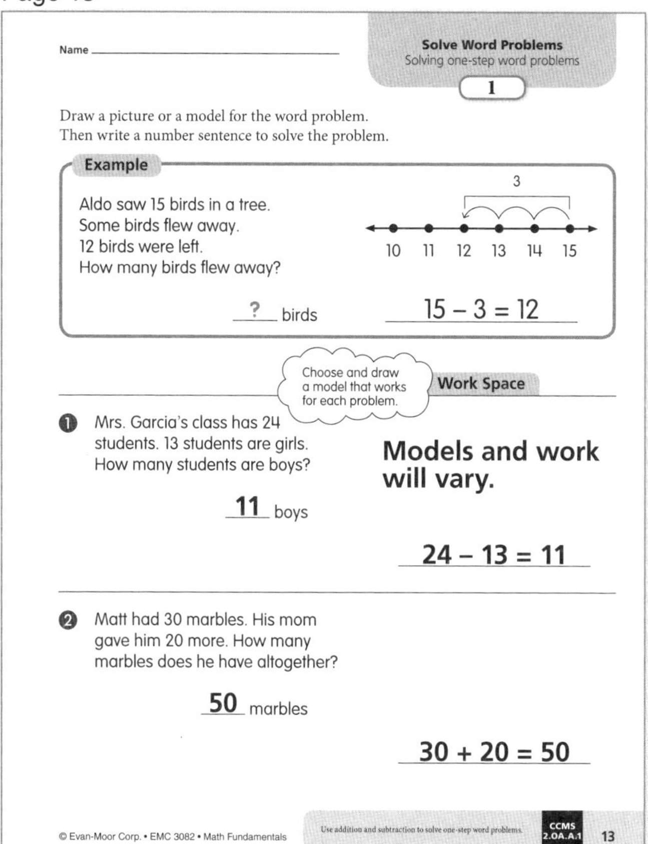

Name ____________

Solve Word Problems
Solving one-step word problems
1

Draw a picture or a model for the word problem.
Then write a number sentence to solve the problem.

Example

Aldo saw 15 birds in a tree.
Some birds flew away.
12 birds were left.
How many birds flew away?

3
10 11 12 13 14 15

? birds

15 – 3 = 12

Choose and draw a model that works for each problem.

Work Space

1. Mrs. Garcia's class has 24 students. 13 students are girls. How many students are boys?

Models and work will vary.

11 boys

24 – 13 = 11

2. Matt had 30 marbles. His mom gave him 20 more. How many marbles does he have altogether?

50 marbles

30 + 20 = 50

© Evan-Moor Corp. • EMC 3082 • Math Fundamentals
Use addition and subtraction to solve one-step word problems. CCMS 2.OA.A.1 13

Page 14

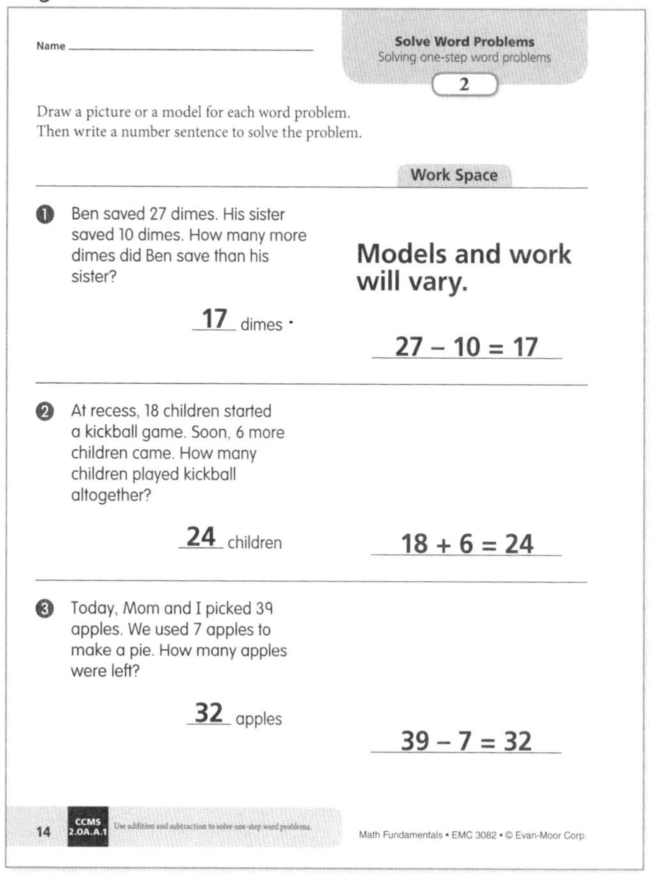

Name ____________

Solve Word Problems
Solving one-step word problems
2

Draw a picture or a model for each word problem.
Then write a number sentence to solve the problem.

Work Space

1. Ben saved 27 dimes. His sister saved 10 dimes. How many more dimes did Ben save than his sister?

Models and work will vary.

17 dimes

27 – 10 = 17

2. At recess, 18 children started a kickball game. Soon, 6 more children came. How many children played kickball altogether?

24 children

18 + 6 = 24

3. Today, Mom and I picked 39 apples. We used 7 apples to make a pie. How many apples were left?

32 apples

39 – 7 = 32

14 CCMS 2.OA.A.1 Use addition and subtraction to solve one-step word problems.
Math Fundamentals • EMC 3082 • © Evan-Moor Corp.

Page 15

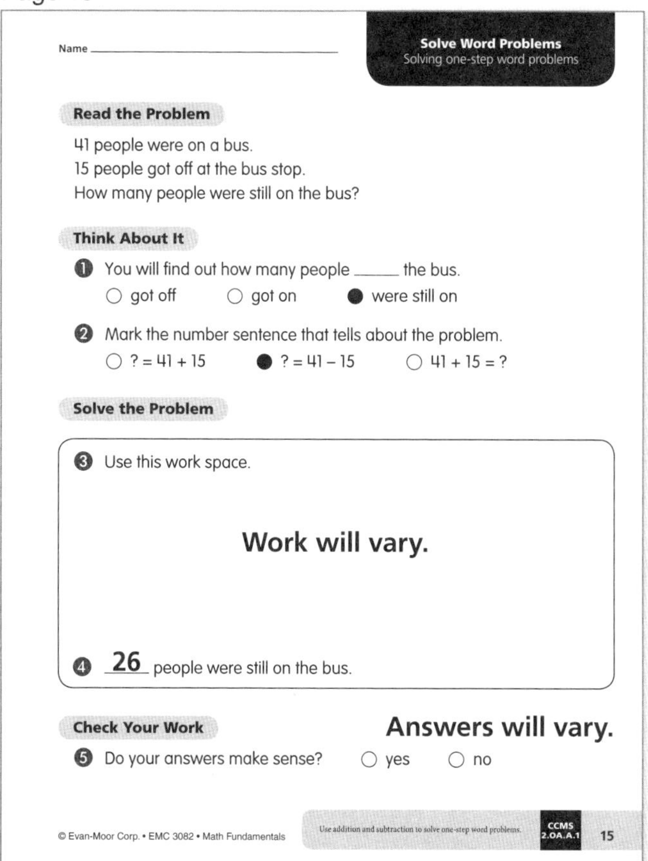

Name ____________

Solve Word Problems
Solving one-step word problems

Read the Problem

41 people were on a bus.
15 people got off at the bus stop.
How many people were still on the bus?

Think About It

1. You will find out how many people ____ the bus.
   ○ got off ○ got on ● were still on
2. Mark the number sentence that tells about the problem.
   ○ ? = 41 + 15 ● ? = 41 – 15 ○ 41 + 15 = ?

Solve the Problem

3. Use this work space.

Work will vary.

4. 26 people were still on the bus.

Check Your Work

Answers will vary.

5. Do your answers make sense? ○ yes ○ no

© Evan-Moor Corp. • EMC 3082 • Math Fundamentals
Use addition and subtraction to solve one-step word problems. CCMS 2.OA.A.1 15

Page 17

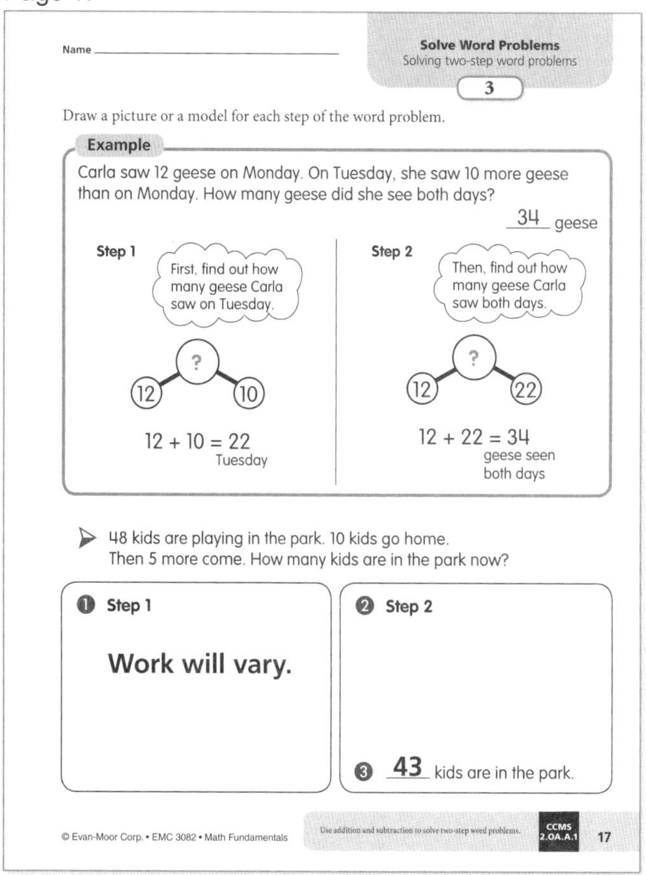

Name ____________

Solve Word Problems
Solving two-step word problems
3

Draw a picture or a model for each step of the word problem.

Example

Carla saw 12 geese on Monday. On Tuesday, she saw 10 more geese than on Monday. How many geese did she see both days?

34 geese

Step 1
First, find out how many geese Carla saw on Tuesday.
? 12 10
12 + 10 = 22
Tuesday

Step 2
Then, find out how many geese Carla saw both days.
? 12 22
12 + 22 = 34
geese seen both days

➤ 48 kids are playing in the park. 10 kids go home.
Then 5 more come. How many kids are in the park now?

1. Step 1

Work will vary.

2. Step 2

3. 43 kids are in the park.

© Evan-Moor Corp. • EMC 3082 • Math Fundamentals
Use addition and subtraction to solve two-step word problems. CCMS 2.OA.A.1 17

There are many ways to model a problem or to word an explanation. Accept any reasonable answer.

Page 18

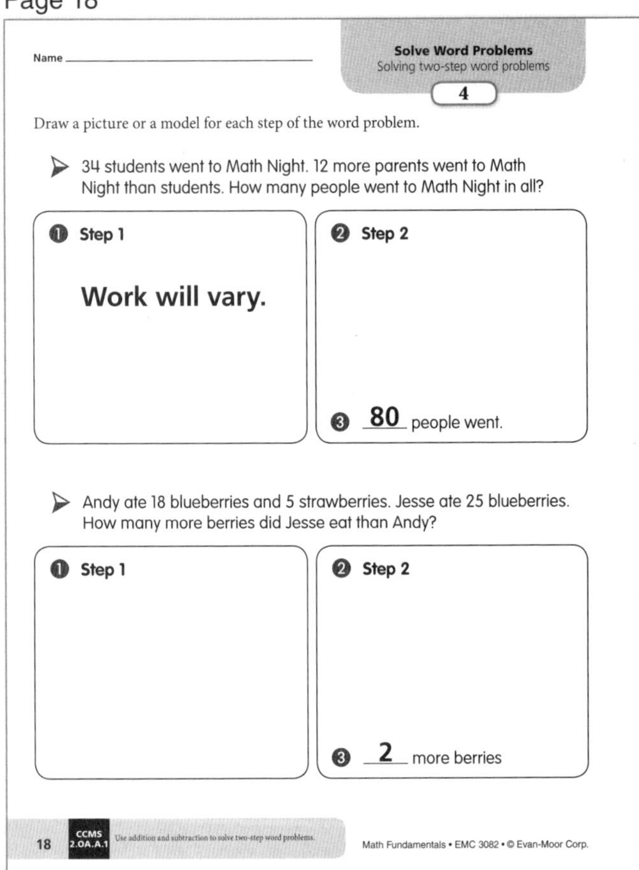

Name ______________________

Solve Word Problems
Solving two-step word problems
4

Draw a picture or a model for each step of the word problem.

➤ 34 students went to Math Night. 12 more parents went to Math Night than students. How many people went to Math Night in all?

❶ Step 1

Work will vary.

❷ Step 2

❸ __80__ people went.

➤ Andy ate 18 blueberries and 5 strawberries. Jesse ate 25 blueberries. How many more berries did Jesse eat than Andy?

❶ Step 1

❷ Step 2

❸ __2__ more berries

18 CCMS 2.OA.A.1 Use addition and subtraction to solve two-step word problems. Math Fundamentals • EMC 3082 • © Evan-Moor Corp.

Page 19

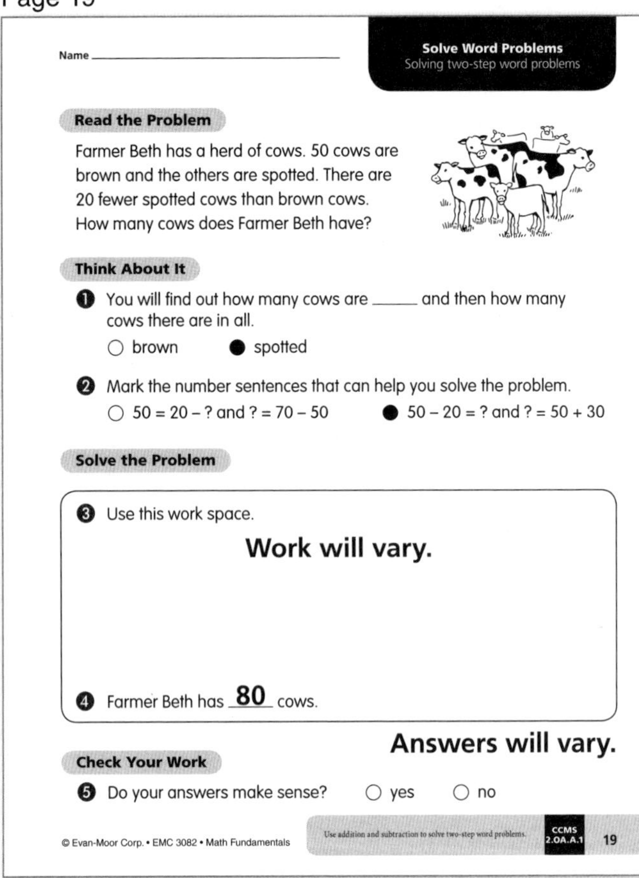

Name ______________________

Solve Word Problems
Solving two-step word problems

Read the Problem

Farmer Beth has a herd of cows. 50 cows are brown and the others are spotted. There are 20 fewer spotted cows than brown cows. How many cows does Farmer Beth have?

Think About It

❶ You will find out how many cows are ______ and then how many cows there are in all.
○ brown ● spotted

❷ Mark the number sentences that can help you solve the problem.
○ 50 = 20 – ? and ? = 70 – 50 ● 50 – 20 = ? and ? = 50 + 30

Solve the Problem

❸ Use this work space.

Work will vary.

❹ Farmer Beth has __80__ cows.

Answers will vary.

Check Your Work

❺ Do your answers make sense? ○ yes ○ no

© Evan-Moor Corp. • EMC 3082 • Math Fundamentals Use addition and subtraction to solve two-step word problems. CCMS 2.OA.A.1 19

Page 21

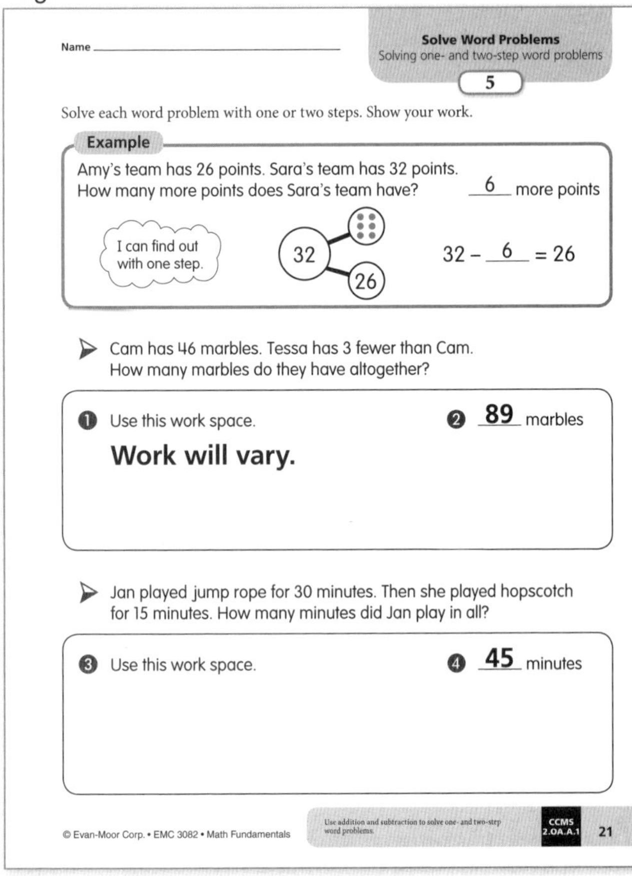

Name ______________________

Solve Word Problems
Solving one- and two-step word problems
5

Solve each word problem with one or two steps. Show your work.

Example

Amy's team has 26 points. Sara's team has 32 points. How many more points does Sara's team have? __6__ more points

I can find out with one step.

32 – __6__ = 26

➤ Cam has 46 marbles. Tessa has 3 fewer than Cam. How many marbles do they have altogether?

❶ Use this work space. ❷ __89__ marbles

Work will vary.

➤ Jan played jump rope for 30 minutes. Then she played hopscotch for 15 minutes. How many minutes did Jan play in all?

❸ Use this work space. ❹ __45__ minutes

© Evan-Moor Corp. • EMC 3082 • Math Fundamentals Use addition and subtraction to solve one- and two-step word problems. CCMS 2.OA.A.1 21

Page 22

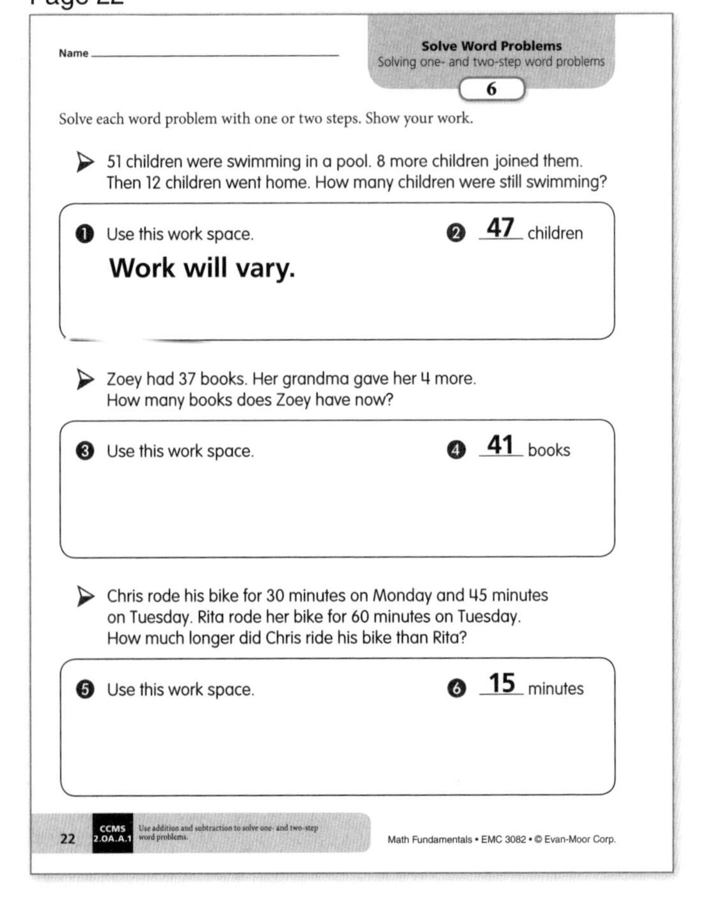

Name ______________________

Solve Word Problems
Solving one- and two-step word problems
6

Solve each word problem with one or two steps. Show your work.

➤ 51 children were swimming in a pool. 8 more children joined them. Then 12 children went home. How many children were still swimming?

❶ Use this work space. ❷ __47__ children

Work will vary.

➤ Zoey had 37 books. Her grandma gave her 4 more. How many books does Zoey have now?

❸ Use this work space. ❹ __41__ books

➤ Chris rode his bike for 30 minutes on Monday and 45 minutes on Tuesday. Rita rode her bike for 60 minutes on Tuesday. How much longer did Chris ride his bike than Rita?

❺ Use this work space. ❻ __15__ minutes

22 CCMS 2.OA.A.1 Use addition and subtraction to solve one- and two-step word problems. Math Fundamentals • EMC 3082 • © Evan-Moor Corp.

There are many ways to model a problem or to word an explanation. Accept any reasonable answer.

Page 23

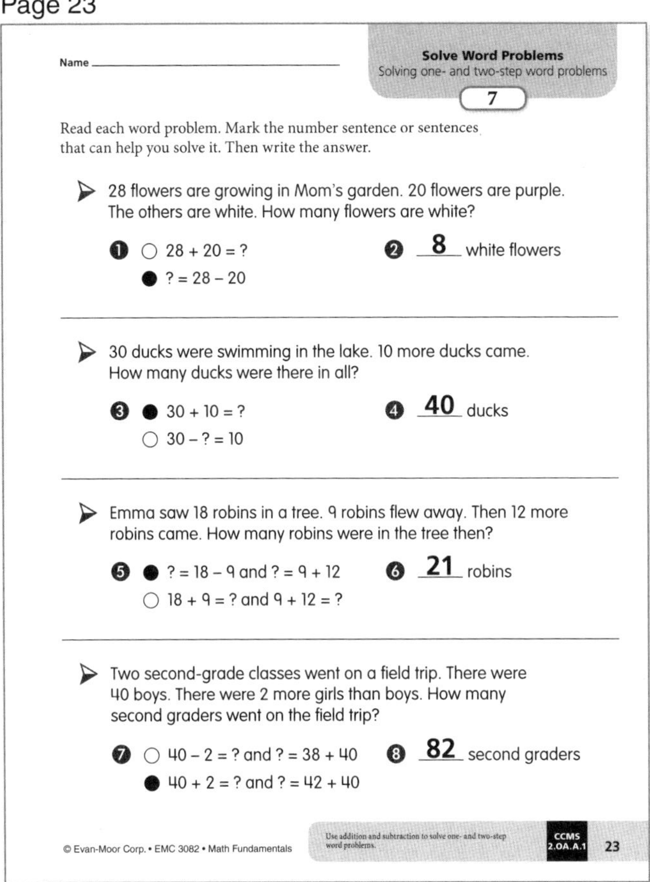

Name ______________________

Solve Word Problems
Solving one- and two-step word problems
7

Read each word problem. Mark the number sentence or sentences that can help you solve it. Then write the answer.

➤ 28 flowers are growing in Mom's garden. 20 flowers are purple. The others are white. How many flowers are white?

❶ ○ 28 + 20 = ?
● ? = 28 − 20

❷ **8** white flowers

➤ 30 ducks were swimming in the lake. 10 more ducks came. How many ducks were there in all?

❸ ● 30 + 10 = ?
○ 30 − ? = 10

❹ **40** ducks

➤ Emma saw 18 robins in a tree. 9 robins flew away. Then 12 more robins came. How many robins were in the tree then?

❺ ● ? = 18 − 9 and ? = 9 + 12
○ 18 + 9 = ? and 9 + 12 = ?

❻ **21** robins

➤ Two second-grade classes went on a field trip. There were 40 boys. There were 2 more girls than boys. How many second graders went on the field trip?

❼ ○ 40 − 2 = ? and ? = 38 + 40
● 40 + 2 = ? and ? = 42 + 40

❽ **82** second graders

© Evan-Moor Corp. • EMC 3082 • Math Fundamentals — Use addition and subtraction to solve one- and two-step word problems. — CCMS 2.OA.A.1 — 23

Page 24

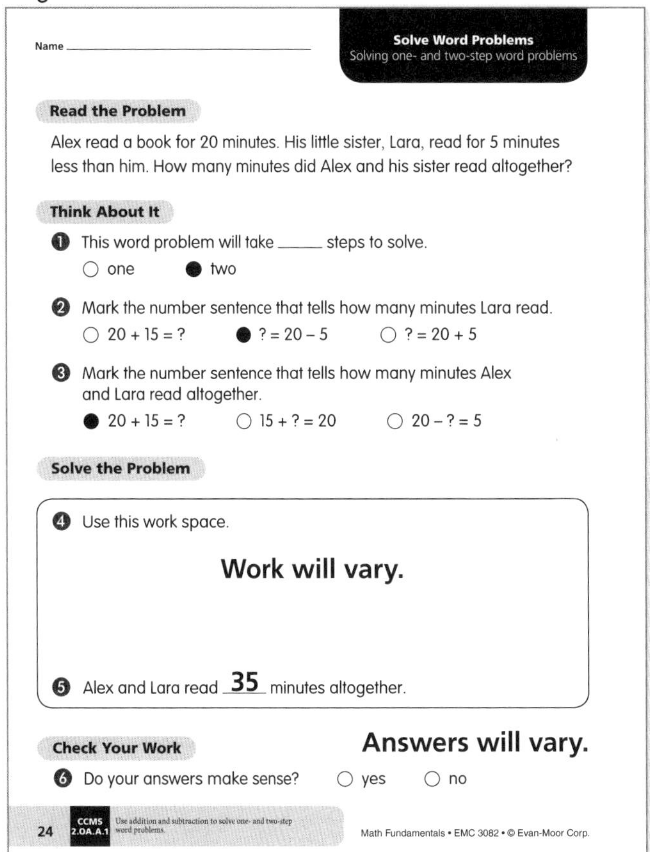

Name ______________________

Solve Word Problems
Solving one- and two-step word problems

Read the Problem

Alex read a book for 20 minutes. His little sister, Lara, read for 5 minutes less than him. How many minutes did Alex and his sister read altogether?

Think About It

❶ This word problem will take _____ steps to solve.
○ one ● two

❷ Mark the number sentence that tells how many minutes Lara read.
○ 20 + 15 = ? ● ? = 20 − 5 ○ ? = 20 + 5

❸ Mark the number sentence that tells how many minutes Alex and Lara read altogether.
● 20 + 15 = ? ○ 15 + ? = 20 ○ 20 − ? = 5

Solve the Problem

❹ Use this work space.

Work will vary.

❺ Alex and Lara read **35** minutes altogether.

Check Your Work **Answers will vary.**

❻ Do your answers make sense? ○ yes ○ no

24 — CCMS 2.OA.A.1 — Use addition and subtraction to solve one- and two-step word problems. — Math Fundamentals • EMC 3082 • © Evan-Moor Corp.

Page 27

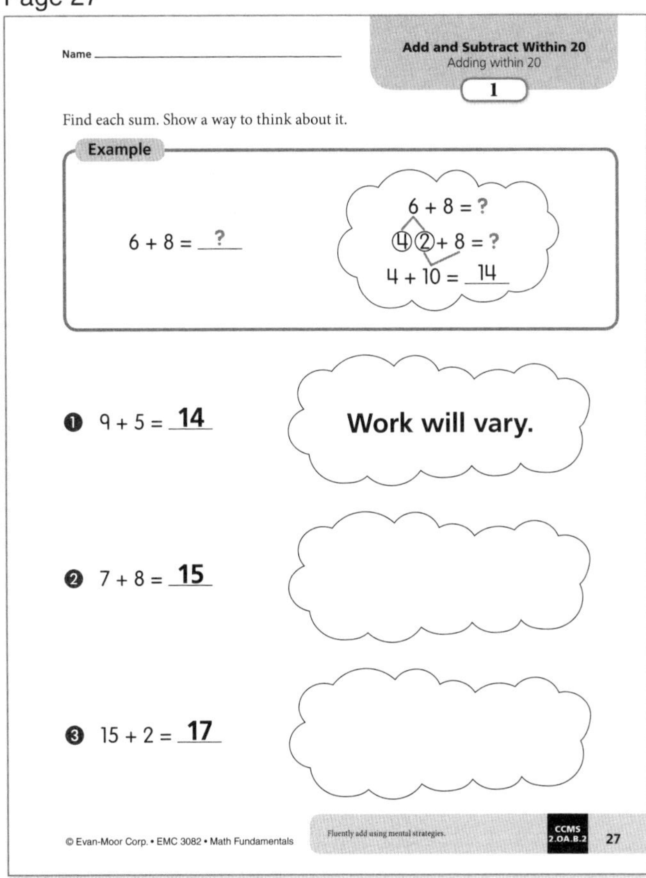

Name ______________________

Add and Subtract Within 20
Adding within 20
1

Find each sum. Show a way to think about it.

Example

6 + 8 = ?

6 + 8 = ?
④②+ 8 = ?
4 + 10 = 14

❶ 9 + 5 = **14** **Work will vary.**

❷ 7 + 8 = **15**

❸ 15 + 2 = **17**

© Evan-Moor Corp. • EMC 3082 • Math Fundamentals — Fluently add using mental strategies. — CCMS 2.OA.B.2 — 27

Page 28

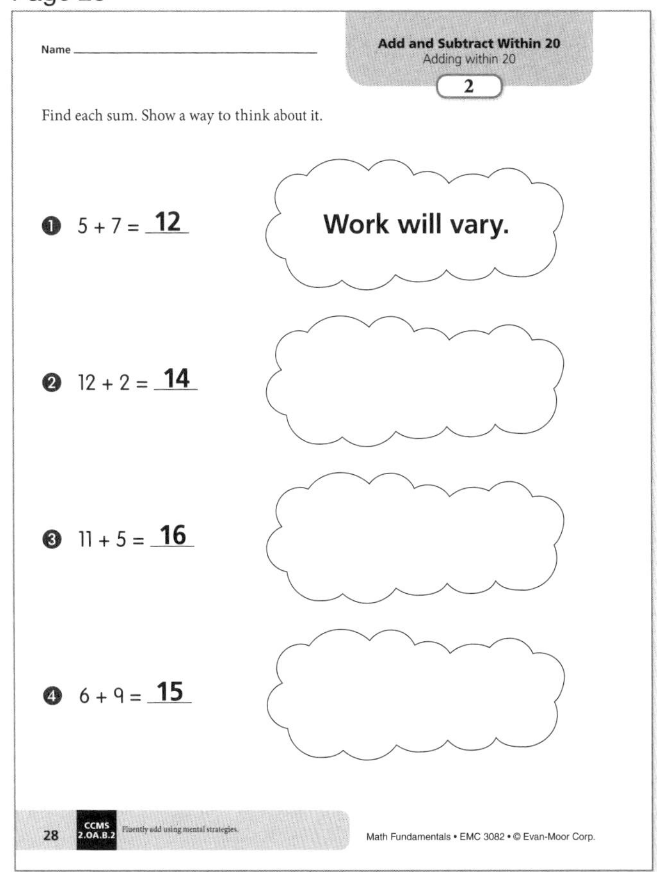

Name ______________________

Add and Subtract Within 20
Adding within 20
2

Find each sum. Show a way to think about it.

❶ 5 + 7 = **12** **Work will vary.**

❷ 12 + 2 = **14**

❸ 11 + 5 = **16**

❹ 6 + 9 = **15**

28 — CCMS 2.OA.B.2 — Fluently add using mental strategies. — Math Fundamentals • EMC 3082 • © Evan-Moor Corp.

There are many ways to model a problem or to word an explanation. Accept any reasonable answer.

Page 29

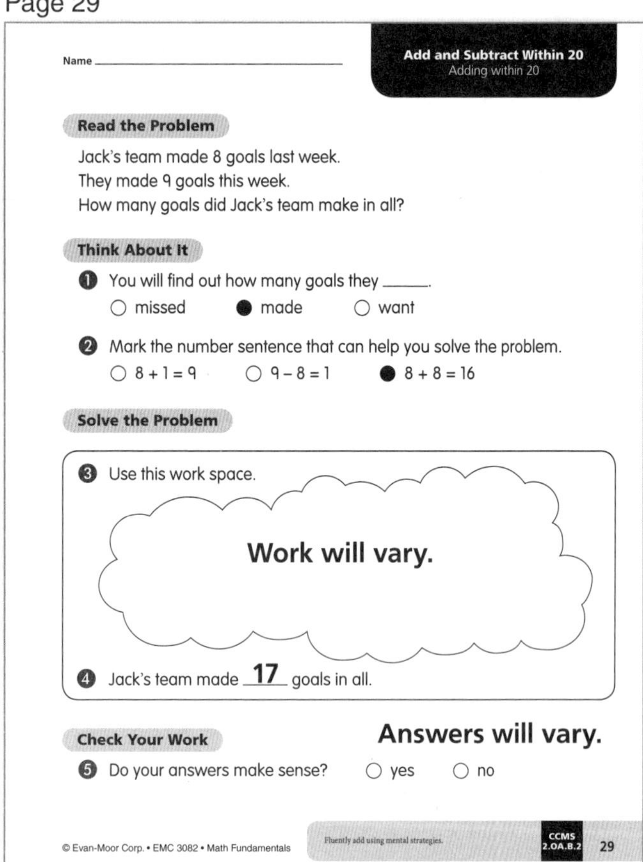

Name ____________

Add and Subtract Within 20
Adding within 20

Read the Problem

Jack's team made 8 goals last week.
They made 9 goals this week.
How many goals did Jack's team make in all?

Think About It

1. You will find out how many goals they ____.
   ○ missed ● made ○ want
2. Mark the number sentence that can help you solve the problem.
   ○ 8 + 1 = 9 ○ 9 − 8 = 1 ● 8 + 8 = 16

Solve the Problem

3. Use this work space.

   Work will vary.

4. Jack's team made **17** goals in all.

Check Your Work Answers will vary.

5. Do your answers make sense? ○ yes ○ no

© Evan-Moor Corp. • EMC 3082 • Math Fundamentals | Fluently add using mental strategies. | CCMS 2.OA.B.2 | 29

Page 31

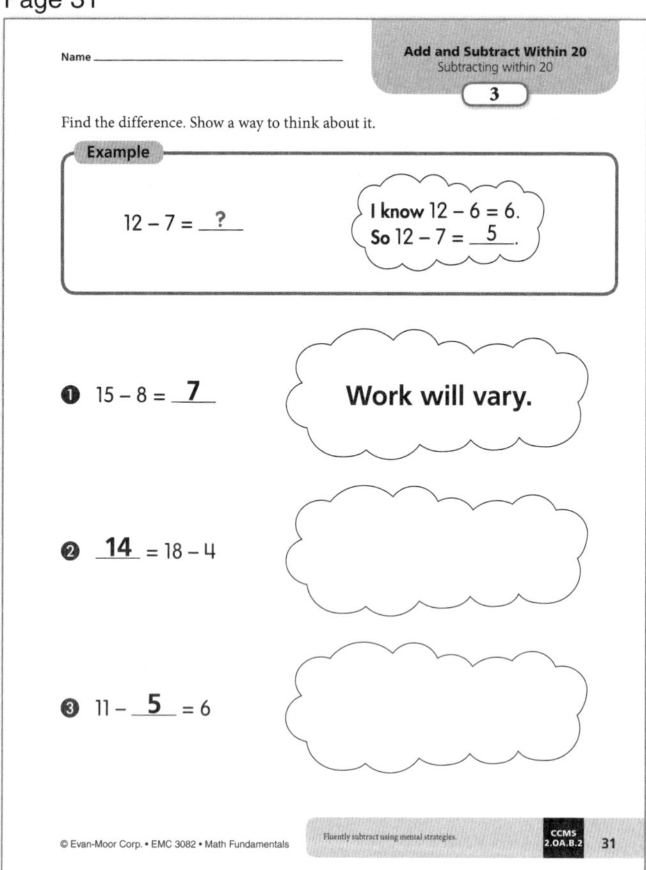

Name ____________

Add and Subtract Within 20
Subtracting within 20
3

Find the difference. Show a way to think about it.

Example

12 − 7 = **?**

I know 12 − 6 = 6.
So 12 − 7 = **5**.

1. 15 − 8 = **7** Work will vary.
2. **14** = 18 − 4
3. 11 − **5** = 6

© Evan-Moor Corp. • EMC 3082 • Math Fundamentals | Fluently subtract using mental strategies. | CCMS 2.OA.B.2 | 31

Page 32

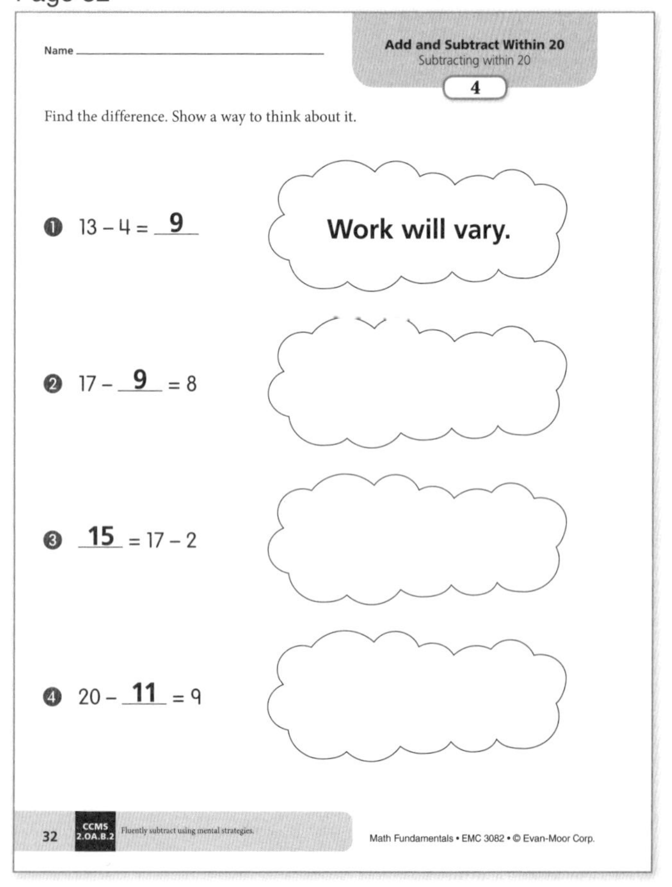

Name ____________

Add and Subtract Within 20
Subtracting within 20
4

Find the difference. Show a way to think about it.

1. 13 − 4 = **9** Work will vary.
2. 17 − **9** = 8
3. **15** = 17 − 2
4. 20 − **11** = 9

32 | CCMS 2.OA.B.2 | Fluently subtract using mental strategies. | Math Fundamentals • EMC 3082 • © Evan-Moor Corp.

Page 33

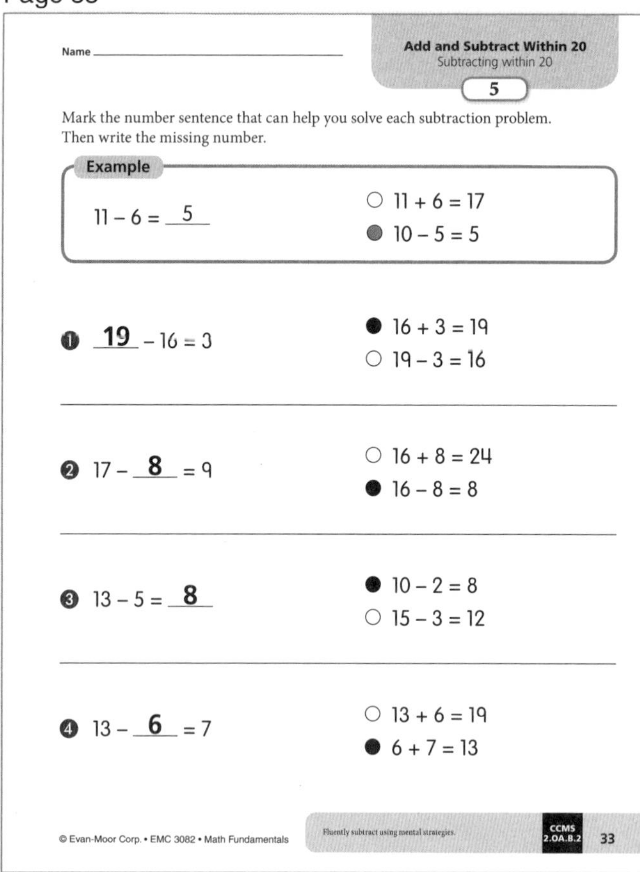

Name ____________

Add and Subtract Within 20
Subtracting within 20
5

Mark the number sentence that can help you solve each subtraction problem.
Then write the missing number.

Example

11 − 6 = **5**
○ 11 + 6 = 17
● 10 − 5 = 5

1. **19** − 16 = 3
   ● 16 + 3 = 19
   ○ 19 − 3 = 16
2. 17 − **8** = 9
   ○ 16 + 8 = 24
   ● 16 − 8 = 8
3. 13 − 5 = **8**
   ● 10 − 2 = 8
   ○ 15 − 3 = 12
4. 13 − **6** = 7
   ○ 13 + 6 = 19
   ● 6 + 7 = 13

© Evan-Moor Corp. • EMC 3082 • Math Fundamentals | Fluently subtract using mental strategies. | CCMS 2.OA.B.2 | 33

There are many ways to model a problem or to word an explanation. Accept any reasonable answer.

Page 34

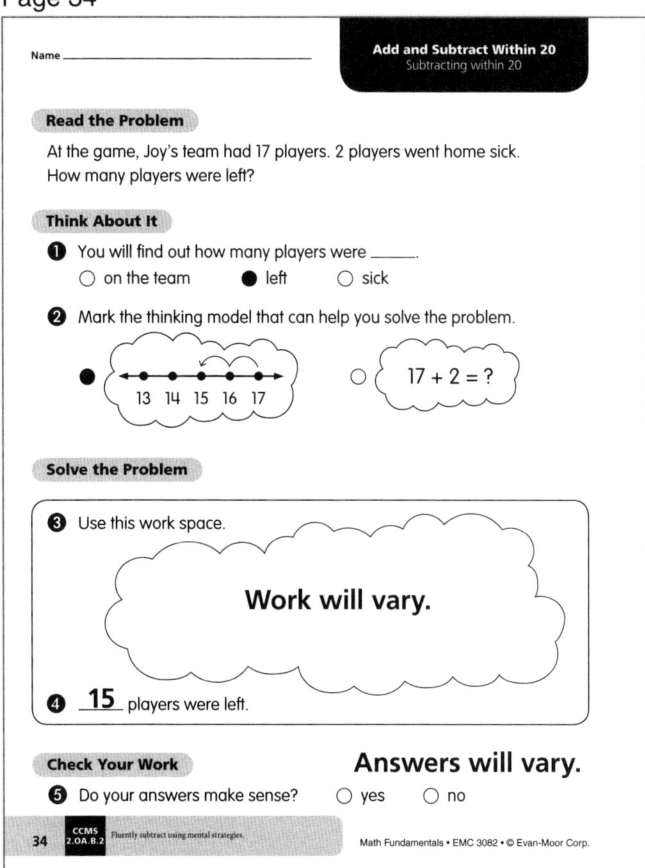

Name ______

Add and Subtract Within 20
Subtracting within 20

Read the Problem

At the game, Joy's team had 17 players. 2 players went home sick. How many players were left?

Think About It

1. You will find out how many players were ______.
   ○ on the team ● left ○ sick
2. Mark the thinking model that can help you solve the problem.
   ● 13 14 15 16 17 ○ 17 + 2 = ?

Solve the Problem

3. Use this work space.
   Work will vary.
4. **15** players were left.

Check Your Work **Answers will vary.**

5. Do your answers make sense? ○ yes ○ no

34 CCMS 2.OA.B.2 Fluently subtract using mental strategies. Math Fundamentals • EMC 3082 • © Evan-Moor Corp.

Page 37

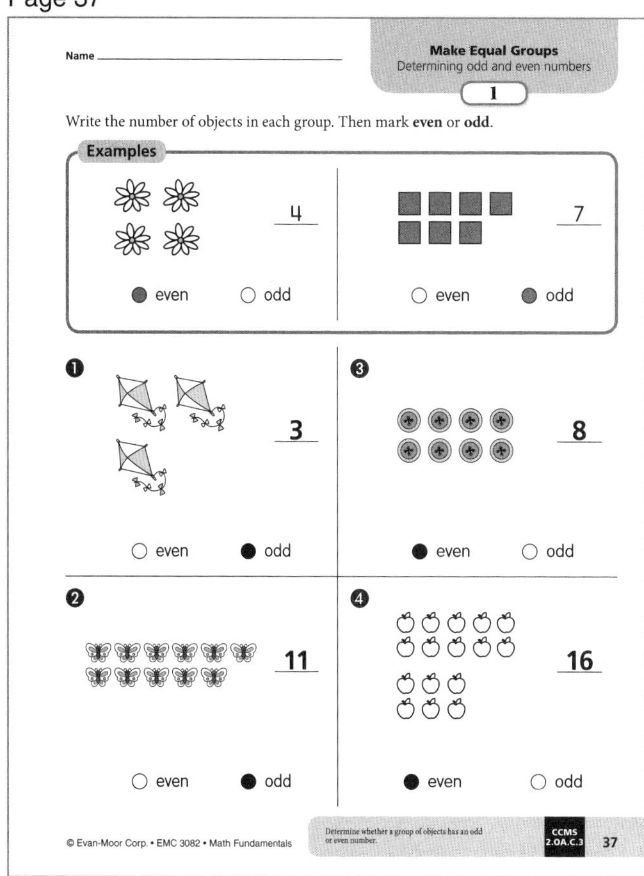

Name ______

Make Equal Groups
Determining odd and even numbers
1

Write the number of objects in each group. Then mark **even** or **odd**.

Examples

4 ● even ○ odd

7 ○ even ● odd

1. **3** ○ even ● odd
2. **11** ○ even ● odd
3. **8** ● even ○ odd
4. **16** ● even ○ odd

© Evan-Moor Corp. • EMC 3082 • Math Fundamentals Determine whether a group of objects has an odd or even number. CCMS 2.OA.C.3 37

Page 38

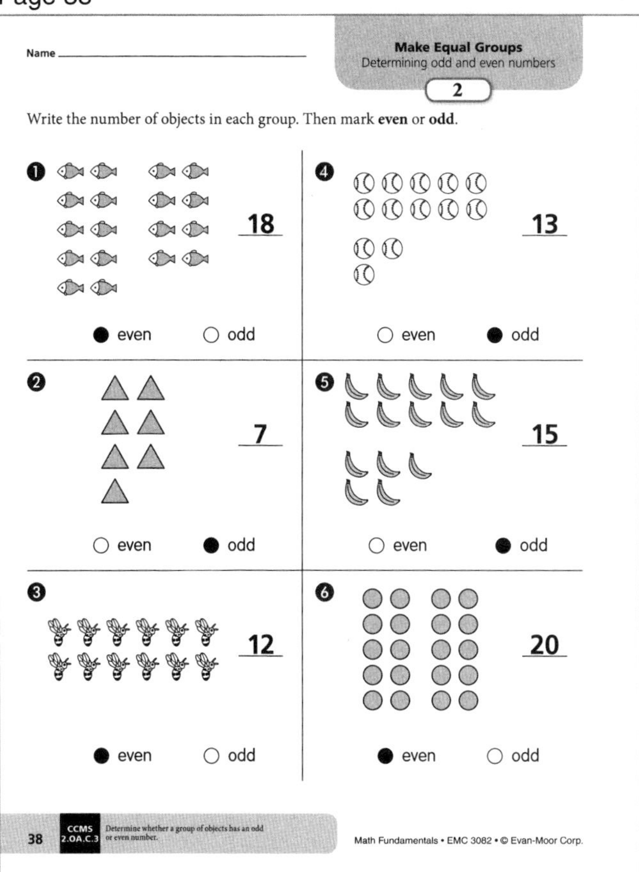

Name ______

Make Equal Groups
Determining odd and even numbers
2

Write the number of objects in each group. Then mark **even** or **odd**.

1. **18** ● even ○ odd
2. **7** ○ even ● odd
3. **12** ● even ○ odd
4. **13** ○ even ● odd
5. **15** ○ even ● odd
6. **20** ● even ○ odd

38 CCMS 2.OA.C.3 Determine whether a group of objects has an odd or even number. Math Fundamentals • EMC 3082 • © Evan-Moor Corp.

Page 39

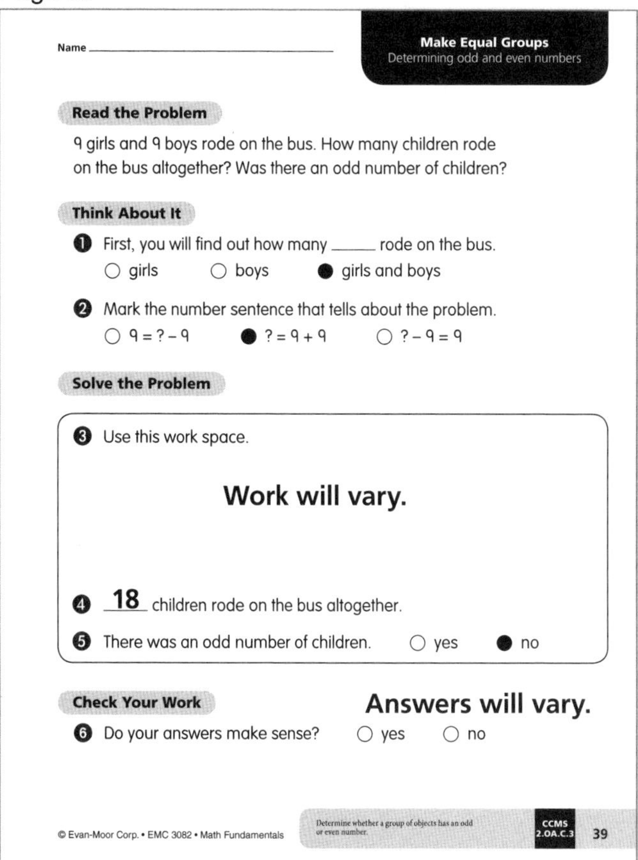

Name ______

Make Equal Groups
Determining odd and even numbers

Read the Problem

9 girls and 9 boys rode on the bus. How many children rode on the bus altogether? Was there an odd number of children?

Think About It

1. First, you will find out how many ______ rode on the bus.
   ○ girls ○ boys ● girls and boys
2. Mark the number sentence that tells about the problem.
   ○ 9 = ? − 9 ● ? = 9 + 9 ○ ? − 9 = 9

Solve the Problem

3. Use this work space.
   Work will vary.
4. **18** children rode on the bus altogether.
5. There was an odd number of children. ○ yes ● no

Check Your Work **Answers will vary.**

6. Do your answers make sense? ○ yes ○ no

© Evan-Moor Corp. • EMC 3082 • Math Fundamentals Determine whether a group of objects has an odd or even number. CCMS 2.OA.C.3 39

There are many ways to model a problem or to word an explanation. Accept any reasonable answer.

Page 41

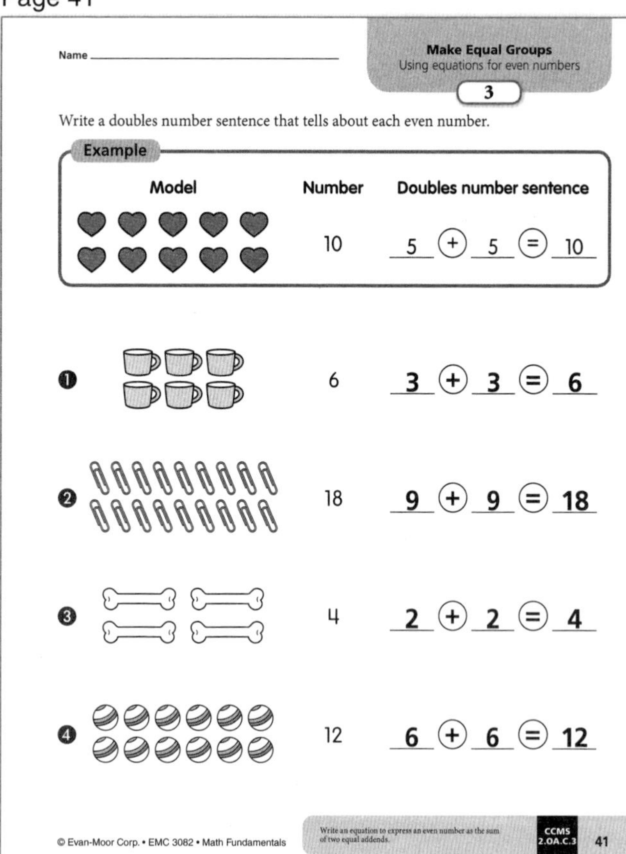

Page 42

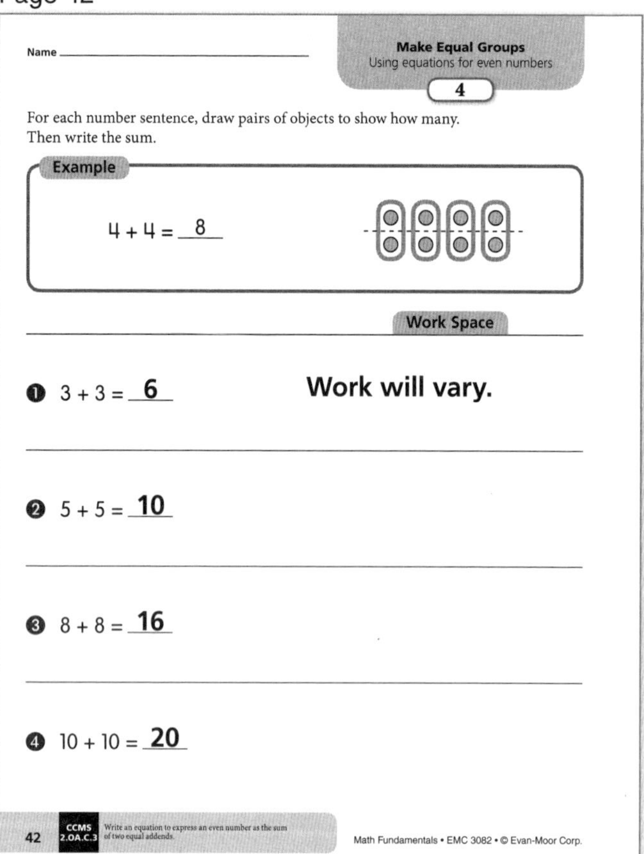

Page 43

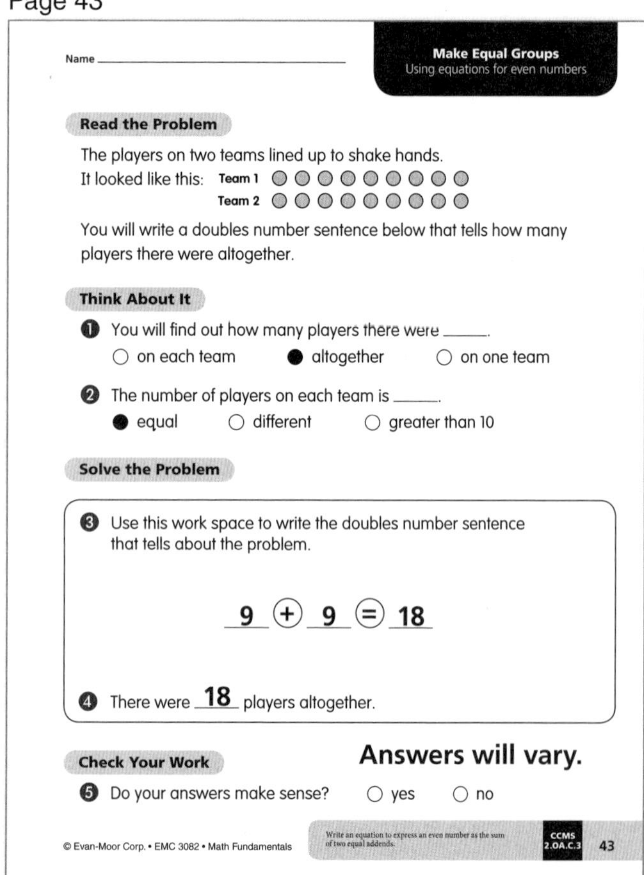

Page 45

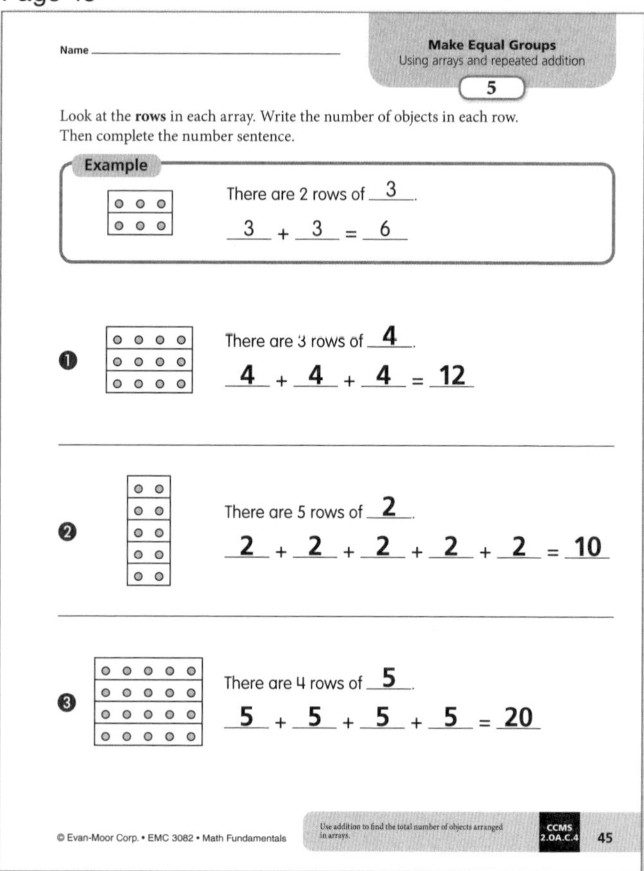

There are many ways to model a problem or to word an explanation. Accept any reasonable answer.

Page 46

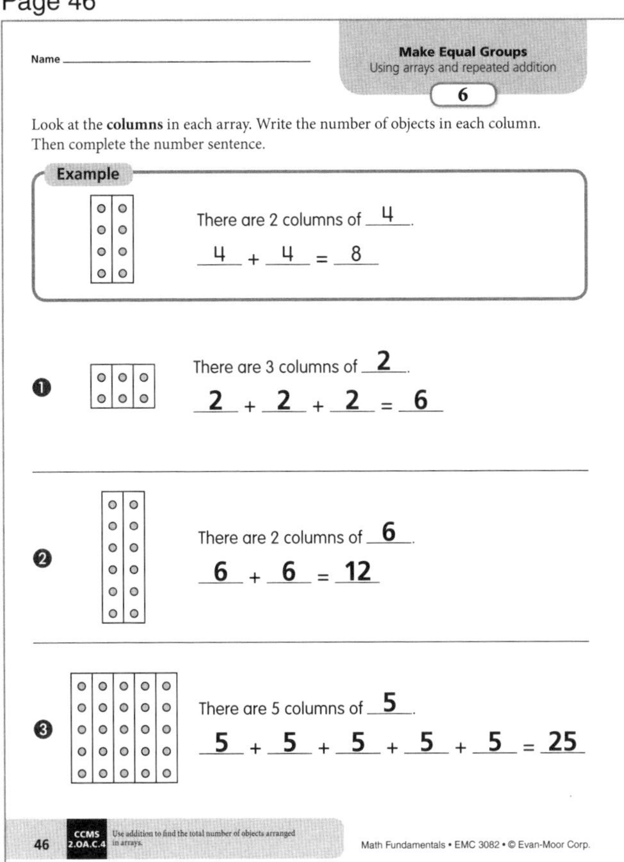

Page 47

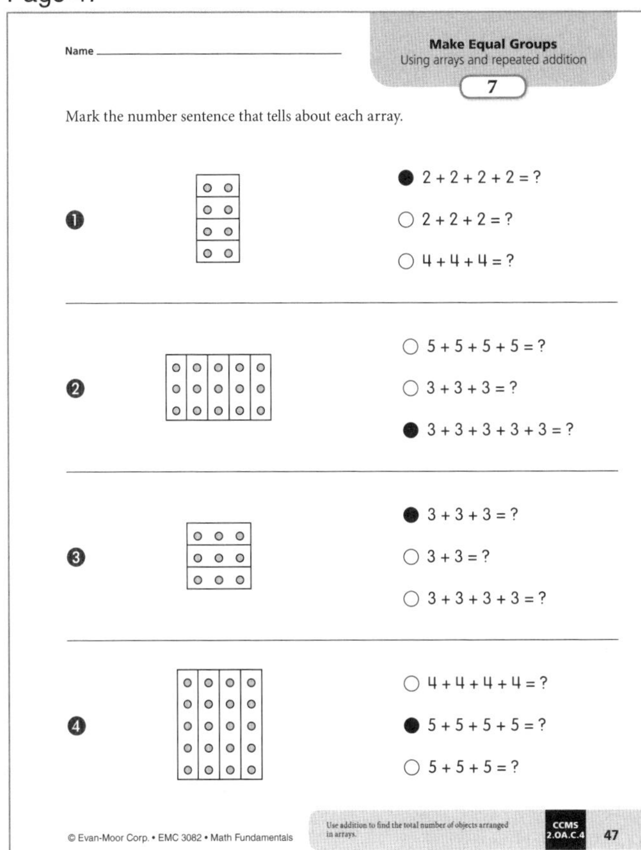

Page 48

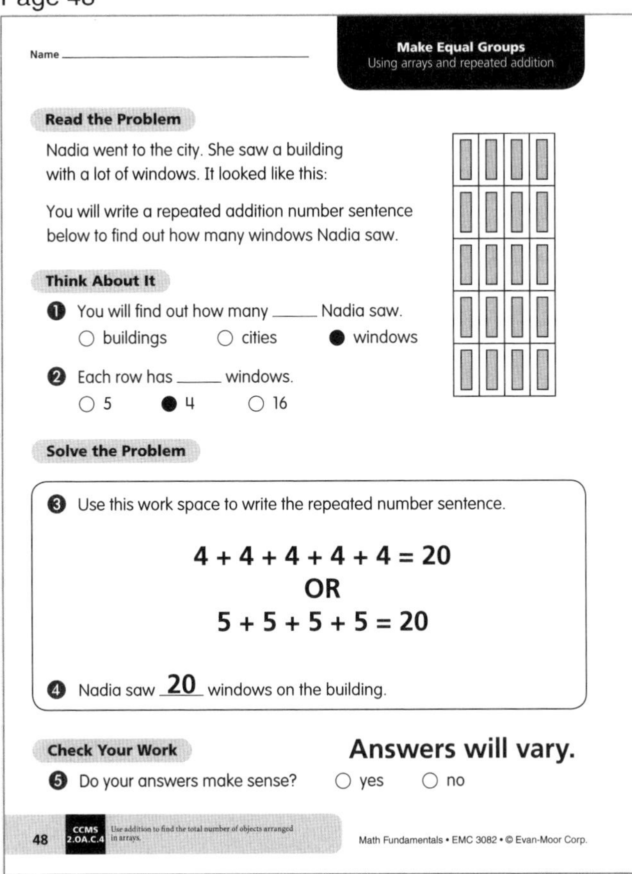

Page 51

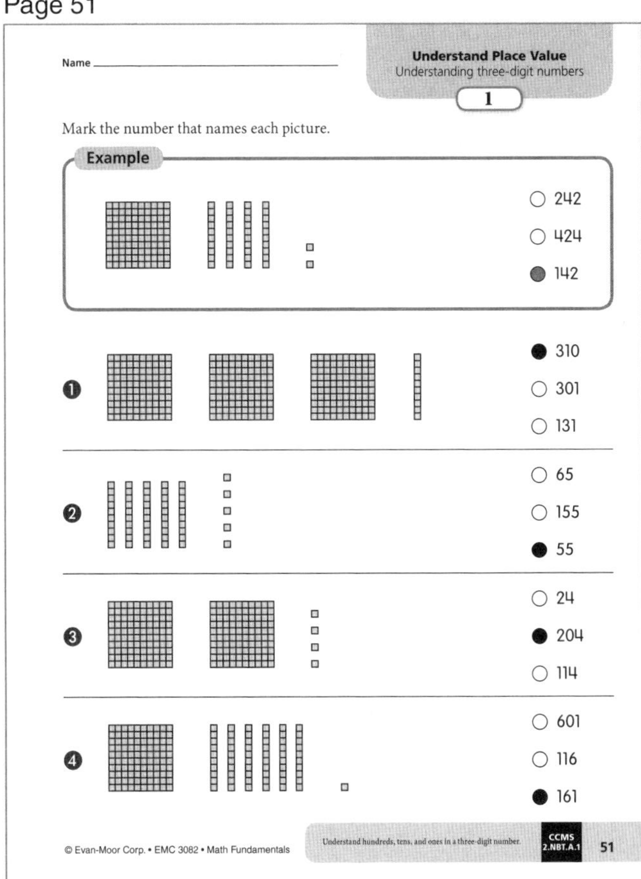

There are many ways to model a problem or to word an explanation. Accept any reasonable answer.

Page 52

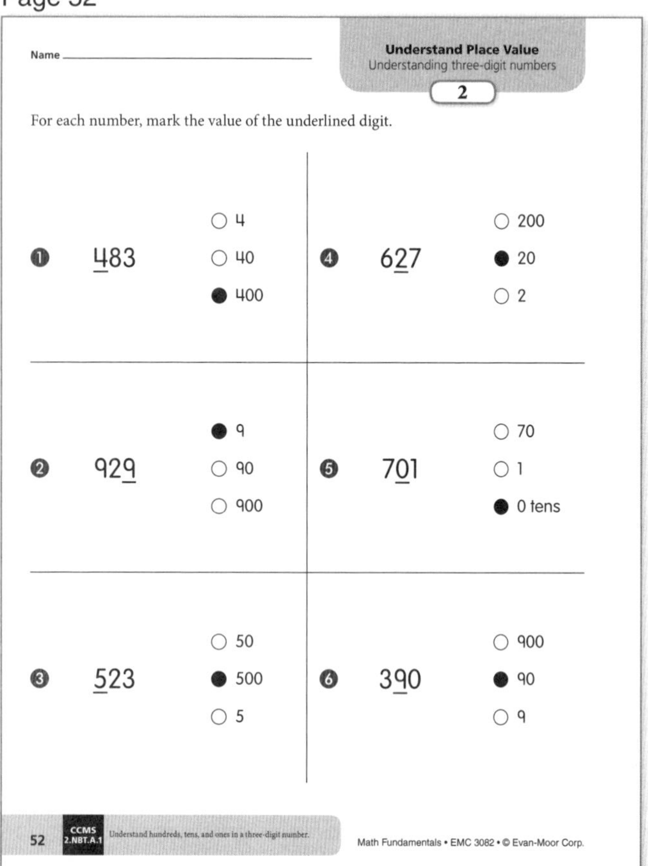

Name ______

Understand Place Value
Understanding three-digit numbers
2

For each number, mark the value of the underlined digit.

1. 483 — ○ 4 ○ 40 ● 400
2. 929 — ● 9 ○ 90 ○ 900
3. 523 — ○ 50 ● 500 ○ 5
4. 627 — ○ 200 ● 20 ○ 2
5. 701 — ○ 70 ○ 1 ● 0 tens
6. 390 — ○ 900 ● 90 ○ 9

52 CCMS 2.NBT.A.1 Understand hundreds, tens, and ones in a three-digit number. Math Fundamentals • EMC 3082 • © Evan-Moor Corp.

Page 53

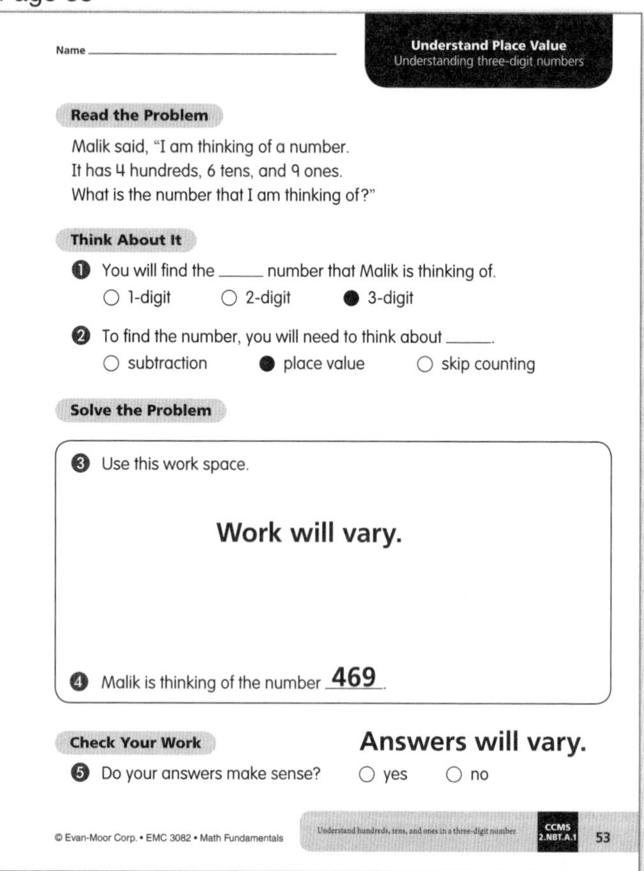

Name ______

Understand Place Value
Understanding three-digit numbers

Read the Problem

Malik said, "I am thinking of a number.
It has 4 hundreds, 6 tens, and 9 ones.
What is the number that I am thinking of?"

Think About It

1. You will find the ____ number that Malik is thinking of.
   ○ 1-digit ○ 2-digit ● 3-digit
2. To find the number, you will need to think about ____.
   ○ subtraction ● place value ○ skip counting

Solve the Problem

3. Use this work space.

Work will vary.

4. Malik is thinking of the number **469**.

Check Your Work **Answers will vary.**

5. Do your answers make sense? ○ yes ○ no

© Evan-Moor Corp. • EMC 3082 • Math Fundamentals Understand hundreds, tens, and ones in a three-digit number. CCMS 2.NBT.A.1 53

Page 55

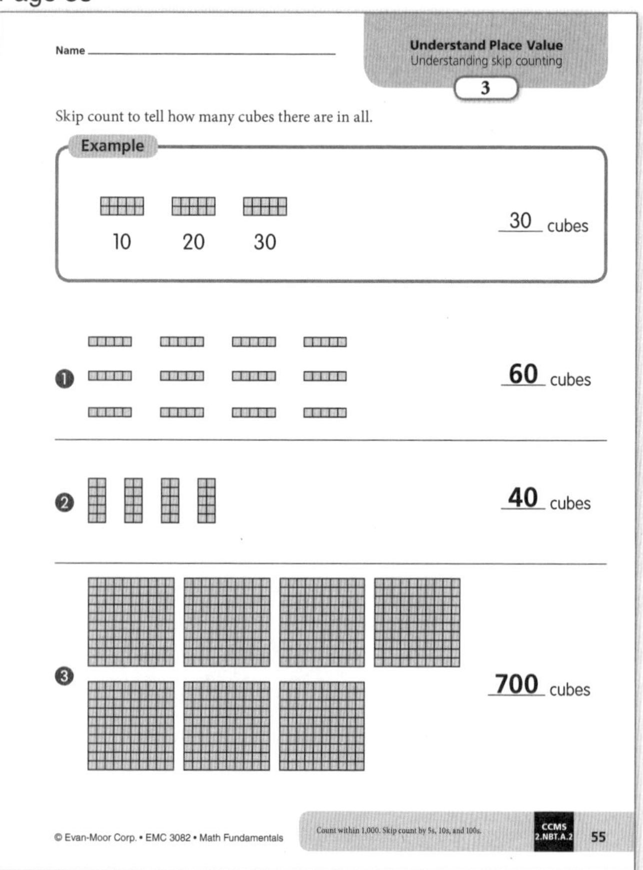

Name ______

Understand Place Value
Understanding skip counting
3

Skip count to tell how many cubes there are in all.

Example

10 20 30 — 30 cubes

1. **60** cubes
2. **40** cubes
3. **700** cubes

© Evan-Moor Corp. • EMC 3082 • Math Fundamentals Count within 1,000. Skip count by 5s, 10s, and 100s. CCMS 2.NBT.A.2 55

Page 56

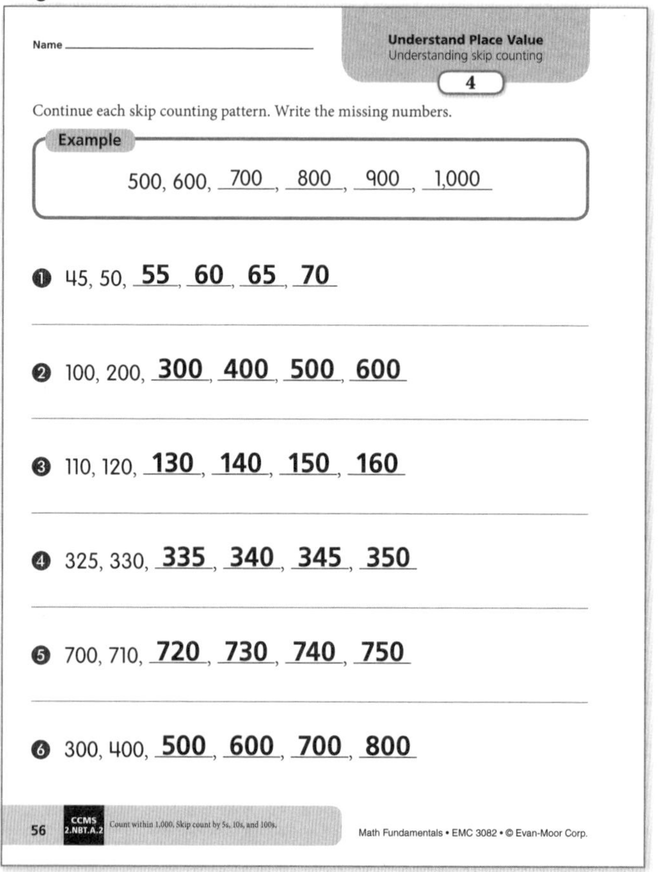

Name ______

Understand Place Value
Understanding skip counting
4

Continue each skip counting pattern. Write the missing numbers.

Example

500, 600, 700, 800, 900, 1,000

1. 45, 50, **55**, **60**, **65**, **70**
2. 100, 200, **300**, **400**, **500**, **600**
3. 110, 120, **130**, **140**, **150**, **160**
4. 325, 330, **335**, **340**, **345**, **350**
5. 700, 710, **720**, **730**, **740**, **750**
6. 300, 400, **500**, **600**, **700**, **800**

56 CCMS 2.NBT.A.2 Count within 1,000. Skip count by 5s, 10s, and 100s. Math Fundamentals • EMC 3082 • © Evan-Moor Corp.

There are many ways to model a problem or to word an explanation. Accept any reasonable answer.

Page 57

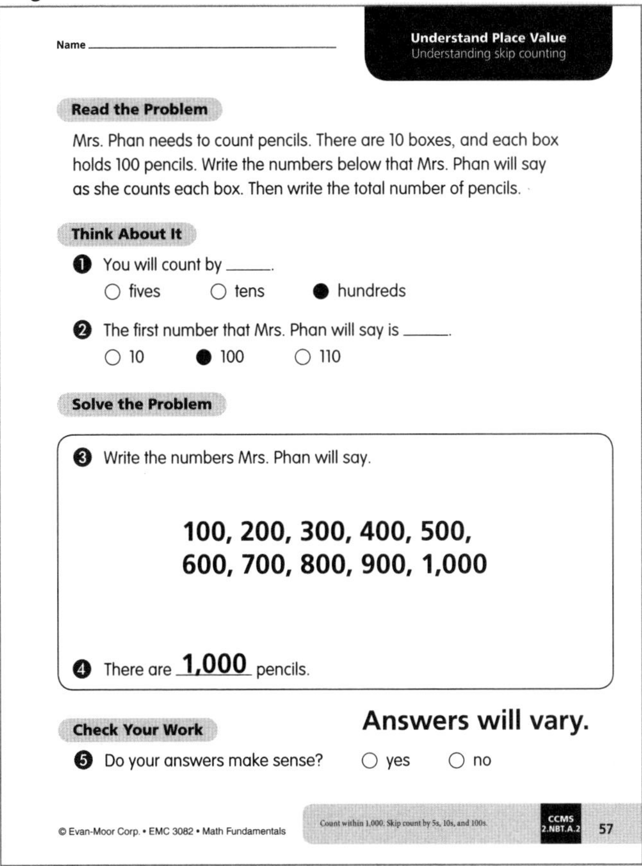

Name ______

Understand Place Value
Understanding skip counting

Read the Problem

Mrs. Phan needs to count pencils. There are 10 boxes, and each box holds 100 pencils. Write the numbers below that Mrs. Phan will say as she counts each box. Then write the total number of pencils.

Think About It

1. You will count by ______.
   ○ fives ○ tens ● hundreds
2. The first number that Mrs. Phan will say is ______.
   ○ 10 ● 100 ○ 110

Solve the Problem

3. Write the numbers Mrs. Phan will say.

   100, 200, 300, 400, 500, 600, 700, 800, 900, 1,000

4. There are **1,000** pencils.

Check Your Work **Answers will vary.**

5. Do your answers make sense? ○ yes ○ no

© Evan-Moor Corp. • EMC 3082 • Math Fundamentals — Count within 1,000. Skip count by 5s, 10s, and 100s. — CCMS 2.NBT.A.2 — 57

Page 59

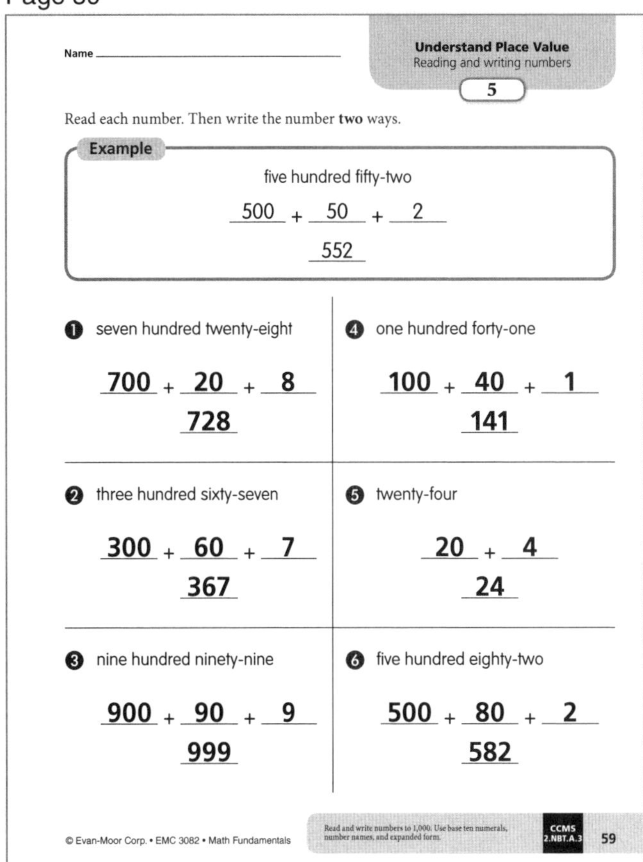

Name ______

Understand Place Value
Reading and writing numbers
5

Read each number. Then write the number **two** ways.

Example
five hundred fifty-two
500 + 50 + 2
552

1. seven hundred twenty-eight
   700 + **20** + **8**
   728
2. three hundred sixty-seven
   300 + **60** + **7**
   367
3. nine hundred ninety-nine
   900 + **90** + **9**
   999
4. one hundred forty-one
   100 + **40** + **1**
   141
5. twenty-four
   20 + **4**
   24
6. five hundred eighty-two
   500 + **80** + **2**
   582

© Evan-Moor Corp. • EMC 3082 • Math Fundamentals — Read and write numbers to 1,000. Use base ten numerals, number names, and expanded form. — CCMS 2.NBT.A.3 — 59

Page 60

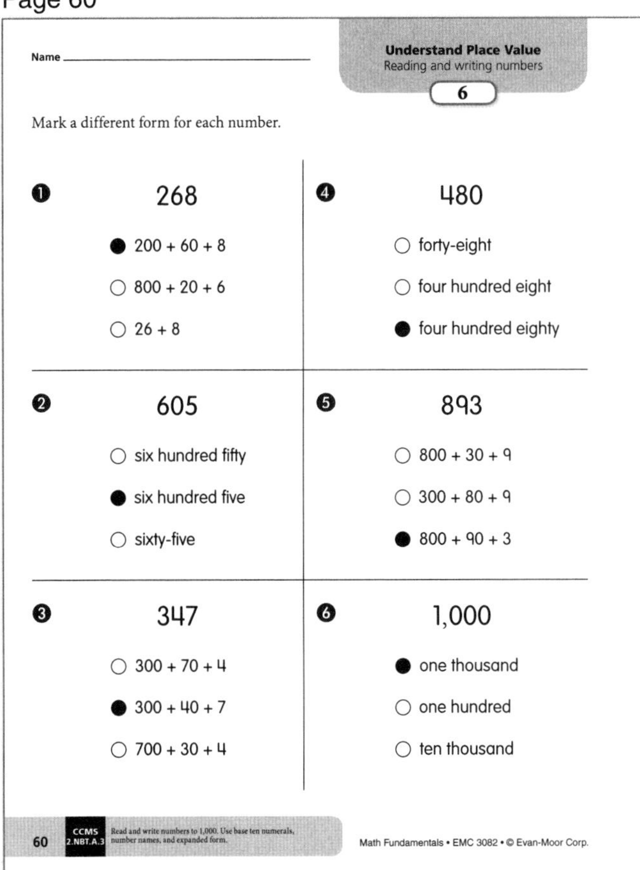

Name ______

Understand Place Value
Reading and writing numbers
6

Mark a different form for each number.

1. 268
   ● 200 + 60 + 8
   ○ 800 + 20 + 6
   ○ 26 + 8
2. 605
   ○ six hundred fifty
   ● six hundred five
   ○ sixty-five
3. 347
   ○ 300 + 70 + 4
   ● 300 + 40 + 7
   ○ 700 + 30 + 4
4. 480
   ○ forty-eight
   ○ four hundred eight
   ● four hundred eighty
5. 893
   ○ 800 + 30 + 9
   ○ 300 + 80 + 9
   ● 800 + 90 + 3
6. 1,000
   ● one thousand
   ○ one hundred
   ○ ten thousand

60 — CCMS 2.NBT.A.3 — Read and write numbers to 1,000. Use base ten numerals, number names, and expanded form. — Math Fundamentals • EMC 3082 • © Evan-Moor Corp.

Page 61

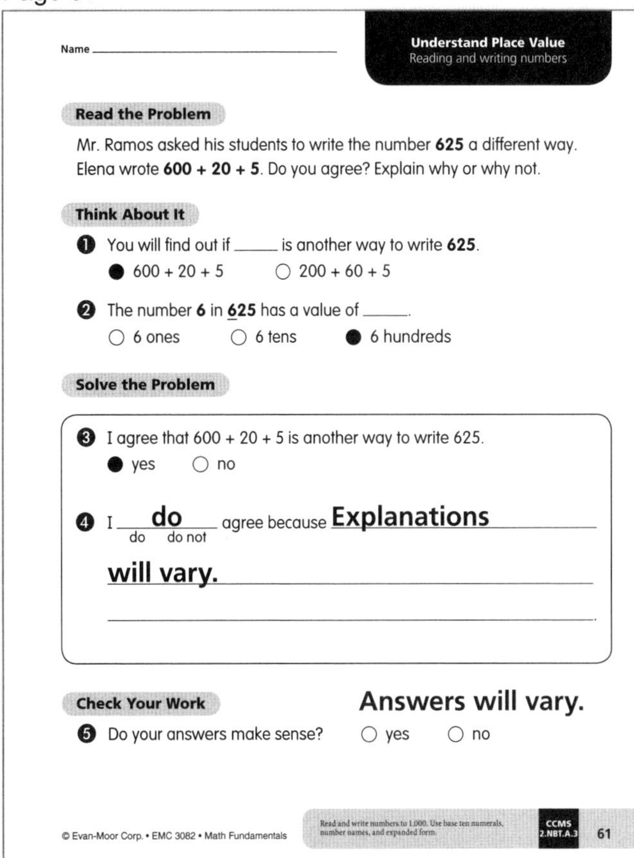

Name ______

Understand Place Value
Reading and writing numbers

Read the Problem

Mr. Ramos asked his students to write the number **625** a different way. Elena wrote **600 + 20 + 5**. Do you agree? Explain why or why not.

Think About It

1. You will find out if ______ is another way to write **625**.
   ● 600 + 20 + 5 ○ 200 + 60 + 5
2. The number **6** in **625** has a value of ______.
   ○ 6 ones ○ 6 tens ● 6 hundreds

Solve the Problem

3. I agree that 600 + 20 + 5 is another way to write 625.
   ● yes ○ no
4. I **do** (do / do not) agree because **Explanations will vary.**

Check Your Work **Answers will vary.**

5. Do your answers make sense? ○ yes ○ no

© Evan-Moor Corp. • EMC 3082 • Math Fundamentals — Read and write numbers to 1,000. Use base ten numerals, number names, and expanded form. — CCMS 2.NBT.A.3 — 61

There are many ways to model a problem or to word an explanation. Accept any reasonable answer.

Page 63

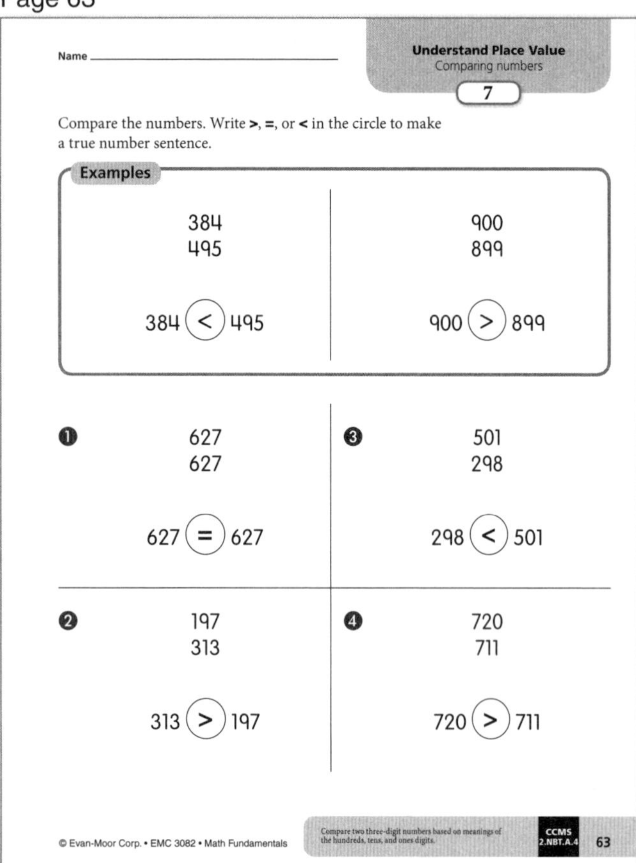

Name ____________

Understand Place Value
Comparing numbers
7

Compare the numbers. Write >, =, or < in the circle to make a true number sentence.

Examples

384 495	900 899
384 (<) 495	900 (>) 899

❶ 627 627 627 (=) 627	❸ 501 298 298 (<) 501
❷ 197 313 313 (>) 197	❹ 720 711 720 (>) 711

© Evan-Moor Corp. • EMC 3082 • Math Fundamentals

Compare two three-digit numbers based on meanings of the hundreds, tens, and ones digits. CCMS 2.NBT.A.4 63

Page 64

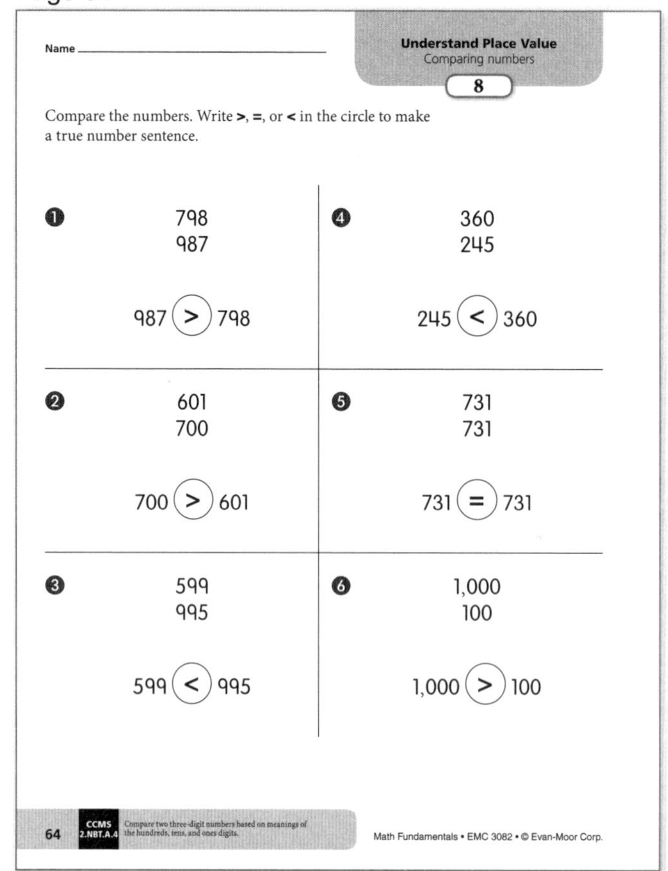

Name ____________

Understand Place Value
Comparing numbers
8

Compare the numbers. Write >, =, or < in the circle to make a true number sentence.

❶ 798 987 987 (>) 798	❹ 360 245 245 (<) 360
❷ 601 700 700 (>) 601	❺ 731 731 731 (=) 731
❸ 599 995 599 (<) 995	❻ 1,000 100 1,000 (>) 100

64 CCMS 2.NBT.A.4 Compare two three-digit numbers based on meanings of the hundreds, tens, and ones digits.

Math Fundamentals • EMC 3082 • © Evan-Moor Corp.

Page 65

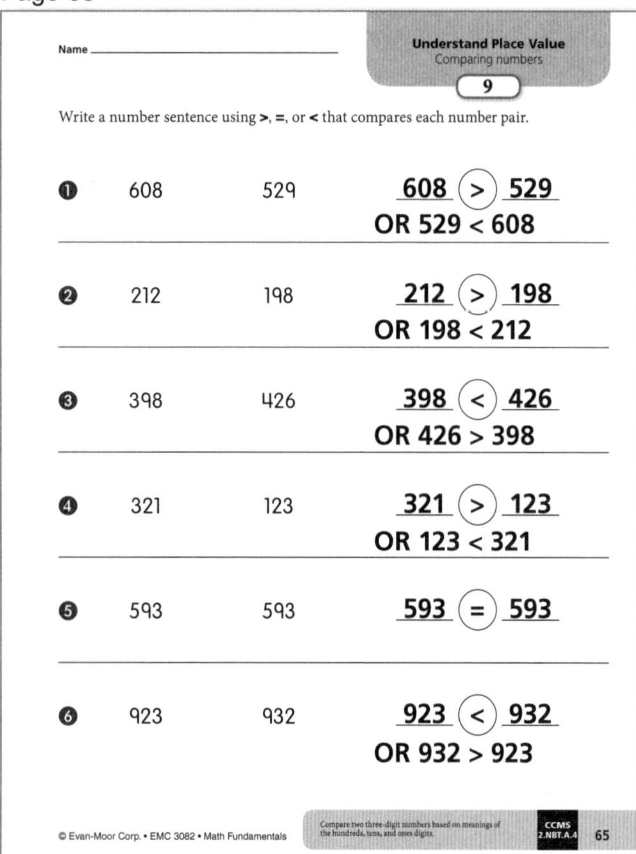

Name ____________

Understand Place Value
Comparing numbers
9

Write a number sentence using >, =, or < that compares each number pair.

❶	608	529	608 (>) 529 OR 529 < 608
❷	212	198	212 (>) 198 OR 198 < 212
❸	398	426	398 (<) 426 OR 426 > 398
❹	321	123	321 (>) 123 OR 123 < 321
❺	593	593	593 (=) 593
❻	923	932	923 (<) 932 OR 932 > 923

© Evan-Moor Corp. • EMC 3082 • Math Fundamentals

Compare two three-digit numbers based on meanings of the hundreds, tens, and ones digits. CCMS 2.NBT.A.4 65

Page 66

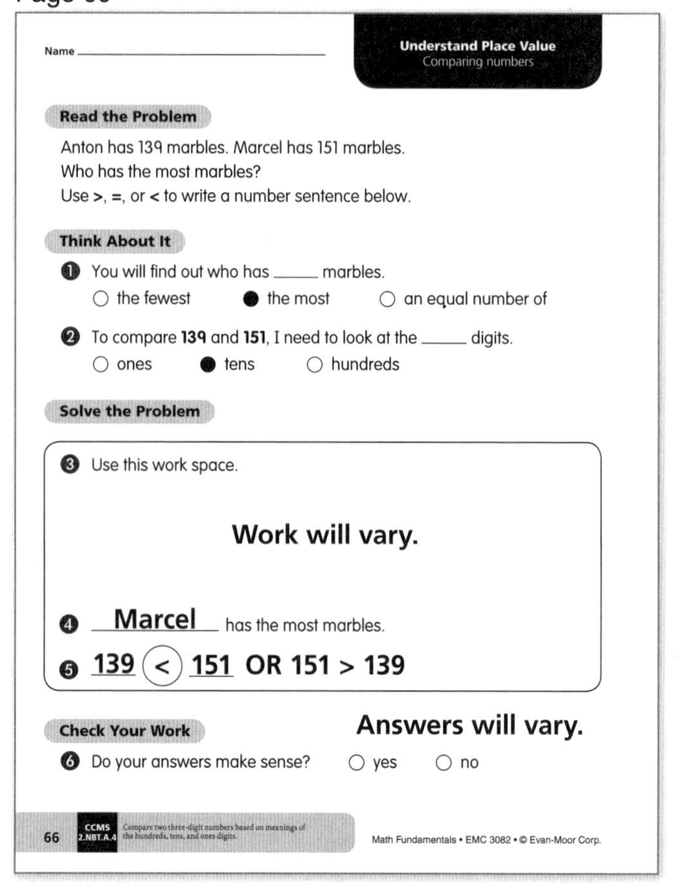

Name ____________

Understand Place Value
Comparing numbers

Read the Problem

Anton has 139 marbles. Marcel has 151 marbles. Who has the most marbles?
Use >, =, or < to write a number sentence below.

Think About It

❶ You will find out who has _____ marbles.
○ the fewest ● the most ○ an equal number of

❷ To compare **139** and **151**, I need to look at the _____ digits.
○ ones ● tens ○ hundreds

Solve the Problem

❸ Use this work space.

Work will vary.

❹ **Marcel** has the most marbles.

❺ **139** (<) **151** **OR 151 > 139**

Check Your Work **Answers will vary.**

❻ Do your answers make sense? ○ yes ○ no

66 CCMS 2.NBT.A.4 Compare two three-digit numbers based on meanings of the hundreds, tens, and ones digits.

Math Fundamentals • EMC 3082 • © Evan-Moor Corp.

There are many ways to model a problem or to word an explanation. Accept any reasonable answer.

Page 69

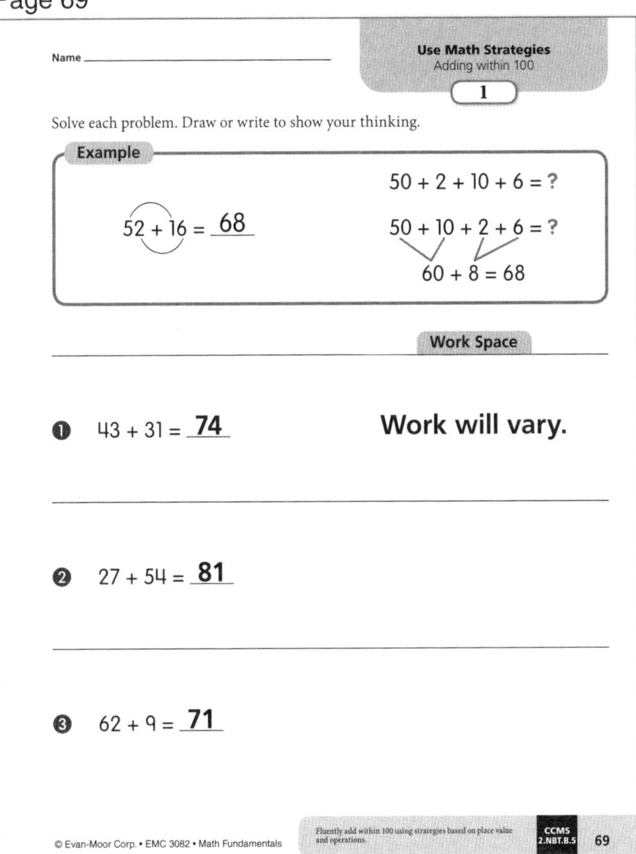

Page 70

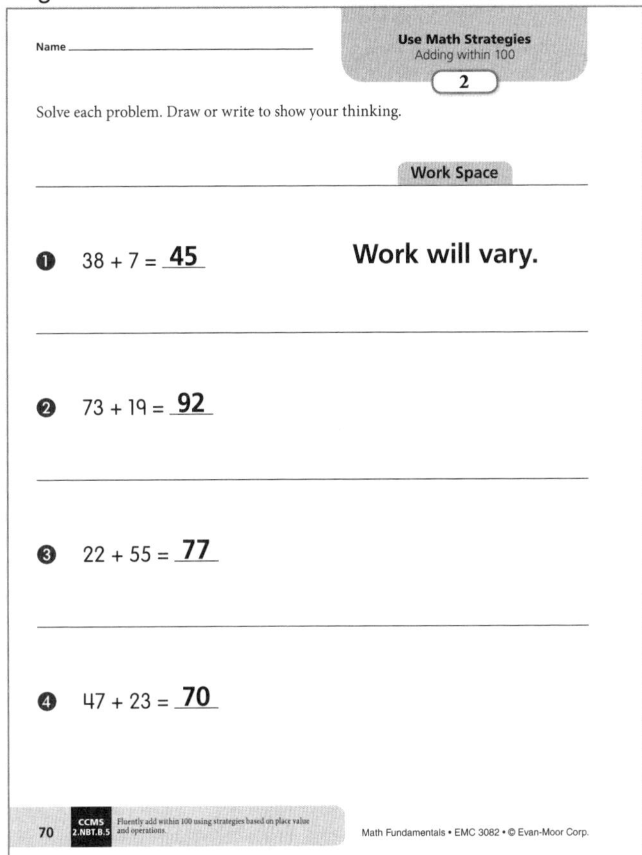

Page 71

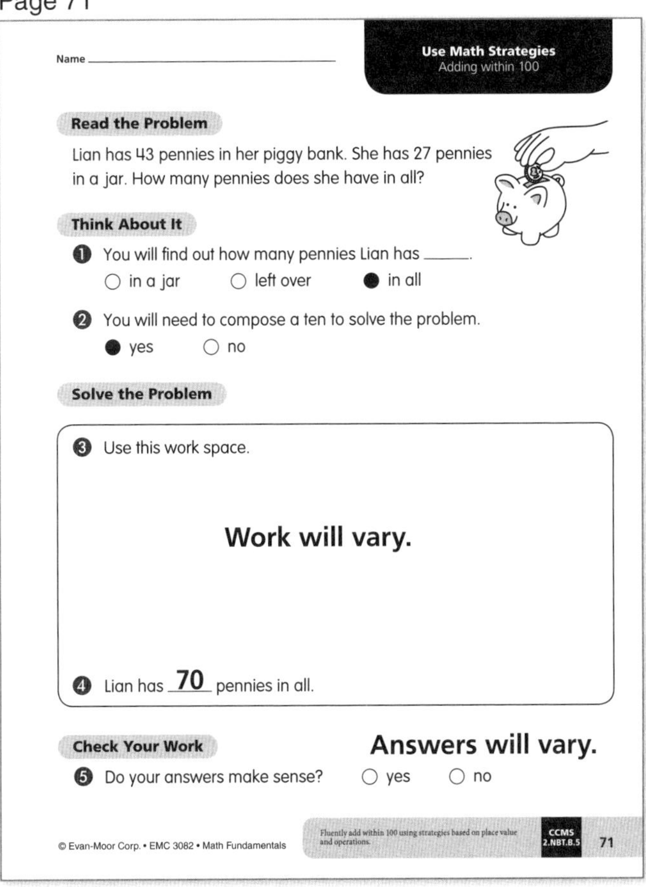

Page 73

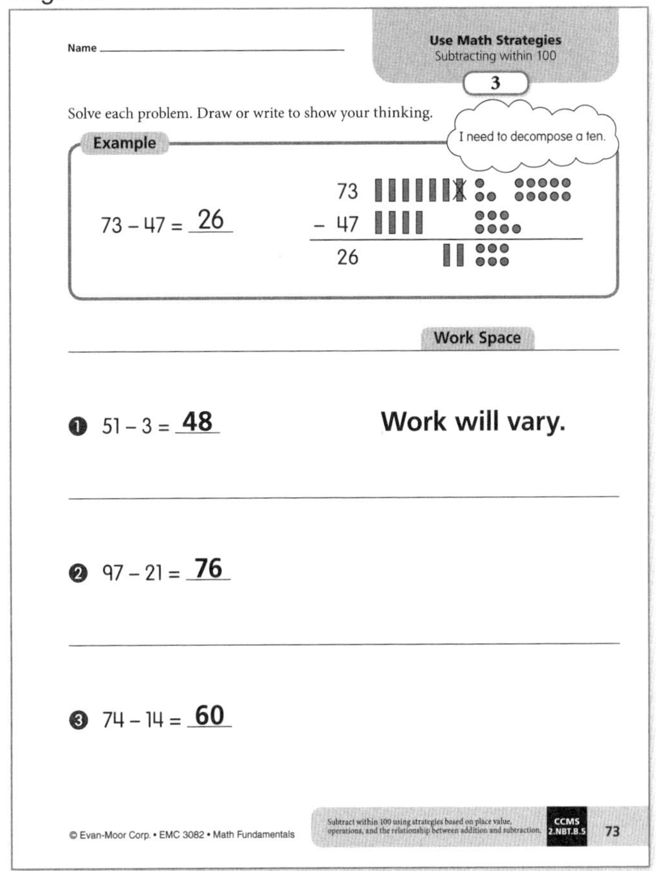

There are many ways to model a problem or to word an explanation. Accept any reasonable answer.

Page 74

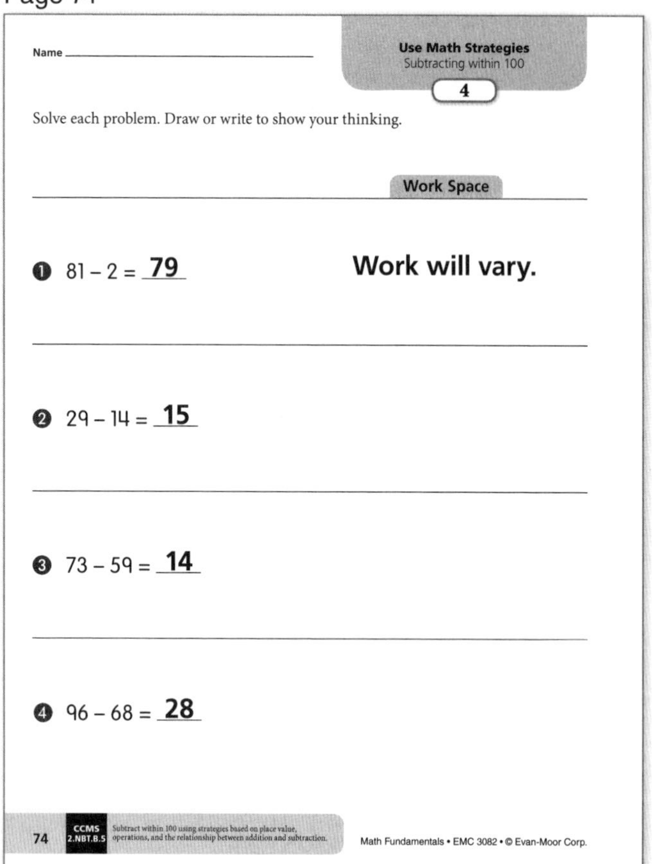

Name ____________

Use Math Strategies
Subtracting within 100
4

Solve each problem. Draw or write to show your thinking.

Work Space

❶ 81 – 2 = **79**

Work will vary.

❷ 29 – 14 = **15**

❸ 73 – 59 = **14**

❹ 96 – 68 = **28**

Page 75

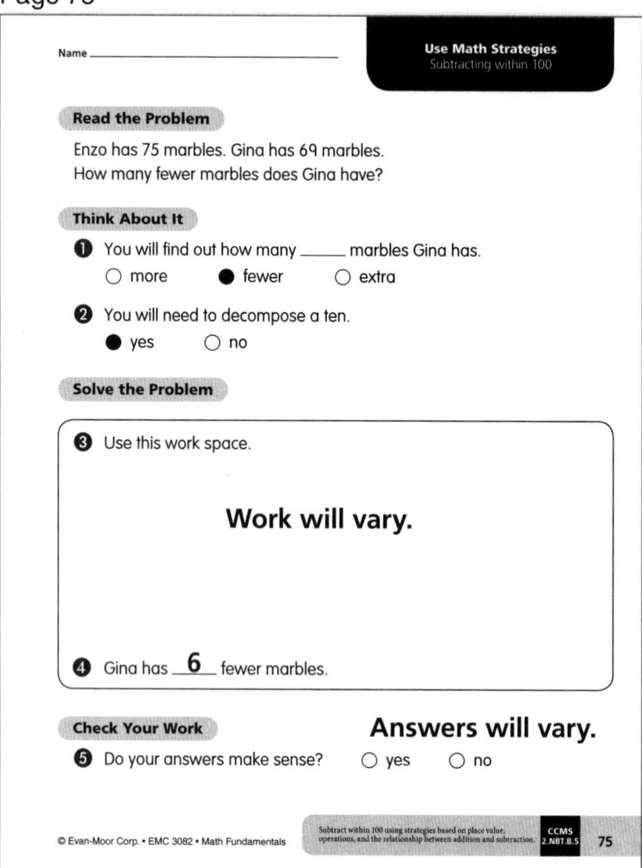

Name ____________

Use Math Strategies
Subtracting within 100

Read the Problem

Enzo has 75 marbles. Gina has 69 marbles.
How many fewer marbles does Gina have?

Think About It

❶ You will find out how many _____ marbles Gina has.
○ more ● fewer ○ extra

❷ You will need to decompose a ten.
● yes ○ no

Solve the Problem

❸ Use this work space.

Work will vary.

❹ Gina has **6** fewer marbles.

Check Your Work

Answers will vary.

❺ Do your answers make sense? ○ yes ○ no

Page 77

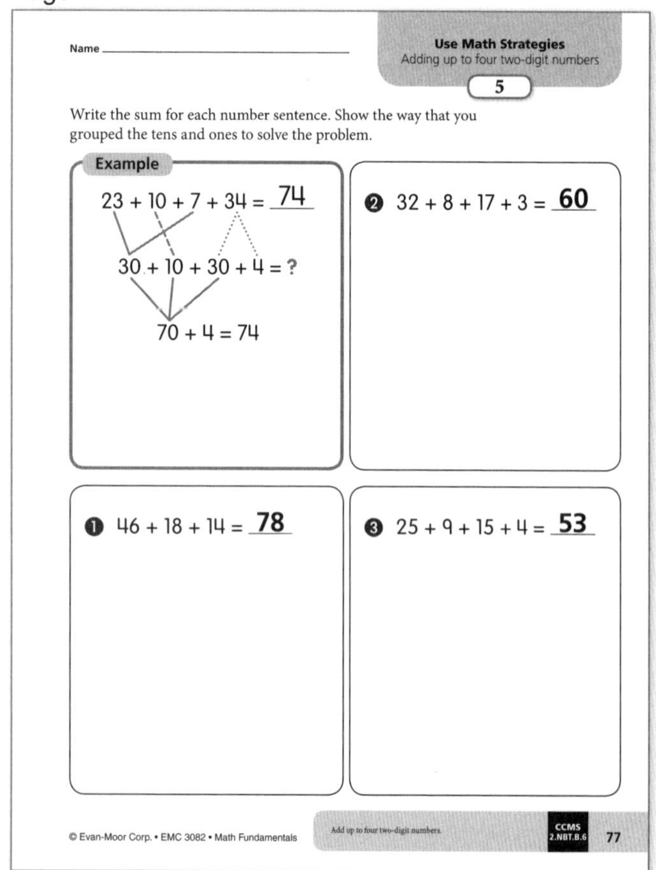

Name ____________

Use Math Strategies
Adding up to four two-digit numbers
5

Write the sum for each number sentence. Show the way that you grouped the tens and ones to solve the problem.

Example

23 + 10 + 7 + 34 = 74
30 + 10 + 30 + 4 = ?
70 + 4 = 74

❷ 32 + 8 + 17 + 3 = **60**

❶ 46 + 18 + 14 = **78**

❸ 25 + 9 + 15 + 4 = **53**

Page 78

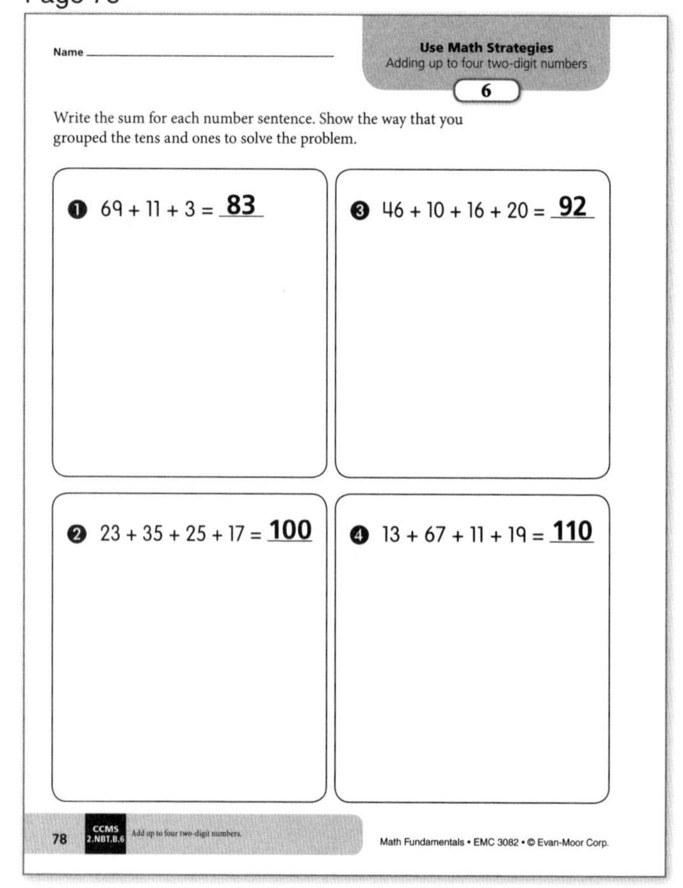

Name ____________

Use Math Strategies
Adding up to four two-digit numbers
6

Write the sum for each number sentence. Show the way that you grouped the tens and ones to solve the problem.

❶ 69 + 11 + 3 = **83**

❸ 46 + 10 + 16 + 20 = **92**

❷ 23 + 35 + 25 + 17 = **100**

❹ 13 + 67 + 11 + 19 = **110**

There are many ways to model a problem or to word an explanation. Accept any reasonable answer.

Page 79

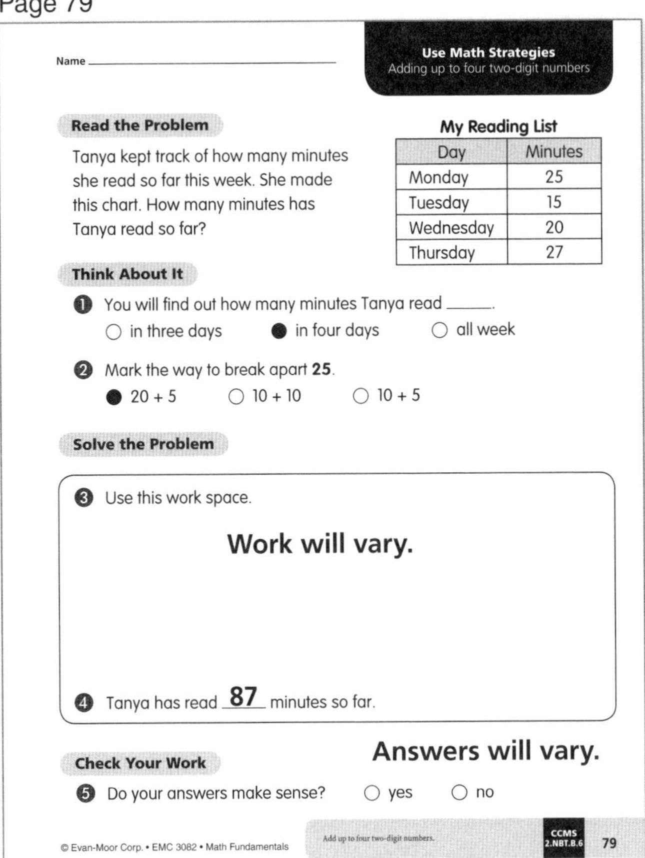
Name ______

Use Math Strategies
Adding up to four two-digit numbers

Read the Problem

Tanya kept track of how many minutes she read so far this week. She made this chart. How many minutes has Tanya read so far?

My Reading List

Day	Minutes
Monday	25
Tuesday	15
Wednesday	20
Thursday	27

Think About It

1. You will find out how many minutes Tanya read ______.
   ○ in three days ● in four days ○ all week
2. Mark the way to break apart **25**.
   ● 20 + 5 ○ 10 + 10 ○ 10 + 5

Solve the Problem

3. Use this work space.
   Work will vary.
4. Tanya has read **87** minutes so far.

Check Your Work **Answers will vary.**

5. Do your answers make sense? ○ yes ○ no

© Evan-Moor Corp. • EMC 3082 • Math Fundamentals · Add up to four two-digit numbers. · CCMS 2.NBT.B.6 · 79

Page 81

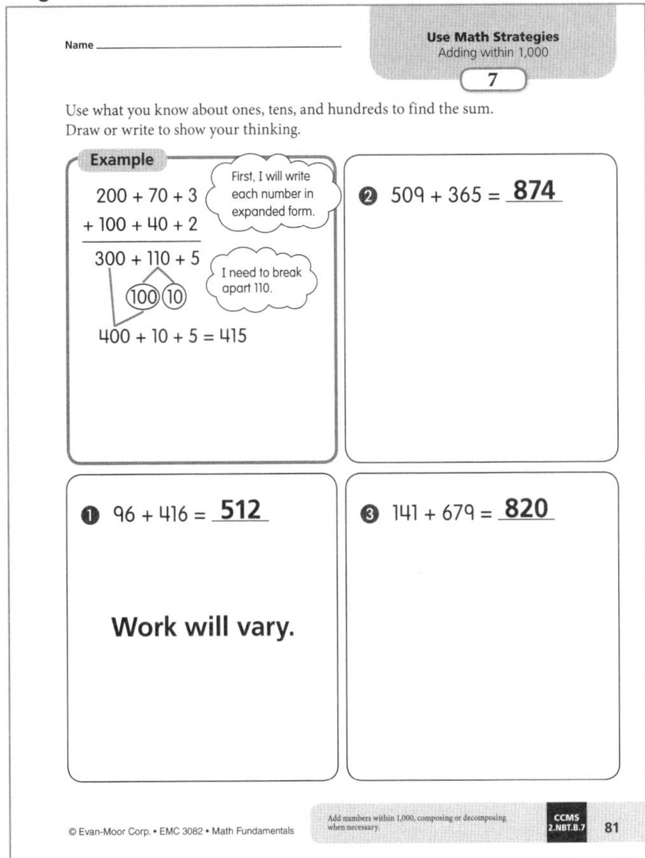
Name ______

Use Math Strategies
Adding within 1,000
7

Use what you know about ones, tens, and hundreds to find the sum. Draw or write to show your thinking.

Example

200 + 70 + 3
+ 100 + 40 + 2
300 + 110 + 5
(100)(10)
400 + 10 + 5 = 415

First, I will write each number in expanded form.
I need to break apart 110.

1. 96 + 416 = **512**
2. 509 + 365 = **874**
3. 141 + 679 = **820**

Work will vary.

© Evan-Moor Corp. • EMC 3082 • Math Fundamentals · Add numbers within 1,000, composing or decomposing when necessary. · CCMS 2.NBT.B.7 · 81

Page 82

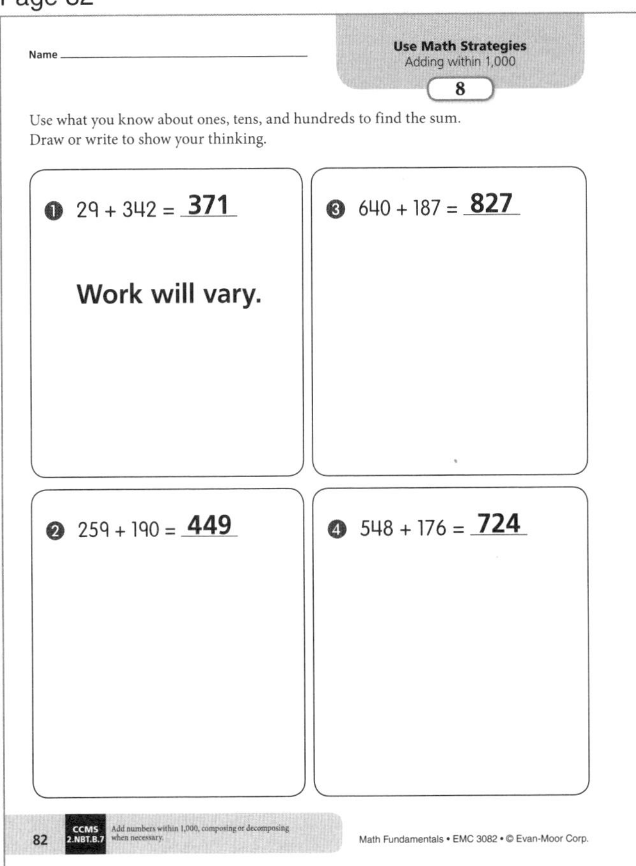
Name ______

Use Math Strategies
Adding within 1,000
8

Use what you know about ones, tens, and hundreds to find the sum. Draw or write to show your thinking.

1. 29 + 342 = **371**
2. 259 + 190 = **449**
3. 640 + 187 = **827**
4. 548 + 176 = **724**

Work will vary.

82 · CCMS 2.NBT.B.7 · Add numbers within 1,000, composing or decomposing when necessary. · Math Fundamentals • EMC 3082 • © Evan-Moor Corp.

Page 83

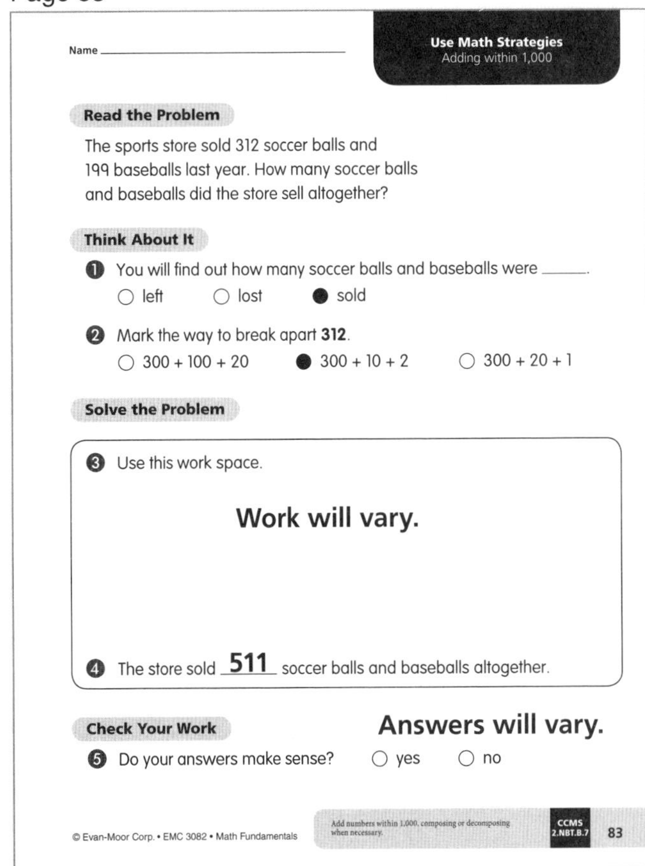
Name ______

Use Math Strategies
Adding within 1,000

Read the Problem

The sports store sold 312 soccer balls and 199 baseballs last year. How many soccer balls and baseballs did the store sell altogether?

Think About It

1. You will find out how many soccer balls and baseballs were ______.
   ○ left ○ lost ● sold
2. Mark the way to break apart **312**.
   ○ 300 + 100 + 20 ● 300 + 10 + 2 ○ 300 + 20 + 1

Solve the Problem

3. Use this work space.
   Work will vary.
4. The store sold **511** soccer balls and baseballs altogether.

Check Your Work **Answers will vary.**

5. Do your answers make sense? ○ yes ○ no

© Evan-Moor Corp. • EMC 3082 • Math Fundamentals · Add numbers within 1,000, composing or decomposing when necessary. · CCMS 2.NBT.B.7 · 83

There are many ways to model a problem or to word an explanation. Accept any reasonable answer.

Page 85

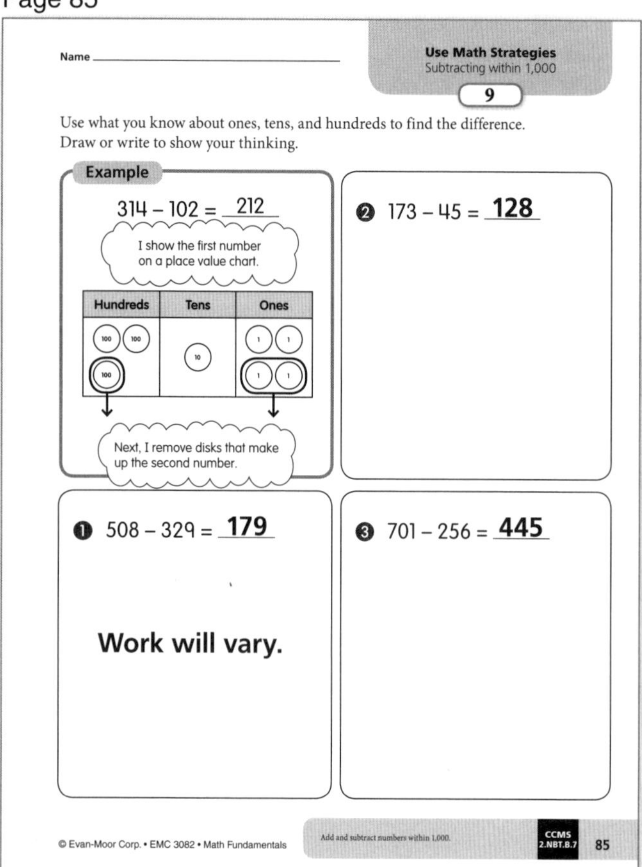

Name ______________________

Use Math Strategies
Subtracting within 1,000
9

Use what you know about ones, tens, and hundreds to find the difference.
Draw or write to show your thinking.

Example

314 – 102 = 212

I show the first number on a place value chart.
Hundreds
Tens
Ones
100
10
1
Next, I remove disks that make up the second number.

❶ 508 – 329 = **179**

❷ 173 – 45 = **128**

❸ 701 – 256 = **445**

Work will vary.

© Evan-Moor Corp. • EMC 3082 • Math Fundamentals | Add and subtract numbers within 1,000. | CCMS 2.NBT.B.7 | 85

Page 86

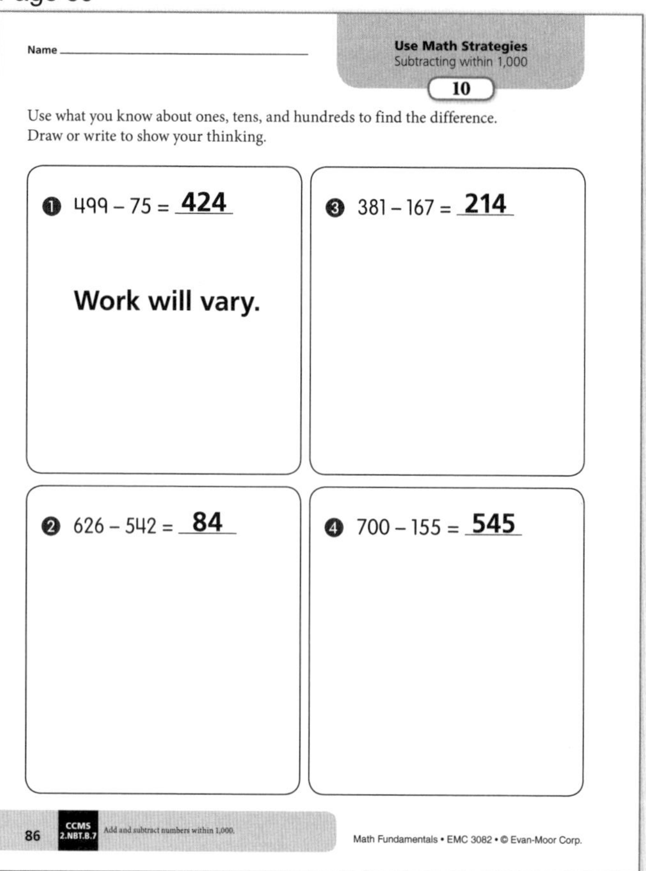

Name ______________________

Use Math Strategies
Subtracting within 1,000
10

Use what you know about ones, tens, and hundreds to find the difference.
Draw or write to show your thinking.

❶ 499 – 75 = **424**

Work will vary.

❷ 626 – 542 = **84**

❸ 381 – 167 = **214**

❹ 700 – 155 = **545**

86 | CCMS 2.NBT.B.7 | Add and subtract numbers within 1,000. | Math Fundamentals • EMC 3082 • © Evan-Moor Corp.

Page 87

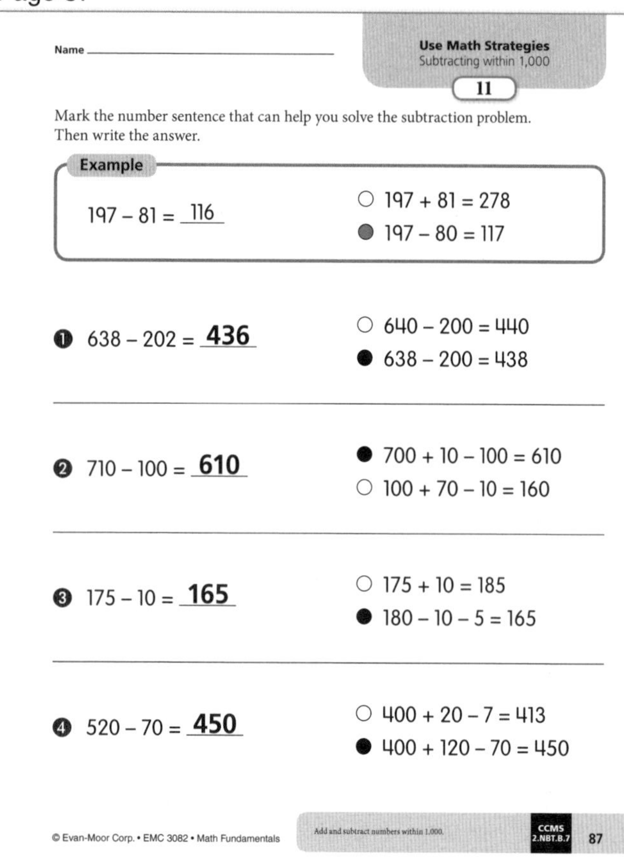

Name ______________________

Use Math Strategies
Subtracting within 1,000
11

Mark the number sentence that can help you solve the subtraction problem.
Then write the answer.

Example

197 – 81 = 116
- ○ 197 + 81 = 278
- ● 197 – 80 = 117

❶ 638 – 202 = **436**
- ○ 640 – 200 = 440
- ● 638 – 200 = 438

❷ 710 – 100 = **610**
- ● 700 + 10 – 100 = 610
- ○ 100 + 70 – 10 = 160

❸ 175 – 10 = **165**
- ○ 175 + 10 = 185
- ● 180 – 10 – 5 = 165

❹ 520 – 70 = **450**
- ○ 400 + 20 – 7 = 413
- ● 400 + 120 – 70 = 450

© Evan-Moor Corp. • EMC 3082 • Math Fundamentals | Add and subtract numbers within 1,000. | CCMS 2.NBT.B.7 | 87

Page 88

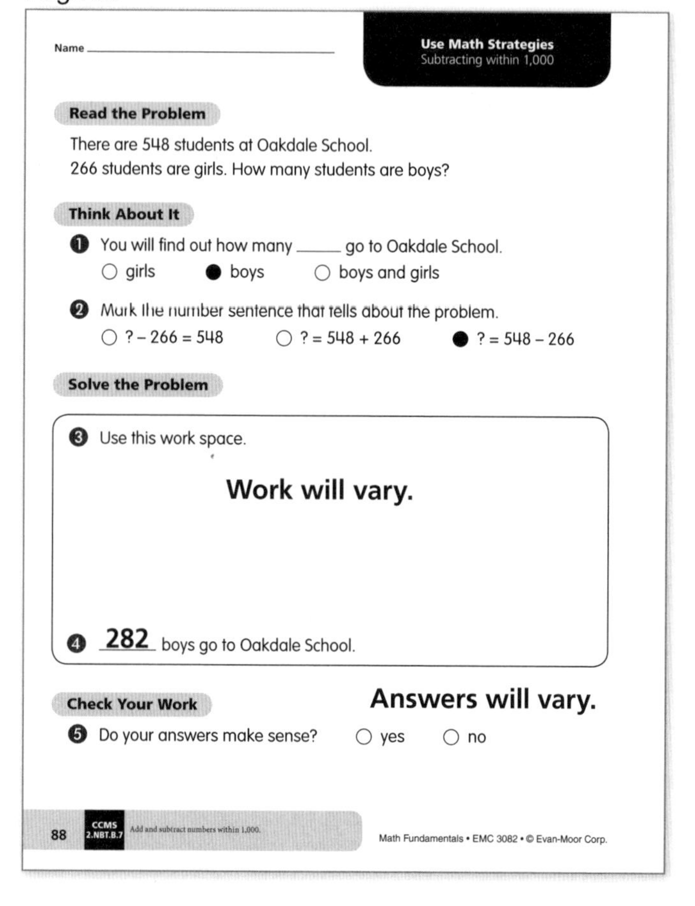

Name ______________________

Use Math Strategies
Subtracting within 1,000

Read the Problem

There are 548 students at Oakdale School.
266 students are girls. How many students are boys?

Think About It

❶ You will find out how many _____ go to Oakdale School.
○ girls ● boys ○ boys and girls

❷ Mark the number sentence that tells about the problem.
○ ? – 266 = 548 ○ ? = 548 + 266 ● ? = 548 – 266

Solve the Problem

❸ Use this work space.

Work will vary.

❹ **282** boys go to Oakdale School.

Check Your Work

❺ Do your answers make sense? ○ yes ○ no

Answers will vary.

88 | CCMS 2.NBT.B.7 | Add and subtract numbers within 1,000. | Math Fundamentals • EMC 3082 • © Evan-Moor Corp.

There are many ways to model a problem or to word an explanation. Accept any reasonable answer.

Page 90

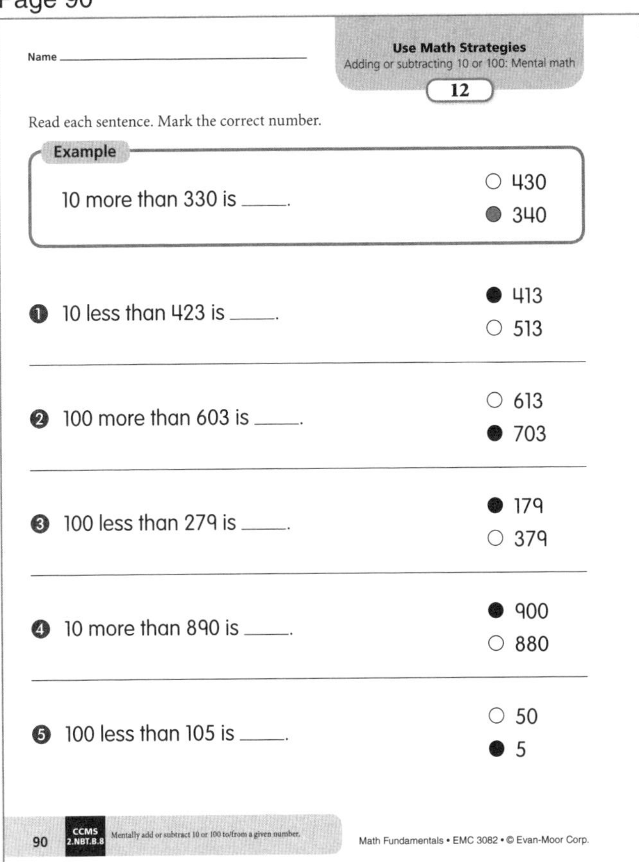

Name ____________

Use Math Strategies
Adding or subtracting 10 or 100: Mental math
12

Read each sentence. Mark the correct number.

Example

10 more than 330 is ____. ○ 430 ● 340

❶ 10 less than 423 is ____. ● 413 ○ 513

❷ 100 more than 603 is ____. ○ 613 ● 703

❸ 100 less than 279 is ____. ● 179 ○ 379

❹ 10 more than 890 is ____. ● 900 ○ 880

❺ 100 less than 105 is ____. ○ 50 ● 5

90 CCMS 2.NBT.B.8 Mentally add or subtract 10 or 100 to/from a given number.   Math Fundamentals • EMC 3082 • © Evan-Moor Corp.

Page 91

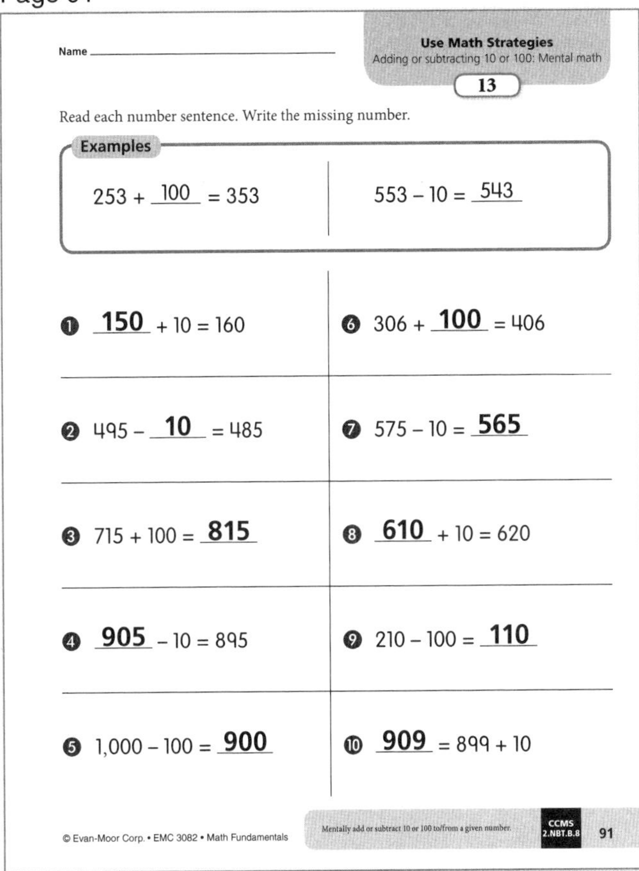

Name ____________

Use Math Strategies
Adding or subtracting 10 or 100: Mental math
13

Read each number sentence. Write the missing number.

Examples

253 + 100 = 353 | 553 − 10 = 543

❶ **150** + 10 = 160

❷ 495 − **10** = 485

❸ 715 + 100 = **815**

❹ **905** − 10 = 895

❺ 1,000 − 100 = **900**

❻ 306 + **100** = 406

❼ 575 − 10 = **565**

❽ **610** + 10 = 620

❾ 210 − 100 = **110**

❿ **909** = 899 + 10

© Evan-Moor Corp. • EMC 3082 • Math Fundamentals   Mentally add or subtract 10 or 100 to/from a given number. CCMS 2.NBT.B.8 91

Page 92

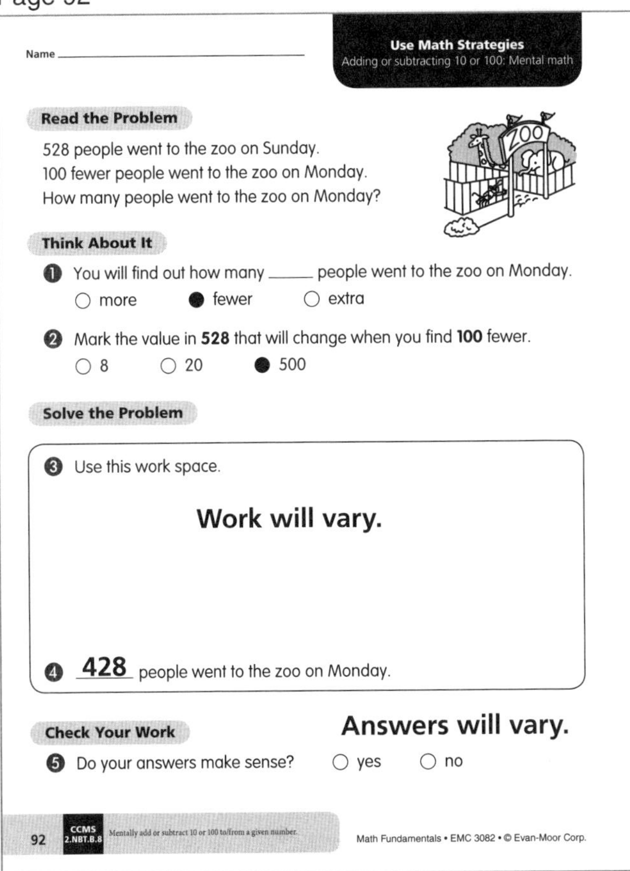

Name ____________

Use Math Strategies
Adding or subtracting 10 or 100: Mental math

Read the Problem

528 people went to the zoo on Sunday.
100 fewer people went to the zoo on Monday.
How many people went to the zoo on Monday?

Think About It

❶ You will find out how many ____ people went to the zoo on Monday.
○ more ● fewer ○ extra

❷ Mark the value in **528** that will change when you find **100** fewer.
○ 8 ○ 20 ● 500

Solve the Problem

❸ Use this work space.

Work will vary.

❹ **428** people went to the zoo on Monday.

Check Your Work

Answers will vary.

❺ Do your answers make sense? ○ yes ○ no

92 CCMS 2.NBT.B.8 Mentally add or subtract 10 or 100 to/from a given number.   Math Fundamentals • EMC 3082 • © Evan-Moor Corp.

Page 94

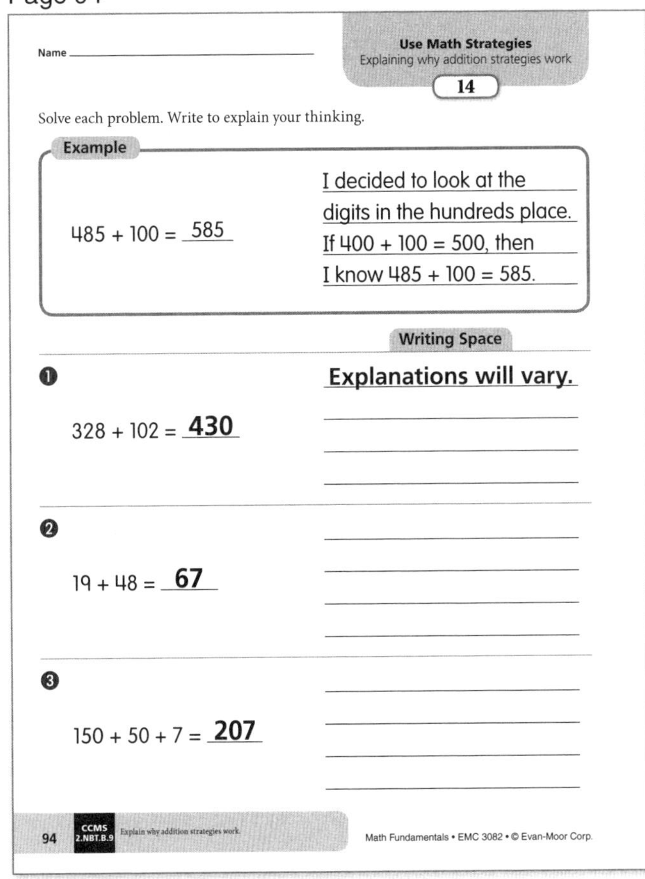

Name ____________

Use Math Strategies
Explaining why addition strategies work
14

Solve each problem. Write to explain your thinking.

Example

485 + 100 = 585

I decided to look at the digits in the hundreds place. If 400 + 100 = 500, then I know 485 + 100 = 585.

Writing Space

❶ 328 + 102 = **430**

Explanations will vary.

❷ 19 + 48 = **67**

❸ 150 + 50 + 7 = **207**

94 CCMS 2.NBT.B.9 Explain why addition strategies work.   Math Fundamentals • EMC 3082 • © Evan-Moor Corp.

There are many ways to model a problem or to word an explanation. Accept any reasonable answer.

Page 95

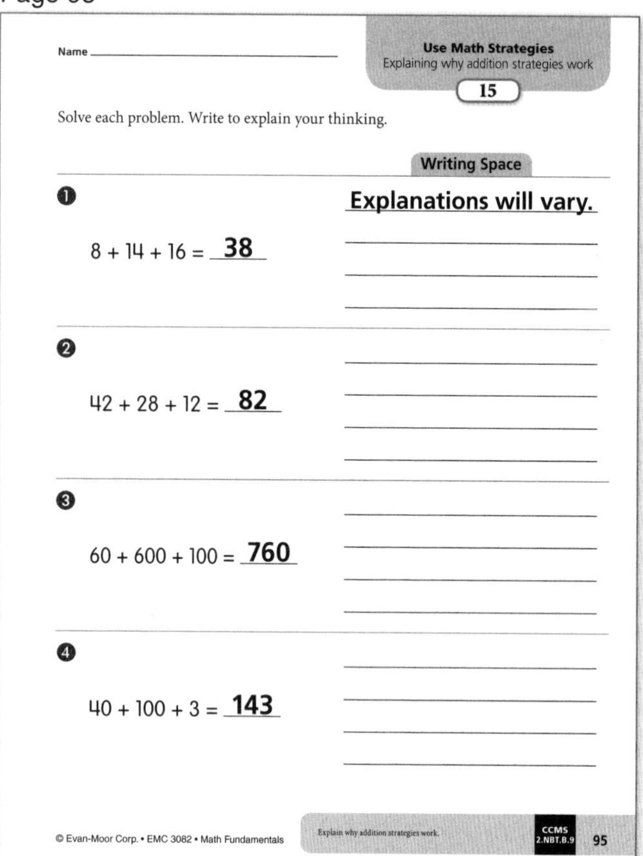

Name ____________

Use Math Strategies
Explaining why addition strategies work
15

Solve each problem. Write to explain your thinking.

Writing Space

1. 8 + 14 + 16 = **38** — **Explanations will vary.**
2. 42 + 28 + 12 = **82**
3. 60 + 600 + 100 = **760**
4. 40 + 100 + 3 = **143**

© Evan-Moor Corp. • EMC 3082 • Math Fundamentals — Explain why addition strategies work. — CCMS 2.NBT.B.9 — 95

Page 96

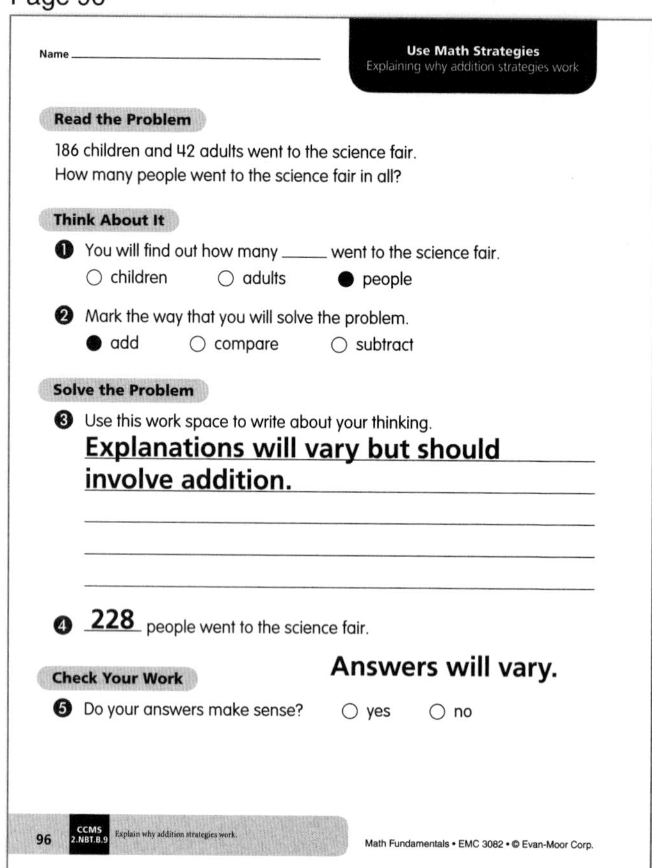

Name ____________

Use Math Strategies
Explaining why addition strategies work

Read the Problem

186 children and 42 adults went to the science fair.
How many people went to the science fair in all?

Think About It

1. You will find out how many _____ went to the science fair.
   ○ children ○ adults ● people
2. Mark the way that you will solve the problem.
   ● add ○ compare ○ subtract

Solve the Problem

3. Use this work space to write about your thinking.
   Explanations will vary but should involve addition.
4. **228** people went to the science fair.

Check Your Work — **Answers will vary.**

5. Do your answers make sense? ○ yes ○ no

96 — CCMS 2.NBT.B.9 — Explain why addition strategies work. — Math Fundamentals • EMC 3082 • © Evan-Moor Corp.

Page 98

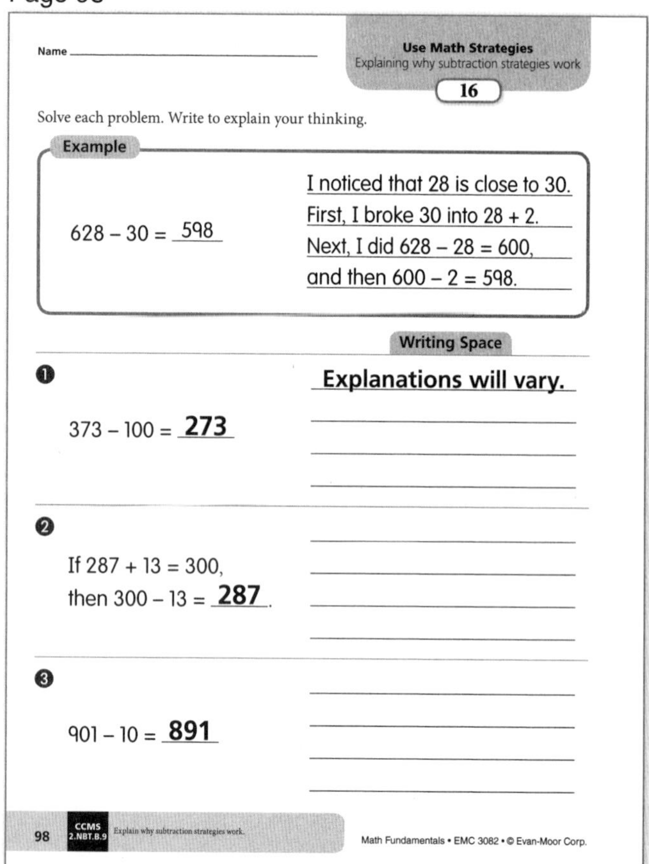

Name ____________

Use Math Strategies
Explaining why subtraction strategies work
16

Solve each problem. Write to explain your thinking.

Example

628 – 30 = 598

I noticed that 28 is close to 30.
First, I broke 30 into 28 + 2.
Next, I did 628 – 28 = 600,
and then 600 – 2 = 598.

Writing Space

1. 373 – 100 = **273** — **Explanations will vary.**
2. If 287 + 13 = 300,
   then 300 – 13 = **287**.
3. 901 – 10 = **891**

98 — CCMS 2.NBT.B.9 — Explain why subtraction strategies work. — Math Fundamentals • EMC 3082 • © Evan-Moor Corp.

Page 99

Name ____________

Use Math Strategies
Explaining why subtraction strategies work
17

Solve each problem. Write to explain your thinking.

Writing Space

1. 482 – 79 = **403** — **Explanations will vary.**
2. 316 – 100 = **216**
3. If 950 + 50 = 1,000,
   then 1,000 – 50 = **950**.
4. 601 – 10 = **591**

© Evan-Moor Corp. • EMC 3082 • Math Fundamentals — Explain why subtraction strategies work. — CCMS 2.NBT.B.9 — 99

There are many ways to model a problem or to word an explanation. Accept any reasonable answer.

Page 100

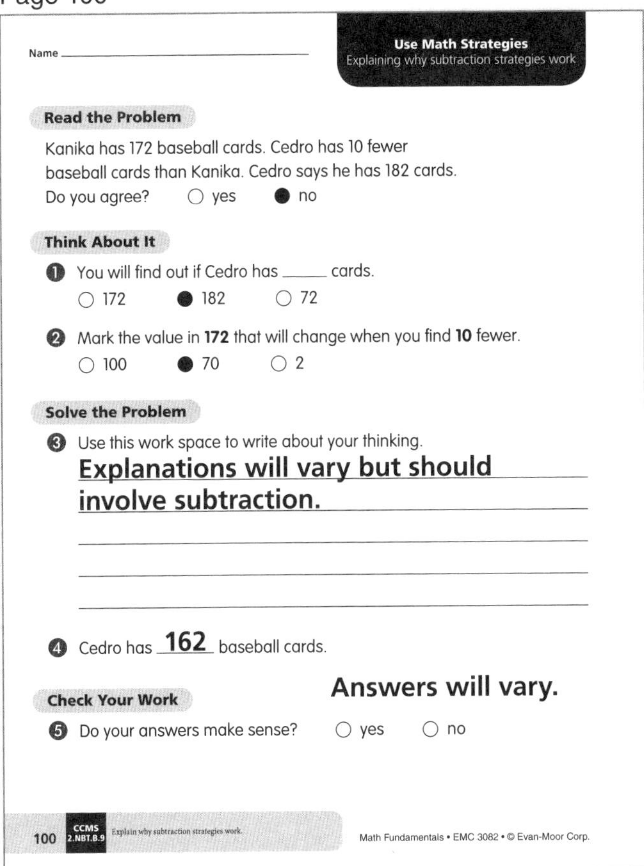

Name ______

Use Math Strategies
Explaining why subtraction strategies work

Read the Problem

Kanika has 172 baseball cards. Cedro has 10 fewer baseball cards than Kanika. Cedro says he has 182 cards. Do you agree? ○ yes ● no

Think About It

1. You will find out if Cedro has ____ cards.
   ○ 172 ● 182 ○ 72
2. Mark the value in **172** that will change when you find **10** fewer.
   ○ 100 ● 70 ○ 2

Solve the Problem

3. Use this work space to write about your thinking.
   Explanations will vary but should involve subtraction.
4. Cedro has **162** baseball cards.

Check Your Work

Answers will vary.

5. Do your answers make sense? ○ yes ○ no

100 CCMS 2.NBT.B.9 Explain why subtraction strategies work. Math Fundamentals • EMC 3082 • © Evan-Moor Corp.

Page 103

Name ______

Measure and Estimate Length
Measuring length in customary units

1

Mark the length that makes sense for each object.

Example

1 2 3 4 5 6 7 8

○ 5 inches ● 7 inches ○ 8 inches

1. 1 2 3 4
   ● 2 feet ○ 3 feet ○ 4 feet
2. 1 2 3 4 5 6 7 8 9 10 11 12 13 14 15 16 17 18
   ○ 16 inches ○ 11 inches ● 14 inches
3. 1 yard 1 yard 1 yard 1 yard 1 yard 1 yard
   ○ 5 yards ● 4 yards ○ 3 yards

© Evan-Moor Corp. • EMC 3082 • Math Fundamentals Select and use appropriate tool to measure the length of an object. CCMS 2.MD.A.1 103

Page 104

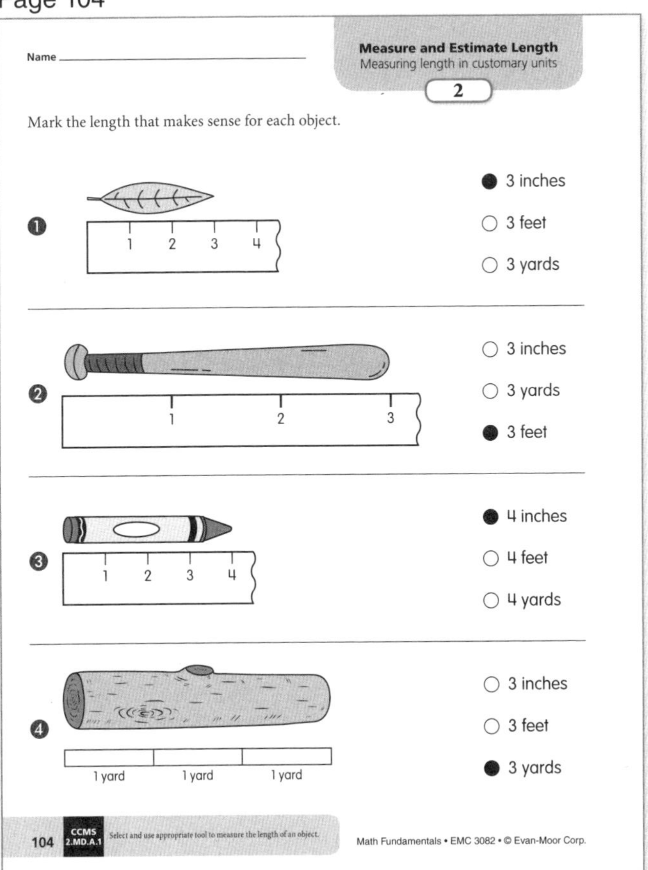

Name ______

Measure and Estimate Length
Measuring length in customary units

2

Mark the length that makes sense for each object.

1. 1 2 3 4
   ● 3 inches ○ 3 feet ○ 3 yards
2. 1 2 3
   ○ 3 inches ○ 3 yards ● 3 feet
3. 1 2 3 4
   ● 4 inches ○ 4 feet ○ 4 yards
4. 1 yard 1 yard 1 yard
   ○ 3 inches ○ 3 feet ● 3 yards

104 CCMS 2.MD.A.1 Select and use appropriate tool to measure the length of an object. Math Fundamentals • EMC 3082 • © Evan-Moor Corp.

Page 105

Name ______

Measure and Estimate Length
Measuring length in customary units

Read the Problem

Jon measured these two plants. He measured one with an inch ruler and one with a centimeter ruler. He thinks the second plant is taller because the number is bigger. Do you agree? Measure the first plant in inches and the second plant in centimeters. Then explain your thinking below.

Think About It

1. You will find out if the second plant's measurement is ____ the first plant's.
   ○ smaller than ● larger than ○ the same as
2. You will need to know that centimeters are ____ inches.
   ● smaller than ○ larger than ○ the same as

Solve the Problem

3. Measure the plants. Explain your thinking.
   2 inches, 5 centimeters
   Explanations will vary.
4. I agree that the second plant is taller. ○ yes ● no

Check Your Work

Answers will vary.

5. Do your answers make sense? ○ yes ○ no

© Evan-Moor Corp. • EMC 3082 • Math Fundamentals Describe how two measurements relate to the size of the unit chosen. CCMS 2.MD.A.2 105

There are many ways to model a problem or to word an explanation. Accept any reasonable answer.

Page 107

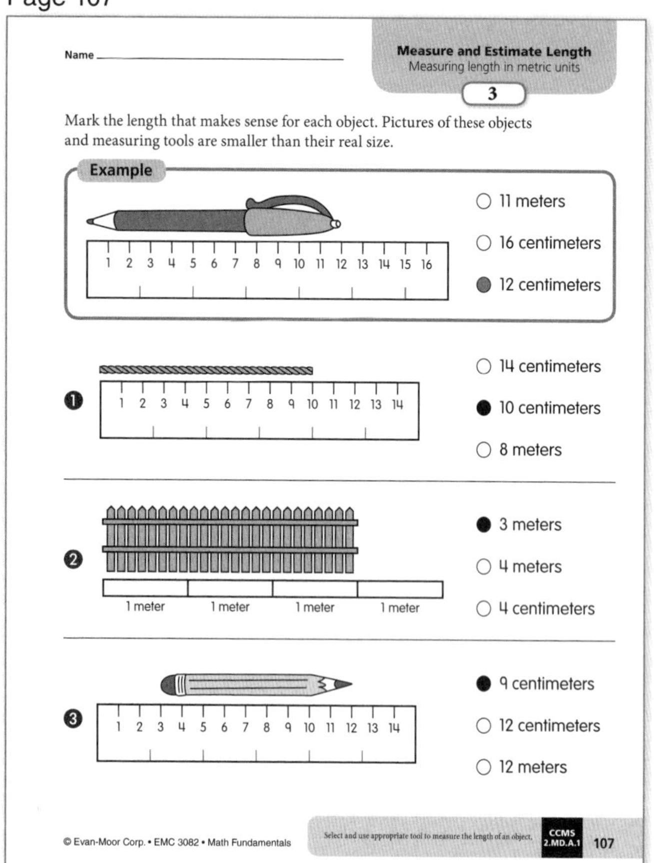
Name ____________

Measure and Estimate Length
Measuring length in metric units
3

Mark the length that makes sense for each object. Pictures of these objects and measuring tools are smaller than their real size.

Example
○ 11 meters
○ 16 centimeters
● 12 centimeters

1.
○ 14 centimeters
● 10 centimeters
○ 8 meters

2.
● 3 meters
○ 4 meters
○ 4 centimeters

3.
● 9 centimeters
○ 12 centimeters
○ 12 meters

© Evan-Moor Corp. • EMC 3082 • Math Fundamentals
Select and use appropriate tool to measure the length of an object. CCMS 2.MD.A.1 107

Page 108

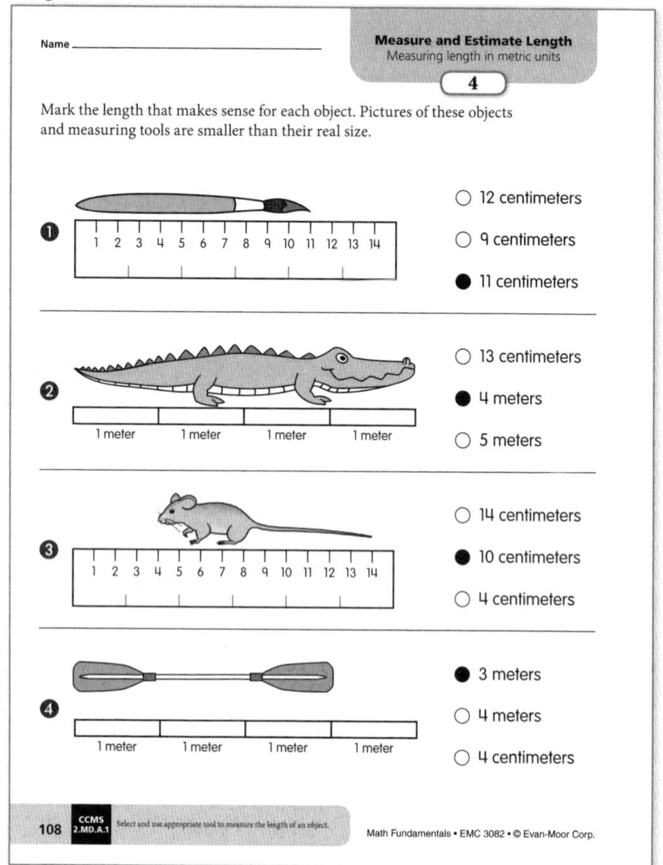
Name ____________

Measure and Estimate Length
Measuring length in metric units
4

Mark the length that makes sense for each object. Pictures of these objects and measuring tools are smaller than their real size.

1.
○ 12 centimeters
○ 9 centimeters
● 11 centimeters

2.
○ 13 centimeters
● 4 meters
○ 5 meters

3.
○ 14 centimeters
● 10 centimeters
○ 4 centimeters

4.
● 3 meters
○ 4 meters
○ 4 centimeters

108 CCMS 2.MD.A.1 Select and use appropriate tool to measure the length of an object.
Math Fundamentals • EMC 3082 • © Evan-Moor Corp.

Page 109

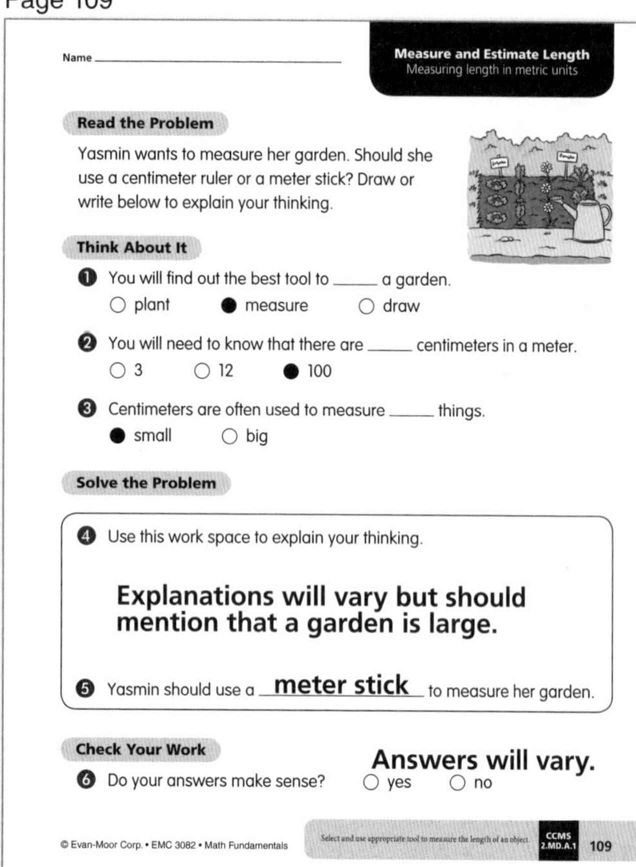
Name ____________

Measure and Estimate Length
Measuring length in metric units

Read the Problem

Yasmin wants to measure her garden. Should she use a centimeter ruler or a meter stick? Draw or write below to explain your thinking.

Think About It

1. You will find out the best tool to ____ a garden.
○ plant ● measure ○ draw

2. You will need to know that there are ____ centimeters in a meter.
○ 3 ○ 12 ● 100

3. Centimeters are often used to measure ____ things.
● small ○ big

Solve the Problem

4. Use this work space to explain your thinking.

Explanations will vary but should mention that a garden is large.

5. Yasmin should use a **meter stick** to measure her garden.

Check Your Work

6. Do your answers make sense? ○ yes ○ no
Answers will vary.

© Evan-Moor Corp. • EMC 3082 • Math Fundamentals
Select and use appropriate tool to measure the length of an object. CCMS 2.MD.A.1 109

Page 111

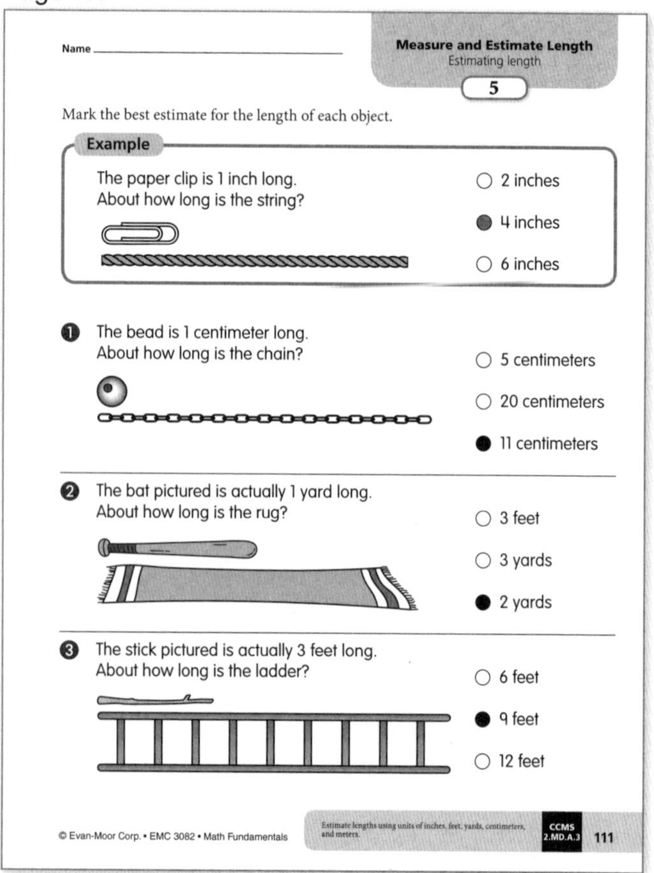
Name ____________

Measure and Estimate Length
Estimating length
5

Mark the best estimate for the length of each object.

Example
The paper clip is 1 inch long.
About how long is the string?
○ 2 inches
● 4 inches
○ 6 inches

1. The bead is 1 centimeter long.
About how long is the chain?
○ 5 centimeters
○ 20 centimeters
● 11 centimeters

2. The bat pictured is actually 1 yard long.
About how long is the rug?
○ 3 feet
○ 3 yards
● 2 yards

3. The stick pictured is actually 3 feet long.
About how long is the ladder?
○ 6 feet
● 9 feet
○ 12 feet

© Evan-Moor Corp. • EMC 3082 • Math Fundamentals
Estimate lengths using units of inches, feet, yards, centimeters, and meters. CCMS 2.MD.A.3 111

There are many ways to model a problem or to word an explanation. Accept any reasonable answer.

Page 112

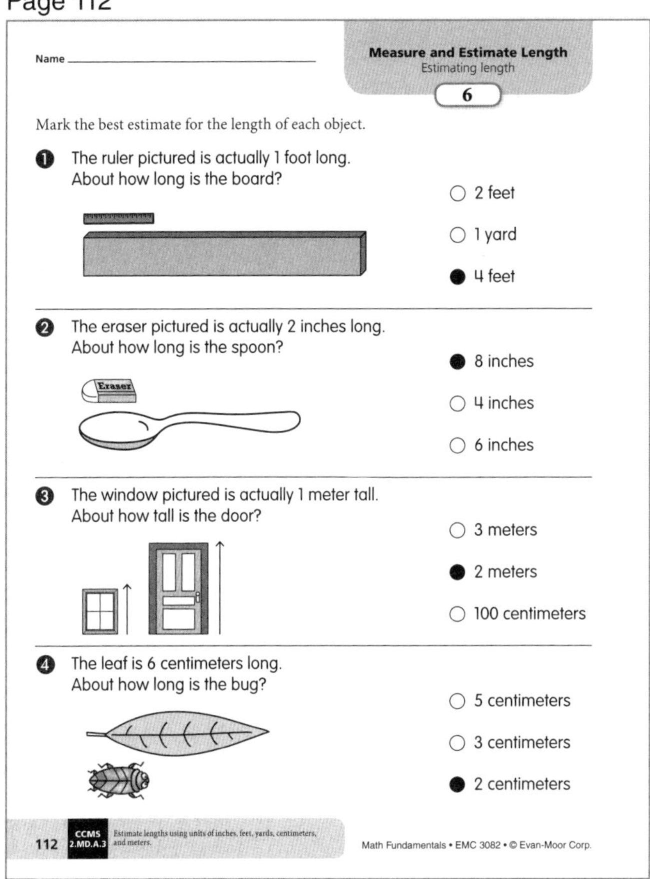

Name ______________________

Measure and Estimate Length
Estimating length
6

Mark the best estimate for the length of each object.

1. The ruler pictured is actually 1 foot long. About how long is the board?
   - ○ 2 feet
   - ○ 1 yard
   - ● 4 feet

2. The eraser pictured is actually 2 inches long. About how long is the spoon?
   - ● 8 inches
   - ○ 4 inches
   - ○ 6 inches

3. The window pictured is actually 1 meter tall. About how tall is the door?
   - ○ 3 meters
   - ● 2 meters
   - ○ 100 centimeters

4. The leaf is 6 centimeters long. About how long is the bug?
   - ○ 5 centimeters
   - ○ 3 centimeters
   - ● 2 centimeters

112 CCMS 2.MD.A.3 Estimate lengths using units of inches, feet, yards, centimeters, and meters. Math Fundamentals • EMC 3082 • © Evan-Moor Corp.

Page 113

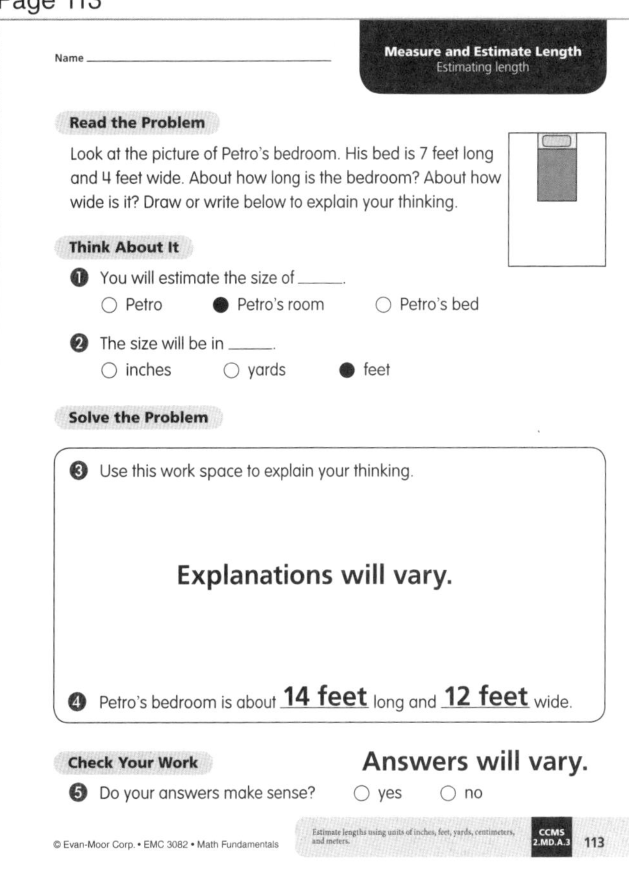

Name ______________________

Measure and Estimate Length
Estimating length

Read the Problem

Look at the picture of Petro's bedroom. His bed is 7 feet long and 4 feet wide. About how long is the bedroom? About how wide is it? Draw or write below to explain your thinking.

Think About It

1. You will estimate the size of ____.
   ○ Petro ● Petro's room ○ Petro's bed

2. The size will be in ____.
   ○ inches ○ yards ● feet

Solve the Problem

3. Use this work space to explain your thinking.

Explanations will vary.

4. Petro's bedroom is about **14 feet** long and **12 feet** wide.

Check Your Work

Answers will vary.

5. Do your answers make sense? ○ yes ○ no

© Evan-Moor Corp. • EMC 3082 • Math Fundamentals Estimate lengths using units of inches, feet, yards, centimeters, and meters. CCMS 2.MD.A.3 113

Page 115

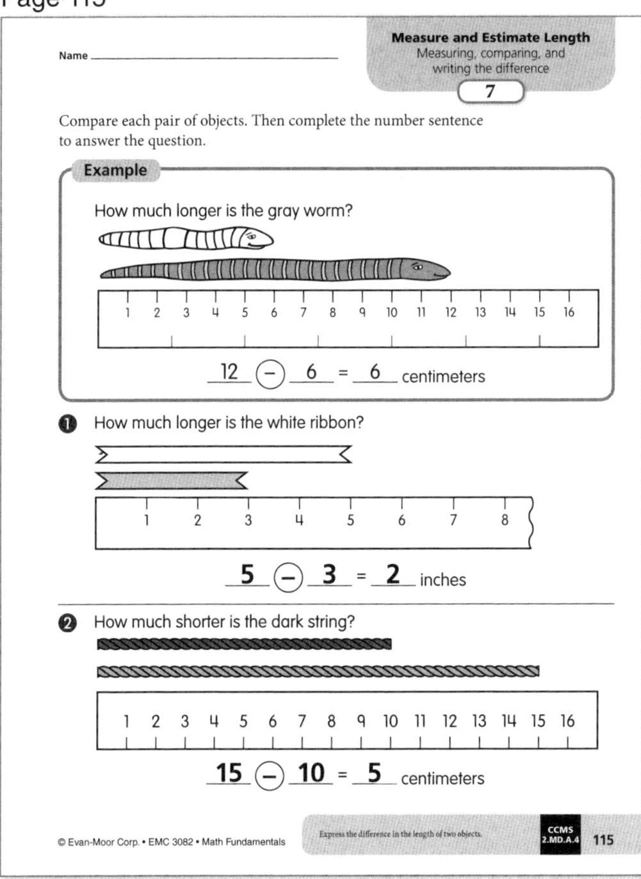

Name ______________________

Measure and Estimate Length
Measuring, comparing, and writing the difference
7

Compare each pair of objects. Then complete the number sentence to answer the question.

Example

How much longer is the gray worm?

12 ⊖ 6 = 6 centimeters

1. How much longer is the white ribbon?

   5 ⊖ **3** = **2** inches

2. How much shorter is the dark string?

   15 ⊖ **10** = **5** centimeters

© Evan-Moor Corp. • EMC 3082 • Math Fundamentals Express the difference in the length of two objects. CCMS 2.MD.A.4 115

Page 116

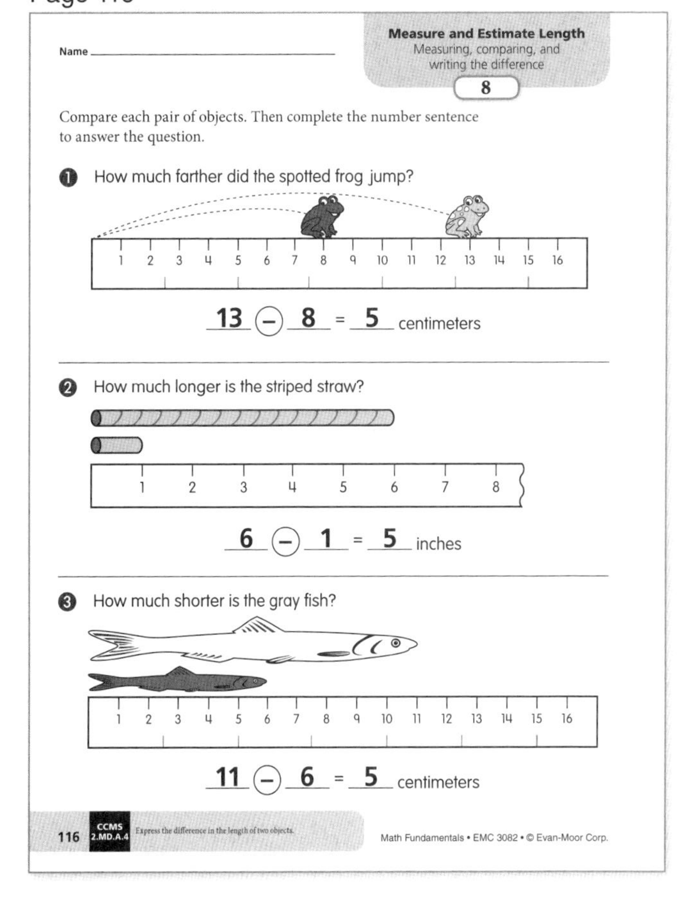

Name ______________________

Measure and Estimate Length
Measuring, comparing, and writing the difference
8

Compare each pair of objects. Then complete the number sentence to answer the question.

1. How much farther did the spotted frog jump?

   13 ⊖ **8** = **5** centimeters

2. How much longer is the striped straw?

   6 ⊖ **1** = **5** inches

3. How much shorter is the gray fish?

   11 ⊖ **6** = **5** centimeters

116 CCMS 2.MD.A.4 Express the difference in the length of two objects. Math Fundamentals • EMC 3082 • © Evan-Moor Corp.

There are many ways to model a problem or to word an explanation. Accept any reasonable answer.

Page 117

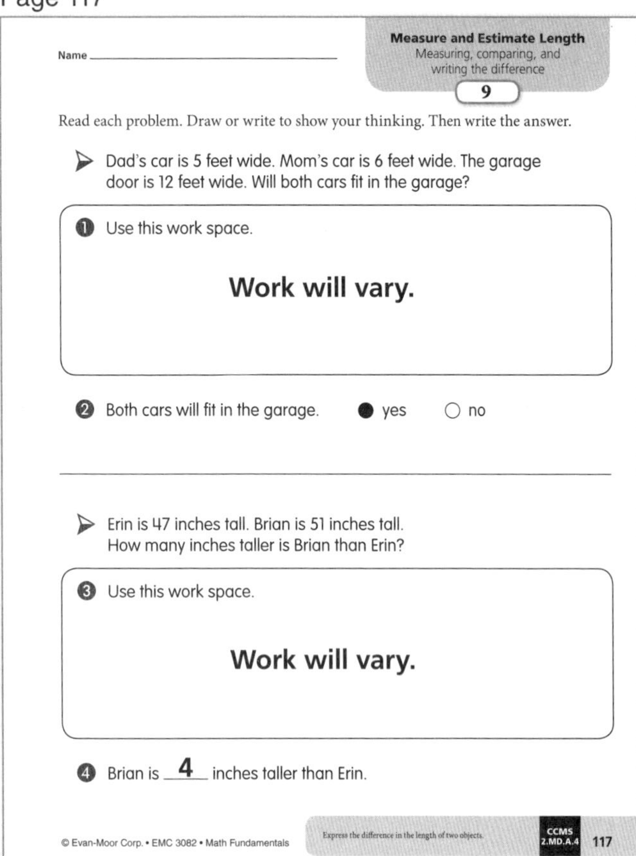

Name ______________________

Measure and Estimate Length
Measuring, comparing, and writing the difference
9

Read each problem. Draw or write to show your thinking. Then write the answer.

➤ Dad's car is 5 feet wide. Mom's car is 6 feet wide. The garage door is 12 feet wide. Will both cars fit in the garage?

1. Use this work space.

Work will vary.

2. Both cars will fit in the garage. ● yes ○ no

➤ Erin is 47 inches tall. Brian is 51 inches tall. How many inches taller is Brian than Erin?

3. Use this work space.

Work will vary.

4. Brian is **4** inches taller than Erin.

© Evan-Moor Corp. • EMC 3082 • Math Fundamentals — Express the difference in the length of two objects. CCMS 2.MD.A.4 — 117

Page 118

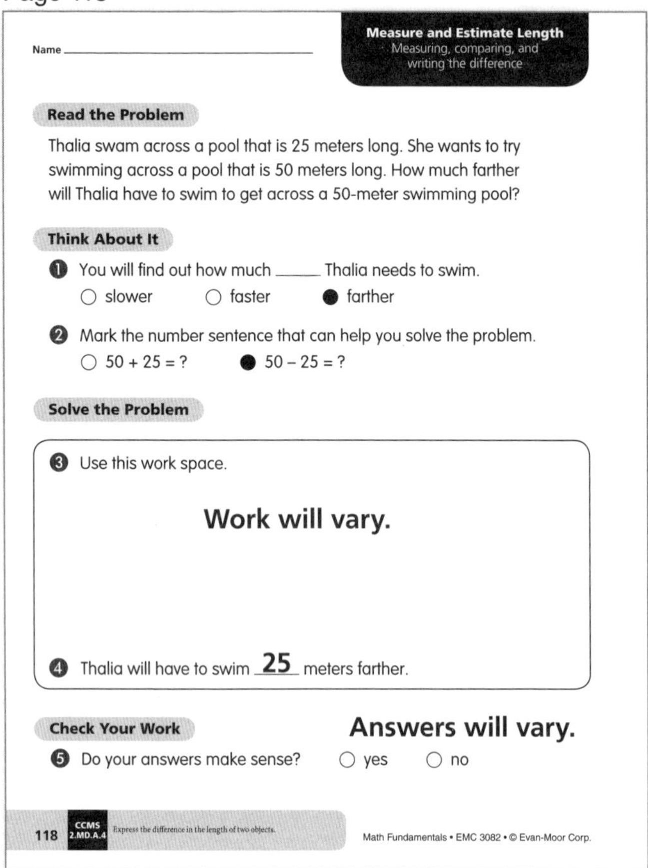

Name ______________________

Measure and Estimate Length
Measuring, comparing, and writing the difference

Read the Problem

Thalia swam across a pool that is 25 meters long. She wants to try swimming across a pool that is 50 meters long. How much farther will Thalia have to swim to get across a 50-meter swimming pool?

Think About It

1. You will find out how much ______ Thalia needs to swim.
○ slower ○ faster ● farther

2. Mark the number sentence that can help you solve the problem.
○ 50 + 25 = ? ● 50 – 25 = ?

Solve the Problem

3. Use this work space.

Work will vary.

4. Thalia will have to swim **25** meters farther.

Check Your Work — **Answers will vary.**

5. Do your answers make sense? ○ yes ○ no

118 — CCMS 2.MD.A.4 — Express the difference in the length of two objects. — Math Fundamentals • EMC 3082 • © Evan-Moor Corp.

Page 121

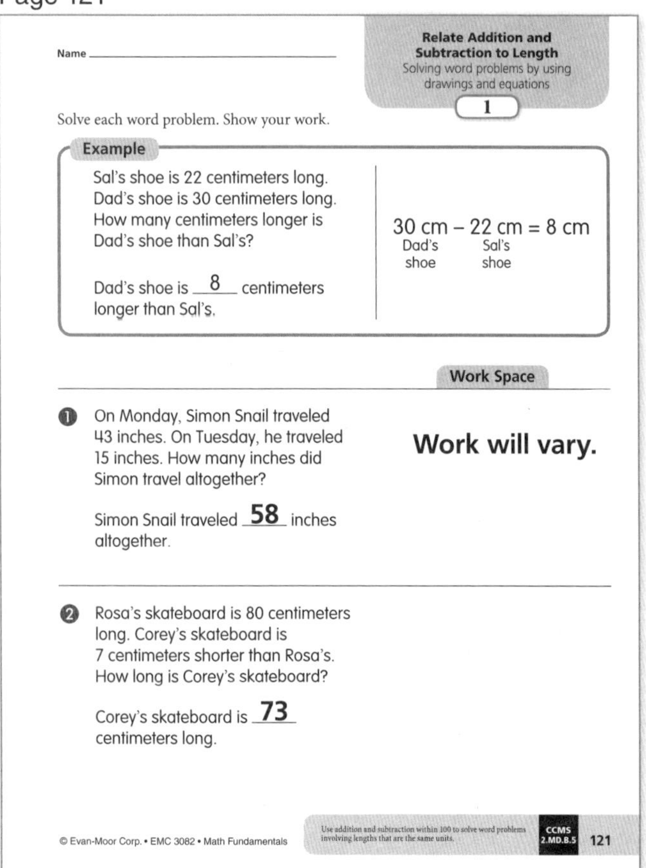

Name ______________________

Relate Addition and Subtraction to Length
Solving word problems by using drawings and equations
1

Solve each word problem. Show your work.

Example

Sal's shoe is 22 centimeters long. Dad's shoe is 30 centimeters long. How many centimeters longer is Dad's shoe than Sal's?

Dad's shoe is 8 centimeters longer than Sal's.

30 cm – 22 cm = 8 cm
(Dad's shoe) (Sal's shoe)

Work Space

1. On Monday, Simon Snail traveled 43 inches. On Tuesday, he traveled 15 inches. How many inches did Simon travel altogether?

Simon Snail traveled **58** inches altogether.

Work will vary.

2. Rosa's skateboard is 80 centimeters long. Corey's skateboard is 7 centimeters shorter than Rosa's. How long is Corey's skateboard?

Corey's skateboard is **73** centimeters long.

© Evan-Moor Corp. • EMC 3082 • Math Fundamentals — Use addition and subtraction within 100 to solve word problems involving lengths that are the same units. CCMS 2.MD.B.5 — 121

Page 122

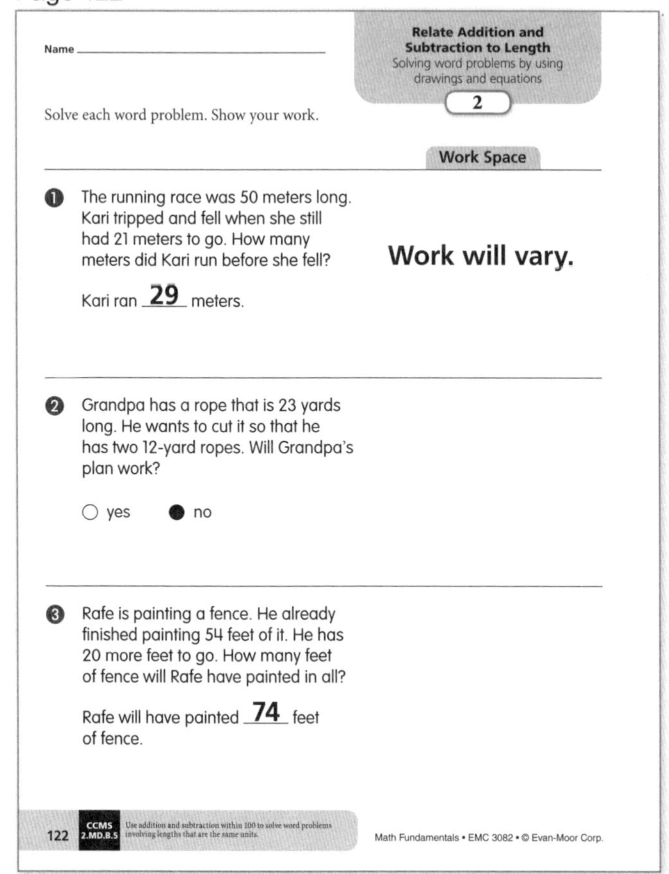

Name ______________________

Relate Addition and Subtraction to Length
Solving word problems by using drawings and equations
2

Solve each word problem. Show your work.

Work Space

1. The running race was 50 meters long. Kari tripped and fell when she still had 21 meters to go. How many meters did Kari run before she fell?

Kari ran **29** meters.

Work will vary.

2. Grandpa has a rope that is 23 yards long. He wants to cut it so that he has two 12-yard ropes. Will Grandpa's plan work?

○ yes ● no

3. Rafe is painting a fence. He already finished painting 54 feet of it. He has 20 more feet to go. How many feet of fence will Rafe have painted in all?

Rafe will have painted **74** feet of fence.

122 — CCMS 2.MD.B.5 — Use addition and subtraction within 100 to solve word problems involving lengths that are the same units. — Math Fundamentals • EMC 3082 • © Evan-Moor Corp.

There are many ways to model a problem or to word an explanation. Accept any reasonable answer.

Page 123

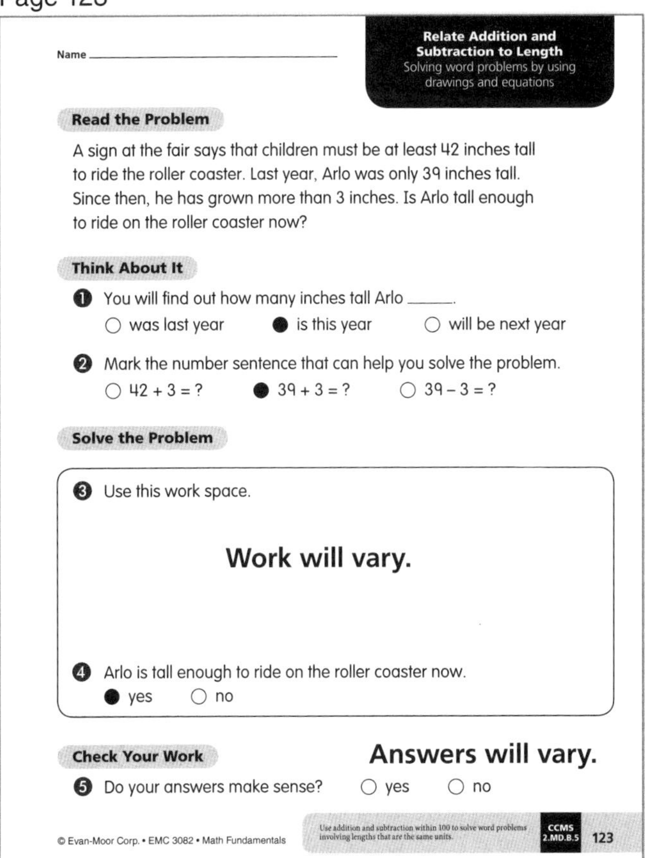

Name ______

Relate Addition and Subtraction to Length
Solving word problems by using drawings and equations

Read the Problem

A sign at the fair says that children must be at least 42 inches tall to ride the roller coaster. Last year, Arlo was only 39 inches tall. Since then, he has grown more than 3 inches. Is Arlo tall enough to ride on the roller coaster now?

Think About It

1. You will find out how many inches tall Arlo ______.
   ○ was last year ● is this year ○ will be next year
2. Mark the number sentence that can help you solve the problem.
   ○ 42 + 3 = ? ● 39 + 3 = ? ○ 39 − 3 = ?

Solve the Problem

3. Use this work space.

Work will vary.

4. Arlo is tall enough to ride on the roller coaster now.
   ● yes ○ no

Check Your Work **Answers will vary.**

5. Do your answers make sense? ○ yes ○ no

© Evan-Moor Corp. • EMC 3082 • Math Fundamentals — Use addition and subtraction within 100 to solve word problems involving lengths that are the same units. CCMS 2.MD.B.5 — 123

Page 125

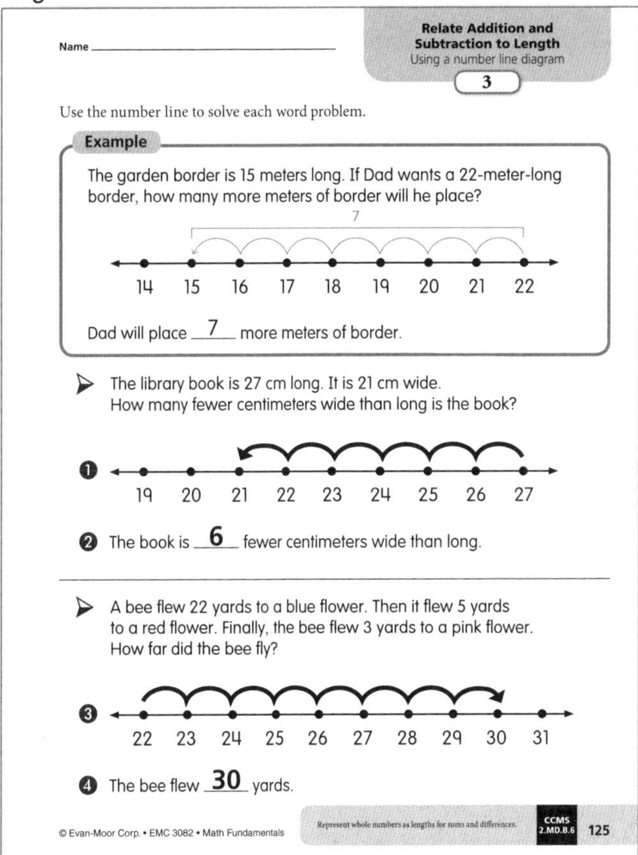

Name ______

Relate Addition and Subtraction to Length
Using a number line diagram
3

Use the number line to solve each word problem.

Example

The garden border is 15 meters long. If Dad wants a 22-meter-long border, how many more meters of border will he place?

7

14 15 16 17 18 19 20 21 22

Dad will place 7 more meters of border.

▷ The library book is 27 cm long. It is 21 cm wide. How many fewer centimeters wide than long is the book?

1. 19 20 21 22 23 24 25 26 27
2. The book is 6 fewer centimeters wide than long.

▷ A bee flew 22 yards to a blue flower. Then it flew 5 yards to a red flower. Finally, the bee flew 3 yards to a pink flower. How far did the bee fly?

3. 22 23 24 25 26 27 28 29 30 31
4. The bee flew 30 yards.

© Evan-Moor Corp. • EMC 3082 • Math Fundamentals — Represent whole numbers as lengths for sums and differences. CCMS 2.MD.B.6 — 125

Page 126

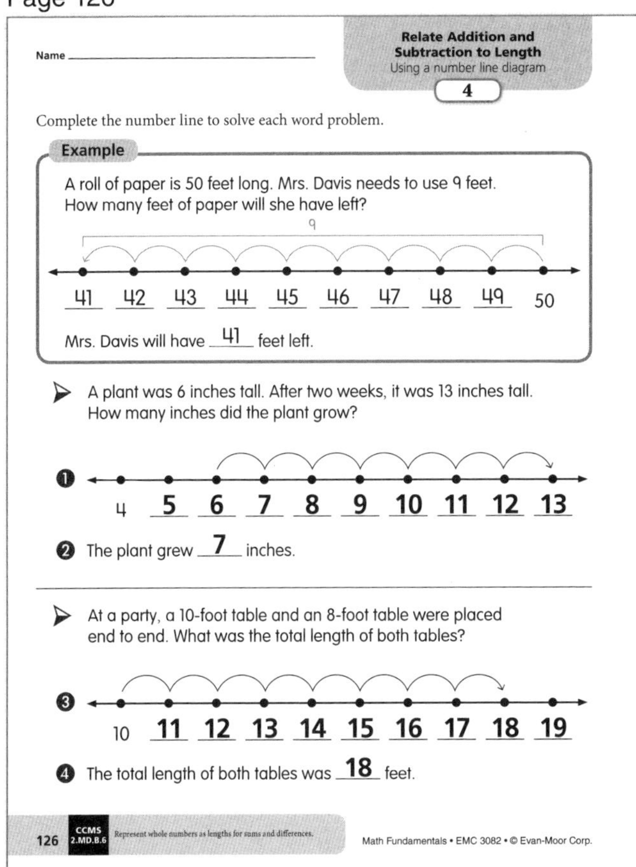

Name ______

Relate Addition and Subtraction to Length
Using a number line diagram
4

Complete the number line to solve each word problem.

Example

A roll of paper is 50 feet long. Mrs. Davis needs to use 9 feet. How many feet of paper will she have left?

9

41 42 43 44 45 46 47 48 49 50

Mrs. Davis will have 41 feet left.

▷ A plant was 6 inches tall. After two weeks, it was 13 inches tall. How many inches did the plant grow?

1. 4 5 6 7 8 9 10 11 12 13
2. The plant grew 7 inches.

▷ At a party, a 10-foot table and an 8-foot table were placed end to end. What was the total length of both tables?

3. 10 11 12 13 14 15 16 17 18 19
4. The total length of both tables was 18 feet.

126 — CCMS 2.MD.B.6 — Represent whole numbers as lengths for sums and differences. — Math Fundamentals • EMC 3082 • © Evan-Moor Corp.

Page 127

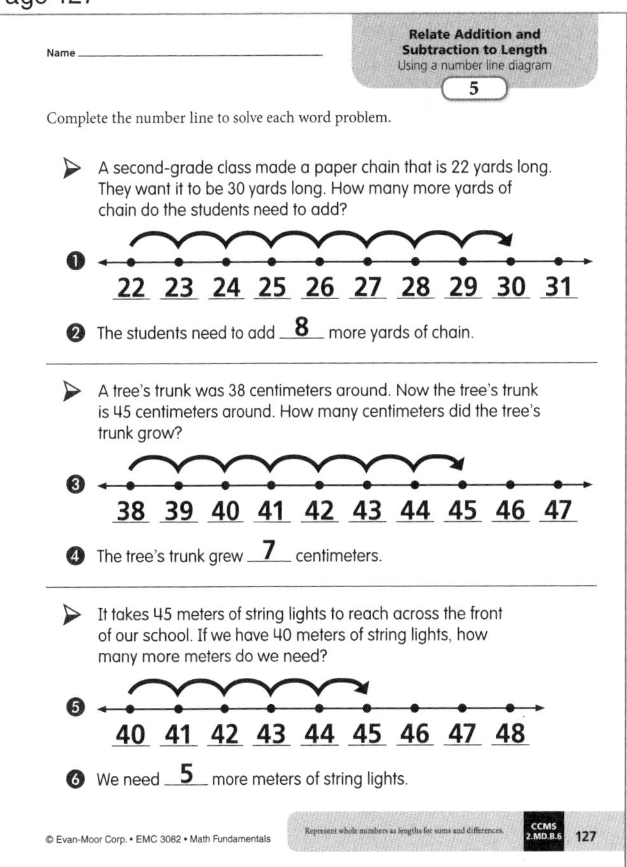

Name ______

Relate Addition and Subtraction to Length
Using a number line diagram
5

Complete the number line to solve each word problem.

▷ A second-grade class made a paper chain that is 22 yards long. They want it to be 30 yards long. How many more yards of chain do the students need to add?

1. 22 23 24 25 26 27 28 29 30 31
2. The students need to add 8 more yards of chain.

▷ A tree's trunk was 38 centimeters around. Now the tree's trunk is 45 centimeters around. How many centimeters did the tree's trunk grow?

3. 38 39 40 41 42 43 44 45 46 47
4. The tree's trunk grew 7 centimeters.

▷ It takes 45 meters of string lights to reach across the front of our school. If we have 40 meters of string lights, how many more meters do we need?

5. 40 41 42 43 44 45 46 47 48
6. We need 5 more meters of string lights.

© Evan-Moor Corp. • EMC 3082 • Math Fundamentals — Represent whole numbers as lengths for sums and differences. CCMS 2.MD.B.6 — 127

There are many ways to model a problem or to word an explanation. Accept any reasonable answer.

Page 128

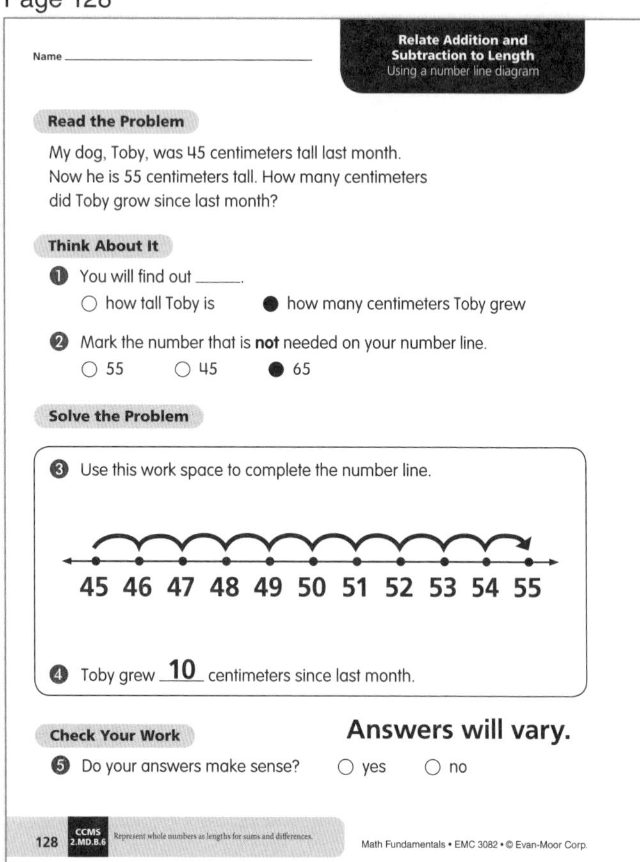

Page 131

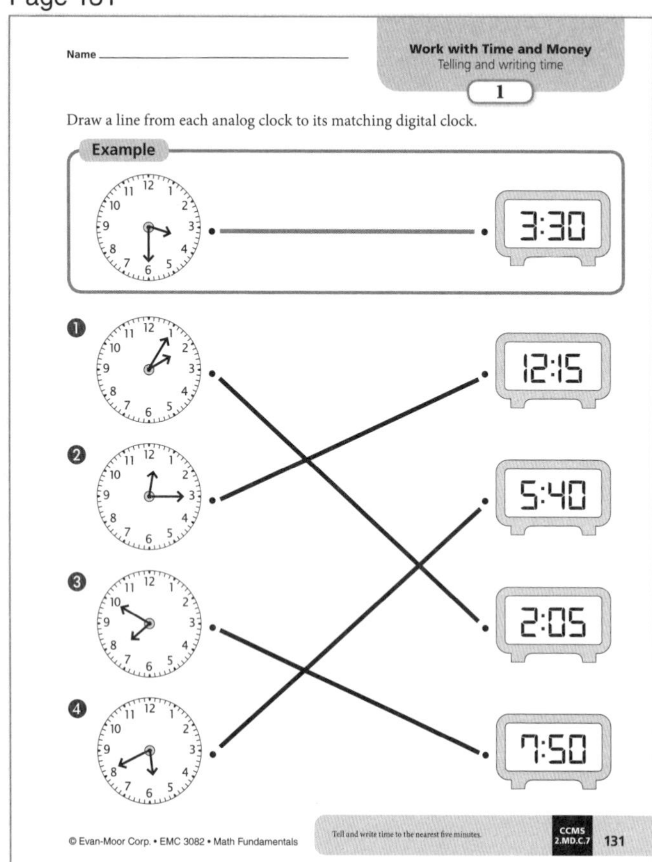

Page 132

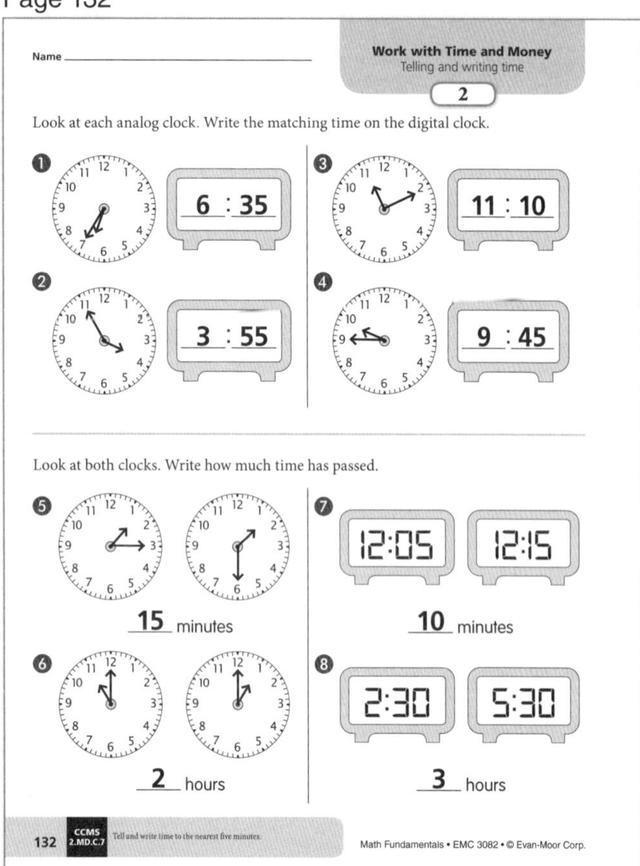

Page 133

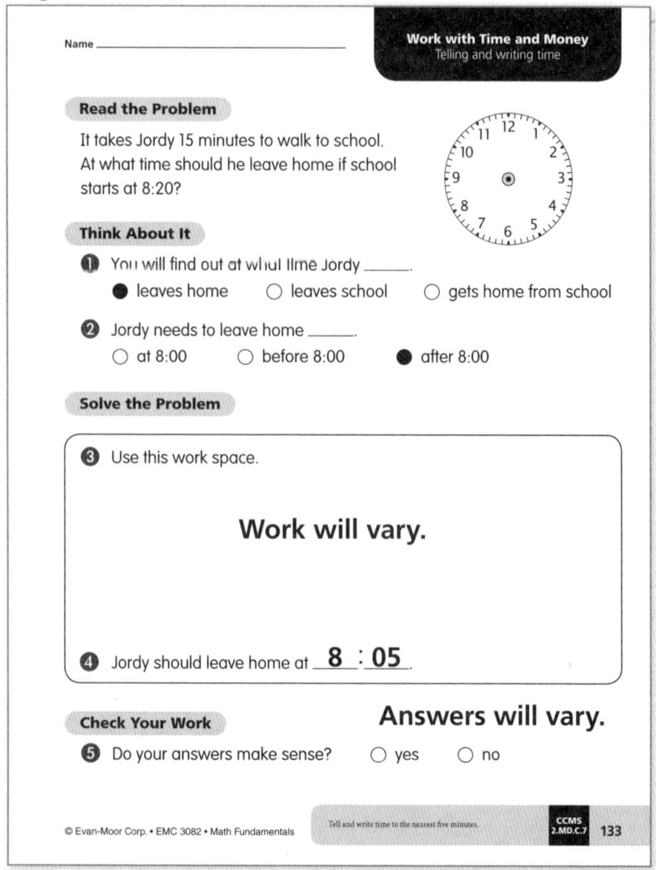

There are many ways to model a problem or to word an explanation. Accept any reasonable answer.

Page 135

Name ______________________

Work with Time and Money
Using a.m. and p.m.
3

Mark **a.m.** or **p.m.** to show when each action is likely to happen.

Example

I eat breakfast. ● a.m. ○ p.m.

1. We see the sunset. ○ a.m. ● p.m.
2. We get up in the morning. ● a.m. ○ p.m.
3. I go to bed at night. ○ a.m. ● p.m.
4. The school day begins. ● a.m. ○ p.m.
5. We sit down for dinner. ○ a.m. ● p.m.

© Evan-Moor Corp. • EMC 3082 • Math Fundamentals — Tell and write time using a.m. and p.m. — CCMS 2.MD.C.7 — 135

Page 136

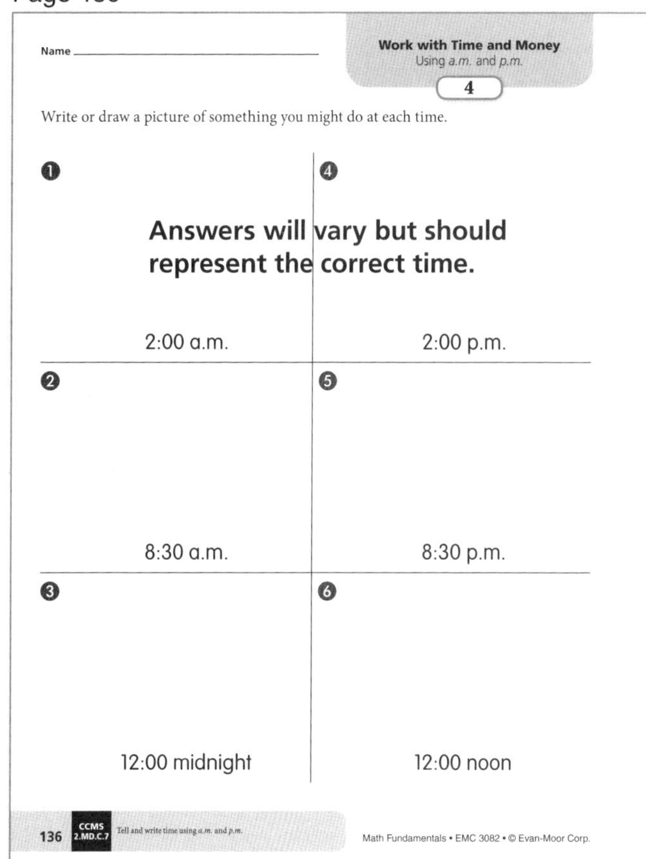

Name ______________________

Work with Time and Money
Using a.m. and p.m.
4

Write or draw a picture of something you might do at each time.

Answers will vary but should represent the correct time.

1. 2:00 a.m.	4. 2:00 p.m.
2. 8:30 a.m.	5. 8:30 p.m.
3. 12:00 midnight	6. 12:00 noon

136 — CCMS 2.MD.C.7 — Tell and write time using a.m. and p.m. — Math Fundamentals • EMC 3082 • © Evan-Moor Corp.

Page137

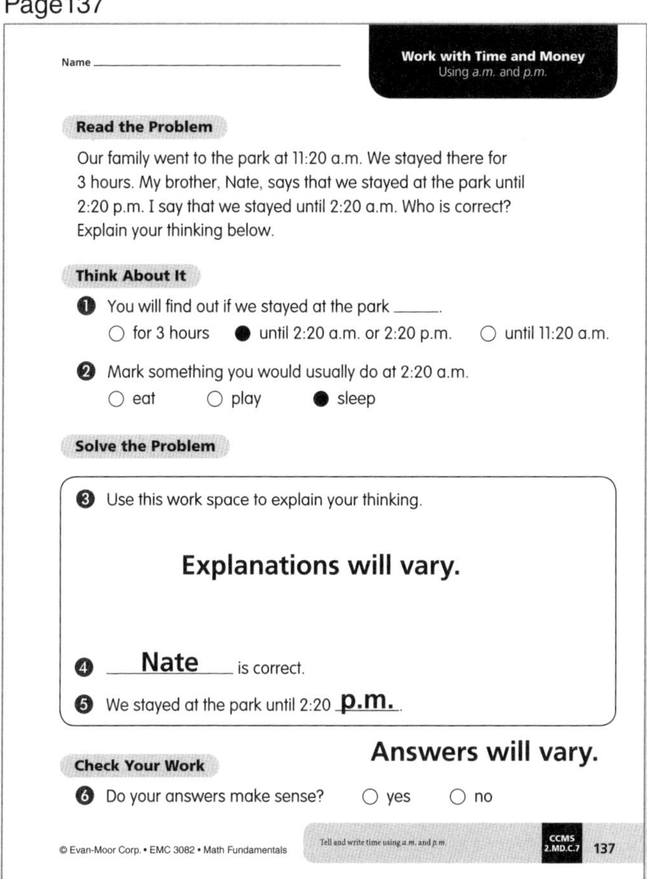

Name ______________________

Work with Time and Money
Using a.m. and p.m.

Read the Problem

Our family went to the park at 11:20 a.m. We stayed there for 3 hours. My brother, Nate, says that we stayed at the park until 2:20 p.m. I say that we stayed until 2:20 a.m. Who is correct? Explain your thinking below.

Think About It

1. You will find out if we stayed at the park ______.
   ○ for 3 hours ● until 2:20 a.m. or 2:20 p.m. ○ until 11:20 a.m.
2. Mark something you would usually do at 2:20 a.m.
   ○ eat ○ play ● sleep

Solve the Problem

3. Use this work space to explain your thinking.

Explanations will vary.

4. **Nate** is correct.
5. We stayed at the park until 2:20 **p.m.**

Check Your Work

Answers will vary.

6. Do your answers make sense? ○ yes ○ no

© Evan-Moor Corp. • EMC 3082 • Math Fundamentals — Tell and write time using a.m. and p.m. — CCMS 2.MD.C.7 — 137

Page 139

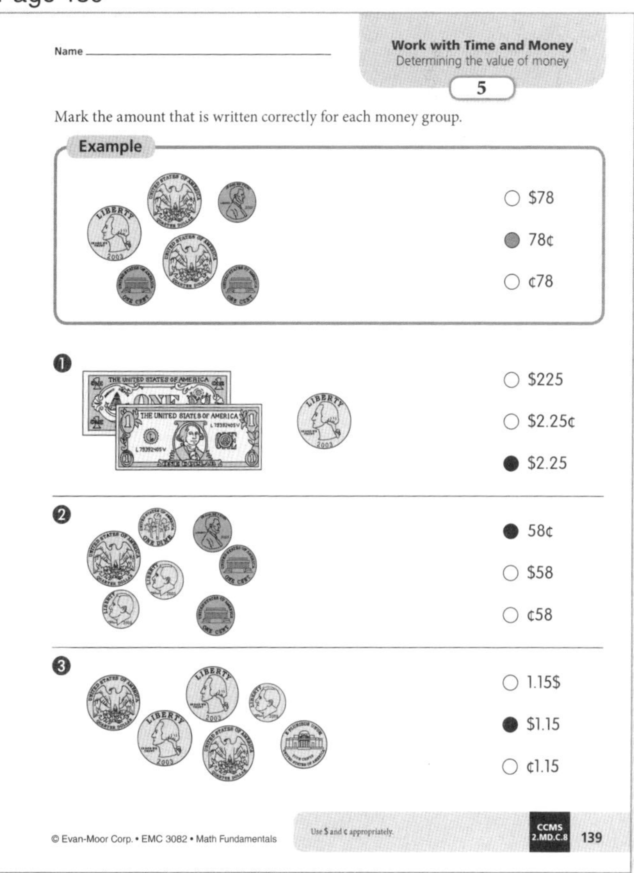

Name ______________________

Work with Time and Money
Determining the value of money
5

Mark the amount that is written correctly for each money group.

Example

○ $78
● 78¢
○ ¢78

1. ○ $225 ○ $2.25¢ ● $2.25
2. ● 58¢ ○ $58 ○ ¢58
3. ○ 1.15$ ● $1.15 ○ ¢1.15

© Evan-Moor Corp. • EMC 3082 • Math Fundamentals — Use $ and ¢ appropriately. — CCMS 2.MD.C.8 — 139

There are many ways to model a problem or to word an explanation. Accept any reasonable answer.

Page 140

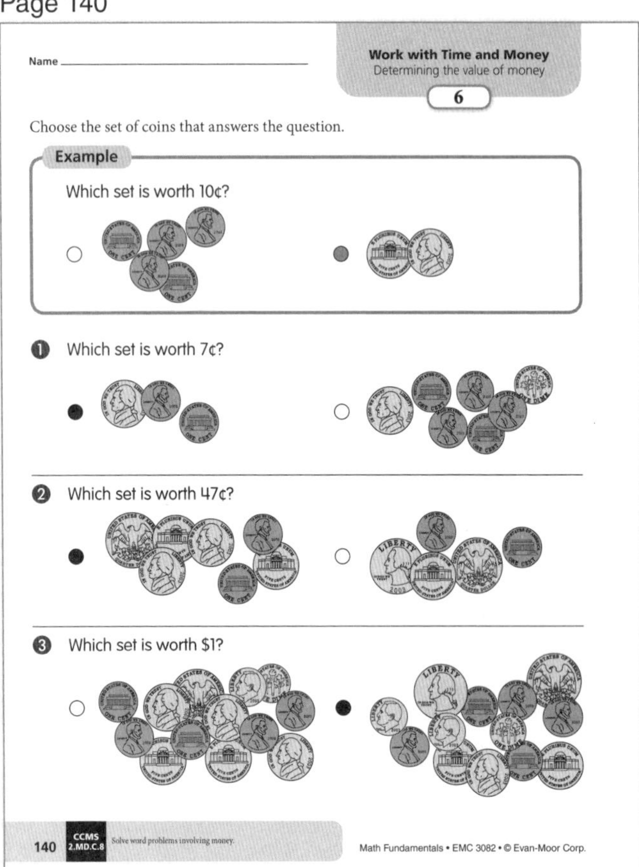

Name ______

Work with Time and Money
Determining the value of money

6

Choose the set of coins that answers the question.

Example

Which set is worth 10¢?

○ ●

❶ Which set is worth 7¢?

● ○

❷ Which set is worth 47¢?

● ○

❸ Which set is worth $1?

○ ●

140 CCMS 2.MD.C.8 Solve word problems involving money. Math Fundamentals • EMC 3082 • © Evan-Moor Corp.

Page 141

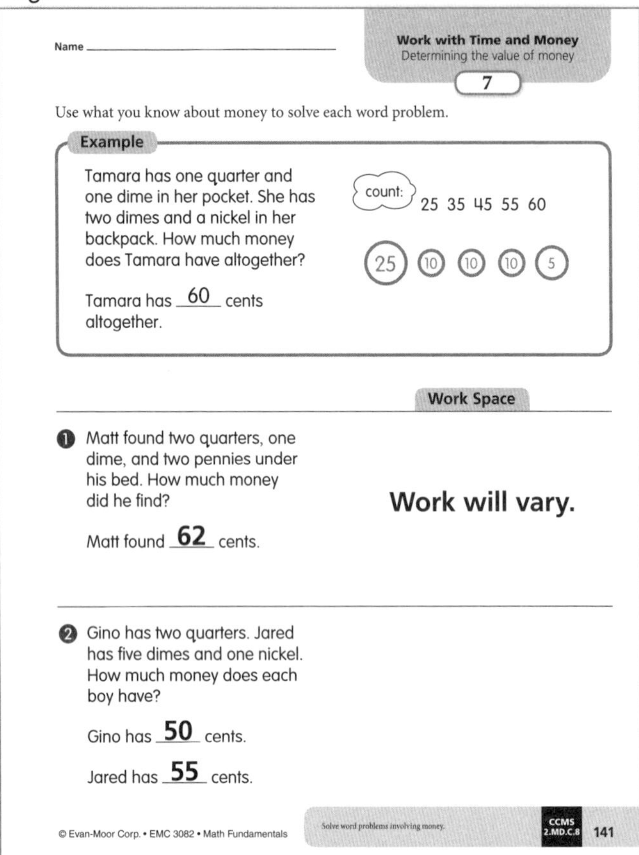

Name ______

Work with Time and Money
Determining the value of money

7

Use what you know about money to solve each word problem.

Example

Tamara has one quarter and one dime in her pocket. She has two dimes and a nickel in her backpack. How much money does Tamara have altogether?

count: 25 35 45 55 60

25 10 10 10 5

Tamara has 60 cents altogether.

Work Space

❶ Matt found two quarters, one dime, and two pennies under his bed. How much money did he find?

Matt found 62 cents.

Work will vary.

❷ Gino has two quarters. Jared has five dimes and one nickel. How much money does each boy have?

Gino has 50 cents.

Jared has 55 cents.

© Evan-Moor Corp. • EMC 3082 • Math Fundamentals Solve word problems involving money. CCMS 2.MD.C.8 141

Page 142

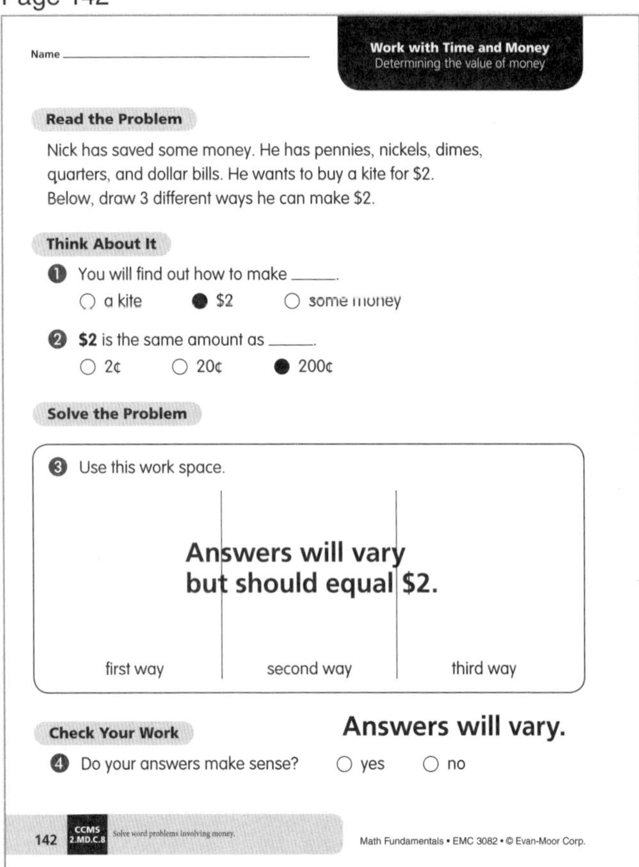

Name ______

Work with Time and Money
Determining the value of money

Read the Problem

Nick has saved some money. He has pennies, nickels, dimes, quarters, and dollar bills. He wants to buy a kite for $2. Below, draw 3 different ways he can make $2.

Think About It

❶ You will find out how to make ______.
○ a kite ● $2 ○ some money

❷ **$2** is the same amount as ______.
○ 2¢ ○ 20¢ ● 200¢

Solve the Problem

❸ Use this work space.

Answers will vary but should equal $2.

first way | second way | third way

Check Your Work

Answers will vary.

❹ Do your answers make sense? ○ yes ○ no

142 CCMS 2.MD.C.8 Solve word problems involving money. Math Fundamentals • EMC 3082 • © Evan-Moor Corp.

Page 144

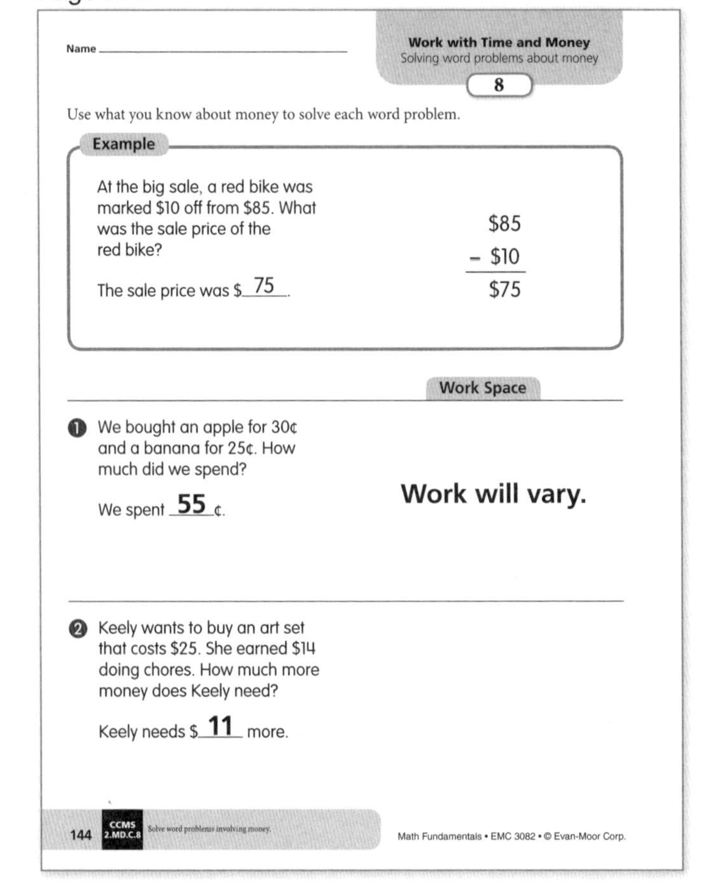

Name ______

Work with Time and Money
Solving word problems about money

8

Use what you know about money to solve each word problem.

Example

At the big sale, a red bike was marked $10 off from $85. What was the sale price of the red bike?

$85
− $10
$75

The sale price was $ 75 .

Work Space

❶ We bought an apple for 30¢ and a banana for 25¢. How much did we spend?

We spent 55 ¢.

Work will vary.

❷ Keely wants to buy an art set that costs $25. She earned $14 doing chores. How much more money does Keely need?

Keely needs $ 11 more.

144 CCMS 2.MD.C.8 Solve word problems involving money. Math Fundamentals • EMC 3082 • © Evan-Moor Corp.

There are many ways to model a problem or to word an explanation. Accept any reasonable answer.

Page 145

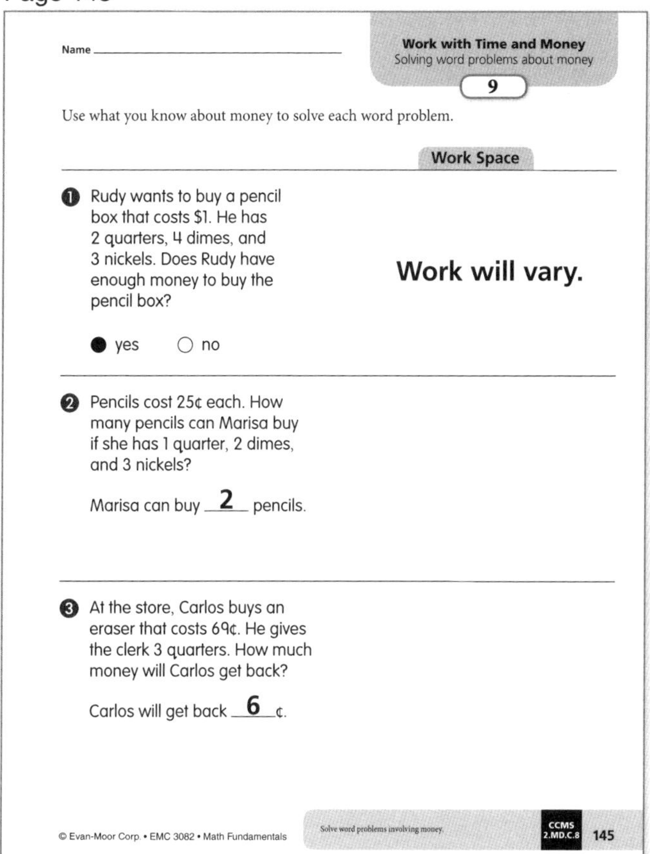

Name ______

Work with Time and Money
Solving word problems about money
9

Use what you know about money to solve each word problem.

Work Space

1. Rudy wants to buy a pencil box that costs $1. He has 2 quarters, 4 dimes, and 3 nickels. Does Rudy have enough money to buy the pencil box?

   ● yes ○ no

Work will vary.

2. Pencils cost 25¢ each. How many pencils can Marisa buy if she has 1 quarter, 2 dimes, and 3 nickels?

   Marisa can buy **2** pencils.

3. At the store, Carlos buys an eraser that costs 69¢. He gives the clerk 3 quarters. How much money will Carlos get back?

   Carlos will get back **6** ¢.

© Evan-Moor Corp. • EMC 3082 • Math Fundamentals — Solve word problems involving money. — CCMS 2.MD.C.8 — 145

Page 146

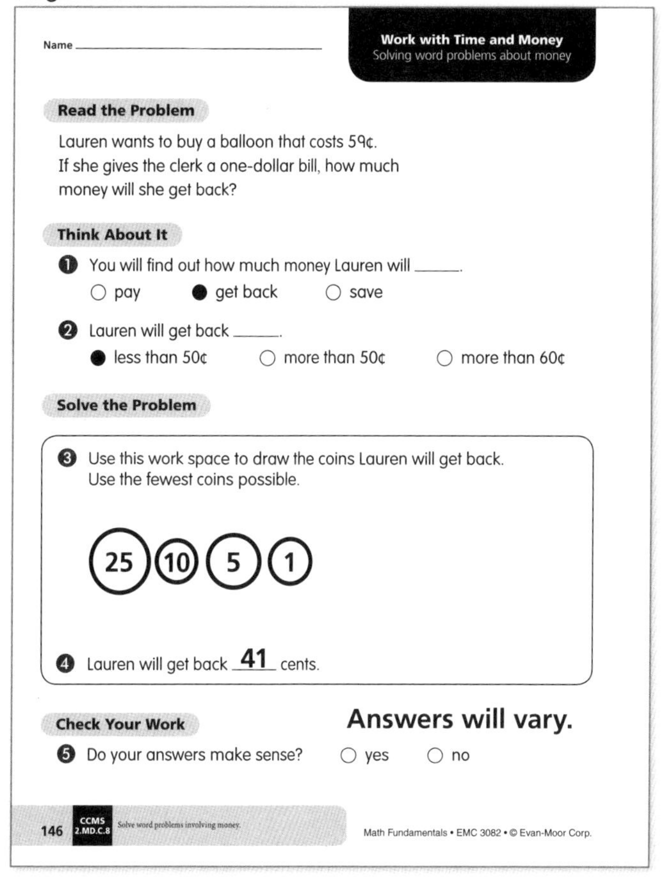

Name ______

Work with Time and Money
Solving word problems about money

Read the Problem

Lauren wants to buy a balloon that costs 59¢. If she gives the clerk a one-dollar bill, how much money will she get back?

Think About It

1. You will find out how much money Lauren will ______.

   ○ pay ● get back ○ save

2. Lauren will get back ______.

   ● less than 50¢ ○ more than 50¢ ○ more than 60¢

Solve the Problem

3. Use this work space to draw the coins Lauren will get back. Use the fewest coins possible.

   (25) (10) (5) (1)

4. Lauren will get back **41** cents.

Check Your Work

Answers will vary.

5. Do your answers make sense? ○ yes ○ no

146 — CCMS 2.MD.C.8 — Solve word problems involving money. — Math Fundamentals • EMC 3082 • © Evan-Moor Corp.

Page 149

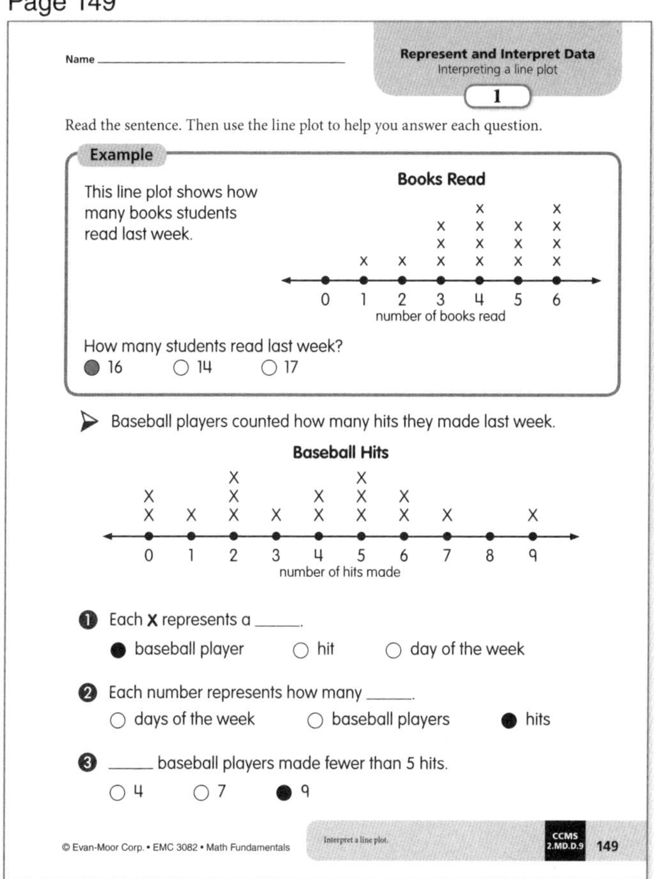

Name ______

Represent and Interpret Data
Interpreting a line plot
1

Read the sentence. Then use the line plot to help you answer each question.

Example

This line plot shows how many books students read last week.

How many students read last week?
● 16 ○ 14 ○ 17

➤ Baseball players counted how many hits they made last week.

1. Each **X** represents a ______.

   ● baseball player ○ hit ○ day of the week

2. Each number represents how many ______.

   ○ days of the week ○ baseball players ● hits

3. ______ baseball players made fewer than 5 hits.

   ○ 4 ○ 7 ● 9

© Evan-Moor Corp. • EMC 3082 • Math Fundamentals — Interpret a line plot. — CCMS 2.MD.D.9 — 149

Page 150

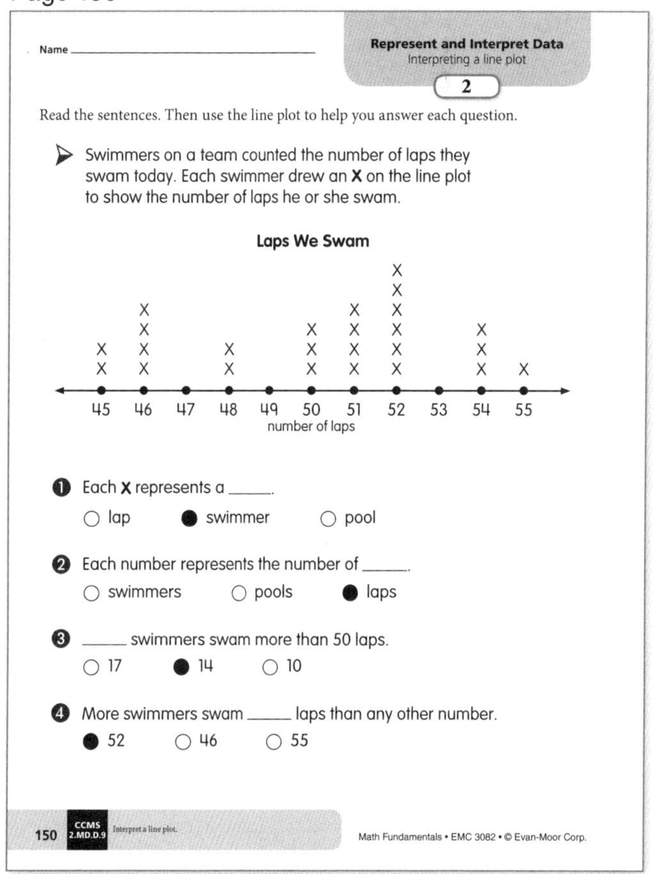

Name ______

Represent and Interpret Data
Interpreting a line plot
2

Read the sentences. Then use the line plot to help you answer each question.

➤ Swimmers on a team counted the number of laps they swam today. Each swimmer drew an **X** on the line plot to show the number of laps he or she swam.

1. Each **X** represents a ______.

   ○ lap ● swimmer ○ pool

2. Each number represents the number of ______.

   ○ swimmers ○ pools ● laps

3. ______ swimmers swam more than 50 laps.

   ○ 17 ● 14 ○ 10

4. More swimmers swam ______ laps than any other number.

   ● 52 ○ 46 ○ 55

150 — CCMS 2.MD.D.9 — Interpret a line plot. — Math Fundamentals • EMC 3082 • © Evan-Moor Corp.

There are many ways to model a problem or to word an explanation. Accept any reasonable answer.

Page 151

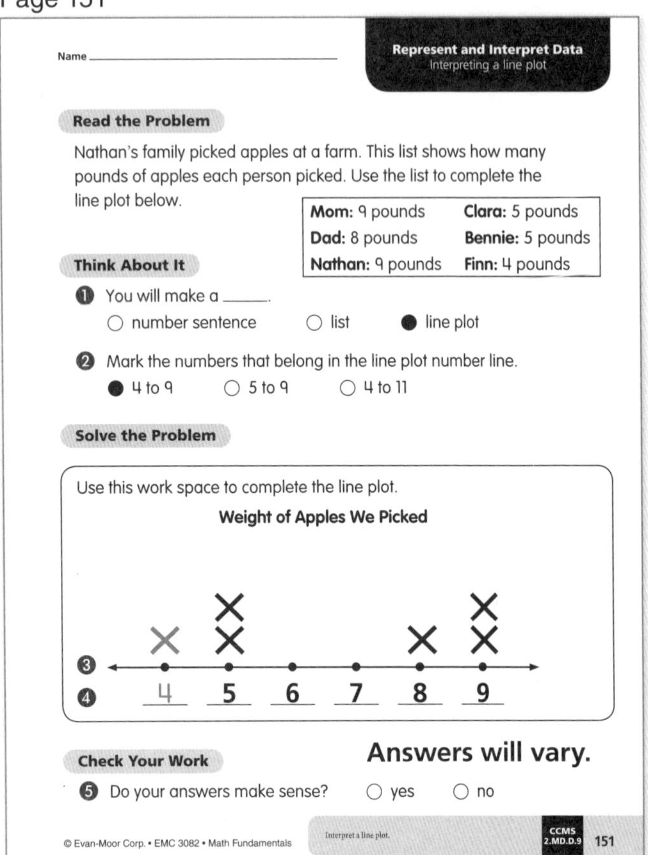

Name ______

Represent and Interpret Data
Interpreting a line plot

Read the Problem

Nathan's family picked apples at a farm. This list shows how many pounds of apples each person picked. Use the list to complete the line plot below.

Mom: 9 pounds	**Clara:** 5 pounds
Dad: 8 pounds	**Bennie:** 5 pounds
Nathan: 9 pounds	**Finn:** 4 pounds

Think About It

1. You will make a ______.
   ○ number sentence ○ list ● line plot
2. Mark the numbers that belong in the line plot number line.
   ● 4 to 9 ○ 5 to 9 ○ 4 to 11

Solve the Problem

Use this work space to complete the line plot.

Weight of Apples We Picked

Check Your Work

5. Do your answers make sense? ○ yes ○ no

Answers will vary.

© Evan-Moor Corp. • EMC 3082 • Math Fundamentals — Interpret a line plot. — CCMS 2.MD.D.9 — 151

Page 153

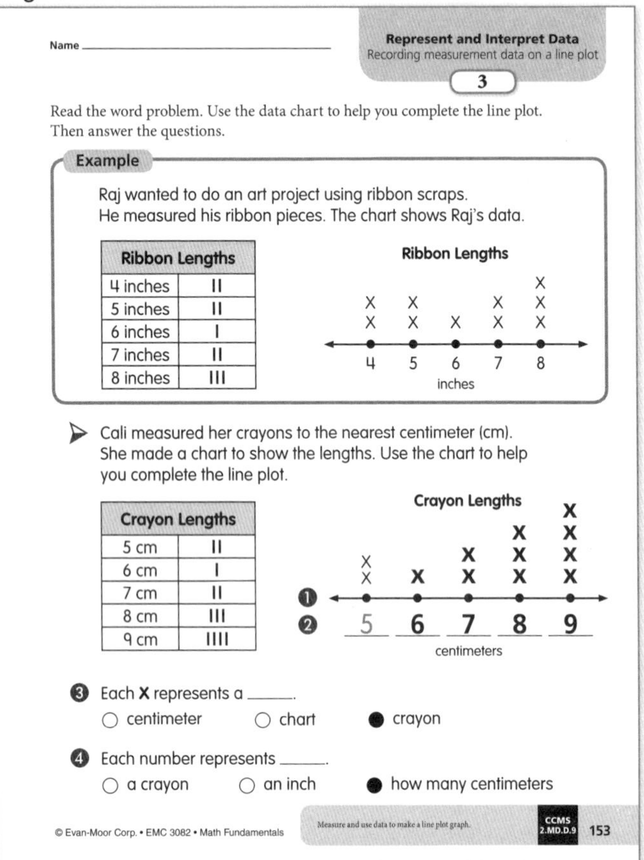

Name ______

Represent and Interpret Data
Recording measurement data on a line plot

3

Read the word problem. Use the data chart to help you complete the line plot. Then answer the questions.

Example

Raj wanted to do an art project using ribbon scraps. He measured his ribbon pieces. The chart shows Raj's data.

Ribbon Lengths	
4 inches	II
5 inches	II
6 inches	I
7 inches	II
8 inches	III

Ribbon Lengths

Cali measured her crayons to the nearest centimeter (cm). She made a chart to show the lengths. Use the chart to help you complete the line plot.

Crayon Lengths	
5 cm	II
6 cm	I
7 cm	II
8 cm	III
9 cm	IIII

Crayon Lengths

3. Each **X** represents a ______.
   ○ centimeter ○ chart ● crayon
4. Each number represents ______.
   ○ a crayon ○ an inch ● how many centimeters

© Evan-Moor Corp. • EMC 3082 • Math Fundamentals — Measure and use data to make a line plot graph. — CCMS 2.MD.D.9 — 153

Page 154

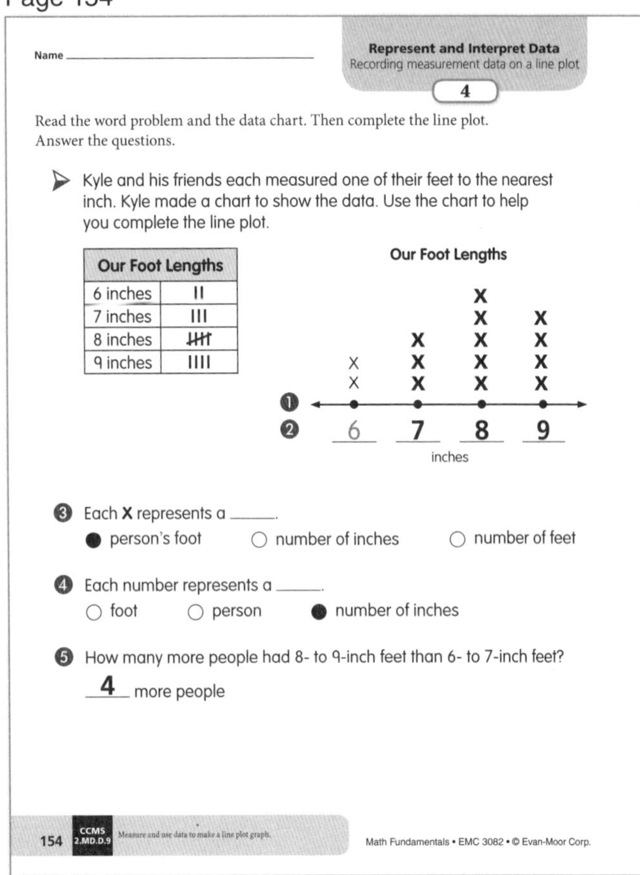

Name ______

Represent and Interpret Data
Recording measurement data on a line plot

4

Read the word problem and the data chart. Then complete the line plot. Answer the questions.

Kyle and his friends each measured one of their feet to the nearest inch. Kyle made a chart to show the data. Use the chart to help you complete the line plot.

Our Foot Lengths	
6 inches	II
7 inches	III
8 inches	卌
9 inches	IIII

Our Foot Lengths

3. Each **X** represents a ______.
   ● person's foot ○ number of inches ○ number of feet
4. Each number represents a ______.
   ○ foot ○ person ● number of inches
5. How many more people had 8- to 9-inch feet than 6- to 7-inch feet?
   4 more people

154 — CCMS 2.MD.D.9 — Measure and use data to make a line plot graph. — Math Fundamentals • EMC 3082 • © Evan-Moor Corp.

Page 155

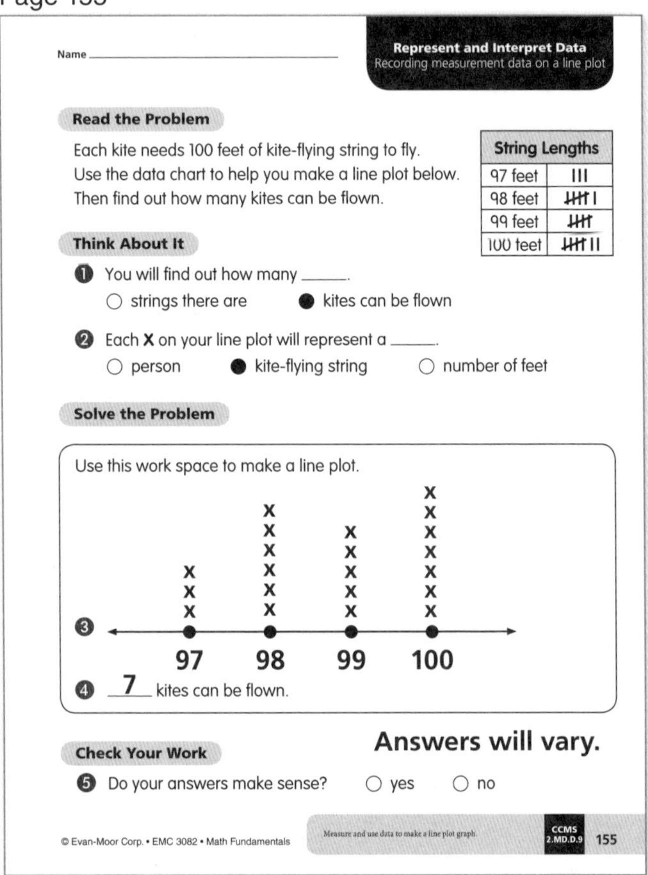

Name ______

Represent and Interpret Data
Recording measurement data on a line plot

Read the Problem

Each kite needs 100 feet of kite-flying string to fly. Use the data chart to help you make a line plot below. Then find out how many kites can be flown.

String Lengths	
97 feet	III
98 feet	卌 I
99 feet	卌
100 feet	卌 II

Think About It

1. You will find out how many ______.
   ○ strings there are ● kites can be flown
2. Each **X** on your line plot will represent a ______.
   ○ person ● kite-flying string ○ number of feet

Solve the Problem

Use this work space to make a line plot.

4. 7 kites can be flown.

Check Your Work

5. Do your answers make sense? ○ yes ○ no

Answers will vary.

© Evan-Moor Corp. • EMC 3082 • Math Fundamentals — Measure and use data to make a line plot graph. — CCMS 2.MD.D.9 — 155

There are many ways to model a problem or to word an explanation. Accept any reasonable answer.

Page 157

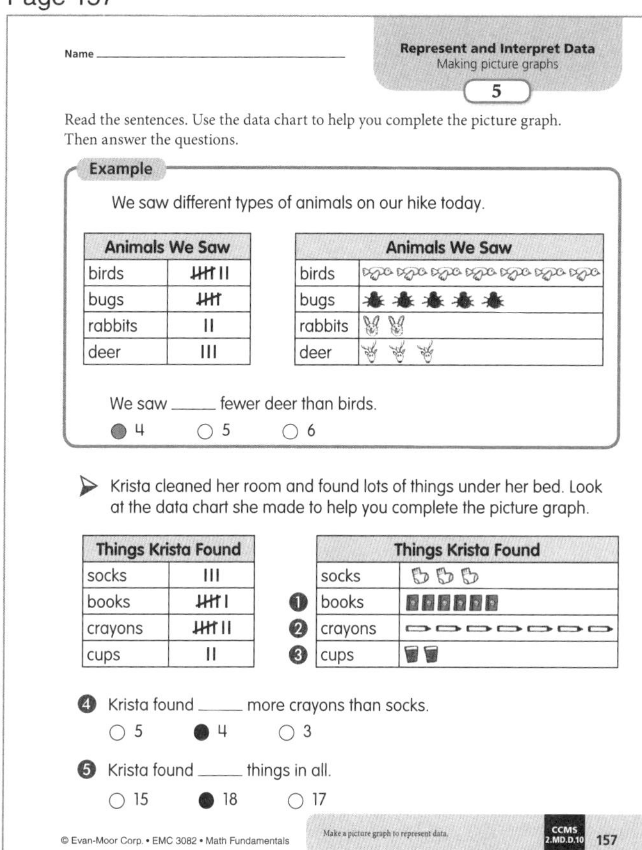
Name ____________

Represent and Interpret Data
Making picture graphs
5

Read the sentences. Use the data chart to help you complete the picture graph. Then answer the questions.

Example

We saw different types of animals on our hike today.

Animals We Saw	
birds	HHT II
bugs	HHT
rabbits	II
deer	III

Animals We Saw	
birds	
bugs	
rabbits	
deer	

We saw _____ fewer deer than birds.
● 4 ○ 5 ○ 6

Krista cleaned her room and found lots of things under her bed. Look at the data chart she made to help you complete the picture graph.

Things Krista Found	
socks	III
books	HHT I
crayons	HHT II
cups	II

Things Krista Found	
socks	
❶ books	
❷ crayons	
❸ cups	

❹ Krista found _____ more crayons than socks.
○ 5 ● 4 ○ 3

❺ Krista found _____ things in all.
○ 15 ● 18 ○ 17

© Evan-Moor Corp. • EMC 3082 • Math Fundamentals — Make a picture graph to represent data. — CCMS 2.MD.D.10 — 157

Page 158

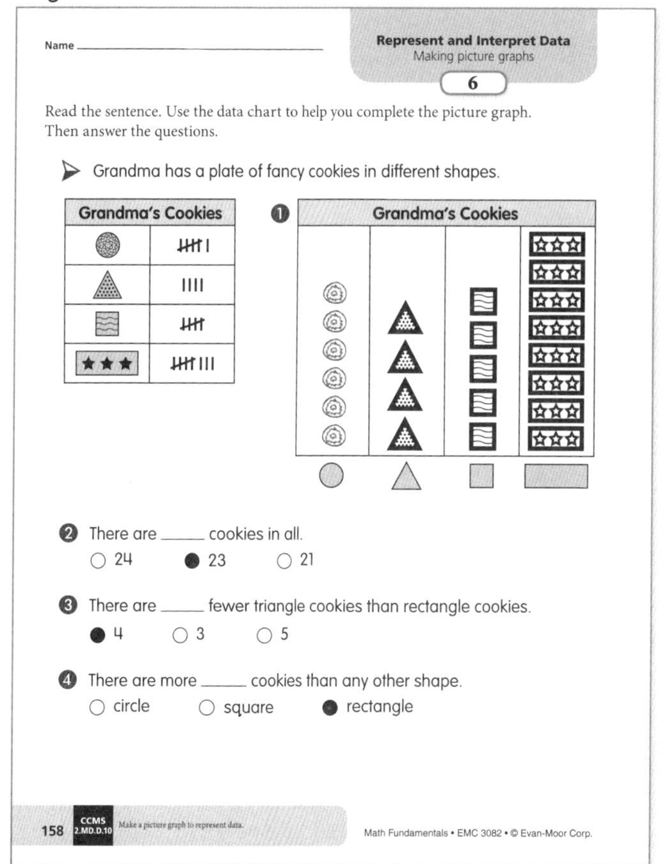
Name ____________

Represent and Interpret Data
Making picture graphs
6

Read the sentence. Use the data chart to help you complete the picture graph. Then answer the questions.

Grandma has a plate of fancy cookies in different shapes.

Grandma's Cookies	
circle	HHT I
triangle	IIII
square	HHT
rectangle	HHT III

❶ Grandma's Cookies

❷ There are _____ cookies in all.
○ 24 ● 23 ○ 21

❸ There are _____ fewer triangle cookies than rectangle cookies.
● 4 ○ 3 ○ 5

❹ There are more _____ cookies than any other shape.
○ circle ○ square ● rectangle

158 — CCMS 2.MD.D.10 — Make a picture graph to represent data. — Math Fundamentals • EMC 3082 • © Evan-Moor Corp.

Page 159

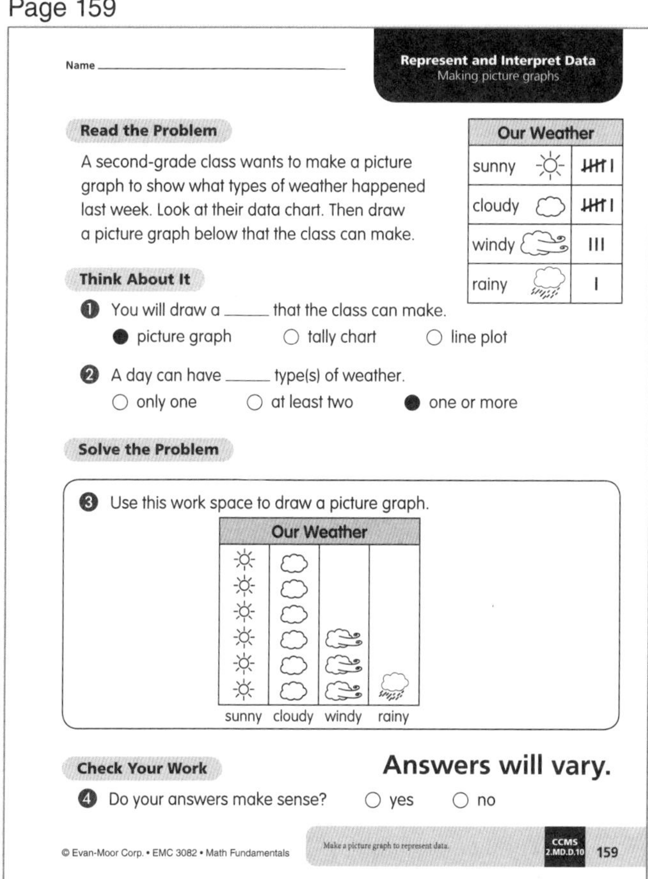
Name ____________

Represent and Interpret Data
Making picture graphs

Read the Problem

A second-grade class wants to make a picture graph to show what types of weather happened last week. Look at their data chart. Then draw a picture graph below that the class can make.

Our Weather	
sunny	HHT I
cloudy	HHT I
windy	III
rainy	I

Think About It

❶ You will draw a _____ that the class can make.
● picture graph ○ tally chart ○ line plot

❷ A day can have _____ type(s) of weather.
○ only one ○ at least two ● one or more

Solve the Problem

❸ Use this work space to draw a picture graph.

Our Weather
sunny cloudy windy rainy

Check Your Work — Answers will vary.

❹ Do your answers make sense? ○ yes ○ no

© Evan-Moor Corp. • EMC 3082 • Math Fundamentals — Make a picture graph to represent data. — CCMS 2.MD.D.10 — 159

Page 161

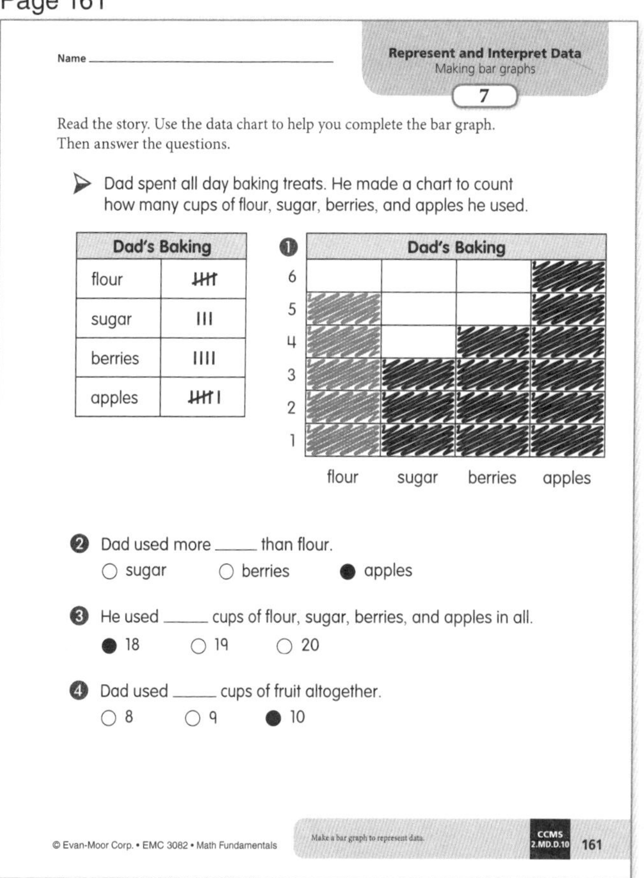
Name ____________

Represent and Interpret Data
Making bar graphs
7

Read the story. Use the data chart to help you complete the bar graph. Then answer the questions.

Dad spent all day baking treats. He made a chart to count how many cups of flour, sugar, berries, and apples he used.

Dad's Baking	
flour	HHT
sugar	III
berries	IIII
apples	HHT I

❶ Dad's Baking
6 5 4 3 2 1
flour sugar berries apples

❷ Dad used more _____ than flour.
○ sugar ○ berries ● apples

❸ He used _____ cups of flour, sugar, berries, and apples in all.
● 18 ○ 19 ○ 20

❹ Dad used _____ cups of fruit altogether.
○ 8 ○ 9 ● 10

© Evan-Moor Corp. • EMC 3082 • Math Fundamentals — Make a bar graph to represent data. — CCMS 2.MD.D.10 — 161

There are many ways to model a problem or to word an explanation. Accept any reasonable answer.

Page 162

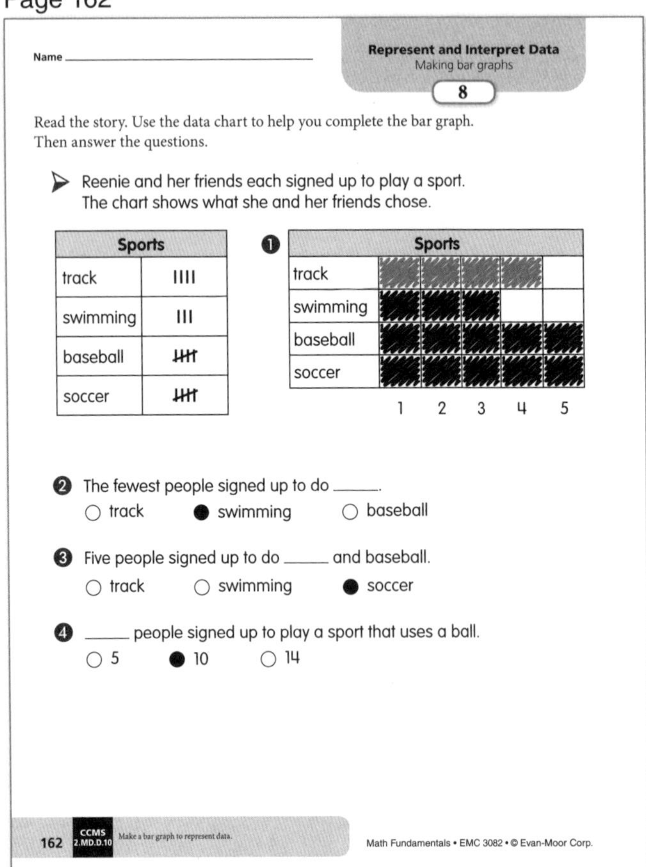

Name ____________________

Represent and Interpret Data
Making bar graphs
8

Read the story. Use the data chart to help you complete the bar graph. Then answer the questions.

Reenie and her friends each signed up to play a sport. The chart shows what she and her friends chose.

Sports	
track	IIII
swimming	III
baseball	𝍸
soccer	𝍸

❶

Sports	1	2	3	4	5
track	■	■	■	■	
swimming	■	■	■		
baseball	■	■	■	■	■
soccer	■	■	■	■	■

❷ The fewest people signed up to do ____.
○ track ● swimming ○ baseball

❸ Five people signed up to do ____ and baseball.
○ track ○ swimming ● soccer

❹ ____ people signed up to play a sport that uses a ball.
○ 5 ● 10 ○ 14

162 CCMS 2.MD.D.10 Make a bar graph to represent data. Math Fundamentals • EMC 3082 • © Evan-Moor Corp.

Page 163

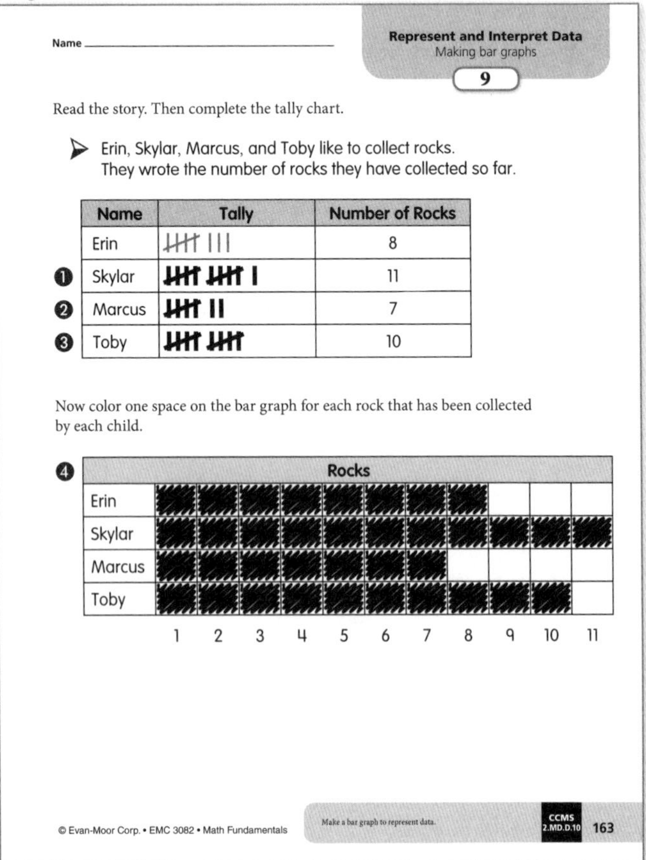

Name ____________________

Represent and Interpret Data
Making bar graphs
9

Read the story. Then complete the tally chart.

Erin, Skylar, Marcus, and Toby like to collect rocks. They wrote the number of rocks they have collected so far.

	Name	Tally	Number of Rocks
	Erin	𝍸 III	8
❶	Skylar	𝍸 𝍸 I	11
❷	Marcus	𝍸 II	7
❸	Toby	𝍸 𝍸	10

Now color one space on the bar graph for each rock that has been collected by each child.

❹

Rocks	1	2	3	4	5	6	7	8	9	10	11
Erin	■	■	■	■	■	■	■	■			
Skylar	■	■	■	■	■	■	■	■	■	■	■
Marcus	■	■	■	■	■	■	■				
Toby	■	■	■	■	■	■	■	■	■	■	

© Evan-Moor Corp. • EMC 3082 • Math Fundamentals Make a bar graph to represent data. CCMS 2.MD.D.10 163

Page 164

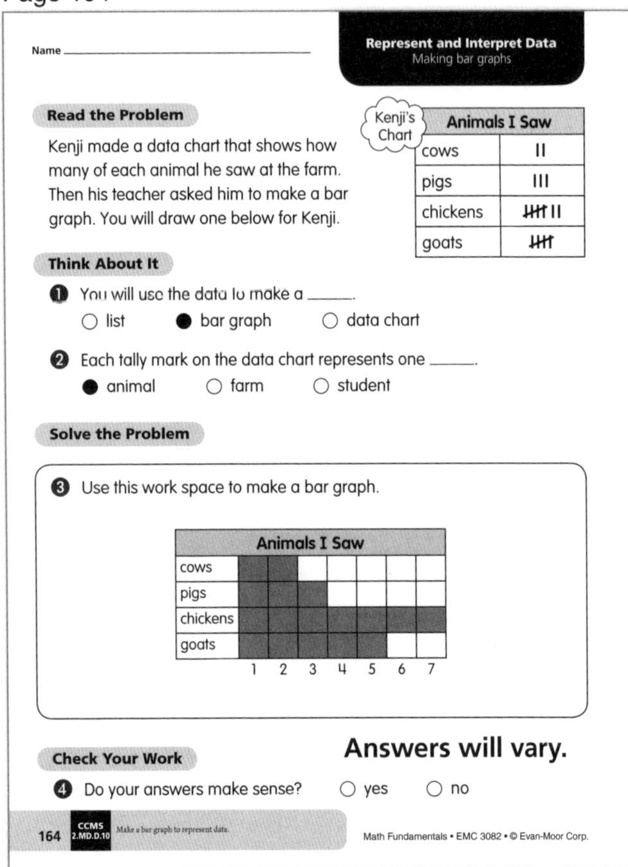

Name ____________________

Represent and Interpret Data
Making bar graphs

Read the Problem

Kenji made a data chart that shows how many of each animal he saw at the farm. Then his teacher asked him to make a bar graph. You will draw one below for Kenji.

Kenji's Chart

Animals I Saw	
cows	II
pigs	III
chickens	𝍸 II
goats	𝍸

Think About It

❶ You will use the data to make a ____.
○ list ● bar graph ○ data chart

❷ Each tally mark on the data chart represents one ____.
● animal ○ farm ○ student

Solve the Problem

❸ Use this work space to make a bar graph.

Animals I Saw	1	2	3	4	5	6	7
cows	■	■					
pigs	■	■	■				
chickens	■	■	■	■	■	■	■
goats	■	■	■	■	■		

Check Your Work

Answers will vary.

❹ Do your answers make sense?
○ yes ○ no

164 CCMS 2.MD.D.10 Make a bar graph to represent data. Math Fundamentals • EMC 3082 • © Evan-Moor Corp.

Page 167

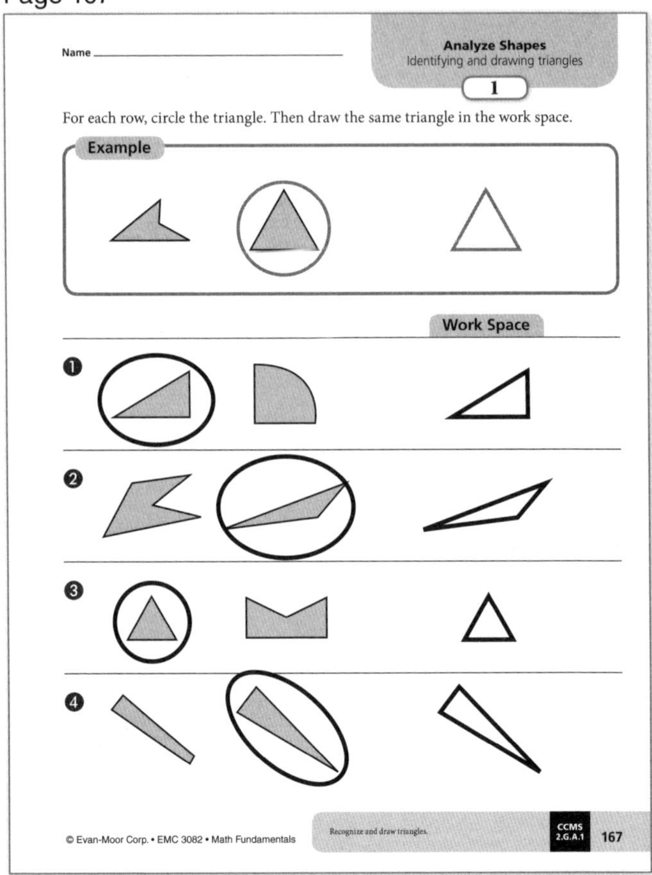

Name ____________________

Analyze Shapes
Identifying and drawing triangles
1

For each row, circle the triangle. Then draw the same triangle in the work space.

Example

Work Space

❶

❷

❸

❹

© Evan-Moor Corp. • EMC 3082 • Math Fundamentals Recognize and draw triangles. CCMS 2.G.A.1 167

There are many ways to model a problem or to word an explanation. Accept any reasonable answer.

Page 168

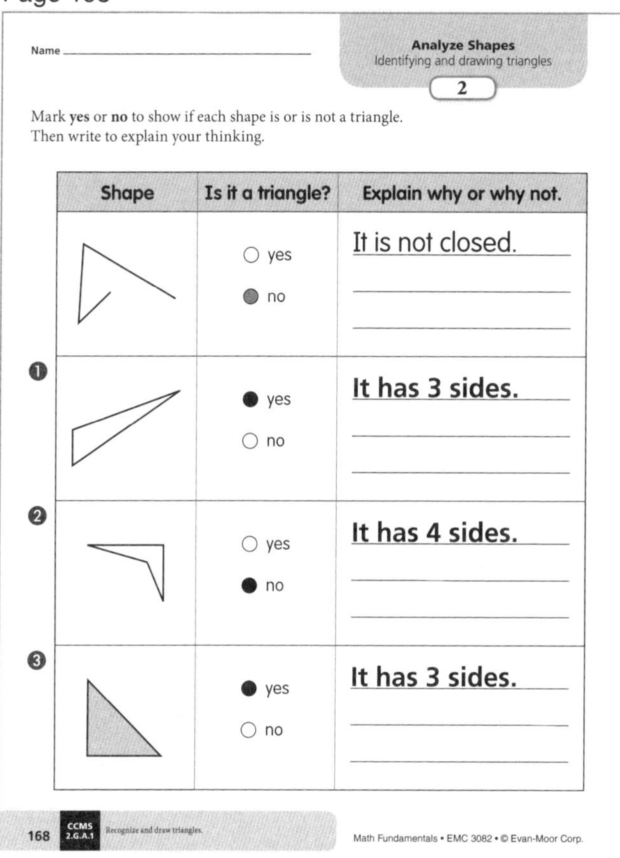

Name ____________

Analyze Shapes
Identifying and drawing triangles

2

Mark **yes** or **no** to show if each shape is or is not a triangle. Then write to explain your thinking.

	Shape	Is it a triangle?	Explain why or why not.
		○ yes ● no	It is not closed.
1		● yes ○ no	It has 3 sides.
2		○ yes ● no	It has 4 sides.
3		● yes ○ no	It has 3 sides.

168 CCMS 2.G.A.1 Recognize and draw triangles. Math Fundamentals • EMC 3082 • © Evan-Moor Corp.

Page 169

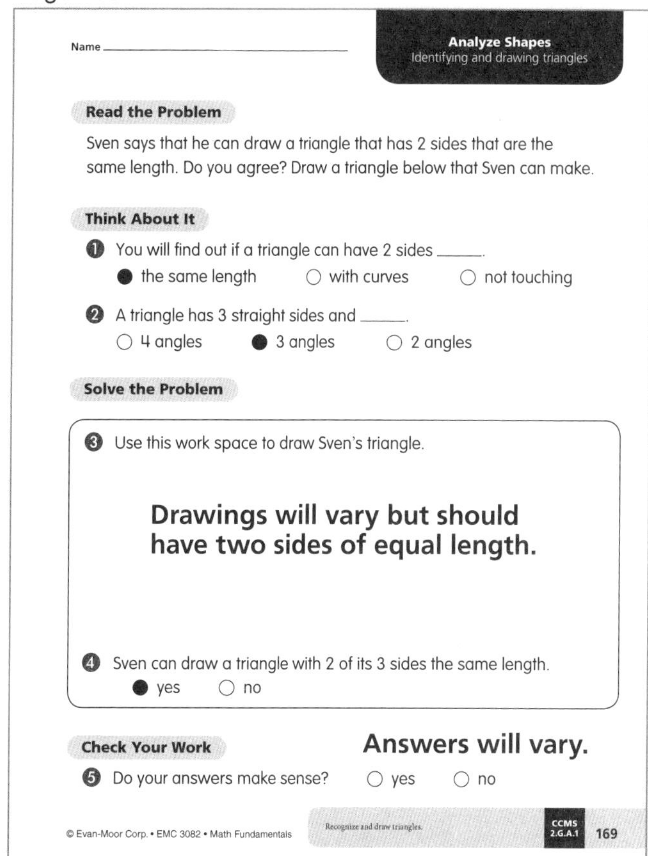

Name ____________

Analyze Shapes
Identifying and drawing triangles

Read the Problem

Sven says that he can draw a triangle that has 2 sides that are the same length. Do you agree? Draw a triangle below that Sven can make.

Think About It

1. You will find out if a triangle can have 2 sides ____.
   ● the same length ○ with curves ○ not touching
2. A triangle has 3 straight sides and ____.
   ○ 4 angles ● 3 angles ○ 2 angles

Solve the Problem

3. Use this work space to draw Sven's triangle.

   Drawings will vary but should have two sides of equal length.

4. Sven can draw a triangle with 2 of its 3 sides the same length.
   ● yes ○ no

Check Your Work

Answers will vary.

5. Do your answers make sense? ○ yes ○ no

© Evan-Moor Corp. • EMC 3082 • Math Fundamentals Recognize and draw triangles. CCMS 2.G.A.1 169

Page 171

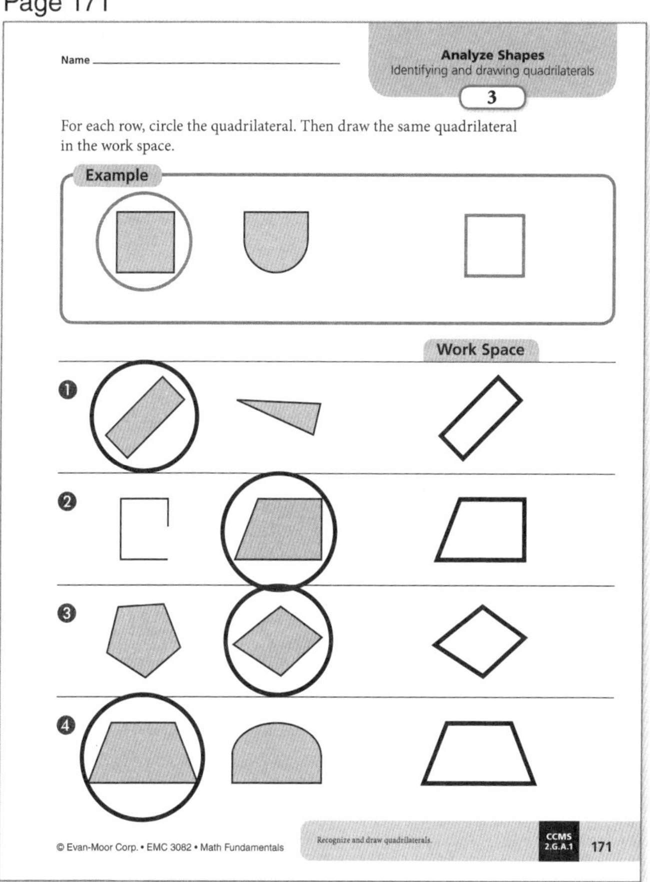

Name ____________

Analyze Shapes
Identifying and drawing quadrilaterals

3

For each row, circle the quadrilateral. Then draw the same quadrilateral in the work space.

Example

Work Space

1

2

3

4

© Evan-Moor Corp. • EMC 3082 • Math Fundamentals Recognize and draw quadrilaterals. CCMS 2.G.A.1 171

Page 172

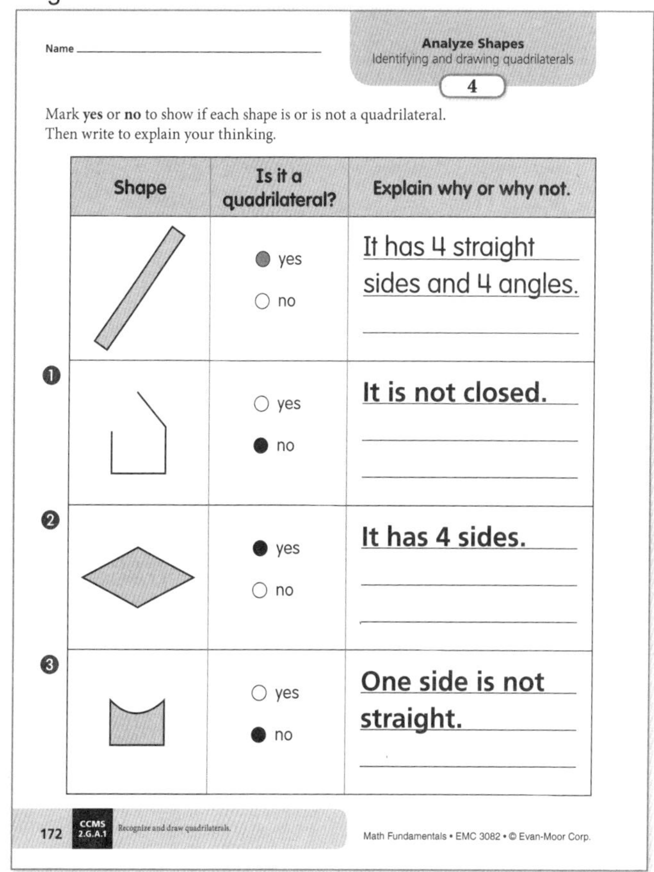

Name ____________

Analyze Shapes
Identifying and drawing quadrilaterals

4

Mark **yes** or **no** to show if each shape is or is not a quadrilateral. Then write to explain your thinking.

	Shape	Is it a quadrilateral?	Explain why or why not.
		● yes ○ no	It has 4 straight sides and 4 angles.
1		○ yes ● no	It is not closed.
2		● yes ○ no	It has 4 sides.
3		○ yes ● no	One side is not straight.

172 CCMS 2.G.A.1 Recognize and draw quadrilaterals. Math Fundamentals • EMC 3082 • © Evan-Moor Corp.

There are many ways to model a problem or to word an explanation. Accept any reasonable answer.

Page 173

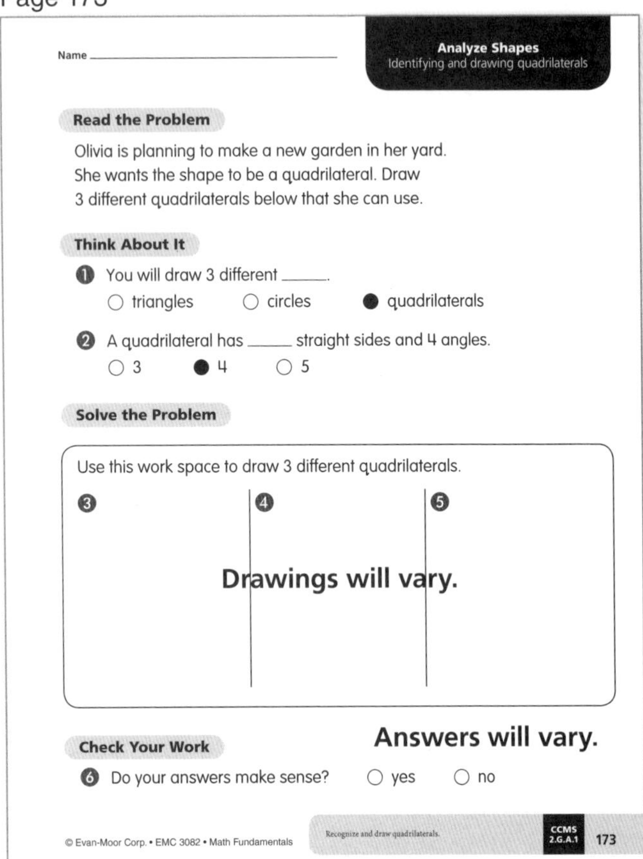

Name

Analyze Shapes
Identifying and drawing quadrilaterals

Read the Problem

Olivia is planning to make a new garden in her yard. She wants the shape to be a quadrilateral. Draw 3 different quadrilaterals below that she can use.

Think About It

1. You will draw 3 different ____.
   ○ triangles ○ circles ● quadrilaterals
2. A quadrilateral has ____ straight sides and 4 angles.
   ○ 3 ● 4 ○ 5

Solve the Problem

Use this work space to draw 3 different quadrilaterals.

3 4 5

Drawings will vary.

Check Your Work

Answers will vary.

6. Do your answers make sense? ○ yes ○ no

© Evan-Moor Corp. • EMC 3082 • Math Fundamentals — Recognize and draw quadrilaterals. — CCMS 2.G.A.1 — 173

Page 175

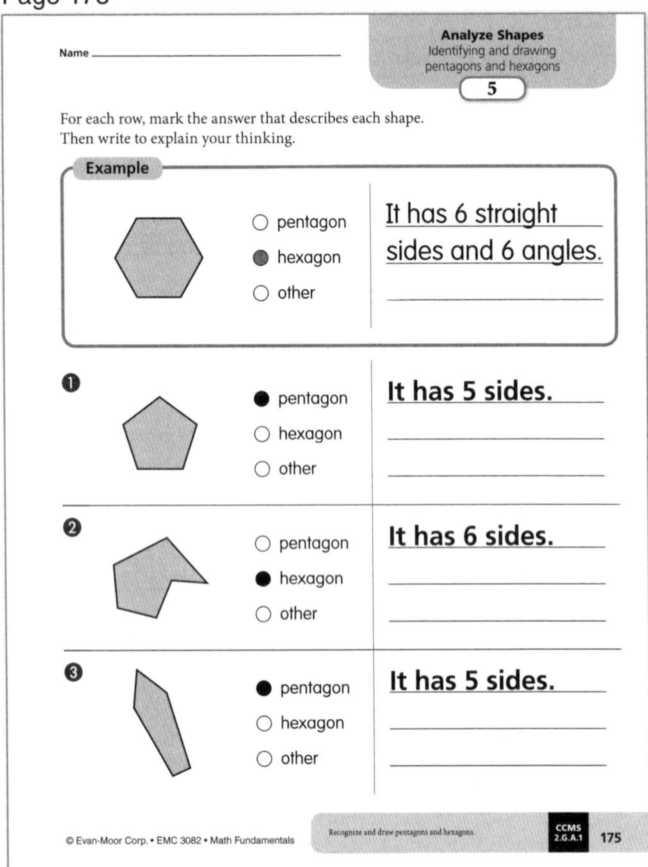

Name

Analyze Shapes
Identifying and drawing pentagons and hexagons

5

For each row, mark the answer that describes each shape. Then write to explain your thinking.

Example

○ pentagon ● hexagon ○ other — It has 6 straight sides and 6 angles.

1. ● pentagon ○ hexagon ○ other — **It has 5 sides.**
2. ○ pentagon ● hexagon ○ other — **It has 6 sides.**
3. ● pentagon ○ hexagon ○ other — **It has 5 sides.**

© Evan-Moor Corp. • EMC 3082 • Math Fundamentals — Recognize and draw pentagons and hexagons. — CCMS 2.G.A.1 — 175

Page 176

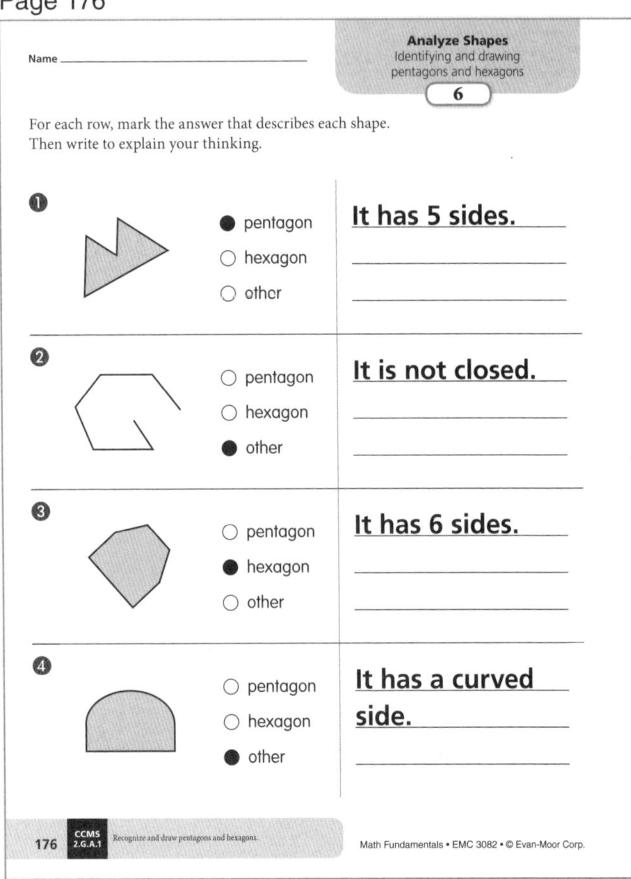

Name

Analyze Shapes
Identifying and drawing pentagons and hexagons

6

For each row, mark the answer that describes each shape. Then write to explain your thinking.

1. ● pentagon ○ hexagon ○ other — **It has 5 sides.**
2. ○ pentagon ○ hexagon ● other — **It is not closed.**
3. ○ pentagon ● hexagon ○ other — **It has 6 sides.**
4. ○ pentagon ○ hexagon ● other — **It has a curved side.**

176 — CCMS 2.G.A.1 — Recognize and draw pentagons and hexagons. — Math Fundamentals • EMC 3082 • © Evan-Moor Corp.

Page 177

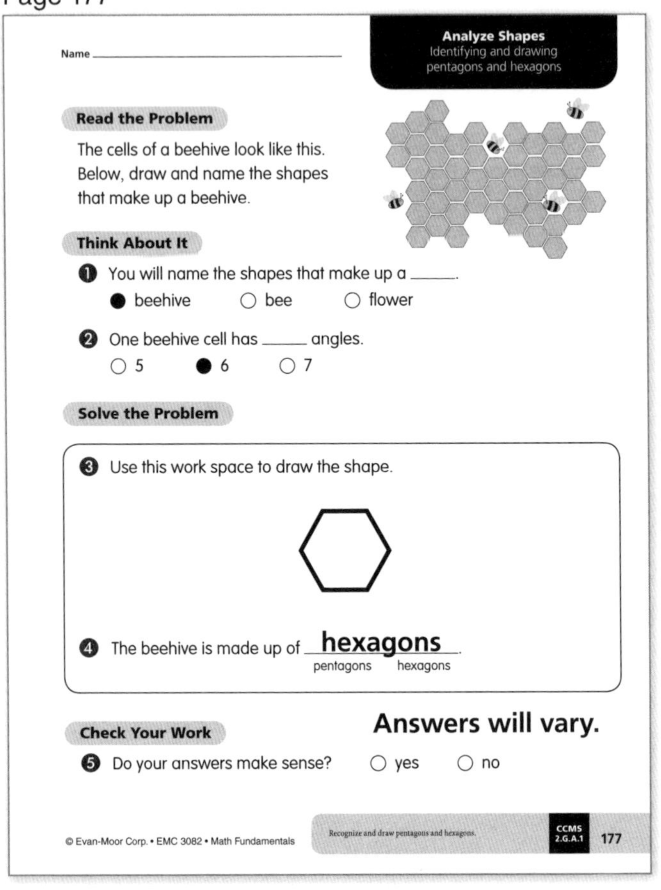

Name

Analyze Shapes
Identifying and drawing pentagons and hexagons

Read the Problem

The cells of a beehive look like this. Below, draw and name the shapes that make up a beehive.

Think About It

1. You will name the shapes that make up a ____.
   ● beehive ○ bee ○ flower
2. One beehive cell has ____ angles.
   ○ 5 ● 6 ○ 7

Solve the Problem

3. Use this work space to draw the shape.
4. The beehive is made up of **hexagons**.
   pentagons hexagons

Check Your Work

Answers will vary.

5. Do your answers make sense? ○ yes ○ no

© Evan-Moor Corp. • EMC 3082 • Math Fundamentals — Recognize and draw pentagons and hexagons. — CCMS 2.G.A.1 — 177

There are many ways to model a problem or to word an explanation. Accept any reasonable answer.

Page 179

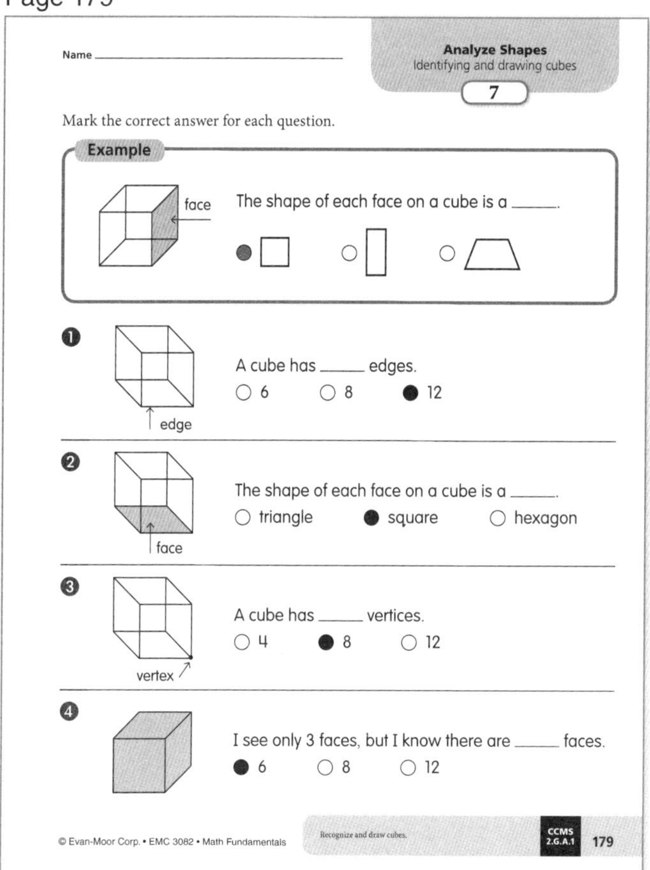
Name ______________________

Analyze Shapes
Identifying and drawing cubes
7

Mark the correct answer for each question.

Example

face

The shape of each face on a cube is a _____.

● (square) ○ (rectangle) ○ (trapezoid)

1. A cube has _____ edges.
○ 6 ○ 8 ● 12
edge

2. The shape of each face on a cube is a _____.
○ triangle ● square ○ hexagon
face

3. A cube has _____ vertices.
○ 4 ● 8 ○ 12
vertex

4. I see only 3 faces, but I know there are _____ faces.
● 6 ○ 8 ○ 12

© Evan-Moor Corp. • EMC 3082 • Math Fundamentals   Recognize and draw cubes.   CCMS 2.G.A.1   179

Page 180

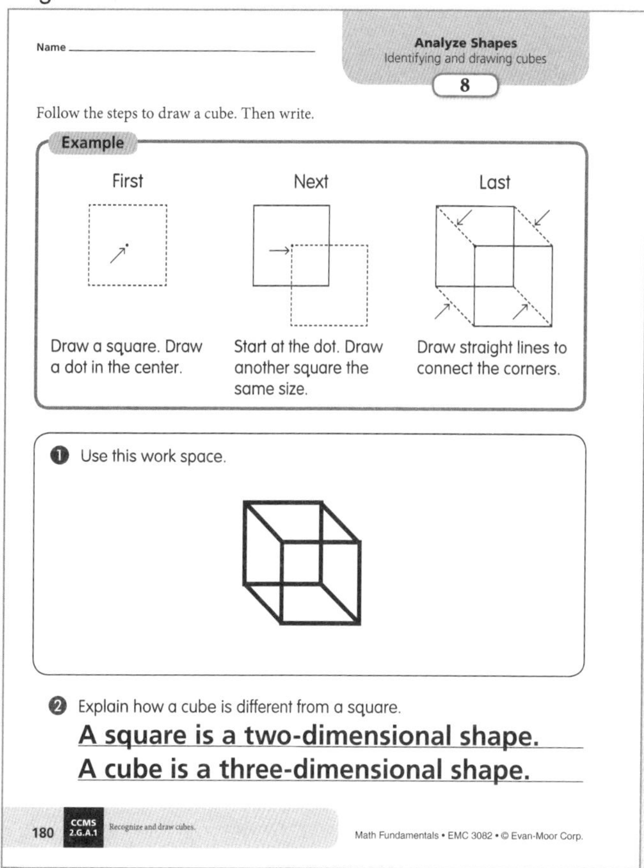
Name ______________________

Analyze Shapes
Identifying and drawing cubes
8

Follow the steps to draw a cube. Then write.

Example

First	Next	Last
Draw a square. Draw a dot in the center.	Start at the dot. Draw another square the same size.	Draw straight lines to connect the corners.

1. Use this work space.

2. Explain how a cube is different from a square.
A square is a two-dimensional shape.
A cube is a three-dimensional shape.

180   CCMS 2.G.A.1   Recognize and draw cubes.   Math Fundamentals • EMC 3082 • © Evan-Moor Corp.

Page 181

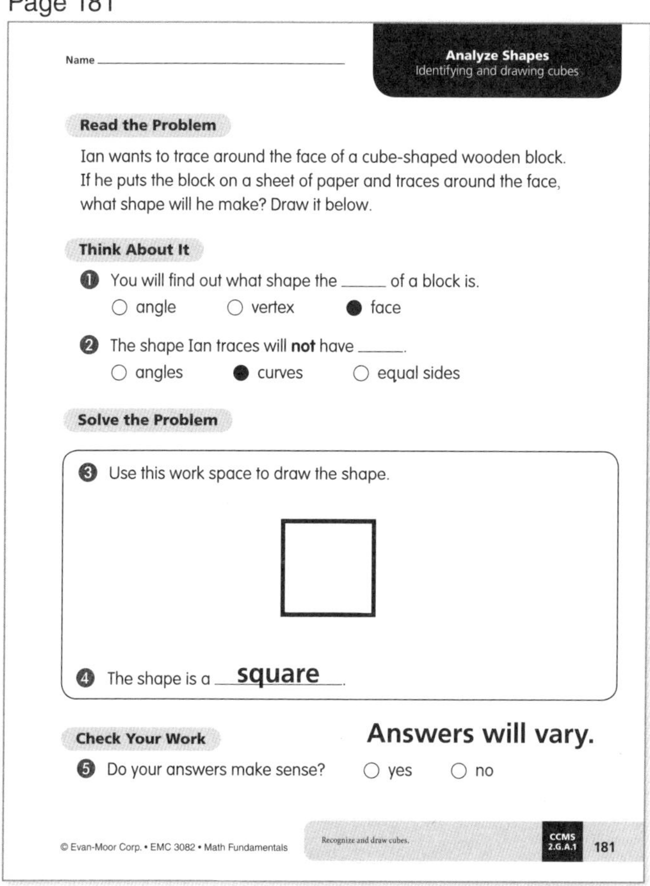
Name ______________________

Analyze Shapes
Identifying and drawing cubes

Read the Problem

Ian wants to trace around the face of a cube-shaped wooden block. If he puts the block on a sheet of paper and traces around the face, what shape will he make? Draw it below.

Think About It

1. You will find out what shape the _____ of a block is.
○ angle ○ vertex ● face

2. The shape Ian traces will **not** have _____.
○ angles ● curves ○ equal sides

Solve the Problem

3. Use this work space to draw the shape.

4. The shape is a **square**.

Check Your Work **Answers will vary.**

5. Do your answers make sense? ○ yes ○ no

© Evan-Moor Corp. • EMC 3082 • Math Fundamentals   Recognize and draw cubes.   CCMS 2.G.A.1   181

Page 183

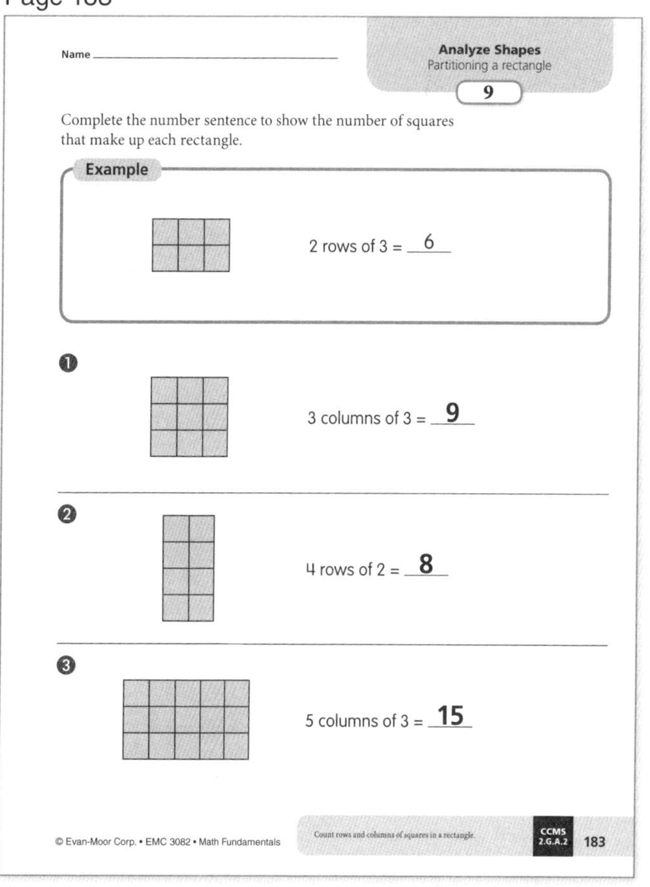
Name ______________________

Analyze Shapes
Partitioning a rectangle
9

Complete the number sentence to show the number of squares that make up each rectangle.

Example

2 rows of 3 = 6

1. 3 columns of 3 = **9**

2. 4 rows of 2 = **8**

3. 5 columns of 3 = **15**

© Evan-Moor Corp. • EMC 3082 • Math Fundamentals   Count rows and columns of squares in a rectangle.   CCMS 2.G.A.2   183

There are many ways to model a problem or to word an explanation. Accept any reasonable answer.

Page 184

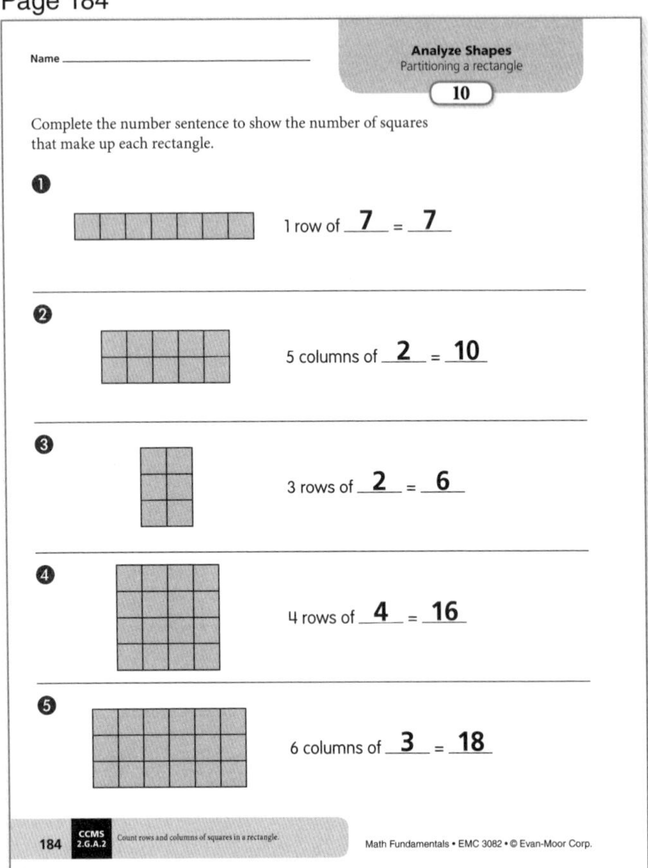
Name ______________________

Analyze Shapes
Partitioning a rectangle
10

Complete the number sentence to show the number of squares that make up each rectangle.

1. 1 row of 7 = 7
2. 5 columns of 2 = 10
3. 3 rows of 2 = 6
4. 4 rows of 4 = 16
5. 6 columns of 3 = 18

184 CCMS 2.G.A.2 Count rows and columns of squares in a rectangle. Math Fundamentals • EMC 3082 • © Evan-Moor Corp.

Page 185

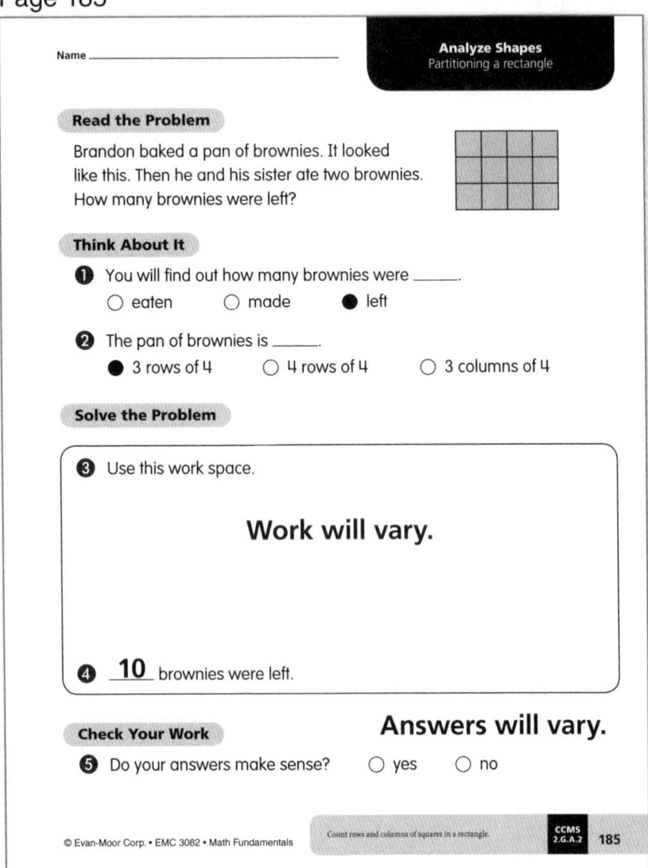
Name ______________________

Analyze Shapes
Partitioning a rectangle

Read the Problem

Brandon baked a pan of brownies. It looked like this. Then he and his sister ate two brownies. How many brownies were left?

Think About It

1. You will find out how many brownies were ______.
   ○ eaten ○ made ● left
2. The pan of brownies is ______.
   ● 3 rows of 4 ○ 4 rows of 4 ○ 3 columns of 4

Solve the Problem

3. Use this work space.

Work will vary.

4. 10 brownies were left.

Check Your Work

Answers will vary.

5. Do your answers make sense? ○ yes ○ no

© Evan-Moor Corp. • EMC 3082 • Math Fundamentals Count rows and columns of squares in a rectangle. CCMS 2.G.A.2 185

Page 187

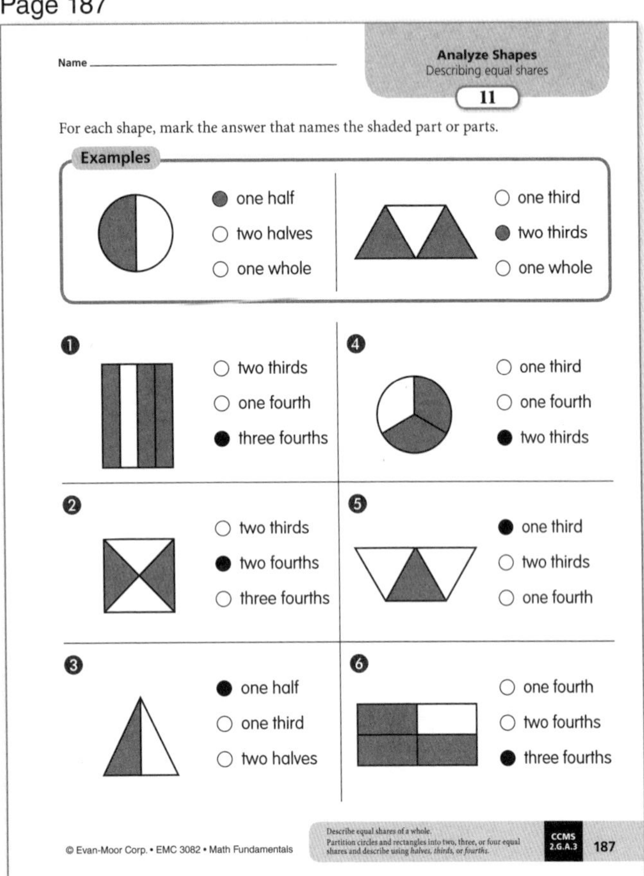
Name ______________________

Analyze Shapes
Describing equal shares
11

For each shape, mark the answer that names the shaded part or parts.

Examples

● one half ○ two halves ○ one whole

○ one third ● two thirds ○ one whole

1. ○ two thirds ○ one fourth ● three fourths
2. ○ two thirds ● two fourths ○ three fourths
3. ● one half ○ one third ○ two halves
4. ○ one third ○ one fourth ● two thirds
5. ● one third ○ two thirds ○ one fourth
6. ○ one fourth ○ two fourths ● three fourths

© Evan-Moor Corp. • EMC 3082 • Math Fundamentals Describe equal shares of a whole. Partition circles and rectangles into two, three, or four equal shares and describe using *halves, thirds, or fourths.* CCMS 2.G.A.3 187

Page 188

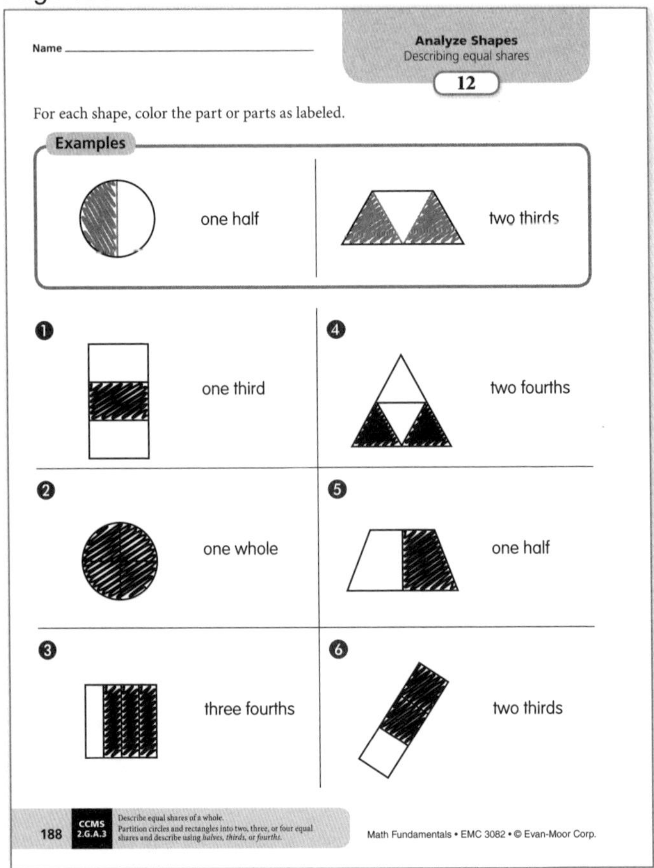
Name ______________________

Analyze Shapes
Describing equal shares
12

For each shape, color the part or parts as labeled.

Examples

one half

two thirds

1. one third
2. one whole
3. three fourths
4. two fourths
5. one half
6. two thirds

188 CCMS 2.G.A.3 Describe equal shares of a whole. Partition circles and rectangles into two, three, or four equal shares and describe using *halves, thirds, or fourths.* Math Fundamentals • EMC 3082 • © Evan-Moor Corp.

There are many ways to model a problem or to word an explanation. Accept any reasonable answer.

Page 189

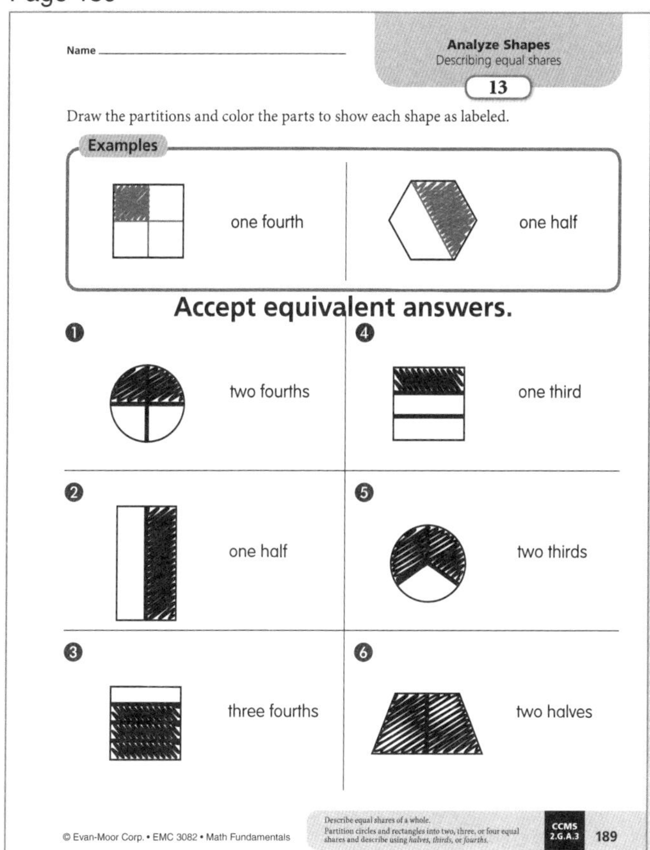

Name

Analyze Shapes
Describing equal shares

13

Draw the partitions and color the parts to show each shape as labeled.

Examples

one fourth

one half

Accept equivalent answers.

1. two fourths
2. one half
3. three fourths
4. one third
5. two thirds
6. two halves

© Evan-Moor Corp. • EMC 3082 • Math Fundamentals

Describe equal shares of a whole. Partition circles and rectangles into two, three, or four equal shares and describe using *halves*, *thirds*, or *fourths*. CCMS 2.G.A.3 189

Page 190

Name

Analyze Shapes
Describing equal shares

Read the Problem

Teri made a sandwich. She ate three fourths of it.
How much was **not** eaten? Draw the sandwich below.
Color the part Teri did **not** eat.

Think About It

1. You will find out how much was ____.
   ○ made ○ eaten ● not eaten
2. The sandwich is cut into ____.
   ● fourths ○ halves ○ thirds

Solve the Problem

3. Use this work space to draw the sandwich.

   OR

4. **One fourth** of the sandwich was **not** eaten.

Check Your Work

Answers will vary.

5. Do your answers make sense? ○ yes ○ no

190 CCMS 2.G.A.3 Describe equal shares of a whole. Partition circles and rectangles into two, three, or four equal shares and describe using *halves*, *thirds*, or *fourths*.

Math Fundamentals • EMC 3082 • © Evan-Moor Corp.

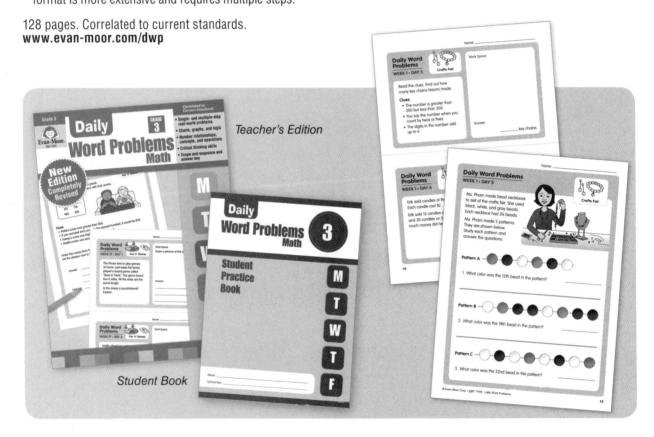

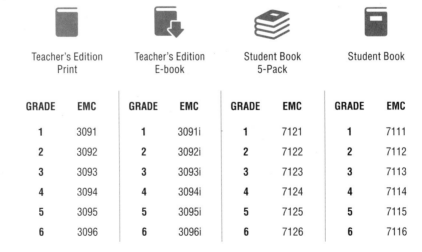